GREEK
THROUGH READING

Head of youth with fair hair

GREEK
through
READING

BY
J.A. Nairn & G.A. Nairn

Published by Bristol Classical Press
General Editor: John H. Betts
(by arrangement with Macmillan Education Ltd.)

First published by Ginn & Co. Ltd, 1952
Second edition published by Macmillan Education Ltd, 1974

Reprinted 1993 by
Bristol Classical Press
an imprint of
Gerald Duckworth & Co. Ltd
The Old Piano Factory
48 Hoxton Square, London N1 6PB

A catalogue record for this book is available
from the British Library

ISBN 1-85399-037-X

Available in USA and Canada from:
Focus Information Group
PO Box 369
Newburyport
MA 01950

Printed & bound by Antony Rowe Ltd, Eastbourne

PREFACE

GREEK is nowadays not usually attempted until a sound foundation has already been laid in Latin. This book aims at making the fullest use of that foundation. We assume that the mechanics of an inflected language are already understood. The structure of Latin and of Greek, both in accidence and syntax, is so similar, that the experience gained in the one language can be readily transferred to the other. Greek, too, is not usually begun until the mind has gained some maturity, when reasoning and observation can be called in to supplement memory. We hope in this book to turn to good account the later start that is generally made in Greek studies.

Greek through Reading has been chosen as a title because we hope that by much early reading of good and varied Greek a sense of idiom will rapidly be gained. The course falls into three parts—grammar, reading passages, and English paraphrases for re-translation into Greek. The essentials of Greek grammar, both in accidence and syntax, are set out in compact form. To the elementary part of this grammar section are joined the exercises on pp. 139 to 174. When these exercises, and those pages of the grammar which they illustrate, have been covered, enough fundamental knowledge will have been gained to tackle the reading passages which form the bulk of the book. Only a few of these are synthetic Greek, and the learner will soon be reading passages from Greek authors, chosen on their merits, and not to exemplify particular grammatical rules.

The systematic study of the grammar must not be abandoned at this stage. But reading, and observation of genuine Greek, should make familiar the normal forms of expression, and any uncertainties in accidence or in syntax can be remedied as they are discovered. The common irregular verbs have been given unusually full treatment in the grammar,

v

as, in the authors' experience, they are apt to remain all too long a nebulous area where rough recognition or guesswork steer the course.

The English passages for translation are based very closely on the Greek from which they are taken. They are meant to provide practice in reproducing the Greek idiom, and in understanding how it differs from the English. But even in the elementary exercises paraphrase has been freely used, to teach the habit of thinking in Greek, and to discourage the word for word style of translation. If a solution can as a rule be readily found by referring once again to the Greek passages, our purpose will have been served, which is to familiarise the Greek form of expression.

The illustrations have been chosen chiefly for their bearing on the subject matter. Both the pictures and the passages for reading are meant to give a foretaste of the variety and range of Greek civilisation. This is the reason for the diversity of the fare provided in this elementary course.

We have called on no friendly scholars for criticism, preferring to bear alone the responsibility for this experimental book. But we cannot conclude without expressing gratitude to our publishers, Messrs. Ginn. Without their enthusiasm, their generosity, and their truly classical concern for detail, this book would not have been carried through. We can but hope it may do something to encourage the study of Greek.

J. A. N.

G. A. N.

CONTENTS

PASSAGES IN GREEK   PAGE
    I. Greece and Athens   1
   II. Gods and Goddesses   13
  III. Heroes   23
  IV. Legends   31
    V. Fables and Fiction   39
  VI. Home Life   51
 VII. Sport and Games   65
VIII. The Sea : Sea Fights, Islands   77
  IX. Land Battles and Sieges   87
    X. Travel   101
  XI. Friendship   111
 XII. Great Men   121
XIII. Love of Country   129
XIV. Peace   137

THE ALPHABET   139

INTRODUCTORY EXERCISES   146

GRAMMAR
  Nouns   175
  Adjectives   188
  Adverbs   195
  Pronouns   199
  Verbs   203
  Prepositions   278
  Syntax   288
  Syntax of Clauses   294
  Table of Irregular Verbs   314

ENGLISH INTO GREEK   319

GREEK-ENGLISH VOCABULARY   339

ENGLISH-GREEK VOCABULARY   371

INDEX   383

AUTHORS

Name and date	Country	Page references
AESCHYLUS (525–456 B.C.)	Athens	133
AESOP[1] (6th century, B.C.)	Samos	41, 42, 43, 44
APOLLODORUS[1] (2nd century B.C.)	Athens	17, 18, 19, 20, 25, 26, 27, 30, 33, 34, 35, 36, 37, 38, 70, 71, 73, 117
ANTHOLOGIA PALATINA A collection from various anthologies made about 950 A.D. The poems range from the 5th century B.C. to the 6th century A.D.	Byzantium	20, 42, 61, 62, 82, 93, 114
ARRIAN (2nd century A.D.)	Bithynia	93, 95, 99, 108, 109, 120
CALLIMACHUS (c. 305–240 B.C.)	Alexandria	115
DEMOSTHENES (384–322 B.C.)	Athens	135
HERODOTUS (c. 480–425 B.C.)	Halicarnassus	54, 69, 79, 80, 86, 89, 103, 104, 105, 106, 107, 118, 119, 124, 131
HOMER (8th century B.C.?)	Ionia. Possibly Smyrna or Chios	53, 67, 97, 113
IAMBLICHUS (c. 250–325 A.D.)	Syria	120
LEONIDAS OF TARENTUM (3rd century B.C.)	Tarentum (Taras), S. Italy	61
LUCIAN (2nd century A.D.)	Samosata, N. Syria	44, 45, 47, 48, 49
LYCURGUS (d. 324 B.C.)	Athens	131
NOSSIS (3rd century B.C.)	Locri, S. Italy	20
PHOCYLIDES (6th century B.C.)	Miletus	28
PINDAR (518–438 B.C.)	Boeotia	8
PLATO (429–347 B.C.)	Athens	56, 57, 60, 117
PLUTARCH (c. 46–120 A.D.)	Chaeronea, in Boeotia	113, 118, 123, 125, 127, 128
POLYBIUS (203–120 B.C.)	Arcadia	83
SAPPHO (born c. 612 B.C.)	Lesbos	22
SIMONIDES (c. 556–468 B.C.)	Ceos	93, 132, 136
SOPHOCLES (c. 496–406 B.C.)	Athens	71, 73
STRABO (63 B.C.–21 A.D.)	Pontus	109
THUCYDIDES (c. 460–400 B.C.)	Athens	80, 81, 85, 90, 97, 99, 133
TYRTAEUS (7th century B.C.)	Sparta	92
XENOPHON (c. 430–354 B.C.)	Athens	57, 59, 62, 75, 83, 91

[1] Late adaptation.

NOTES ON ILLUSTRATIONS

PHOTOGRAPHS

Throughout this book familiar names are written with the traditional Latinised spelling. Names less familiar have been approximated to the Greek spelling. Dates are B.C. *unless otherwise stated.*

PAGE

Head of youth with fair hair. Fragment of a statue found on the Acropolis at Athens. *c.* 480. Alinari photograph from Mansell   *Frontis.*

The Acropolis at Athens with the so called Theseum (probably the temple of Hephaestus) in the foreground. l. to r. on the Acropolis are the Erechtheum, the Parthenon, the Propylaea, and the temple of Athena Nike. Parthenon 447–432, Propylaea (entrance-gate) 437–432, Theseum 428, Athena Nike 425, Erechtheum 421. Photograph by K. Scowen   2

Horsemen riding in the Panathenaic procession. From the west side of the Ionic frieze of the Parthenon, *c.* 432. British Museum   7

Theatre of Dionysus, cut in the south side of the Acropolis rock at Athens. As it survives, the auditorium dates from the last quarter of the fourth century B.C., when the orchestra and seating of 499 were reconstructed. Photograph by Nancy Crawshaw   10

Athena wearing the snake-fringed aegis. Bronze plaque about 14 in. high, *c.* 510. Alinari photograph from Mansell   14

Apollo. Central figure of the west pediment of the temple of Zeus at Olympia. Around the calm figure of the god struggle Lapiths and centaurs. Their fights are represented also in the metopes of the Parthenon. *c.* 460. Paul Popper photograph   17

Aphrodite on a goose. From the interior of an Attic white-ground cup in the British Museum. *c.* 460   21

Athena, Heracles, and Atlas. Metope from the temple of Zeus at Olympia. Heracles, with some help from Athena, supports the

ix

PAGE

heavens on a cushion, while Atlas brings him the golden apples of
the Hesperides. *c.* 460. Alinari photograph from Mansell   24

Odysseus and the Sirens. Attic red-figure amphora in the British
Museum. In this ware the figures are " reserved " in the orange-red
of the glazed clay, while background and details are painted in brilliant black glaze. It begins to supplant black figure ware (see Boxing Contest below) about 525. *c.* 475   29

Aesop and the fox. Red-figure Attic cup, *c.* 460. Anderson photograph from Mansell   40

Griffins. Bronze plaque in oriental style found at Olympia. Sixth
century. Alinari photograph from Mansell   46

Flute-player and older man. Interior of Attic red-figure cup in style
of Brygos. *c.* 485. In British Museum. Mansell photograph   52

Woman with necklace and wool-basket. From white-ground Attic
lekythos (λήκυθος, oil flask) in British Museum. *c.* 470   55

Marble girl dedicated by Euthydicus. Many figures of this type have
been found on the Acropolis at Athens. They are called *korae* (κόρη,
a maiden), and are always clothed, often in the height of fashion.
They were the commonest dedicatory offering to Athena. The
equivalent male statue is the naked boy (κοῦρος) connected with
Apollo worship. The frontispiece is from a slightly later version of
this male type. The *korae* belong to the forty years immediately
preceding the sack of Athens by the Persians in 480. The statue
here shown is probably the latest of the series, just before 480.
Alinari photograph from Mansell   58

Flute-player and dancing girl. She is dancing with κρόταλα, casta-
nets, to a flute accompaniment. From an Attic red-figure cup by
Epiktētos. *c.* 510. British Museum   63

Boxing contest. Two boxers with trainer, and another athlete holding ἁλτῆρες, weights used to facilitate long jumping. Attic black

figure amphora. The figures are painted in black glaze on the orange-red background of the clay. Details are rendered by incised lines. This technique is developed at Athens in the sixth century till gradually ousted by the red-figure ware towards the close of the century. *c.* 530. British Museum photograph   66

Boar hunt. Relief decorating one side of a Lycian sarcophagus found at Sidon. On the other side is a lion hunt. This Greek School of S.E. Asia Minor is clearly influenced by the Parthenon reliefs. Early fourth century. Istanbul.   68

Delphic charioteer. Bronze figure holding reins, originally forming part of a large chariot group, of a kind often set up at Delphi by victors. Dedicated in 4/6. Mansell photograph   72

Four-horse chariot group with ἀποβάτης, dismounted rider. Relief, forming one of a pair. In a private collection at Lisbon, and believed to have come from Herculaneum. Perhaps a neo-Attic, 2nd or 1st century B.C. copy of a 4th-century original. Other versions of this scene exist. Giraudon photograph from Mansell   74

Funeral relief (στήλη) of one Democleides, seated on the prow of a ship. Late fifth century B.C. Alinari photograph from Mansell   78

Throne room of the Palace of Minos at Cnossos in Crete. The last important addition made to the palace before disaster either by earthquake, or by enemy hands, overtook it about 1400. The gypsum throne of " Minos " can be seen where it was found. The frescoes of wingless griffins and papyrus reeds are largely restored. Green, red, blue, and white are used on a red background. The room was used for cult purposes and was found in a state of confusion, sacrificial vessels and oil flasks overturned, as though suddenly overtaken by disaster. " It looks as if the king had been hurried here to undergo too late some last ceremony in the hopes of saving the people. Theseus and the Minotaur! Dare we believe that he wore the mask of a bull? Such imaginings may not be suitable to archaeology, but . . . I defy anyone to enter the Throne Room without a strange thrill."[1] The disaster, whether sack or earthquake,

---

[1] *The Archaeology of Crete* by J. D. S. Pendlebury (Methuen). This archaeologist was killed during the fighting in Crete in 1941.

took place about 1400, probably in May, to judge by the spread of
fire before a strong south wind. Mansell photograph   84

Kneeling archer representing Heracles. This figure forms part of the
battle group of the east pediment of the temple to Aphaea on Aegina.
The figures, as usual, are grouped to fit the wide triangle of the
pediment. Erect figures occupy the centre, recumbent figures the
corners ; cf. Apollo from Olympia, p. 17. *c.* 480. Munich
Museum   88

Battle of Issus, 333. Mosaic from Pompeii showing Alexander on
the left, and the Persian king Darius, fleeing on the right. The
mosaic, which may itself be as early as the third century, is held to
be a good copy of a wall-painting by Philoxenos of Eretria made
c. 300 and described by the Elder Pliny. Anderson photograph
from Mansell   94

Winged Victory of Samothrace. Gigantic marble statue, now in the
Louvre, showing Nike alighting on the prow of a ship. Made by a
Rhodian artist, possibly *c.* 250. Alinari photograph from Mansell 98

Arkesilas of Cyrene. The king is on board ship, supervising the
weighing of silphium. This herb provided a much-prized spice,
and was a royal monopoly at Cyrene. Note the African atmosphere
imparted by the ape on the yard-arm, and the hunting leopard under
the king's chair. The ship's hold can be seen below. Interior of a
cup of Laconian ware, *c.* 560. Giraudon photograph from Mansell   102

Sailing ships. Exterior of a black figure Attic vase. Note the oars
that serve as rudders, and the landing ladders. *c.* 520. Giraudon
photograph from Mansell   106

Achilles binding up Patroclus' wounded arm. Patroclus wears the
protective fur cap worn under the helmet. The shoulder flap of his
corselet has been undone. One man shows attentive concentration ;
the other turns away in pain. Interior of an Attic red-figure cup by
Sōsias, *c.* 490. Berlin State Museum photograph   112

Socrates. Statuette in marble, 14 in. high. Roman copy made
about the second century A.D. from a full-size marble statue of the
fourth century B.C. British Museum   116

PAGE

Pericles. Marble copy made about 100 from a bronze original by Cresilas set up on the Acropolis soon after the death of Pericles in 429. British Museum 122

Demosthenes. Later marble copy of bronze full-length statue made in 280 by Polyeuctes. Demosthenes died in 322. Ashmolean Museum, Oxford 126

Mourning Athena. Relief showing Athena gazing solemnly at what is perhaps a funerary inscription, *c.* 450. Alinari photograph from Mansell 130

Attic stele. The dead man is represented as a warrior with his horse. Note the snake often used to represent the soul of the dead. *c.* 390. Alinari photograph from Mansell 134

Delphi is most strikingly set among the lower spurs of Mt. Parnassus. The theatre (*c.* 160) was used for the performances that formed a part of the Delphic festival.
Photograph by Nancy Crawshaw 318

Sunium. The ruins of this temple (*c.* 425), appropriately dedicated to Poseidon, stand on the edge of the steep promontory which is the most southerly point of Attica.
Photograph by Cassavetti, by kind permission of the Greek Embassy 320

Olympia. Part of the Altis or sacred grove, with the temple of Hera. This, the earliest Doric temple, dates from the first part of the seventh century. The columns, originally of wood, were replaced in marble at widely different dates. E.N.A. photograph 328

DRAWINGS

Athena and voters. Athena supervises the voting which is to decide whether to award the arms of the dead Achilles to Ajax or to Odysseus. From an Attic red-figure cup by Douris, *c.* 490. Drawn from Pl. 63, *Masterpieces of Greek Drawing and Painting* : Pfuhl (Chatto & Windus Ltd.) by kind permission 1

Birth of Athena. Hephaestus has proudly produced with his axe Athena, armed with shield, from the head of Zeus, who holds the thunderbolt. From an Attic black-figure cup. *c.* 550. British Museum 12

PAGE

Hermes. Clad in characteristic hat (πέτασος) and sandals, and carrying his herald's staff (κηρύκειον), he is warding off a satyr. Part
of a scene from an Attic red-figure cup by Brygos. *c.* 480. British
Museum   13

Girl picking apples. From a white-ground Attic cup by Sotades. *c.*
450. British Museum   22

Heracles feasting. Part of a scene from a large Attic black-figure amphora. The hero's characteristic lion-skin and club can be seen. *c.*
520.   23

Introduction of Heracles to Olympus. Athena, clad in snake-fringed
aegis, firmly leads Heracles, with characteristic lion-skin, bow and
club, before Zeus. This type of black-figure cup is called " little
master ". The small and animated figures are about the size of the
reproduction. Women's flesh is generally shown as white. From
the same cup in the British Museum, as the Birth of Athena, page 12.
c. 550.   30

Theseus killing the Minotaur. From an Attic black-figure cup. *c.* 550.
British Museum   31

The home-coming of Castor and Polydeuces (Διὸς κοῦροι). A domestic
scene by Exēkias, perhaps the greatest Attic vase painter. Black-
figure amphora in Vatican Museum. *c.* 530. Drawn from Pl. 22,
Masterpieces of Greek Drawing and Painting: Pfuhl (Chatto &
Windus Ltd.) by kind permission   32

Heracles wrestling with the Nemean lion. This, the first of the hero's
labours, is a favourite theme on Attic vases. This scene is drawn
above the reclining Heracles, shown on page 23   38

Sphinx. This terracotta figure, moulded in the round, forms the
base of a rhyton or drinking-horn in the red-figure style and is about
9 in. high. *c.* 460. British Museum   39

Olive pickers. From a late black-figure Attic vase. *c.* 510. British
Museum   51

PAGE

Athletes in the palaestra. One is pouring oil, another receiving massage. From an Attic red-figure crater (κρατήρ, mixing bowl for wine and water) by Euphronios. *c.* 500. Berlin State Museum   65

Hunter with dog. He carries a dead hare and fox. From an Attic black-figure cup. *c.* 530. Drawn from *Greek Pottery:* Lane (Faber and Faber Ltd.) by kind permission   76

Ship. Part of a scene with ships on a black-figure cup. *c.* 530. British Museum   77

Theseus landing from a ship. Detail from the huge 2 ft. crater by Klitias and Ergotimos called the François vase. It is ornamented by five continuous bands of black-figure painting. The volute handles and the base are also painted. *c.* 565. In Florence   86

Achilles carrying the body of Patroclus. Scene from one of the two handles of the François vase. (See previous picture.)   87

Achilles and Hector fighting. Taken from a small scene ornamenting the neck of a large black volute crater. Red-figure style. *c.* 480. British Museum   100

Persian archer. From a plate by Epiktētos. *c.* 520. British Museum   101

Dionysus in a boat. From the mast springs a vine. The sea is rendered by dolphins. Painted by Exēkias. *c.* 530. Drawn from *Greek Pottery*: Lane (Faber & Faber Ltd.) by kind permission   110

Bandaging scene. Forms part of the battle over Achilles' body, shown on a Chalcidian amphora now lost. Early sixth century. Drawn from Pl. 13, *Masterpieces of Greek Drawing and Painting*: Pfuhl (Chatto & Windus Ltd.) by kind permission   111

Dismounted rider. Painted in red-figure style by Epiktētos. *c.* 520. British Museum   121

Rider on horseback. Black-figure style by Epiktētos. *c.* 520. British Museum. Cf. page 121 and note how this artist works in both red- and black-figure styles   128

PAGE

Warrior, arming, with his parents' help.   From red-figure vase by
Euthymides.   *c.* 500   129

Warrior's farewell.   From a white-ground funeral lekythos, of a type
used for offering to the dead.   The painting is in coloured outline on a
white ground.   Hair, etc., is filled in.   Much use is made of red.   As
in this picture, the dead person is usually represented, often in company with mourner.   *c.* 450.   Drawn from Pl. 94, *Masterpieces of
Greek Drawing and Painting* : Pfuhl (Chatto & Windus Ltd.) by
kind permission   136

MAPS AND DIAGRAMS
Greece.   Prepared by Emery Walker Ltd.   5

Alphabets.   Based on Maunde Thompson, *Introduction to Greek
and Latin Palaeography* (Kegan Paul), by Emery Walker Ltd.   140

I
GREECE AND ATHENS

1

Greece

Ἡ Ἑλλὰς μέρος τί ἐστι τῆς Εὐρώπης. οἰκοῦσι δ᾽ αὐτὴν
οἱ Ἕλληνες. τοὺς δ᾽ Ἕλληνας τοὺς πάλαι διὰ τοῦτο καὶ νῦν
τιμῶμεν, ὅτι τήν τ᾽ ἐλευθερίαν ἐφίλουν, καὶ τὴν ἀλήθειαν,
καὶ τὸ καλόν. καὶ ὑπὲρ μὲν τῆς ἐλευθερίας ὀλίγοι πρὸς πολλοὺς πολεμοῦντες πολλάκις ἐνίκησαν, τὴν δ᾽ ἀλήθειαν καὶ τὸ 5
καλὸν ζητοῦντες ποιήματα καὶ δράματα καὶ ἱστορίας ἔγραψαν,
καὶ ἀνδριάντας ἔγλυψαν καὶ ἱερὰ ᾠκοδόμησαν, ὧν ἔνια καὶ
ἐφ᾽ ἡμῶν περίεστι.
αὕτη ἡ βίβλος περὶ τῶν θ᾽ Ἑλλήνων καὶ περὶ τῶν ἔργων
ἀπαγγελεῖ.   10

J. A. N.

2

The sea

Τῆς Ἑλλάδος οὐδὲν μέρος πολὺ τῆς θαλάττης ἀπέχει.
μεταξὺ γὰρ τῆς Εὐρώπης καὶ τῆς Ἀσίας πολλαὶ νῆσοί εἰσι,
καὶ ἐν τῇ χώρᾳ αὐτῇ πολλοὶ λιμένες, ὥστε οἱ ἀπ᾽ Εὐρώπης
πρὸς Ἀσίαν πλέοντες γῆν ἀεί ποθ᾽ ὁρῶσιν· ἀγαθοὶ δ᾽ ὄντες
ναῦται οἱ Ἕλληνες ἦλθον ἐπὶ τὴν Ἰωνίαν καὶ τὴν Λιβύην, 5
καὶ Αἴγυπτον, καὶ δὴ καὶ ἐπὶ τὴν Βρεταννικήν, καὶ διὰ τοῦ
Ἑλλησπόντου ἐπὶ τὸν Εὔξεινον πόντον, καὶ ἀποικίας ᾤκισαν.
ὡς καλὸν τὸ χρῶμα τῆς ἐκεῖ, τῆς Αἰγαίας θαλάττης! τῷ
οἴνῳ προσόμοιον ἔφασαν εἶναι οἱ ποιηταί.

J. A. N.

l. 1. θαλάττης. Later Attic writes ττ for σσ. Both forms will be
found throughout this book.

3

3

The land

Μικρὰ δὴ χώρα ἡ Ἑλλάς· καὶ πολλὰ μὲν ὄρη ὀλίγα δὲ πεδία
ἔχει, ποταμοὺς δ' οὐ μακρούς. τὰ δ' ὄρη, τοὺς Ἕλληνας ἀπ'
ἀλλήλων ἀποτέμνοντα, ἀπίστους πρὸς τοὺς ὁμόρους ἐποίει,
ῥᾴδιον γὰρ οὐκ ἦν συνελθεῖν. καὶ πρὸς τοὺς ἔξω πολεμίους
τοῦτο μέγαν κίνδυνον παρεῖχεν, ἐπεὶ οὐχ ὡς ἐν ἔθνος ἀλλ' ὡς   5
πόλεις ἑκάστη καθ' ἑκάστην διῆγον. τῶν δὲ πόλεων ὀνόματα
τῶν λαμπροτάτων γράψω· Σπάρτη, Ἀθῆναι, Θῆβαι, Ἄργος,
Κόρινθος. ἐπολέμουν πρὸς ἀλλήλας αὗται αἱ πόλεις πολλάκις,
εἰρήνην δ' ἦγον οὐ πολλάκις.

J. A. N.

4

Sparta and Athens

Ἡ μὲν Σπάρτη ἔνεστιν ἐν τῇ τοῦ Πέλοπος νήσῳ, ἣν οἱ Ἕλληνες Πελοπόννησον ἐκάλουν· ἀπέχει δέ τι τῆς θαλάττης.
στρατιώτας δ' ἔτρεφεν ἀνδρείους, οἳ πόλεμον ἀπὸ παιδὸς
ἤσκουν. ἔτι δ' αἱ γυναῖκες αὐτῶν ἐν τοῖς γυμνασίοις ἔμαθον
ἰσχυραὶ εἶναι, ὡς πρέπει ταῖς μητράσι στρατιωτῶν.   5
Ἀθῆναι δὲ τοὐναντίον πρὸς τῇ θαλάττῃ εἰσιν, οἱ δ' Ἀθηναῖοι πλεῖν τὴν θάλατταν ἔμαθον, ὡς ναῦται καὶ ἔμποροι.
ἀπὸ δὲ τῶν νεῶν ἐμάχοντο, καὶ μεγάλην δύναμιν ἔσχον,
θαλαττοκράτορες ὄντες.

J. A. N.

1. 2. τι, somewhat.
   3. ἀπὸ παιδός, from boyhood.
   4. ἔμαθον, str. aor. of μανθάνω.
   6. τοὐναντίον, for τὸ ἐναντίον : on the contrary.
   7. πλεῖν, infin. of πλέω.

Horsemen riding in the Panathenaic procession

5

Athens

Ἔτι καὶ νῦν αἱ Ἀθῆναι λαμπροτάτη τῆς Ἑλλάδος πόλις·
πῶς Ἀθήναζε ἐρχόμεθα ; κατὰ θάλατταν ῥᾷον ἢ κατὰ γῆν.
πλέοντες οὖν εἰς Πειραιᾶ ἀφικνούμεθα, τῶν Ἀθηνῶν λιμένα.
ἆρα μέλλομεν, ὡς Σωκράτης χρόνῳ ποτέ, πομπὴν ὁρᾶν ;
Πλάτων γὰρ ἔγραψεν ὡς ἐν Πειραιεῖ, ἐν τῇ θυσίᾳ θεοῦ τινος, 5
Σωκράτους παρόντος, νεανίαι ἔδραμον, δᾷδας ἔχοντες ἐν
ταῖς χερσί, καὶ τρέχοντες παρέδοσαν τὰς δᾷδας ἕκαστος τῷ
πλησίον, καὶ ἐκεῖνος ὡσαύτως τῷ πλησίον, τοῦτο δὲ τῆς νυκτὸς
ἐγένετο.

J. A. N.

l. 1. ἔτι καὶ νῦν, *even now.*
   2. Ἀθήναζε, *to Athens.* -δε, place to (Ἀθήνασ-δε). e.g. οἴκαδε, *homewards.*
      Ἀθήνηθεν,, *from Athens.* -θεν, place from which. e.g. οἴκοθεν, *from home.*
      Ἀθήνησι, *at Athens.* -ι sing. ; -σι, plural, old locative forms. e.g. οἴκοι, *at home.*
   3. Πειραιᾶ, nominative Πειραιεύς. The chief harbour of Athens. It was at one time linked to Athens by the Long Walls, μακρὰ τείχη, 40 stades, or 5 miles, in length.
   4. μέλλομεν : this verb gives a sense of futurity, *to be about to, to intend.* χρόνῳ ποτέ, *once upon a time.*
   6. Σωκράτους παρόντος, genitive absolute (Par. 98).
      ἔδραμον, strong aorist of τρέχω (Par. 71).
   8. τῆς νυκτός, *by night.*

6

The Acropolis

Ἐν δὲ ταῖς Ἀθήναις ἄκρα τίς ἐστιν, ἣν Ἀκρόπολιν ὀνομά-
ζουσι· διατείνει δ᾽ ἀφ᾽ ἡλίου ἀνατέλλοντος ἐφ᾽ ἥλιον δύνοντα·

Η ΕΛΛΑΣ

ΜΑΚΕΔΟΝΙΑ

Στρυμών

Πέλλα

Ἀμφίπολις

ΧΑΛΚΙΔΙΚΗ

Ὄλυνθος

Ποτίδαια

Ἄθως

Ὄλυμπος

Τὰ Τέμπη

Ὄσσα

Ὁ Αἰγαῖος
Πόντος

Δωδώνη

Πηνειός

Λάρισσα

ΗΠΕΙΡΟΣ

ΘΕΣΣΑΛΙΑ

Πήλιον

Κέρκυρα

Ἀμβρακία

ΑΙΤΩΛΙΑ

Θερμοπύλαι

Λευκάς

Ἐλατεία

Πάρνασσος

Ὀρχόμενος

Χαλκὶς τῆς Εὐβοίας

Χαλκὶς τῆς
Αἰτωλίας

Δελφοί

ΒΟΙΩΤΙΑ

Θῆβαι

Ἐρέτρια

Ἰθάκη

Ἑλικών

Κύθαιρών

Πλάταια

ΕΥΒΟΙΑ

Πάτραι

Κεφαλληνία

ΑΧΑΙΑ

Μέγαρα

Ἀθῆναι

ΑΤΤΙΚΗ

Μαραθών

Ζάκυνθος

ΗΛΙ

Ὀλυμπία

Νέμεα

Κόρινθος

Μυκῆναι

ΑΡΓΟΛΙΣ

Σαλαμίς

Πειραιεύς

Αἴγινα

Σούνιον

Μαντίνεια

Ἄργος

Ἀλφειός

Τεγέα

ΑΡΚΑΔΙΑ

Μεγαλόπολις

Μεσσήνη

ΜΕΣΣΗΝΙΑ

Εὐρώτας

Σπάρτη

Πύλος

Σφακτηρία

ΛΑΚΩΝΙΑ

Μῆλος

Κύθηρα

Στάδια

0 100 200 300 400 500 600 700 800 900

Miles

0 10 20 30 40 50 60 70 80 90 100

ἐπὶ δὲ ταύτης τῆς ἄκρας ἱερά ἐστιν, ὧν τὸ μέγιστον Παρθενὼν
καλεῖται, ἱερὸν γάρ ἐστιν τῆς θεοῦ ᾿Αθηνᾶς, ἣ παρθένος
διέμεινεν. τετράγωνον δὲ τὸ ἱερόν, καὶ πολλοὺς ἔχει στύλους. 5
ἐν δὲ τῷ ἄνωθεν μέρει ξόανα ἐστιν, ἔργον τοῦ Φειδίου. τῇ
μὲν ἡ ᾿Αθηνᾶ γεννᾶται, θυγάτηρ οὖσα τοῦ Διός, τῇ δ᾿ ἐρίζει
πρὸς τὸν Ποσειδῶνα, πότερος ἄρξει τῆς ᾿Αττικῆς.

J. A. N.

l. 3. ἱερά, neuter plural, therefore with singular verb.
   6. ἐν τῷ ἄνωθεν μέρει, in the upper part, i.e. the two pediments at
      the east and west end of the building.
   7. τῇ μέν . . . τῇ δέ, on the one side . . . on the other.
   8. πότερος, which of the two (Par. 88).

7

Pindar, the Theban poet, praises Athens

Αἵ τε λιπαραὶ καὶ ἰοστέφανοι καὶ ἀοίδιμοι,
῾Ελλάδος ἔρεισμα, κλειναὶ ᾿Αθᾶναι, δαιμόνιον πτολίεθρον.

Pindar : Sandys (Locb edition), fr. 76, p. 556

*O, the gleaming, and the violet-crowned, and sung in story : the
bulwark of Hellas, famous Athens, city divine* (translation by
Sandys).

This is a fragment from the works of Pindar, best known for
his odes in praise of victors in the great Greek games.

l. 2. ᾿Αθᾶναι, for ᾿Αθῆναι, shows that the poem is in the Doric dialect :
Pindar's home was in Thebes in Boeotia, where Doric was
spoken. The chief Greek dialects besides Doric are : Attic
(from ᾿Αττική, of which Athens is the capital ; this ultimately
prevailed over the other dialects) and Aeolic (spoken in Lesbos,
and used by the poets Alcaeus and Sappho).
ἰοστέφανος, " violet-crowned " may apply to the purple glow
seen in Athens at sunset upon Mount Hymettus, or it may
mark Athens as semi-divine, for certain divinities, such as the
Muses, are also called " violet-crowned ".

8

Athens : the Parthenon

Ἐπὶ δὲ τῶν τοῦ ἱεροῦ τειχῶν ἄνω λίθινα ζῷά ἐστιν, ἐν πομπῇ,
τιμὴν φέροντα τῇ θεῷ Ἀθηνᾷ. ἐνθάδε μὲν οἱ θεοὶ ὁρῶσι τὴν
πομπήν, Ζεύς τε καὶ Ἥρα καὶ Ἥφαιστος. καὶ μὴν καὶ ὁ
Ἄρης, καίπερ τοῦ πολέμου θεὸς ὤν, μένει ἡσυχῇ. ἐκεῖ δ᾽ ὁ
ἱερεὺς τῆς θεοῦ, πέπλον λαβὼν ἐν ταῖς χερσί, δίδωσι παιδί· 5
νέος δ᾽ οὗτος ὁ πέπλος, ἀντὶ τοῦ παλαιοῦ τῇ θεῷ φερόμενος.
πέμπουσι δὲ τὸν πέπλον νεανίαι, καὶ παρθένοι, καὶ ἱππῆς, καὶ
αὐληρίδες, καὶ κιθαριστρίαι. ἆρ᾽ ἑώρακας ; ἔνεστι γὰρ
ἔνια τῶν ζῴων ἐν τῇ πατρίδι ἡμῶν.

J. A. N.

l. 1. ζῷα, figures of marble (λίθινα). The procession forms a frieze
high up on the temple wall.

2. τιμὴν φέροντα, *doing honour*. The procession was to bring a
new robe to the goddess in place of her old one.

7. πέμπουσι here means *escort*.

8. ἑώρακας, perfect of ὁρῶ.

9. ἐν τῇ πατρίδι ἡμῶν, *in our own country*. The Parthenon
sculptures in the British Museum are called the Elgin Marbles,
from Lord Elgin who brought them to London early in the
nineteenth century to save them from destruction.

9

Athens : the market place

Ἰδοὺ ἡ τῶν Ἀθηνῶν ἀγορά· μεστὴ δὲ περὶ μεσημβρίαν
τῶν ὠνουμένων. πρῲ δ᾽ ἥκοντες ἑστᾶσι βλέποντες τό τ᾽
ἔλαιον καὶ τὸ ὄξος καὶ τοὺς πρὸς τὸ πῦρ ἄνθρακας, καὶ τοὺς
πρὸς τὸ δεῖπνον ἰχθῦς. πολλοὶ δὲ τῶν παρόντων διαλέ-
γονται ἀλλήλοις, νεώτερόν τι ἢ λέγειν ἢ ἀκούειν βουλόμενοι. 5

Theatre of Dionysus, Athens

ἴσως δ' ἀκούουσι τῶν σοφιστῶν τῶν διδασκόντων δὴ τὴν
σοφίαν. ἆρα πάρεστι Σωκράτης ; ναί, καὶ περιεστᾶσι πολλοί,
ἐλέγχει γὰρ τοὺς σοφιστάς, καὶ φανερὸν ποιεῖ ὅτι δοκοῦντες
εἰδέναι τι τῷ ὄντι οὐκ ἴσασιν.

J. A. N.

l. 1. μεστή, supply ἐστί.
l. 2. ἑστᾶσι, perfect of ἵστημι (p. 248).
l. 3. πρὸς τὸ πῦρ, for the fire.
l. 5. νεώτερόν τι, something rather new, some novelty.
l. 6. δὴ is here ironical—professing to teach.
l. 8. ὅτι, that. Syntax F2, p. 298.
l. 9. τῷ ὄντι, in reality. ἴσασιν (Par. 73).

10

Athens : the Theatre of Dionysus

Ἔστιν ἔτι καὶ νῦν Ἀθήνησι θέατρον ὃ Διονύσου καλεῖται·
φέρει δὲ τὸ ὄνομα τοῦ θεοῦ ὃν ἐτίμων ἐν τοῖς δράμασιν. τούτων
δὲ τῶν δραμάτων τὰ μὲν τραγῳδίαι, τὰ δὲ κωμῳδίαι. ἤθελον
γὰρ οἱ Ἀθηναῖοι οὐ μόνον δακρύειν ἐπὶ ταῖς τραγῳδίαις, ἀλλὰ
καὶ γελᾶν ἐπὶ ταῖς κωμῳδίαις.   5

.Ἆρα γιγνώσκετε τάδε τὰ ὀνόματα ; Αἰσχύλος, Σοφοκλῆς,
Εὐριπίδης. οὗτοι τραγῳδίας ἔγραψαν· καὶ Ἀριστοφάνην
ἀκήκοας ; οὗτος λαμπρὸς ἦν κωμῳδοποιός. πολλὰ τῶν
ἔργων αὐτῶν ἔτι καὶ νῦν περίεστιν, ἄλλα δὲ διὰ τὸν χρόνον
διέφθαρται.   10

J. A. N.

l. 3. τὰ μὲν, some (were)..., τὰ δὲ, others (were)...
   4. οὐ μόνον, not only..., ἀλλὰ καί, but also.
   8. ἀκήκοας, from ἀκούω.
   9. ἄλλα, others, from ἄλλος. Distinguished by its accent from
      ἀλλά, but.
  10. διέφθαρται, perf. pass. 3rd pers. sing. of διαφθείρω, I destroy.
      Translate have perished.

II

Athens head of a League of Nations

Μετὰ τὴν ἐν Σαλαμῖνι μάχην, οἱ Ἀθηναῖοι, τῷ ναυτικῷ
ὑπερέχοντες, συμμάχους εἶχον πολλὰς πόλεις, μάλιστα δὲ τῶν
νησιωτῶν. καὶ ὅμοια ἐφρόνουν διὰ τὸν τῶν Περσῶν φόβον.
ἦν δὲ τεταγμένον ἑκάστην πόλιν ναῦς τινας τοῖς Ἀθηναίοις
παρέχειν, καὶ τὰς ναῦς κωλύειν τοὺς Πέρσας μὴ εἰς τὴν 5
Ἑλλάδα εἰσβάλλειν· ὕστερον δὲ ἀντὶ νεῶν χρήματα εἰσέφερον,
φόρον ἐνιαύσιον.

Ἀλλ' οἱ Ἀθηναῖοι τοῖς συμμάχοις οὐ πρεπόντως ἐχρήσαντο.
τὰ γὰρ χρήματα τὰ πρὸς πόλεμον διδόμενα εἰς ἑαυτοὺς ἀνήλισκον, ὥστε οὐκέτι συμμαχία ἀλλ' Ἀθηναίων ἀρχὴ κατέστη. 10
τέλος δ' ἀπέστησαν οἱ σύμμαχοι, καὶ μετὰ Σπάρτης τε καὶ
Κορίνθου εἷλον τὰς Ἀθήνας. οὕτως ἠφανίσθη ἡ τῶν Ἀθηναίων ἀρχή.

J. A. N.

The battle of Salamis was fought in 480 B.C.
The surrender of Athens took place in 404 B.C.
l. 3. ὅμοια ἐφρόνουν translate *they were in agreement*.
   9. ἀνήλισκον from ἀναλίσκω, *spend*.
10. κατέστη and ἀπέστησαν, p. 246.   12. εἷλον (Par. 72).

II

GODS AND GODDESSES

Athena wearing the snake-fringed aegis

12

Zeus and Hera

Μέγιστος δὲ τῶν Ἑλλήνων θεὸς ὁ Ζεύς, πατὴρ θεῶν τε
καὶ ἀνθρώπων καλούμενος. ἔλεξαν δ᾽ ὅτι μετὰ τῶν ἄλλων
θεῶν ἐπὶ κορυφῆς ὄρους τινὸς διάγει, ᾧ ὄνομα Ὄλυμπος. οἱ
δ᾽ ἄλλοι θεοὶ περικάθηνται αὐτόν, καὶ συμβουλεύουσιν, κρίνει
δ᾽ ὁ Ζεύς. κεραυνὸν δὲ φέρει, δι᾽ οὗ κολάζει τοὺς ἁμαρτάνοντας. 5
ἀδελφοὺς δ᾽ ἔχει δύο, τὸν μὲν Ἀΐδην, τῶν νερτέρων θεόν, τὸν
δὲ Ποσειδῶνα, θεὸν τῆς θαλάσσης. ἀδελφὴν δ᾽ ἔχει, ἣ καὶ
γυνὴ ἦν τοῦ Διός, τὴν Ἥραν. ὄρνις δὲ Διὸς ὁ ἀετός.

J. A. N.

l. 2. Syntax F2, p. 298.   l. 4. περικάθηνται, p. 272.
  3. Ὄλυμπος, a mountain in north of Greece. Do not confuse
    with Olympia in the Peloponnese, where the Olympic games
    were held.
  8. ὁ ἀετός. Which noun is predicative? (See Par. 93, § b.)

13

Athena

Μεγάλην εἶχε τιμὴν Ἀθήνησιν ἡ Ἀθηνᾶ, ἣ καὶ τὸ ὄνομα
ἔδωκε τῇ πόλει. εἶπον δὲ ὅτι ἐκ τῆς κεφαλῆς τοῦ πατρὸς
αὐτῆς, τοῦ Διός, ἐξῆλθε. καὶ ὡς πρὸς τὸν πόλεμον δόρυ
ἔφερεν ἡ Ἀθηνᾶ ἐν τῇ δεξιᾷ, ἐν δὲ τῇ ἀριστερᾷ ἀσπίδα· ἐπὶ δὲ
τοῦ κράνους ἐκάθητο γλαῦξ· σημεῖον δ᾽ αὕτη ἡ ὄρνις τῆς 5
σοφίας, θεὸς δὲ σοφίας ἡ Ἀθηνᾶ.

15

τῶν δ' ἀνθρώπων φίλτατος τῇ Ἀθηνᾷ ὁ Ὀδυσσεύς, ὡς
εὑρεῖν πάρεστιν ἐν τῇ Ὀδυσσείᾳ τοῦ Ὁμήρου.

J. A. N.

l. 5. ἐκάθητο (see Par. 82).
σημεῖον (Par. 93 b).
γλαῦκ' Ἀθήναζε, *an owl to Athens.* Proverbial, like " coals to
Newcastle ".
8. εὑρεῖν, aor. infin. act., from εὑρίσκω. εὑρεῖν πάρεστιν, *one
can find.*

14

Poseidon

θεὸς ἦν τῆς θαλάσσης ὁ Ποσειδῶν, περὶ οὗ ἔλεξαν ὅτι
κυανέας ἔχοι τὰς τρίχας, καὶ ὅτι ἐν ὀχήματι αὐτὸν θηρία
θαλάσσια φέροι ἐπὶ τῶν κυμάτων, τρίαιναν δ' ἔχοι, σημεῖον
τῆς ἀρχῆς. καὶ σεισμούς — πολλοὺς δ' ἔχει ἡ Ἑλλάς —
ἐποίει, ὡς ἐνόμιζον, ὁ Ποσειδῶν σείων τὴν τρίαιναν. λέλεκται 5
δ' ἄνωθεν ὅτι ἤρισε πρὸς τὴν Ἀθηνᾶν πότερος ἄρξοι τῆς
Ἀττικῆς. τότε δ' ἐνίκησεν Ἀθηνᾶ, ἐλάαν γενέσθαι ποιοῦσα,
ὁ δὲ Ποσειδῶν τῇ τριαίνῃ θαλάσσιον ὕδωρ ἐν τῇ Ἀκροπόλει
ἐποίησεν.

J. A. N.

l. 1. For tenses and moods with ὅτι see F2, p. 298.
2. τρίχας, see θρίξ.
6. ἤρισεν from ἐρίζω.
7. γενέσθαι, aor. infin. of γίγνομαι, *come into being.*

15

Phoebus Apollo and Artemis

ὁ Ἀπόλλων, Διὸς υἱὸς καὶ Λητοῦς, θεὸς ἦν φέγγους. τοῦ
δ' ἡλίου ζωὴν διδόντος, τῶν νεανιῶν φύλαξ ἦν Ἀπόλλων,
ἀγῶσί τε καὶ τῇ παλαίστρᾳ ἐπισκοπῶν. σημεῖον δὲ τούτου

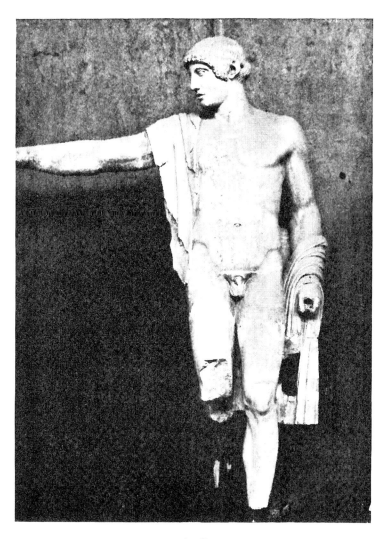

Apollo

τόξον φέρει καὶ φαρέτραν. ἔτι δὲ καὶ τῆς μαντικῆς θεὸς ὢν
Δελφοὺς ᾤκει, ἡ δ' ἱέρεια αὐτοῦ τοῖς ἀνθρώποις τὰ μέλλοντα 5
ἔυεσθαι προεῖπεν. ἐπεὶ δὲ ἡ μαντικὴ καὶ ἡ μουσικὴ κοινόν
τι ἔχειν φαίνονται, λύραν φέρει, καὶ ἐν ταῖς τῶν θεῶν θυσίαις
φορμίζει, καὶ τὸν τῶν Μουσῶν χορὸν εἰσάγει. καὶ μὴν τοῖς
ἰατροῖς, ὡς μάντις, τέχνην ἐντίθησι τοῦ τὰς νόσους
εὑρίσκειν, καὶ ἰᾶσθαι. 10

Ἄρτεμις, ἡ τοῦ Ἀπόλλωνος ἀδελφή, κυνηγέτις οὖσα, τὰς
ὕλας ᾤκει, φαρέτραν καὶ τόξον καὶ αὐτὴ ἔχουσα.

Apollodorus, *The Library*, I. iv. 1, etc.

l. 1. Διός, gen. of Zeus (see Par. 23).
Λητοῦς, from Λητώ (see Par. 23).
5. τὰ μέλλοντα ἔσεσθαι, *future events*. Often τὰ μέλλοντα alone.
6. προεῖπεν, aor. Used with πρόφημι, *tell beforehand, prophesy*,
the word from which *prophesy* derives.
ἡ μαντικὴ καὶ ἡ μουσικὴ. These are adjectives. Supply τέχνη,
art. Translate *prophecy* and *music*.
10. τοῦ ... εὑρίσκειν, *of discovering*. The infinitive with the article
serves as a noun in Greek (Par. 93 d).
ἰᾶσθαι, infin. of ἰῶμαι, dep. *cure*. Cf. ἰατρός.

16

Hermes

Ὁ δ' Ἑρμῆς Διὸς καὶ Μαίας υἱὸς ἦν, ἐν Ἀρκαδίᾳ, ποιμνῶν
τε καὶ ἀγελῶν χώρα, γεγονώς. ἔῳ δὲ γεννηθείς, μεσημβρίᾳ
ἐφόρμιζεν, ἑσπέρᾳ δὲ τοὺς τοῦ Ἀπόλλωνος βοῦς ἔκλεψε. τὴν
δὲ λύραν ἐποίησεν ἐκ νώτου χελώνης, ἐπὶ τούτου τὰς ἑπτὰ
χορδὰς τανύσας. τοὺς δὲ βοῦς ἔκλεψεν ἐπ' ὀπίσω ἐλάσας, 5
ὥστε τὰ ἴχνη αὐτῶν πρὸς οἶκον τρέπεσθαι δοκεῖν. πρὸς δὲ τῇ

λύρᾳ καὶ τὴν σύριγγα ἐξεῦρε. καὶ μὴν τῶν θεῶν ἄγγελος ὢν
τοὺς ἀνθρώπους ἦγε τὴν ἐσχάτην εἰς Ἀΐδου πορείαν.

Apollodorus, III. x. 2

l. 2. γεγονώς, perf. partic. nom. of γέγονα, strong perf. of γίγνομαι,
having been born. ἕῳ, from ἕως, *at dawn.* γεννηθείς, aor.
pass. partic., *having been born.*
5. ἐλάσας, aor. part. of ἐλαύνω, *driving.*
8. ἦγε, from ἄγω. τὴν . . . πορείαν. This acc. defines the scope of
the verb. This type is common in Greek. See acc. Par. 96.
Note there is also an object acc. with this verb.

17

Demeter

Τὴν Δήμητρα ἐνόμιζον οἱ Ἕλληνες γῆν μητέρα εἶναι.
ἐδίδαξε δ᾽ ἡ θεὸς αὕτη ἀνθρώπους τὸν σῖτον θεραπεύειν, ἔν
τε τῇ Θετταλίᾳ καὶ τῇ Σικελίᾳ, ἐκεῖ γὰρ πολὺς ἦν σῖτος. θυγατέρα δ᾽ εἶχε τὴν Περσεφόνην· παρθένος δ᾽ οὖσα ἥδε συνέλεγεν
ἄνθη, ἥρπασε δ᾽ αὐτὴν Ἀΐδης, ὁ νερτέρων θεός. ἀγανακτοῦσα 5
δ᾽ ἡ Δημήτηρ οὐκ εἴα τὸν σῖτον ἀκμάζειν, ὥστε λιμῷ παθεῖν
τοὺς ἀνθρώπους. ἔπαυσαν δὲ τοῦτο οἱ θεοί, ὑποσχόμενοι
τὴν Περσεφόνην ἑκάστου ἔτους μέρος μετὰ τῆς μητρὸς
διάξειν.

Apollodorus, I. v. 1

l. 6. εἴα, imperf. 3rd pers. of ἐῶ. Note irregular augment, and
contraction of α (see p. 315).
ὥστε . . . παθεῖν, consecutive clause, *so that . . .* (Syntax H1,
p. 302). παθεῖν, str. aor. infin. of πάσχειν, (p. 316).
7. ὑποσχόμενοι, aor. partic. of ὑπισχνοῦμαι, *promise* (see Syntax
F1, p. 298). The myth of Demeter and Persephone is no
doubt based on the return to life in springtime of the seed
sown in the previous autumn.

18

Aphrodite

Ἡ Ἀφροδίτη, Διὸς καὶ Διώνης θυγάτηρ, θεὸς ἦν τοῦ ἔρωτος. Ἡσίοδος δὲ ὁ ποιητὴς λέγει ὅτι ἀπ᾽ ἀφροῦ τῆς θαλάττης ἐγένετο, καὶ ἐπὶ τὴν Κύπρον — φιλτάτη δὲ ἡ νῆσος τῇ θεῷ — ὑπὸ τῶν κυμάτων ἠνέχθη. ἐρῶσα δὲ καλοῦ νεανίου, τοῦ Ἀδώνιδος, ἀποθανόντος ὑπὸ κάπρου ἐκείνου, βαρέως 5 ἔφερεν. καὶ μὴν πρὸς Ἥραν καὶ Ἀθηνᾶν ἤρισεν ἡ Ἀφροδίτη περὶ τοῦ κάλλους· ἔκρινε δὲ Πάρις, Πριάμου υἱός, ὃς τὸ μῆλον Ἀφροδίτη ἔνειμεν. ἡ δ᾽ αὐτῷ Ἑλένην, καλλίστην γυναικῶν, ἔδωκεν. ἡ δὲ θεὸς ἢ μῆλον φέρει, ἢ κάτοπτρον, ἢ πελειάδα, ὁ δ᾽ υἱός, Ἔρως, τόξον καὶ φαρέτραν ἔχει. 10

Apollodorus, I. iii. 1

l. 3. ἐγένετο, aor. of γίγνομαι, *was born.*
4. ἠνέχθη, aor. pass. 3rd pers. of φέρω (Par. 71, and 72).
5. ἀποθανόντος, gen. sing. aor. partic. of ἀποθνῄσκω.

19

Love's sweetness

Ἥδιον οὐδὲν Ἔρωτος, ἃ δ᾽ ὄλβια, δεύτερα πάντα
ἐστίν· ἀπὸ στόματος δ᾽ ἔπτυσα καὶ τὸ μέλι.
Τοῦτο λέγει Νοσσίς· τὴν δ᾽ ἡ Κύπρις οὐκ ἐφίλησεν
οὐκ οἶδεν κείνης τἄνθεα ποῖα ῥόδα.

Anthologia Palatina, v. 170

This poem and the next were written by women. Sappho wrote in the 6th, Nossis in the 3rd century B.C.

l. 1. ἃ δ᾽ ὄλβια, lit. *things which are blessed, blessings.*
3. τὴν δ᾽, *she whom.*
4. κείνης for ἐκείνης, τἄνθεα for τὰ ἄνθη.

Aphrodite on a goose

20

The apple pickers

Οἶον τὸ γλυκύμαλον ἐρεύθεται ἄκρῳ ἐπ' ὄσδῳ,
ἄκρον ἐπ' ἀκροτάτῳ, λελάθοντο δὲ μαλοδροπῆες,
οὐ μὰν ἐκλελάθοντ', ἀλλ' οὐκ ἐδύναντ' ἐπίκεσθαι.

Sappho : Smyth, *Greek Melic Poets*, p. 33

This poem is written in the Aeolic dialect, current on Lesbos. η is mostly changed to α. Aspirates are few.

l. 1. οἶον, *such, so.* ὄσδῳ for ὄζῳ.
   2. λελάθοντο, strong aor. of λανθάνομαι. Usually ἐλάθοντο. μαλοδροπῆες for μηλοδροπῆς. 3. μὰν for μὴν. ἐπίκεσθαι for ἐφικέσθαι, str. aor. of ἐφικνοῦμαι, *reach.*

III

HEROES

Athena, Heracles, and Atlas

Heracles

Ἡρακλῆς ἦν Διὸς καὶ Ἀλκμήνης υἱός, καὶ ἐν σπαργάνοις
ἔτι ὢν οὕτως ἰσχυρὸς ἦν ὥστε ὄφεις ἄγχειν δύνασθαι οὓς
ἔπεμψεν Ἥρα ὡς διαφθεροῦντας αὐτόν. φιλάνθρωπος δ' ὤν,
πολλὰ καὶ ἀγαθὰ ἔργα ἔδρασεν ἵνα οἱ ἄνθρωποι βίον ἔχοιεν
εὐδαιμονέστερον. ἐν δὲ τῇ Ἡρακλέους αἱρέσει Ξενοφῶν 5
λέγει ὅτι νεανίᾳ ὄντι τῷ Ἡρακλεῖ δύο γυναῖκες ἠπάντησαν,
ὧν ἡ μὲν ἡδονὴν ἡ δὲ ἀρετὴν προύθηκεν. ἀρετὴν δ' ἀνθ'
ἡδονῆς ἑλομένῳ φύλαξ ἐγένετο Ἀθηνᾶ. ἀλλ' Ἥρα, ἀεὶ δυσ-
μενὴς οὖσα, δώδεκα ἄθλους ὑπομένειν ἠνάγκασεν, ὧν εἷς ἦν
τὸν λέοντα τὸν τῆς Νεμέας ἀποκτείνειν. λέοντος δὲ δορὰν 10
περιεβάλετο καὶ ῥόπαλον ἔφερεν.

Apollodorus, II. iv. 9

Read Syntax G on Final clauses.

l. 4. πολλὰ καὶ ἀγαθὰ, compare and contrast use of καὶ here with
Latin and English.

5. αἱρέσει. *The Choice of Heracles* was the title given to a section
of Xenophon's *Memorabilia Socratis*.

7. προύθηκεν, aor. of προτίθημι, *offer*.

8. ἑλομένῳ, str. aor. mid. of αἱροῦμαι, *choose*.

11. περιεβάλετο, mid. *put on, wear*.

Theseus

Δεύτερος — ὡς ἔπος εἰπεῖν — Ἡρακλῆς ἦν ὁ Θησεύς· καὶ

γὰρ οὗτος γίγαντας καὶ ἄλλα θηρία διέφθειρε, σφόδρα ἰσχυρὸς
ὤν. πατὴρ δὲ Θησέως Αἰγεύς, τῶν Ἀθηναίων βασιλεύς.
ἄθλους δ᾽ ὑπέμεινεν ἓξ ὁ Θησεύς, ἀκίνδυνον ποιῶν τὴν ἀπ᾽
Ἰσθμοῦ πρὸς Ἀθήνας ὁδόν. πρὸς δὲ τὰς Ἀμαζόνας πολεμῶν, 5
Ἱππολύτην τὴν Ἀμαζόνων βασίλισσαν ἔγημε. καὶ μὴν μετὰ
τοῦ φίλου Πειριθόου εἰς Ἅιδου κατῆλθεν, ὡς Περσεφόνην
ἁρπάσων.

Apollodorus, III. xvi. 2

l. 1. ὡς ἔπος εἰπεῖν, so to speak.
2. καὶ ἄλλα θηρία, and beasts besides.
6. ἔγημε, aor. of γαμῶ.
8. ἁρπάσων, syntax G. 2, p. 300.

23

Castor and Polydeuces

Ἀδελφοὶ ἦσαν Κάστωρ καὶ Πολυδεύκης, Διὸς καὶ Λήδας
υἱοί, ἀδελφοὶ δ᾽ ἦσαν καὶ τῆς Ἑλένης. οὗτοι δὲ μετ᾽ ἄλλων
τὸν κάπρον τὸν Καλυδώνιον ἐδίωξαν, καὶ ἐν τῇ Ἀργοῖ μετὰ
Ἰάσονος εἰς Κολχίδα ἔβησαν, τὸν χρυσοῦν μαλλὸν ζητοῦντες.
Κάστορος δ᾽ ἀποθανόντος οὐκ ἤθελεν ὁ Πολυδεύκης ἀθάνατος 5
εἶναι, καὶ ἄλλοτε μὲν μετὰ τῶν θεῶν, ἄλλοτε δὲ μετ᾽
ἀνθρώπων διάγει. περὶ δὲ τῶν ἀδελφῶν τούτων εἴρηκεν
Ὅμηρος,

Κάστορά θ᾽ ἱππόδαμον καὶ πὺξ ἀγαθὸν Πολυδεύκην.

Apollodorus, III. xi. 2

l. 3. Homer tells the story of the hunting of the Calydonian boar in
Iliad, IX.
4. ἔβησαν, aor. of βαίνω, go (Par. 72).
4. χρυσοῦν, golden (Par. 26). 7. εἴρηκεν, has said (Par. 71).

24

Agamemnon

Ἀγαμέμνων υἱὸς ἦν Ἀτρέως, ἀδελφὸς δὲ Μενελάου. ἀποθανόντος δ᾽ Ἀτρέως ἐβασίλευσεν ἐν Μυκήναις. ἔγημε δὲ
Κλυταιμνήστραν, ἀφ᾽ ἧς ἐγένοντο τρεῖς παῖδες, Ἰφιγένεια,
καὶ Ἠλέκτρα, καὶ Ὀρέστης.

ἐπεὶ δὲ Πάρις, υἱὸς Πριάμου τοῦ ἐν Ἰλίῳ βασιλέως, Ἑλένην 5
ἥρπασε, γυναῖκα Μενελάου, διῆλθε τὴν Ἑλλάδα ὁ Ἀγαμέμνων, παροξύνων τοὺς πανταχοῦ ἡγεμόνας στέλλεσθαι πρὸς
Ἴλιον. ἔπειτε δὲ πολλούς, καὶ τῶν Ἀχαιῶν συναγερθέντων
ἐν Αὐλίδι τῆς Βοιωτίας, τῶν ἀνέμων ἐναντίων ὄντων,
ἔσφαξε τὴν Ἰφιγένειαν. Ἰλίου δ᾽ ἁλόντος, κατελθὼν εἰς 10
Μυκήνας ἀπέθανεν ὑπὸ Κλυταιμνήστρας καὶ Αἰγίσθου.
χρόνῳ δ᾽ ὕστερον ἀπέκτεινεν ἄμφω ὁ Ὀρέστης, δίκην τοῦ
πατρὸς λαβών.

Apollodorus, *Epitome*, III. 6

l. 8. συναγερθέντων, aor. pass. part. of συναγείρω, *collect together*.
   10. ἁλόντος, *being captured*. See ἁλίσκομαι (Par. 72).

25

Achilles

Υἱὸς ἦν δ᾽ Ἀχιλλεὺς Πηλέως, ἀνθρώπου, καὶ Θέτιδος, θεοῦ
ποντίας. ἐν Θετταλίᾳ δὲ γεγονὼς Μυρμιδόνων ἦν βασιλεύς.
ἀπὸ δὲ Θετταλίας ἐπὶ Ἴλιον ἐλθὼν μετ᾽ Ἀγαμέμνονος ἀνδρειό-
τατον ἑαυτὸν παρέσχεν· ὡσαύτως δὲ καὶ Πάτροκλος, ἑταῖρος
αὐτοῦ, ὃς ἐν τοῖς τοῦ Ἀχιλλέως ὅπλοις πρὸς τοὺς Τρῶας 5

ἐμαχέσατο. Ἕκτορος δ' ἀποκτείναντος τὸν Πάτροκλον, ἀγανακτήσας ὁ Ἀχιλλεύς, ἐν ὅπλοις ἃ ἐποίησεν Ἥφαιστος, ἀποκτείνει τὸν Ἕκτορα. τέλος δ' οἰστῷ ὃν ἔβαλε Πάρις τραυματισθεὶς ἀπέθανεν.

Apollodorus, *Epitome*, iv. 4

The story of Achilles is largely contained in Homer's *Iliad*.

26

Inter caecos luscus rex

Πάντες μὲν Κίλικες κακοὶ ἀνέρες, ἐν δὲ Κίλιξιν
εἷς ἀγαθὸς Κινύρης, καὶ Κινύρης δὲ Κίλιξ.

compare this saying of Phocylides :

καὶ τόδε Φωκυλίδεω· Λέριοι κακοί, οὐχ ὁ μέν, ὃς δ' οὔ,
πάντες, πλὴν Προκλέους, καὶ Προκλέης Λέριος :

and of Richard Porson on the German professor Hermann :

The Germans in Greek
are sadly to seek :
not five in five score,
but ninety-five more.
All save only Hermann,
and Hermann's a German.

This was turned into Greek by Porson :

Νήιδες ἐστὲ μέτρων, ὦ Τεύτονες, οὐχ ὁ μέν, ὃς δ' οὔ,
πάντες πλὴν Ἕρμαννος, ὁ δ' Ἕρμαννος πάνυ Τεύτων.

Odysseus and the Sirens

27

Odysseus

'Οδυσσεὺς ἦν υἱὸς Λαέρτου, 'Ιθάκην δ' ᾤκει, νῆσον
ὀλίγην μέν, φίλην δέ. ἔγημε δὲ Πηνελόπην, καὶ υἱὸν εἶχε
Τηλέμαχον. ἐκ δὲ τῶν θεῶν 'Αθηνᾶν μάλιστ' ἐτίμησεν.
ἐπὶ δὲ "Ιλιον ἐλθὼν ἐν μὲν πολέμῳ ἀνδρεῖον ἐν δὲ βουλῇ σοφὸν 5
ἑαυτὸν παρεῖχε, καὶ ἐν τοῖς κινδύνοις οὕτως εὔπορος ἦν ὥστε
ὑπὸ 'Ομήρου πολύτροπος καλεῖσθαι.

μετὰ δὲ τὴν 'Ιλίου ἅλωσιν ἐπανῆλθεν εἰς 'Ιθάκην, ὅπου ηὗρε
πολλοὺς νεανίας, τῆς Πηνελόπης μνηστῆρας, συνειλεγμένους.
τούτους δέ, συνεργάτας ἔχων Τηλέμαχον, καὶ Εὔμαιον τὸν 10
πιστὸν συφορβόν, ἀπέκτεινεν.

Apollodorus, Epitome, vii. 26

The story of Odysseus is largely contained in Homer's Odyssey.

l. 2. Homer speaks of " a small gift but a dear one " : δόσις δ'
ὀλίγη τε φίλη τε.

9. συνειλεγμένους, perf. pass. partic. of συλλέγω, I collect together.

IV

LEGENDS

The home-coming of Castor and Polydeuces

28

The Argonauts

Βασιλεὺς ἦν τῶν Κόλχων Αἰήτης, τούτῳ δ᾽ ἐδόθη χρησμὸς ὅτι τελευτήσει τὸν βίον ὅταν ξένοι καταπλέοντες τὸ χρυσόμαλλον δέρος ἀπενέγκωσι. διὰ τοῦτο διέδωκεν εἰς ἅπαντα τόπον τὴν φήμην τῆς Κόλχων ἀγριότητος, ἵνα μηδεὶς τῶν ξένων ἐπιβαίνειν τολμήσῃ τῆς χώρας. ἐν δὲ τῷ αὐτῷ καιρῷ 5 Πελίᾳ, βασιλεῖ Ἰωλκοῦ ἐν Θετταλίᾳ, χρησμὸς ἐδόθη ὅτι Ἰάσων μέλλει φονεύσειν αὐτόν. δείσας τοίνυν Ἰάσονα, ἐκέλευσεν αὐτὸν τὸ χρυσόμαλλον δέρος φέρειν αὐτῷ. τὸ δὲ δέρος ἔκειτο ἐν Ἄρεος ἄλσει ἐν Κόλχοις, ὅπου ἐφρουρεῖτο ὑπὸ δράκοντος ἀΰπνου. ἐπὶ τοῦτο πεμπόμενος Ἰάσων πρῶτον 10 μὲν ναῦν κατεσκεύασεν, ἣ προσηγορεύθη Ἀργώ. ἔπειτα δὲ συνήγειρε τοὺς ἀρίστους τῆς Ἑλλάδος, ὧν ἦσαν Ἡρακλῆς καὶ Κάστωρ καὶ Πολυδεύκης.

Apollodorus, I. ix. 22

29

The Argonauts (continued)

Εἷς δὲ τῶν κινδύνων οὓς ὑπέμειναν οἱ Ἀργοναῦται ἦν ἀπὸ τῶν Συμπληγάδων πετρῶν. ἦσαν δ᾽ αὗται κατὰ τὴν τοῦ Πόντου εἴσοδον, ὑπερμεγέθεις· συγκρουόμεναι δ᾽ ὑπὸ τῶν πνευμάτων τὸν διὰ θαλάττης πόρον ἀπέκλειον. χαλεπὸν δ᾽ ἦν καὶ τοῖς ὄρνισι δι᾽ αὐτῶν ἐλθεῖν· ἐκέλευσεν οὖν Ἰάσων ἀφεῖναι 5

33

πελειάδα διὰ τῶν πετρῶν. ταύτης δὲ τῆς πελειάδος τὰ ἄκρα
τῶν πτερῶν ἡ σύμπτωσις τῶν πετρῶν ἀπέκοψεν· ὕστερον
δ' οἱ ἑταῖροι, ἐπιτηρήσαντες τὰς πέτρας διασχιζομένας,
διῆλθον. ἐκ δὲ τούτου τοῦ χρόνου αἱ Συμπληγάδες ἔστησαν
ἀκίνητοι.   10

Apollodorus, I. ix. 22

l. 5. ἀφεῖναι, aor. infin. act. of ἀφίημι (Par. 78, p. 264).

30

The Argonauts (continued)

Οὕτως οἱ 'Αργοναῦται ἦλθον ἐπὶ Κολχίδα. καὶ ἧκε πρὸς
Αἰήτην 'Ιάσων, παρακαλῶν δοῦναι τὸ δέρας αὐτῷ, ὁ δ' ὑπέσ-
χετο δώσειν ὅταν τοὺς χαλκόποδας ταύρους μόνος καταζεύξῃ·
ἦσαν δὲ ἄγριοι παρ' Αἰήτῃ ταῦροι δύο, οἳ χαλκοῦς μὲν εἶχον
πόδας, πῦρ δ' ἐκ στομάτων ἐφύσων. ἀποροῦντι δὲ τῷ 'Ιάσονι   5
ὅπως καταζεύξει τοὺς ταύρους, Μήδεια, θυγάτηρ Αἰήτου
ἐρῶσα 'Ιάσονος, ἔδειξεν ὅπως χρὴ τοῦτο ποιεῖν, ὤμοσε δ'
'Ιάσων αὐτὴν ἕξειν γυναῖκα, καὶ εἰς 'Ελλάδα ἄξειν· οὕτως
φάρμακον ἔδωκε Μήδεια ᾧ ἐκέλευσε χρῖσαι τὸ σῶμα· οὐδὲν
γὰρ πείσεσθαι ὑπὸ τῶν ταύρων.   10

Apollodorus, I. ix. 23

l. 7. ὤμοσε, swore, from ὄμνυμι ; see Syntax F1, p. 298.
10. πείσεσθαι ; see πάσχω.
Indirect statement—supply from ἐκέλευσε, " she said ".

31

The Argonauts (continued)

Ἰάσων δὲ τοῦτο ἀκούσας, καὶ χρισάμενος τῷ φαρμάκῳ, κατέζευξε τοὺς ταύρους, καίπερ μετὰ πολλοῦ πυρὸς ὁρμήσαντας πρὸς αὐτόν. ἔπειτα ἐκέλευσεν Αἰήτης σπείρειν ὀδόντας δράκοντος· σπείροντος δὲ τοῦ Ἰάσονος ἐπανῆλθον ἐκ τῆς γῆς ἄνδρες ἔνοπλοι. ὁ δέ, ὅπου πλείστους ἑώρα, λίθοις ἔβαλλε· 5 καὶ μαχομένους πρὸς ἀλλήλους, προσιὼν διέφθειρεν.

ἔπειτα Μήδεια νυκτὸς ἐπὶ τὸ δέρας ἤγαγε, καὶ τὸν φύλακα, τὸν δράκοντα, κατακοιμίσασα τοῖς φαρμάκοις ἔλαβε τὸ δέρας. καὶ κατελθὼν ἐπὶ τὴν Ἑλλάδα τὸ μὲν δέρας Ἰάσων Πελίᾳ ἔδωκε, τὴν δὲ ναῦν ἀνέθηκε Ποσειδῶνι. 10

Apollodorus, I. ix. 22

l. 1. χρισάμενος, middle, *anointing himself.*
7. Supply αὐτὸν with ἤγαγε.

32

Perseus and Andromeda

Περσεὺς υἱὸς ἦν Διὸς καὶ Δανάης. μετὰ δὲ ἄλλους πόνους πορευόμενος πρὸς Αἰθιοπίαν, ἧς ἐβασίλευσε Κηφεύς, ηὗρε τὴν τούτου θυγατέρα, Ἀνδρομέδαν, δοθεῖσαν βορὰν θαλασσίῳ κήτει. Κασσιόπεια γάρ, ἡ Κηφέως γυνή, Νήρῃσιν ἤρισε περὶ κάλλους, καὶ πασῶν εἶναι κρείσσων ηὔχησεν· αἱ δ' οὖν 5 Νηρῃδες βαρέως ἔφερον, καὶ Ποσειδῶν συνοργισθεὶς κῆτος ἔπεμψεν ἐπὶ τὴν Αἰθιοπίαν· ἀναγκασθεὶς δ' ὑπὸ τῶν πολιτῶν Κηφεὺς προὔθηκεν Ἀνδρομέδαν τῷ κήτει. ταύτην θεασάμενος ὁ Περσεύς, καὶ ἐρασθείς, διέφθειρε τὸ κῆτος, καὶ ἔλαβεν Ἀνδρομέδαν γυναῖκα. Apollodorus, II. iv. 3

l 5. ηὔχησεν from αὐχέω, *boast.* Syntax F 1, p. 298.

33

Deucalion and Pyrrha

Δευκαλίων παῖς ἦν Προμηθέως, καὶ ἔγημε Πύρραν. ἐπεὶ
δὲ Ζεὺς ἤθελε τὸ χαλκοῦν γένος ἀνθρώπων, διὰ τὴν ἀδικίαν
αὐτῶν, ἀφανίσαι, Δευκαλίων ἐποίησε λάρνακα, καὶ τὰ ἐπιτήδεια ἐνθεὶς μετὰ Πύρρας ἐνέβη. Ζεὺς δὲ πολὺν ὑετὸν ἀπ᾽
οὐρανοῦ πέμψας, τὰ πλεῖστα μέρη τῆς Ἑλλάδος κατέκλυσε.   5
διεφθάρησαν δ᾽ οἱ ἄνθρωποι πλὴν ὀλίγων, οἳ κατέφυγον ἐπὶ τὰ
ὕψιστα ὄρη. Δευκαλίων δὲ διὰ τῆς θαλάσσης φερόμενος ἡμέρας
καὶ νύκτας ἐννέα, τῷ Παρνασῷ προσίσχει, καὶ ἐκβὰς τῆς
λάρνακος ἔθυσε Διί.

Apollodorus, I. vii. 2

34

Orpheus

Ὀρφεύς, Καλλιόπης καὶ Οἰάγρου υἱός, ᾄδων ἐκήλει
λίθους τὲ καὶ δένδρα ὥστε ἕπεσθαι αὐτῷ. ἡ δὲ γυνὴ αὐτοῦ,
Εὐρυδίκη, δηχθεῖσα ὑπ᾽ ὄφεως ἀπέθανεν· ὁ δ᾽ Ὀρφεὺς κατελθὼν εἰς Ἅδου Πλούτωνα ἔπεισεν ἀναπέμψαι αὐτήν, ἀλλ᾽
ἐπὶ τούτῳ, ὅτι οὐ χρὴ Ὀρφέα, πρὸς τὸ φῶς πορευόμενον, ἐπι-   5
στραφῆναι πρὶν ἂν εἰς τὴν οἰκίαν γένηται. Ὀρφεὺς δὲ διὰ
πόθον τῆς γυναικὸς ἐπεστράφη, ἡ δὲ πάλιν εἰς Ἅδου κατηνέχθη.

Apollodorus, I. iii. 2

l. 3. δηχθεῖσα, aor. pass. partic. of δάκνω, bite.
   5. ἐπὶ τούτῳ, on this condition.   ἐπὶ + dat. often has this sense.
ἐπιστραφῆναι, strong aor. pass. infin. of ἐπιστρέφω, turn back
(himself).   πρὶν ἄν, see Syntax O 3, p. 306.   κατηνέχθη, aor.
pass. of καταφέρω.

35

Prometheus

Προμηθεύς, Ἰαπέτου υἱός, ἐξ ὕδατος καὶ πηλοῦ ἀνθρώπους
ἔπλασε, καὶ πῦρ ἔδωκε, παρὰ Διὸς κλέψας. ὡς δ' ᾔσθετο Ζεύς,
προσέταξεν Ἡφαίστῳ προσηλοῦν τὸ σῶμα Προμηθέως τῷ
Καυκάσῳ ὄρει. καὶ ἐκεῖ Προμηθεὺς πολλῶν ἐτῶν ἀριθμὸν
διετέλεσε· καθ' ἑκάστην δ' ἡμέραν ἀετὸς ἐλθὼν τὸ ἧπαρ αὐτοῦ 5
κατέφαγεν, ἀλλ' ηὐξάνετο τὸ ἧπαρ νυκτός. τέλος δὲ Ἡρακλῆς
ἔλυσεν αὐτόν.

Apollodorus, I. vii. 1

l. 2. ᾔσθετο from αἰσθάνομαι, *perceive.*
6. κατέφαγεν from κατεσθίω.
τέλος δέ, adverbially, *at the end, finally.*

Great poets have worked on this theme. Aeschylus wrote
Προμηθεὺς Δεσμώτης (*Prometheus Bound*), which we still have :
the first of a trilogy, i.e. three plays presented to the Athenian
public together (the other two plays—Π. Λυόμενος and Π.
Πυρφόρος—have been lost). Inspired by Aeschylus, Shelley
wrote *Prometheus Unbound,* in which mankind is viewed as set
free from tyranny.

36

The Sphinx

Ἡ Σφὶγξ θηρίον δίμορφον ἦν, ἔχουσα τὴν μὲν κεφαλὴν
γυναικὸς τὸ δὲ σῶμα λεαίνης. καὶ εἰς τὰς Θήβας τῆς Βοιωτίας
ἐλθοῦσα αἴνιγμα προύθηκε τοῖς πειρωμένοις λῦσαι, καὶ πολλοὺς οὐ δυναμένους διέφθειρε.

Ἦν δὲ τὸ αἴνιγμα οὕτως ἔχον· τί ἐστι τῶν ζῴων τὸ αὐτὸ 5
δίπουν καὶ τρίπουν καὶ τετράπουν, ἀσθενέστατον δὲ ὅταν τετράπουν. ἀπορούντων δὲ τῶν ἄλλων ἔλυσεν ὁ Οἰδίπους, εἰπὼν
ἄνθρωπον εἶναι· νήπιον γὰρ ὄντα τετράπουν εἶναι, καὶ ἀσθε-
νέστατον· αὐξηθέντα δὲ δίπουν εἶναι· γηράσαντα δὲ τρίπουν,
βακτηρίᾳ χρώμενον ὥστ᾽ ἐπερείδεσθαι. ἐνταῦθα ἡ μὲν Σφίγξ 10
διέφθειρεν ἑαυτήν, ὁ δ᾽ Οἰδίπους Ἰοκάστην γαμεῖ, τοῦ
λύσαντος ἆθλον.

Apollodorus, III. v. 8

l. 3. τοῖς πειρωμένοις λῦσαι, *for men to try to solve*.

10. βακτηρία, *rod, staff*. Bacteria were so named as rod-like creatures
under the microscope.

The story of Oedipus forms the subject of some of the greatest
of the Greek plays that have come down to us : such as the
Oedipus Rex, the *Oedipus Coloneus*, and the *Antigone* (all by
Sophocles).

V

FABLES AND FICTION

Aesop and the fox

37

The frogs ask for a king

Οἱ βάτραχοι, λυπούμενοι ἐπὶ τῇ ἑαυτῶν ἀναρχίᾳ, πρέσβεις ἔπεμψαν ἐπὶ τὸν Δία, αἰτοῦντες βασιλέα αὐτοῖς παρασχεῖν. ὁ δέ, αἰσθόμενος τὴν εὐήθειαν αὐτῶν, ξύλον εἰς τὴν λίμνην καθῆκε. καὶ οἱ βάτραχοι τὸ μὲν πρῶτον καταπλαγέντες τὸν ψόφον, ἑαυτοὺς εἰς τὰ βάθη τῆς λίμνης ἔρριψαν· ὕστερον δέ,   5
ὡς ἀκίνητον ἦν τὸ ξύλον, ἀνῆλθον πάλιν, καὶ ἐς τοσοῦτο τῆς καταφρονήσεως ἦλθον ὥστε ἐπιβαίνοντες ἐκαθίζοντο. καὶ ἀνάξιον νομίζοντες τοιοῦτον βασιλέα, ἦλθον αὖθις πρὸς τὸν Δία, καὶ παρεκάλουν ἀλλάξαι αὐτοῖς τὸν ἄρχοντα. καὶ ὁ Ζεὺς ἀγανακτήσας ὕδραν αὐτοῖς ἔπεμψεν, ἣ συλλαβοῦσα κατή-   10
σθιεν αὐτούς.

Ὁ λόγος δηλοῖ ὅτι ἄμεινόν ἐστιν ἀργὸν εἶναι τὸν ἄρχοντα ἢ φίλεργον καὶ πονηρόν.

Aesop (Halm, 76)

l. 4. καταπλαγέντες, str. aor. pass. of καταπλήσσω, *terrify*.
  τὸν ψόφον, adverbial acc. *at the sound*.
  5. ἔρριψαν, aor. of ῥίπτειν, *to throw*. Initial ρ doubles after the augment.
  7. ἐκαθίζοντο, from καθίζομαι, *sit down*, augmented as though not a compound.

38

The town mouse and the country mouse

Μύες δύο, ὁ μὲν ἀρουραῖος ὁ δ' ἀστικός, κοινὸν εἶχον τὸν βίον.

41

καὶ ὁ ἀρουραῖος πρῶτος εἰς ἀγρὸν τὸν ἀστικὸν παρελάμβανε,
καὶ ξενίαν αὐτῷ παρεῖχε καὶ τράπεζαν, οἷα φέρει τοῖς ἐνοι-
κοῦσιν ἀγρός. ἀμειβόμενος δὲ τὴν ξενίαν ὁ ἀστικὸς τὸν
ἀρουραῖον μῦν εἰς ἀνδρὸς εὐπόρου παρελάμβανεν οἶκον. ὡς 5
δὲ τῶν ὄντων ἅπτεσθαι ἤρχοντο, ἀνέῳξέ τις τὴν θύραν, οἱ δ᾽
ἔφυγον εἰς στενὴν τρώγλην· ὡς δὲ πάλιν ἤμελλον ἐκκύψειν καὶ
μικρὰν ἰσχάδα λήψεσθαι, ἕτερος ἦλθεν, οἱ δ᾽ ἔνδον ἐκρύπτοντο.
ὁ δ᾽ ἀρουραῖος εἶπε, Καίπερ τοσαῦτα δειπνῶν, χαῖρε, ἔχων
τὰ πάντα μετὰ κινδύνων. ἐγὼ δὲ βοτάνας καὶ ῥίζας τρώγων 10
ἀφόβως βιώσομαι.

 ῾Ο λόγος δηλοῖ ὅτι οἱ μέτρια κτώμενοι πολλάκις εὐδαιμονέστεροί εἰσι τῶν πλουτούντων.

Aesop (Halm, 297)

l. 6. τῶν ὄντων, *what there was*. ἅπτομαι, takes gen.
    ἀνέῳξε from ἀνοίγνυμι. Note double augment.
 7. ἤμελλον from μέλλω. Note augment ἠ.
 9. τοσαῦτα, internal acc., *feeding off so much*.
 11. βιώσομαι. See ζῶ (Par. 71).

39

The mouse and the miser

Μῦν ᾿Ασκληπιάδης ὁ φιλάργυρος εἶδεν ἐν οἴκῳ,
    καί, Τί ποιεῖς ; φησίν, φίλτατε μῦ, παρ᾽ ἐμοί ;
ἡδὺ δ᾽ ὁ μῦς γελάσας, Μηδέν, φίλε, φησί, φοβήθῃς,
    οὐχὶ τροφῆς παρὰ σοὶ χρῄζομεν, ἀλλὰ μόνης.

Anth. Pal. xi. 391

l. 3. ἡδύ, neuter adj. as adverb. cf. *dulce ridentem Lalagen*.

40

The farmer and his sons

Γεωργός τις, μέλλων τελευτᾶν τὸν βίον, καὶ βουλόμενος
τοὺς παῖδας πεῖραν λαβεῖν τῆς γεωργίας καὶ μὴ πρὸς ἄλλα
τρέπεσθαι, προσκαλέσας ἔφη· Ἐγὼ μέν, ὦ παῖδες, ἤδη τοῦ
βίου ἔξειμι· ὑμεῖς δὲ ζητοῦντες ἃ ἐν τῷ ἀμπελῶνι κέκρυπται
εὑρήσετε πάντα. οἱ μὲν οὖν, οἰόμενοι θησαυρὸν ἐκεῖ κατω-   5
ρύχθαι, πᾶσαν τὴν τοῦ ἀμπελῶνος γῆν ἀποθανόντος τοῦ πατρὸς
κατέσκαψαν, καὶ θησαυρὸν μὲν οὐχ ηὗρον, ὁ δ' ἀμπελών, καλῶς
σκαφάντων αὐτῶν, πολὺν τὸν καρπὸν ἀπέδωκεν.
Ὁ λόγος δηλοῖ ὅτι ὁ πόνος θησαυρός ἐστι τοῖς ἀνθρώποις.

Aesop (Halm, 98)

l. 2. πεῖραν λαβεῖν, make an attempt at +gen.
5. κατωρύχθαι, perf. pass. infin. of κατορύσσω.

41

The North Wind and the Sun

Βορρᾶς καὶ Ἥλιος περὶ δυνάμεως ἤριζον· ἔδοξε δὲ αὐτοῖς
τὴν νίκην ἐκείνῳ ἀπονεῖμαι ὃς ἂν αὐτῶν ἄνθρωπον ὁδοιπόρον
ἐκδύσῃ. καὶ ὁ Βορρᾶς ἀρξάμενος σφοδρὸς ἦν, τοῦ δ' ἀνθρώπου
ἀντεχομένου τῆς ἐσθῆτος μᾶλλον ἔπνει. ὁ δ' ὑπὸ τοῦ ψύχους
πονῶν ἑτέραν ἐσθῆτα προσελάμβανεν, ἕως ἀποκαμὼν ὁ   5
Βορρᾶς τῷ Ἡλίῳ μετὰ ταῦτα παρέδωκε. καὶ ἐκεῖνος τὸ μὲν
πρῶτον μετρίως ἔλαμψε, τοῦ δ' ἀνθρώπου τὰ περισσὰ τῶν

ἱματίων ἀποθέντος, σφοδρότερον τὸ καῦμα ἐποίησε, μέχρις
οὗ, πρὸς τὴν θερμότητα ἀντέχειν οὐ δυνάμενος, ἀποδυσάμενος ἐπὶ λουτρὸν ἀπῄει. 10
ὁ μῦθος δηλοῖ ὅτι πειθὼ βίαν νικᾷ.

Aesop (Halm, 82)

l. 2. ὃς ἂν ἐκδύσῃ, indefinite construction (Syntax N 1, p. 306).

42
The Lion, the Ass, and the Fox

Λέων καὶ ὄνος καὶ ἀλώπηξ κοινωνίαν ποιησάμενοι ἐξῆλθον
πρὸς ἄγραν· πολλῆς οὖν θήρας συλληφθείσης, προσέταξεν ὁ
λέων τῷ ὄνῳ διελεῖν αὐτοῖς. ὁ δὲ τρεῖς μερίδας ποιήσας ἴσας,
ἐκδέξασθαι ἐκέλευσε. καὶ ὁ λέων ὀργισθεὶς τὸν ὄνον κατέφαγεν. εἶτα τῇ ἀλώπεκι προσέταξε διελεῖν, ἡ δέ, μίαν μερίδα 5
μεγάλην ποιήσασα, ἑαυτῇ βραχύ τι κατέλιπε. καὶ ὁ λέων,
Τίς σε, ὦ βελτίστη, ἔφη, οὕτως διαιρεῖν ἐδίδαξεν ; ἡ δ’
εἶπεν, Ἡ τοῦ ὄνου συμφορά.

Aesop (Halm, 260)

l. 2. συλληφθείσης from συλλαμβάνω (p. 316).
3. διελεῖν from διαιρέω, divide.

43
Voyage to the Moon

Ἑπτὰ δ’ ἡμέρας καὶ τὰς ἴσας νύκτας ἀεροδρομήσαντες καθ-
ορῶμεν γῆν τινα μεγάλην ἐν τῷ ἀέρι ὥσπερ νῆσον, λαμπρὰν καὶ
σφαιροειδῆ· προσενεχθέντες δ’ αὐτῇ καὶ ὁρμισάμενοι ἀπέ-

βημεν, ἐπισκοποῦντες δὲ τὴν χώραν εὑρίσκομεν οἰκουμένην
τε καὶ γεωργουμένην. ἡμέρας μὲν οὐδὲν ἄλλο καθεωρῶμεν, 5
νυκτὸς δ' ἐπιγενομένης ἐφαίνοντο ἡμῖν καὶ ἄλλαι πολλαὶ νῆσοι
πλησίον, καὶ γῆ τις κάτω, καὶ πόλεις ἐν αὐτῇ ἔχουσα καὶ ποταμοὺς καὶ πελάγη καὶ ὕλας καὶ ὄρη. ταύτην οὖν τὴν καθ' ἡμᾶς
οἰκουμένην ἠκάζομεν. δόξαν δὲ ἡμῖν καὶ ἔτι πορρωτέρω
προελθεῖν, τοῖς Ἱππογύπαις ἠπαντήσαμεν· οὗτοι δέ εἰσιν 10
ἄνδρες ἐπὶ γυπῶν μεγάλων ὀχούμενοι, καὶ καθάπερ ἵπποις τοῖς
ὄρνισι χρώμενοι. μάθοι δ' ἄν τις τὸ μέγεθος αὐτῶν ἐντεῦθεν·
νεὼς γὰρ μεγάλης ἱστίου ἕκαστον τῶν πτερῶν μακρότερον καὶ
παχύτερον φαίνεται.

Lucian, Vera Historia, I. 10

The Ἀληθὴς Ἱστορία of Lucian is a forerunner of *Gulliver's Travels*.

l. 5. ἡμέρας, *by day.*
  8. τὴν καθ' ἡμᾶς οἰκουμένην : *our world.*
  9. ἠκάζομεν from εἰκάζω, *guess to be.*
    δόξαν, acc. abs. from δοκεῖ, *as it seemed good* (Par. 98).
 12. μάθοι δ' ἄν τις. Potential, *one might learn* (Syntax R 1, p. 312).
 13. ἱστίου, comparative gen.

44

Voyage to the Moon (continued)

Τούτοις οὖν τοῖς Ἱππογύπαις προσετάχθη περιπετομένοις
τὴν γῆν, εἴ τις εὑρεθείη ξένος, ἀνάγειν ὡς τὸν βασιλέα. καὶ δὴ
καὶ ἡμᾶς συλλαβόντες ἀνάγουσιν ὡς αὐτόν. ὁ δὲ θεασάμενος
καὶ ἀπὸ τῆς θέας καὶ τῆς στολῆς εἰκάσας, Ἕλληνες ἄρα,
ἔφη, ὑμεῖς, ὦ ξένοι. συμφησάντων δέ, Πῶς οὖν ἀφίκεσθε, 5

Griffins

ἔφη, τοσοῦτον ἀέρα διελθόντες ; καὶ ἡμεῖς τὸ πᾶν αὐτῷ διηγησάμεθα. καὶ ἐκεῖνος αὖ τὰ καθ' ἑαυτὸν ἡμῖν διεξῄει, ὡς καὶ αὐτὸς ἄνθρωπος ὤν, τοὔνομα Ἐνδυμίων, ὃς ἀπὸ τῆς ἡμετέρας γῆς καθεύδων ἀνηρπάσθη, καὶ ἀφικόμενος ἐβασίλευσε τῆς χώρας.   10

Lucian, *Vera Historia*, 11

l. 2. εὑρεθείη, conditional clause in indirect statement (Syntax Q 2, p. 310).
7. διεξῄει from διέξειμι, *to go through, tell*.
8. τοὔνομα for τὸ ὄνομα, adverbial, *by name*.
Ἐνδυμίων, the youth Endymion while asleep was admired by Σελήνη, the moon.

45

Sea monsters

Ἡμεῖς δὲ δύο μόνον ἡμέρας πλεύσαντες πρὸς ἀνίσχοντα τὸν ἥλιον ὁρῶμεν θηρία καὶ κήτη πολλὰ μὲν καὶ ἄλλα, ἐν δὲ μέγιστον ἁπάντων, ὅσον σταδίων χιλίων τὸ μέγεθος. ἐπῄει δὲ κεχηνὸς καὶ πρὸ πολλοῦ τάρασσον τὴν θάλασσαν, ἀφρῷ τε περικλυζόμενον καὶ τοὺς ὀδόντας ἐκφαῖνον ὀξεῖς ὥσπερ σκόλοπας 5 καὶ λευκοὺς ὥσπερ ἐλεφαντίνους. ἡμεῖς δὲ τὸ ὕστατον ἀλλήλους προσειπόντες καὶ περιβαλόντες ἐμένομεν, τὸ δ' ἤδη παρῆν, καὶ ἡμᾶς αὐτῇ νηὶ κατέπιεν. ἐπεὶ δ' ἔνδον ἦμεν, τὸ μὲν πρῶτον σκότος ἦν καὶ οὐδὲν ἑωρῶμεν, ὕστερον δέ, αὐτοῦ ἀναχανόντος, εἴδομεν κύτος μέγα καὶ πάντη πλατὺ καὶ 10 ὑψηλόν, ἱκανὸν μυριάνδρῳ πόλει ἐνοικεῖν· ἔκειντο δ' ἐν μέσῳ καὶ μακροὶ ἰχθύες καὶ ἄλλα πολλὰ θηρία, καὶ πλοίων ἱστία, καὶ ἄγκυραι.

Lucian, *Vera Historia*, i. 30

l. 1. πλεύσαντες, aor. partic. of πλέω, *sail*.
   3. ἐπῄει from ἔπειμι (Par. 81, p. 272).
   4. κεχηνός, perf. partic. of χάσκω, *gape*, p. 317.
   πρὸ πολλοῦ, *far in front*.
   8. αὐτῇ νηὶ, *ship and all*.
   10. ἀναχανόντος, strong aor. of ἀναχάσκω, *yawn*.

46

A woman changes herself into a bird, by means of a magical ointment

Ἡμέραις δὲ ὕστερον οὐ πολλαῖς ἀγγέλλει μοι ἡ Παλαίστρα ὡς ἡ δέσποινα αὐτῆς μέλλει, ὄρνις γενομένη, πέτεσθαι πρὸς τὸν ἐρώμενον. καὶ ἐγώ, Νῦν, ἔφην, ὦ Παλαίστρα, ὁ καιρὸς τῆς σῆς εἰς ἐμὲ χάριτος. Θάρρει, ἔφη. καὶ ἐπειδὴ ἑσπέρα ἦν ἄγει με πρὸς τὴν θύραν τοῦ δωματίου ἔνθα ἐκείνη ἐκάθευδε, 5 καὶ κελεύει με προσελθεῖν ὀπῇ τινι τῆς θύρας λεπτῇ, καὶ σκοπεῖν τὰ γιγνόμενα ἔνδον. ὁρῶ οὖν τὴν γυναῖκα. ἡ δὲ κιβώτιον μέγα ἀνοίξασα, πάνυ πολλὰς πυξίδας ἔχον ἐν αὐτῷ, ἐντεῦθεν προφέρει μίαν. ἐνῆν δ' οἶμαι ἔλαιον, καὶ τούτου λαβοῦσα χρίεται ὅλη. καὶ ἄφνω πτερὰ ἐκφύεται αὐτῇ, καὶ ἡ ῥὶς κερατίνη καὶ 10 γρυπὴ ἐγένετο, καὶ τὰ ἄλλα εἶχεν ὅσα ὀρνίθων κτήματά ἐστιν. καὶ ἦν οὐδὲν ἄλλο ἢ κόραξ.

Lucian: Λούκιος ἢ Ὄνος 12
(*Lucius, or The Ass*)

l. 3. τὸν ἐρώμενον, *lover*. Pres. pass. partic. of ἐράω.
   ὁ καιρός, supply *has come*. (Notes continued overleaf.)

4. Θάρρει, *be confident, cheer up.* Sometimes written θάρσει. Pres. imper. of θαρρέω.

7. τὰ γιγνόμενα, *the happenings.*

8. ἀνοίξασα from ἀνοίγνυμι, *open.*

9. οἶμαι, *I think,* for οἴομαι.
τούτου λαβοῦσα, partitive genitive, *taking some of this.*
χρίεται, middle, *to anoint oneself.*

11. τὰ ἄλλα . . . ὅσα . . . κτήματα, *all the other characteristics.*

47

A man is changed into an ass

Ἐγὼ δ' ὄναρ ἐκεῖνο οἰόμενος ὁρᾶν, τοῖς δακτύλοις τῶν ἐμαυτοῦ βλεφάρων ἡπτόμην, οὐ πιστεύων τοῖς ἐμοῖς ὀφθαλμοῖς. ὡς δὲ μόλις ἐπείσθην ὅτι οὐ καθεύδω, ᾔτησα τὴν Παλαίστραν καὶ ἐμὲ πτερῶσαι, καὶ χρίσασαν ἐκείνῳ τῷ φαρμάκῳ ἐᾶσαι πέτεσθαί με. ἐβουλόμην γὰρ μαθεῖν εἰ τὴν 5 μορφὴν λαβὼν ὄρνιθος καὶ τὴν ψυχὴν ὄρνις ἔσομαι. ἡ δὲ κομίζει τὴν πυξίδα, ἐγὼ δ' ἀποδυσάμενος χρίω ὅλον ἐμαυτόν. καὶ ὄρνις μὲν οὐ γίγνομαι ὁ δυστυχής, ἀλλά μοι οὐρὰ ὄπισθεν ἐξῆλθε, καὶ οἱ δάκτυλοι ᾤχοντο οὐκ οἶδ' ὅπου, ὄνυχας δὲ τοὺς πάντας τέσσαρας εἶχον, καὶ τούτους οὐδὲν ἄλλο ἢ ὁπλὰς καὶ αἱ 10 χεῖρες καὶ οἱ πόδες κτήνους πόδες ἐγένοντο, καὶ τὰ ὦτα μακρά, καὶ τὸ πρόσωπον μέγα, φωνὴν δ' ἀνθρώπου εἰς τὸ μέμφεσθαι τῇ Παλαίστρᾳ, οὐκέτι εἶχον· ἐπεὶ δὲ κύκλῳ περιεσκόπουν, ἐμαυτὸν ἑώρων ὄνον.

Lucian, *ibidem,* 13

l. 6. τὴν ψυχήν, adverbial acc., *in soul.*

9. τοὺς πάντας τέσσαρας, *four altogether.* Note position of πάντας.

48

The Rhodian Swallow-song

Ἦλθ᾽ ἦλθε χελιδών
καλὰς ὥρας ἄγουσα,
καλοὺς ἐνιαυτούς,
ἐπὶ γαστέρα λευκά,
ἐπὶ νῶτα μέλαινα.   5
παλάθαν σὺ προκύκλει
ἐκ πίονος οἴκου,
οἴνου τε δέπαστρον,
τυροῦ τε κάνυστρον.
καὶ πύρνα χελιδὼν   10
καὶ λεκιθίταν
οὐκ ἀπωθεῖται. πότερ᾽ ἀπίωμες ἢ λαβώμεθα ;
εἰ μέν τι δώσεις, εἰ δὲ μή, οὐκ ἐάσομες.
ἢ τὰν θύραν φέρωμες, ἢ θοὐπέρθυρον,
ἢ τὰν γυναῖκα τὰν ἔσω καθημέναν.   15
μικρὰ μέν ἐστι, ῥᾳδίως μιν οἴσομες.
ἂν δὲ φέρῃς τι
μέγα δή τι φέροιο.
ἄνοιγ᾽ ἄνοιγε τὰν θύραν χελιδόνι·
οὐ γὰρ γέροντές ἐσμεν, ἀλλὰ παιδία.   20

Smythe, *Greek Melic Poets*, p. 159

Boys went from house to house soliciting gifts on the appearance of the swallow, as they did in England on Boxing Day.
Note Doric α for η, and -ες for -εν, 1st pers. plur. as φέρωμες.

14. φέρωμες, *are we to carry off*, deliberative (Syntax, B 5, p. 294).
θοὐπέρθυρον = τὸ ὑπέρθυρον.   16. μιν, *her*.

18. φέροιο is a wish ; φέρομαι, middle = *win*, *gain*.

VI

HOME LIFE

Flute-player and older man

49

The tent of Achilles before Troy

Οὗτοι μέν — ὅ τ᾽ Ὀδυσσεὺς καὶ ὁ Αἴας καὶ ὁ Φοῖνιξ —
προσῆλθον τῇ τοῦ Ἀχιλλέως κλισίᾳ· ἐκεῖνον δ᾽ ηὗρον τερπό-
μενον φόρμιγγι, ᾄδοντά τε ἀνδρῶν ἐν μάχῃ ἀρετήν, καὶ
κελεύοντος Ἀχιλλέως ἐκαθίζοντο ἐν ἕδραις ἐπὶ τάπησι· καὶ
ἐνέχεε πιεῖν Πάτροκλος, Ἀχιλλέως ἑταῖρος. ἔπειτα κρέας 5
συὸς καὶ αἰγὸς νῶτον ἔταμεν Ἀχιλλεύς, καὶ ὀβελοῖς ἔπειρε.
Πάτροκλος δὲ ὑπὲρ τοῦ πυρὸς τοὺς ὀβελοὺς ἔχων ὤπτησε τὸ
κρέας. οἱ δὲ τοῖς θεοῖς θύσαντες εἶτα κρέως καὶ σίτου εἷλον.

After Homer, *Iliad*, IX. 182

l. 5. πιεῖν. 2 aor. : πίνω, *drink.*
  6. ἔταμεν from τέμνω, *cut.*
  8. κρέως καὶ σίτου, partitive genitive.

50

At the Court of Menelaus, King of Sparta

Ὁ Τηλέμαχος καὶ ὁ Πεισίστρατος ἦλθον εἰς Λακεδαίμονα.
ἰδόντες δὲ οἱ Μενελάου ὑπηρέται τοὺς μὲν ἵππους ἔλυσαν,
αὐτοὺς δ᾽ εἰσήγαγον. καὶ πρῶτον μὲν ἔλουσαν καὶ ἔχρισαν
ἐλαίῳ αἱ θεράπαιναι, εἶτα καθήμενοι ἐκεῖνοι παρὰ τῷ βασιλεῖ
ἔφαγόν τε καὶ ἔπιον. ἔπειτα τοῦ Μενελάου ἤκουσαν ἄλλους 5
τε πολλοὺς τῶν περὶ Ἴλιον πολεμησάντων πενθοῦντος, καὶ
δὴ καὶ Ὀδυσσέα, ὥστε δακρῦσαι τὸν Τηλέμαχον. εἶτα
εἰσῆλθεν ἡ Ἑλένη· παρέθεσαν δ᾽ αὐτῇ θεράπαιναι ἠλακάτην

53

καὶ τάλαρον, ἵνα ἔρια ἐργάζοιτο· ὕστερον δε ἐν τῷ οἴνῳ,
πινόντων αὐτῶν, φάρμακα ἐνέβαλεν, ὡς τὰς ὀδύνας παύσουσα 10
καὶ λήθην ἐνθήσουσα ὧν ἔπαθον. καὶ ὁ μὲν Τηλέμαχος καὶ
ὁ φίλος ἐν προθύρῳ οἴκου ἐκοιμήσαντο, ἐν δὲ αὐτῷ τῷ οἴκῳ
Μενέλαος καὶ ἡ γυνή.

After Homer, Odyssey, IV

51

Epitaph on a baby

Ἄρτι με γενόμενον ζωῆς βρέφος ἥρπασε δαίμων,
    οὐκ οἶδ' εἴτ' ἀγαθῶν αἴτιος εἴτε κακῶν.
ἀπλήρωτ' Ἀΐδα, τί με νήπιον ἥρπασας ἐχθρῶς;
    τί σπεύδεις; οὐ σοὶ πάντες ὀφειλόμεθα;

Kaibel, Epigrammata Graeca, 576

52

How a baby was saved from a cruel death

Τοῖς Βακχιάδαις — λαμπροὶ δ' ἦσαν οὗτοι ἐν τῇ Κορίνθῳ
— χρησμὸς ἐδόθη ὅτι ὁ Ἠετίωνος υἱὸς τὴν ἀρχὴν αὐτῶν
καταλύσει. ἐπεὶ δ' ἔτεκεν ἡ Ἠετίωνος γυνή, ὡς τάχιστα
πέμπουσι δέκα ἄνδρας εἰς τὸν οἶκον αὐτῆς τὸ βρέφος ἀπο-
κτενοῦντας. καὶ παρελθόντες εἰς τὴν αὐλὴν ᾔτουν τὸ παιδίον
ἑλεῖν· ἡ δὲ γυνή, οὐδὲν εἰδυῖα ἐκείνων ὧν ἕνεκα ἦλθον, 5
ἐνεχείρισεν αὐτὸ ἑνί. καὶ τοῖς μὲν δέκα ἔδοξεν ἤδη τὸν πρῶτον
αὐτῶν λαβόντα τὸ παιδίον εὐθὺς ἀποκτεῖναι· ἀλλὰ τῷ λαβόντι
προσεγέλασεν, ὥστε αὐτὸν κατοικτείρειν. καὶ ἀντὶ τοῦ

Woman with necklace and wool-basket

ἀποκτεῖναι παραδίδωσι τῷ δευτέρῳ, καὶ οὗτος τῷ τρίτῳ· καὶ
οὕτω διεξῆλθε διὰ πάντων τῶν δέκα, οὐδενὸς βουλομένου 10
διαφθεῖραι.

Herodotus, v. 92 (adapted)

53

In a house in Athens where Protagoras was staying

Ἐπειδὴ δὲ ἐν τῷ προθύρῳ ἐγενόμεθα, τέως μὲν στάντες
διελεγόμεθα· ἔπειτα ἐκρούσαμεν· καὶ ὁ θυρωρὸς ἀχθεσθεὶς
οἶμαι διὰ τὸ πλῆθος τῶν φοιτώντων ἐπὶ τὴν οἰκίαν ἀνέῳξε,
καὶ ἰδὼν ἡμᾶς, "Ἔα, ἔφη, σοφισταί τινές· οὐ σχολὴ αὐτῷ.
καὶ ἅμα ἀμφοῖν τοῖν χεροῖν τὴν θύραν πάνυ προθύμως ὡς οἷός 5
τ᾽ ἦν ἐπήραξε. καὶ ἡμεῖς πάλιν ἐκρούομεν· ὁ δὲ πρὶν ἀνοῖξαι,
Ὦ ἄνθρωποι, ἔφη, οὐκ ἀκηκόατε ὅτι οὐ σχολὴ αὐτῷ;
Ἀλλ᾽ ὦ ἀγαθέ, ἔφην, οὔτε παρὰ Καλλίαν τὸν σὸν δεσπότην ἥκομεν οὔτε σοφισταί ἐσμεν, ἀλλὰ θάρρει. Πρωταγόραν γὰρ βουλόμενοι ἰδεῖν ἥκομεν. εἰσάγγειλον οὖν. μόγις 10
οὖν ποτε ὁ ἄνθρωπος ἀνέῳξε τὴν θύραν.

Plato, *Protagoras*, 314 c

l. 4. οὐ σχολὴ αὐτῷ. *Master has no time to spare.*

54

Protagoras (continued)

Ἐπειδὴ δ᾽ εἰσήλθομεν, κατελάβομεν Πρωταγόραν ἐν τῷ
προθύρῳ περιπατοῦντα μετὰ πολλῶν ἄλλων, οἳ αὐτῷ συμ-
περιεπάτουν.

τούτων οἳ ὄπισθεν ἠκολούθουν, ἐπακούοντες τῶν λεγο-
μένων, οἱ πολλοὶ ξένοι ἐφαίνοντο, οὓς ἄγει ἐξ ἑκάστης πόλεως 5
Πρωταγόρας, κηλῶν τῇ φωνῇ ὥσπερ Ὀρφεύς. ἦσαν δέ τινες
τῶν ἐπιχωρίων ἐκεῖ. περὶ τούτων μάλιστ᾽ ἐθαύμασα ἰδὼν
ὡς καλῶς εὐλαβοῦντο μηδέποτ᾽ ἐμποδὼν ἐν τῷ ἔμπροσθεν εἶναι
Πρωταγόρου· ἀλλ᾽ ἐπειδὴ ἐκεῖνος ἀναστρέφοι, καὶ οἱ μετ᾽
ἐκείνου εὖ πως καὶ ἐν κόσμῳ περιεσχίζοντο ἔνθα καὶ ἔνθα, καὶ 10
ἐν κύκλῳ περιϊόντες ἀεὶ εἰς τὸ ὄπισθεν κάλλιστα καθίσταντο.

Plato, Protagoras, 315 B

l. 2. περιπατοῦντα. The Peripatetic philosophers followed Aristotle, whose school contained a covered walk, περίπατος. The
name Peripatetic was from early times erroneously derived from
Aristotle's alleged habit of pacing up and down while he taught.
4. οἱ, distinguish between οἱ article and οἳ relative.
11. καθίσταντο, middle, *took their places, set themselves.*

55

The training of a young wife

Ἀλλὰ καὶ τοῦτο, ἔφην, ὦ Ἰσχόμαχε, πάνυ ἂν ἡδέως
σου πυθοίμην, πότερον αὐτὸς σὺ ἐπαίδευσας τὴν γυναῖκα
ὥστε εἶναι οἵαν δεῖ, ἢ ἐπισταμένην ἔλαβες παρὰ τοῦ πατρὸς
καὶ τῆς μητρὸς διοικεῖν τὰ προσήκοντα αὐτῇ. Καὶ τί
ἠπίστατο, ὦ Σώκρατες, ἢ ἔτη μὲν οὔπω πεντεκαίδεκα γεγονυῖα 5
ἦλθε πρὸς ἐμέ, τὸν δ᾽ ἔμπροσθεν χρόνον ἔζη πολλῶν ἐπιμελουμένων ὅπως ὡς ἐλάχιστα μὲν ὄψοιτο, ἐλάχιστα δ᾽ ἀκούσοιτο,
ἐλάχιστα δ᾽ ἔροιτο ; ἀγαπητὸν δ᾽ ἂν εἴη εἰ ἐπίσταιτο περὶ
ἐρίων ὡς θεραπαίναις δέδοται πρὸς τὸ ἐργάζεσθαι. ἀλλὰ τά
γ᾽ ἀμφὶ γαστέρα πάνυ καλῶς, ὦ Σώκρατες, πεπαιδευμένη 10

Marble girl dedicated by Euthydicus

ἦλθεν, ὅπερ μέγιστον ἔμοιγε δοκεῖ παίδευμα εἶναι καὶ ἀνδρὶ
καὶ γυναικί.

Xenophon, *Oeconomicus*, VII. 4

l. 3. ἐπισταμένην ἔλαβες, *did she know, when you took her, etc.?*
(Par. 90, p. 286). 6. πολλῶν ἐπιμελουμένων, gen. abs., *with
many to take charge.* 7. ὄψοιτο, etc. Syntax K4, p. 302, and
footnote 2, p. 207. 8. ἀγαπητὸν ἂν εἴη, *one would be thankful.*

56

A young wife (continued)

Πρὸς θεῶν, ἔφην, ὦ Ἰσχόμαχε, τί πρῶτον ἤρχου
διδάσκειν αὐτήν; ὡς ἐγὼ τοῦτ' ἂν ἥδιόν σου ἀκούοιμι ἢ εἴ
μοι γυμνικὸν ἢ ἱππικὸν ἀγῶνα τὸν κάλλιστον διηγοῖο. καὶ
ὁ Ἰσχόμαχος ἀπεκρίνατο· Ἐπειδὴ ἤδη μοι χειροήθης ἦν,
ἠρώτων αὐτὴν ὧδέ πως· εἰπέ μοι, ὦ γύναι, τίνος ἕνεκα ἐγώ 5
τέ σε ἔλαβον, καὶ οἱ γονεῖς ἔδοσάν σε ἐμοί; καταφανὲς γὰρ
τοῦτο ὅτι οὐκ ἀπορία ἦν τῶν ἄλλων μεθ' ὧν τὸν βίον διά-
γοιμεν ἄν. ἀλλ' ἐγώ τέ σε ἐξελεξάμην καὶ οἱ σοὶ γονεῖς ἐμέ,
ὡς κοινωνὸν βέλτιστον, ἐκ τῶν δυνατῶν, περὶ οἴκου τε καὶ
τέκνων. ἢν δὲ θεὸς διδῷ ἡμῖν τέκνα, τότε βουλευσόμεθα περὶ 10
αὐτῶν ὅπως ὡς βέλτιστα παιδεύσομεν αὐτά. κοινὸν γὰρ
ἡμῖν τοῦτο ἀγαθόν, συμμάχων καὶ γηροβοσκῶν ὅτι βελτίστων
τυγχάνειν.

Xenophon, *Oeconomicus*, VII. 9

57

A well-ordered household and its joys

Ἄλλαι δὲ ἴδιαι ἡδοναί, ἔφην ἐγὼ τῇ γυναικί, ἔσονται

60 GATE-CRASHERS

ὅταν θεράπαιναν ἀνεπιστήμονα ταλασίας λαβοῦσα ἐπιστήμονα
ποιήσῃς, καὶ διπλασίου σοι ἀξία γένηται, ὡσαύτως δὲ ὅταν
ταμιείας καὶ διακονίας ἀνεπιστήμονα λαβοῦσα ἐπιστήμονα
ποιήσῃς. ἰδίᾳ δὲ καὶ ἡδονή σοι ἔσται ὅταν ἐξῇ σοι εὖ ποιῆσαι   5
τοὺς σώφρονας καὶ ὠφελίμους, καὶ ὅταν ἐξῇ σοι τοὺς πονηροὺς
κολάσαι. τὸ δὲ πάντων ἥδιστον ἔσται, ὅταν βελτίων ἐμοῦ
φανῇς, καὶ ἐμὲ σὸν θεράποντα ποιήσῃς. οὕτως γὰρ οὐ δεῖ σε
φοβεῖσθαι μὴ προιούσης τῆς ἡλικίας ἀτιμοτέρα ἐν τῷ οἴκῳ
γένῃ, ἀλλὰ πιστεύσεις ὅτι πρεσβυτέρα γιγνομένη τοσούτῳ τιμιω-   10
τέρα ἐν τῷ οἴκῳ ἔσει ὅσῳ ἂν ἐμοὶ ἀμείνων κοινωνὸς γένῃ, καὶ
τοῖς παισὶ φύλαξ.

Xenophon, *Oeconomicus*, VII. 41

58
Revellers " gate-crash " a feast

Εἰπόντος δὲ ταῦτα τοῦ Σωκράτους, οἱ μὲν ἐπήνεσαν, ὁ δ᾽
Ἀριστοφάνης μέμφεσθαί τι ἤρχετο. καὶ ἐξαίφνης ἡ αὐλεία
θύρα κρουομένη πολὺν ψόφον παρεῖχεν ὡς κωμαστῶν, καὶ
αὐλητρίδος φωνῆς ἠκούομεν. ὁ Ἀγάθων τοίνυν, Οὐ σκέ-
ψεσθε, παῖδες ; ἔφη, καὶ ἐὰν μέν τις τῶν ἐπιτηδείων ᾖ,   5
καλεῖτε, εἰ δὲ μὴ λέγετε ὡς ἀναπαυόμεθα. καὶ οὐ πολὺ
ὕστερον Ἀλκιβιάδου φωνῆς ἠκούσαμεν ἐν τῇ αὐλῇ, σφόδρα
μεθύοντος, καὶ μέγα βοῶντος· ἠρώτα δ᾽ ὅπου Ἀγάθων εἴη
καὶ ἐκέλευεν ἄγειν παρ᾽ Ἀγάθωνα. ἦγον οὖν αὐτὸν ἥ τ᾽ αὐλητρὶς καὶ ἄλλοι τινὲς τῶν ἀκολούθων, καὶ παρῆν ἐστεφα-   10
νωμένος κιττοῦ καὶ ἴων στεφάνῳ, καὶ ταινίας ἔχων ἐπὶ τῆς
κεφαλῆς.

Plato, *Symposium*, 212 c

59

Rose and Thorn

Τὸ ῥόδον ἀκμάζει βαιὸν χρόνον· ἢν δὲ παρέλθῃ,
ζητῶν εὑρήσεις οὐ ῥόδον ἀλλὰ βάτον.

Anthologia Palatina, XI. 53

l. 1. Σαπφοῦς βαιὰ μὲν ἀλλὰ ῥόδα. Said by Meleager, of Sappho's
poems. παρέλθῃ, *pass, fade.*

Epitaph on a boy aged twelve

Δωδεκετῆ τὸν παῖδα πατὴρ ἀπέθηκε Φίλιππος
ἐνθάδε, τὴν πολλὴν ἐλπίδα, Νικοτέλην.

Anthologia Palatina, VII. 453

The little sister

Ἡ παῖς ᾤχετ᾽ ἄωρος ἐν ἑβδόμῳ ἦδ᾽ ἐνιαυτῷ
εἰς Ἀΐδην, πολλῆς ἡλικίης προτέρη·
δειλαία ποθέουσα τὸν εἰκοσάμηνον ἀδελφόν,
νήπιον ἀργαλέου γενόμενον θανάτου.
αἰαῖ, λυγρὰ παθοῦσα Περιστερί, ὡς ἐν ἑτοίμῳ   5
ἀνθρώποις δαίμων θῆκε τὰ δεινότατα.

Leonidas of Tarentum, *Anthologia Palatina*, VII. 662

l. 2. ἡλικίης : Ionic form of ἡλικίας, with η for α, *her companions.*
προτέρη : Ionic, for προτέρα, as with ἡλικίης.
3. ποθέουσα : uncontracted.
5. Περιστερί, voc. ἐν ἑτοίμῳ, *close at hand.*
6. θῆκε : note poetical omission of augment.

60

A kiss within the cup

Εἰμὶ μὲν οὐ φιλόοινος· ὅταν δ' ἐθέλῃς με μεθύσσαι,
 πρῶτα σὺ γευομένη πρόσφερε, καὶ δέχομαι.
εἰ γὰρ ἐπιψαύσεις τοῖς χείλεσιν, οὐκέτι νήφειν
 εὐμαρές, οὐδὲ φυγεῖν τὸν γλυκὺν οἰνοχόον.
πορθμεύει γὰρ ἔμοιγε κύλιξ παρὰ σοῦ τὸ φίλημα,   5
 καί μοι ἀπαγγέλλει τὴν χάριν ἣν ἔλαβεν.

Anthologia Palatina, v. 261

Hence Ben Jonson's lines to Celia :

> *Drink to me only with thine eyes,*
> *And I will pledge with mine.*
> *Or leave a kiss within the cup*
> *And I'll not ask for wine.*
> *The thirst that from the soul doth rise*
> *Doth ask a drink divine.*
> *But might I of Jove's nectar sup*
> *I would not change for thine.*

l. 1. φιλόοινος : note uncontracted form for φίλοινος.
 μεθύσσαι, infin. aor. of μεθύσκω, *I make drunk.*

61

A cabaret show

'Ως δ' ἀφῃρέθησαν αἱ τράπεζαι, καὶ ἔσπεισαν τοῖς θεοῖς, καὶ
ἐπαιάνισαν, ἔρχεται αὐτοῖς Συρακόσιός τις ἄνθρωπος, ἔχων
αὐλητρίδα, καὶ ὀρχηστρίδα τῶν τὰ θαύματα δυναμένων ποιεῖν,

Flute-player and dancing girl

καὶ παῖδα πάνυ γε ὡραῖον καὶ πάνυ καλῶς κιθαρίζοντα καὶ
ὀρχούμενον. καὶ ἡ μὲν αὐλητρὶς ηὔλησεν, ὁ δὲ παῖς ἐκιθάρισε, 5
καὶ ἀμφότεροι ἐδόκουν μάλα ἱκανῶς εὐφραίνειν τοὺς παρόντας·
ἔπειτα εἶπεν ὁ Σωκράτης, Νὴ Δία, ὦ Καλλία, τελέως ἡμᾶς
ἑστιᾷς· οὐ γὰρ μόνον δεῖπνον ἄμεμπτον παρέθηκας, ἀλλὰ καὶ
θαύματα καὶ ἀκροάματα ἥδιστα παρέχεις. ἐκ τούτου ηὔλει
τῇ ὀρχηστρίδι ἡ αὐλητρίς, παρεστηκὼς δέ τις ἀνεδίδου τροχοὺς 10
μέχρι δώδεκα, ἡ δὲ λαμβάνουσα ἅμα μὲν ὠρχεῖτο καὶ ἀνέρ-
ριπτε, συντεκμαιρομένη ὅσον ἔδει ῥίπτειν ὕψος ὥστ' ἐν ῥυθμῷ
δέχεσθαι τοὺς τροχούς.

Xenophon, Symposium, 11

l. 1. ἔσπεισαν from σπένδω, often σπένδομαι, pour a libation.
  3. ὀρχηστρίδα τῶν ... ποιεῖν, a kind of dancer who could do
     marvels, an acrobatic dancer.
  9. ηὔλει τῇ ὀρχηστρίδι, played a flute accompaniment for the dancer.

62

A skolion, or drinking song : the scale of blessings

Ὑγιαίνειν μὲν ἄριστον ἀνδρὶ θνητῷ,
δεύτερον δὲ φυὰν καλὸν γενέσθαι·
τὸ τρίτον δὲ πλουτεῖν ἀδόλως,
καὶ τὸ τέταρτον ἡβᾶν μετὰ τῶν φίλων.

Smyth, Greek Melic Poets, p. 149

l. 2. φυάν : note poetical form for φυήν = φύσιν. To be fine in stature.
Adv. acc. with καλόν.

VII

SPORT AND GAMES

Boxing contest

63

In the Greek camp before Troy

Ὁ μὲν Ἀχιλλεὺς ἆθλον ἔθηκε πυγμαχίας ἐπὶ τῷ Πατρόκλου
νεκρῷ· τὰ δὲ ἔπαθλα ἦν τῷ μὲν νικήσαντι ἡμίονος τῷ δὲ νικη-
θέντι κύλιξ. κελεύσαντος δὲ παρεῖναι πυγμάχους, πρῶτος
ἀνέστη Ἐπειός, ὃς ἐπίστευεν ὅτι νικήσει. εἶτα ἀνέστη
Εὐρύαλος, καὶ ἐς χεῖρας ἦλθον, ἔρρει δ' ἱδρὼς ἀπὸ τῶν γυίων. 5
τὸν δ' Εὐρύαλον μέλλοντα τὸν ἕτερον τύπτειν ἐπάταξεν Ἐπειὸς
κατὰ τὴν παρειάν. Εὐρύαλος δὲ πρῶτον μὲν ἤλατο ὑπὸ τῆς
πληγῆς, ἔπειτα κατέπεσεν, ὡς ἰχθὺς ἐκπηδήσας ἐκ τῆς θαλάττης
εἶτα πάλιν καλύπτεται. οἱ δ' ἑταῖροι ἀπήγαγον, οὐ μάλα
κύριον ὄνθ' ἑαυτοῦ. 10

After Homer, Iliad, XXIII. 262

l. 7. ἤλατο, aor. of ἅλλομαι, *leap in the air.*
8. κατέπεσεν, str. aor. of καταπίπτω, *fall down.*

64

At the Court of Alcinous in Phaeacia

Παρὰ τοῖς Φαίαξιν ἦν ἀγὼν γυμνικός, πρῶτον μὲν δρόμου,
ἔπειτα δ' ἅλματος, καὶ δισκοβολίας, καὶ πυγμῆς. ἐρωτῶντος δέ τινος πότερον Ὀδυσσεὺς ἀθλήσει, ἀπεκρίνατο, Οὐ
μέλει μοι ἄθλων, ἐπεὶ τοσαῦτα ἔπαθον· ἀλλὰ τοῦτό μοι μέλει
ὅπως οἴκαδε εἰς Ἰθάκην κάτειμι. ἔπειτα ὠνείδισεν Ὀδυσσεῖ 5

A boar hunt

ὁ ἕτερος ὡς ἄθλων ἀνεπιστήμονι. ἀλλ᾽ Ὀδυσσεύς, Ἵνα
ἴδῃς, ἔφη, ὡς οὐκ ἄπειρος εἰμι ἄθλων, πειράσομαι καὶ
ἐγώ. λαβὼν δὲ δίσκον ἔβαλε· καὶ ὑπερέβαλε τοὺς ἄλλους.
εἶτα προὐκαλέσατο ἐκείνους ἢ πὺξ ἢ πάλῃ ἢ δρόμῳ, ἢ καὶ
τόξῳ. ἀλλ᾽ ἀνθίστατο οὐδείς.   10

After Homer, *Odyssey*, viii. 104 ff.

65

A boar hunt

Ἀφικνεῖται ἐς τὰς Σάρδεις παρὰ Κροῖσον, βασιλέα τῶν
Λυδῶν, ἀνὴρ ᾧ ὄνομα Ἄδραστος, μεγάλῃ συμφορᾷ ἐχόμενος,
ἐπεὶ ἄνδρα ἀπέκτεινε. Κροῖσος δὲ φιλικῶς ἐδέξατο καὶ ἔφη,
Ἐνθάδε μένων οὐδενὸς χρήματος ἀπορήσεις. ἐν δὲ τῷ
αὐτῷ χρόνῳ εἰς τὸ Μυσῶν ὄρος παραγίγνεται κάπρος, ὅς 5
ὁρμώμενος ἐκ τοῦ ὄρους τοὺς τῶν Μυσῶν ἀγροὺς διέφθειρεν.
οἱ δὲ Μυσοί, καίπερ πολλάκις ἐξελθόντες ἐπ᾽ αὐτὸν οὐδὲν
κακὸν ἐποίουν, ἀλλὰ μᾶλλον κακὰ ἔπασχον πρὸς αὐτοῦ.
τέλος οὖν πέμψαντες πρὸς τὸν βασιλέα ἐδέοντο τὸν παῖδα καὶ
λογάδας νεανίας καὶ κύνας πορίζειν, ἵνα ἐξελαύνωσι τὸν 10
κάπρον ἐκ τῆς χώρας.

Herodotus, i. 35 (adapted)

66

A boar hunt (continued)

Τῷ δὲ Κροίσῳ ἐπέστη ὄνειρον, σημαῖνον ὅτι ὁ παῖς ἀπο-
λεῖται, αἰχμῇ σιδηρᾷ βληθείς. διὰ τοῦτο οὐκ ἤθελε τὸν υἱόν,
Ἄτυν ὀνομαζόμενον, ἐκπέμπειν. ἀλλ᾽ ἱκετεύοντος Ἄτυος

ἐνέδωκε, καὶ φύλακα τοῦ παιδὸς τὸν "Αδραστον ἐπιστήσας
ἐξέπεμψεν.   5

'Αφικόμενοι οὖν εἰς τὸν "Ολυμπον τὸν κάπρον ἐζήτουν καὶ
εὑρόντες περιέστησαν κύκλῳ, καὶ ἐσηκόντιζον. ἔνθα δὴ ὁ
"Αδραστος ἀκοντίζων τοῦ μὲν κάπρου ἥμαρτε, τυγχάνει δὲ
τοῦ Κροίσου παιδός. οὕτως ἐξέπλησε τὸ ὄνειρον. ὁ δὲ
Κροῖσος, Οὐ σὺ τοῦδε τοῦ κακοῦ αἴτιος, ἔφη, ἀλλὰ θεός 10
τις ὅς μοι προὐσήμαινε τὰ μέλλοντ' ἔσεσθαι."

Herodotus, I. 35 (adapted)

l. 9. ἐξέπλησε from ἐκπίμπλημι, he fulfilled.

67
The Olympic Games

Τὰ 'Ολύμπια διὰ πεμπτοῦ ἔτους ἐγένετο ἐν 'Ολυμπίᾳ τῆς
"Ηλιδος· κεῖται δὲ ἡ πόλις ἥδε ἐπὶ τοῖς 'Αλφειοῦ ποταμοῦ
ὄχθοις. ὁ δὲ χρόνος ἐν ᾧ ἐγίγνετο οὗτος ὁ ἀγὼν ἱερὸς ἦν,
καὶ ἐκεχειρίαν ἦγον οἱ "Ελληνες, ὥστε μὴ πολεμεῖν πρὸς
ἀλλήλους. πέντε δ' ἡμέρας ἤθλουν, τῶν δ' ἄθλων τὰ λαμ- 5
πρότατα ἦν ταῦτα· δρόμος, δίαυλος (ἀνὰ καὶ κατὰ τὸ στάδιον),
δολιχός (ἔτι μακρότερος τοῦ διαύλου), πάλη, πένταθλον (ἅλμα,
ποδώκειαν, δίσκον, ἄκοντα, πάλην), ἔτι δὲ καὶ πυγμή, καὶ
ἵππος κέλης (ἐνὶ ἵππῳ καὶ ἱππεῖ ἆθλον), καὶ ἅρμα (δρόμος
τεττάρων ἵππων μεθ' ἅρματος). τὸ δ' ἔπαθλον, στέφανος 10
κοτίνου, τῷ δὲ νικήσαντι μέγα ἦν τὸ κλέος, ὡς 'Ολυμπιονίκη.

Apollodorus

l. 1. διὰ πεμπτοῦ ἔτους, every fifth year, i.e. once in four years.
    Note inclusive reckoning.
  4. ἐκεχειρία, lit. a holding of one's hand, truce. ἄγειν, keep.

68

The Pythian Games

Τὰ Πύθια ἐγίγνετο ἐν τῷ Κρισαίῳ πεδίῳ, πρὸς Πυθοῖ
(Δελφοὺς δ’ ὠνόμασαν ὕστερον). ἐλέγετο ὅτι ὁ θεὸς ὁ θεὶς
τὸν ἀγῶνα ἦν ’Απόλλων. ὡς δὲ τὰ ’Ολύμπια, οὕτω καὶ τὰ
Πύθια διὰ πεμπτοῦ ἔτους ἠγωνίζοντο, τὰ δ’ ἆθλα προσόμοια
ἦν τοῖς ’Ολυμπίοις.　　　　　　　　　　　　　　　　5

Περὶ δὲ τούτων τῶν ἀγώνων πόλλ’ εἴρηκεν ὁ Πίνδαρος ἐν
ταῖς ᾠδαῖς, ἐπαινῶν τοὺς νικήσαντας. τὰς δὲ ᾠδὰς ᾖδον ἐν
τῇ τοῦ νενικηκότος πόλει ἐπεὶ οἴκαδε κατῆλθεν. τὸ δ’ ἔπαθλον
Πυθοῖ ἦν δάφνη, ἢ ἦν ἱερὰ τοῦ ’Απόλλωνος.

Apollodorus

69

Chariot race at the Pythian Games

‘Ο δ’ ’Ορέστης, ὡς λέγεται ὑπὸ Σοφοκλέους ἐν τῷ δράματι
τῇ ’Ηλέκτρᾳ, ἦλθε πρὸς Δελφοὺς τῶν ἄθλων χάριν. καὶ ὑπὸ
τοῦ κήρυκος ἀνεκαλεῖτο ὀνομαστί, ὡς ’Αργεῖός τις, ὄνομα
’Ορέστης, υἱὸς ’Αγαμέμνονος, τοῦ τὸ κλεινὸν στράτευμα
ἐπ’ ῎Ιλιον συναγείραντος. ἄλλῃ δ’ ἡμέρᾳ, ἡλίου ἀνατέλλοντος, 5
ἐγένετο ἱππικὸς ἀγών. εἰσῆλθε δ’ ’Ορέστης, μετὰ πολλῶν
ἄλλων ἁρματηλατῶν δέκατος αὐτός. κλήρῳ δὲ τεταγμένον
τόπον εἶχον. εἶτα ὑπὸ σάλπιγγος ᾖξαν, καὶ τὰς ἡνίας σείοντες
ἐπώτρυνον τοὺς ἵππους. πολὺς ἦν ὁ ψόφος, πολλὴ δ’ ἡ
κόνις.　　　　　　　　　　　　　　　　　　　　　10

After Sophocles, Electra, 680 ff.

l. 7. δέκατος αὐτός, lit. *himself the tenth*, i.e. *with nine others.*
Note this idiom. 8. ᾖξαν from ἄσσω, *I rush.* (ἀίσσω.)

Delphic charioteer

70

Chariot race (continued)

Καὶ ὁ Ὀρέστης τὸν μὲν δεξιὸν ἵππον ἀνῆκε, τὸν δ' ἀριστερὸν
κατεῖργεν· ἐχρῆν γὰρ τὴν στήλην ἐπὶ τῇ ἐσχατιᾷ τοῦ δρόμου
ἐπ' ἀριστερὰ καταλείπειν. τοῦ δὲ Θετταλοῦ ἀνδρὸς οἱ ἵπποι,
βίᾳ φερόμενοι, ὠθοῦνται πρὸς τὸ ὄχημα τοῦ Λιβύου ἀνδρός.
ἄλλοι δ' εἰς ἀμφότερα τὰ ἅρματα ταῦτα ἐφέροντο. μόνοι ἄρα 5
περιεγένοντο τῶν δέκα ὅ τ' Ἀθηναῖος καὶ ὁ Ὀρέστης. οὗτος
δέ, κάμπτοντος τοῦ ἀριστεροῦ ἵππου, ἀντὶ τοῦ κατείργειν
ἀνῆκεν, ὥστε τῆς στήλης ἔθιγε τὸ ἅρμα, αὐτὸς δὲ πρὸς τὴν
γῆν κατέπεσεν. ἐνοχλούμενοι δ' ἐν ταῖς ἡνίαις οἱ ἵπποι εἰς
μέσον δρόμον διεσπάρησαν, ὥστε μὴ οἷόν τ' εἶναι λῦσαι αὐτόν. 10
ἀλλὰ τέλος, κατασχόντες τὸ ἅρμα, ἔλυσαν, οὐκέτι ζῶντα.

After Sophocles, *Electra*, 680 ff.

l. 1. ἀνίημι means *release*, opposite of κατείργω, *rein in*.
   4. βίᾳ φερόμενοι, *being carried violently*, i.e. *out of control*.
      ὠθοῦνται, *were being forced*, historic pres.
   7. κάμπτοντος, on the inner horse fell the duty κάμπτειν, *turning
      the post*. For this he had to be reined in.
   8. ἔθιγε, str. aor. of θιγγάνω, *to touch or graze*.
      ἅρμα : it is a two-horse chariot.
  10. διεσπάρησαν, *were scattered*, str. aor. pass. from διασπείρω.

71

The Nemean and Isthmian Games

Ἐγίγνετο τὰ Νέμεια ἐν Νεμέᾳ τῆς Ἀργολίδος· ἐλέγετο δ'
ὅτι ὑπὸ τῶν Ἑπτὰ ἐπὶ Θήβας ἤγετο τὸ πρῶτον, ὕστερον δ'
ὑπὸ Ἡρακλέους, ἐπεὶ τὸν λέοντα τὸν Νέμειον ἀπέκτεινε. τὸ

Four-horse chariot group

δ' ἔπαθλον χλωροῦ σελίνου στέφανος ἦν. καὶ δὶς ἑκάστης
'Ολυμπιάδος, τοῦτ' ἐστι διὰ τρίτου ἔτους, ἐγίγνετο ταῦτα τὰ 5
ἆθλα.

Τὰ δ' Ἴσθμια τὸ ὄνομα ἔχει ὑπὸ τοῦ Κορινθιακοῦ ἰσθμοῦ,
ὅπου ἤγετο τὰ ἆθλα ἐπὶ τίμῃ τοῦ Ποσειδῶνος. ἦγον δὲ Κορίν-
θιοι, κατὰ δὲ τὸν τοῦ ἀγῶνος χρόνον ἱερομηνία ἦν Κορινθίοις
πρὸς 'Αθηναίους. δὶς δ' ἑκάστης τῆς 'Ολυμπιάδος καὶ τὰ 10
Ἴσθμια ἦν. τὸ δ' ἔπαθλον πίτυος φύλλα, ἢ καὶ κιττοῦ
στέφανος.

Apollodorus

l. 2. Ἑπτὰ ἐπὶ Θήβας, the seven champions who unsuccessfully
attacked Thebes to assert the right of Polynices, son of Oedipus,
to reign jointly with his brother Eteocles.

5. διὰ τρίτου ἔτους, *at two-yearly intervals.* See on Olympic
Games, 67.

72

Games held by the Ten Thousand

Ἐντεῦθεν δ' ἦλθον οἱ μύριοι ἐπὶ θάλατταν εἰς Τραπεζοῦντα,
πόλιν Ἑλληνίδα, πρὸς τῷ Εὐξείνῳ πόντῳ. οἱ δὲ Τραπεζούντιοι ἐδέξαντο τοὺς Ἕλληνας, καὶ ξένια ἔδοσαν, βοῦς καὶ
ἄλφιτα καὶ οἶνον. ἐποίησαν δὲ ἀγῶνα γυμνικὸν ἐν τῷ ὄρει
ἔνθαπερ ἐσκήνουν. εἵλοντο δὲ Δρακόντιον Σπαρτιάτην 5
δρόμου ἐπιμελεῖσθαι καὶ τοῦ ἀγῶνος προστατεῖν. ἐπεὶ δὲ ἡ
θυσία τοῖς θεοῖς ἐγένετο, ἡγεῖσθαι αὐτὸν ἐκέλευον πρὸς τὸν
τόπον ὅπου τὸν δρόμον πεποιηκὼς εἴη. ὁ δὲ δείξας τὸν τόπον
οὗπερ ἑστηκότες ἐτύγχανον, Οὗτος ὁ λόφος, ἔφη, κάλλιστος τρέχειν ὅπου ἄν τις βούληται. ἠγωνίζοντο δὲ παῖδες 10
μὲν στάδιον, δολιχὸν δ' ἄνδρες τέλειοι. καὶ καλὴ θέα ἐγένετο·
πολλοὶ γὰρ κατέβησαν, καὶ ἅτε θεωμένων τῶν ἑταίρων πολλὴ
φιλονεικία ἐγένετο. ἔτρεχον δὲ καὶ ἵπποι· καὶ ἔδει αὐτοὺς

κατὰ τοῦ λόφου ἐλάσαντας ἐν τῇ θαλάττῃ ὑποστρέφειν καὶ
πάλιν ἀνὼ πρὸς τὸν βωμὸν ἄγειν.   15

Xenophon, Anabasis, IV. 8, 25

1. 1. οἱ μύριοι. The 10,000 Greek mercenaries who tried to make
   Cyrus king of Persia, 401 B.C.
   8. πεποιηκὼς εἴη : this compound form is commoner than the
   πεποιήκοιμι form given in paradigms. So, too, for the subjunctive.
   9. ἑστηκότες ἐτύγχανον, *they happened to be standing.* Note this
   idiom of participle with τυγχάνω, *happen,* λανθάνω, *escape
   notice,* and φθάνω, *anticipate.*
   κάλλιστος τρέχειν, *most suitable for running.*
   14. ἐλάσαντας, verbs of driving are used intransitively.

VIII

THE SEA : SEA FIGHTS : ISLANDS

Funeral relief

73

Story of the minstrel Arion

Ἀρίων ἦν κιθαρωδὸς τῶν τότε οὐδενὸς ὕστερος, λαβὼν δὲ
χρήματα μεγάλα ἠθέλησεν ἀπ᾽ Ἰταλίας ἐς Κόρινθον ἀφικέσθαι.
οἱ δὲ ἐν τῷ πλοίῳ ἐπεβούλευσαν τὸν Ἀρίονα ἐκβαλόντες ἔχειν
τὰ χρήματα. οὗτος δ᾽ ᾔτησεν ἐᾶν ἐν τῇ σκευῇ πάσῃ στάντα ἐν
τοῖς ἐδωλίοις τὸ ἔσχατον ᾆσαι. ἐκεῖνοι δὲ μέλλοντες ἀκού- 5
σεσθαι του ἀρίστου ἀοιδοῦ ἀνεχώρησαν ἐκ τῆς πρύμνης ἐς
μέσην ναῦν. ὁ δ᾽ Ἀρίων ἐνδὺς πᾶσαν τὴν σκευήν, καὶ τὴν
κιθάραν λαβών, στὰς ἐν τοῖς ἐδωλίοις ᾖσε, τελευτώσης δὲ τῆς
ᾠδῆς ἔρριψεν ἑαυτὸν εἰς τὴν θάλατταν, δελφὶς δ᾽ ὑπολαβὼν
ἤνεγκεν εἰς Ταίναρον. 10

Herodotus, I. 23 (adapted)

l. 4. σκευή, *singing robes*.
7. ἐνδύς, str. aor. partic. from ἐνδύομαι, *don*.
8. ᾖσε from ᾄδειν.

74

The battle of Salamis, 480 B.C.

Ὁ δ᾽ Ἀριστείδης ἐξ Αἰγίνης ἥκων μόγις ἔλαθε τοὺς ἐφορ-
μοῦντας Πέρσας. περιείχετο γὰρ τὸ στρατόπεδον τὸ Ἑλλη-
νικὸν ὑπὸ τῶν νεῶν τοῦ Ξέρξου. οἱ οὖν Ἕλληνες παρεσκευάζοντο ὡς ναυμαχήσοντες. ἐπεὶ δὲ ἕως διέφαινε, Θεμιστοκλῆς
ἐκέλευσεν εἰσβαίνειν εἰς τὰς ναῦς. ἐνταῦθα ἀνῆγον τὰς ναῦς 5
ἁπάσας οἱ Ἕλληνες, ἀναγομένοις δ᾽ ἐπέκειντο οἱ βάρβαροι.

μὲν δὴ ἄλλοι Ἕλληνες ἐπὶ πρύμναν ἀνακρούειν ἤρξαντο καὶ
ὀκέλλειν τὰς ναῦς. ᾿Αμεινίας δὲ ἀνὴρ ᾿Αθηναῖος νηὶ τῶν
Περσῶν ἐμβάλλει, συμπλακείσης δὲ τῆς νεὼς καὶ οὐκέτι
δυναμένης ἀπαλλάσσεσθαι οὕτω δὴ οἱ ἄλλοι ᾿Αμεινίᾳ ἐβοή- 10
θουν.

Herodotus, VIII. 79 (adapted)

75

Exploit of Queen Artemisia at Salamis

Κατὰ δ' ᾿Αρτεμισίαν, Κάρων βασίλισσαν, τάδε ἐγένετο, ὥστε
εὐδοκιμεῖν μᾶλλον παρὰ βασιλεῖ Ξέρξῃ. ἡ γὰρ ναῦς ἡ ᾿Αρτε-
μισίας ἐδιώκετο ὑπὸ νεὼς ᾿Αττικῆς, καὶ οὐκ εἶχε διαφυγεῖν,
ἔμπροσθε γὰρ αὐτῆς ἦσαν νῆες φίλιαι. ἐμβάλλει τοίνυν εἰς
ναῦν φιλίαν, καὶ κατέδυσε. καὶ διπλᾶ ἑαυτὴν ἀγαθὰ εἰργάσατο. 5
ὁ μὲν γὰρ τῆς ᾿Αττικῆς νεὼς τριήραρχος ἐνόμισεν ᾿Αρτεμισίαν
αὐτομολεῖν ἐκ τῶν βαρβάρων, καὶ ἀποστρέψας πρὸς ἄλλας
ἐτρέπετο. ὁ δὲ Ξέρξης, νομίσας τὴν ναῦν τὴν καταδυθεῖσαν
῾Ελληνίδα εἶναι, ἐπήνεσε τὴν ᾿Αρτεμισίαν. καὶ εἰπεῖν λέγεται,
Οἱ μὲν ἄνδρες μοι γεγόνασι γυναῖκες, αἱ δὲ γυναῖκες 10
ἄνδρες.

Herodotus, VIII. 87 (adapted)

l. 1. κατὰ A . . . τάδε : *This is what befell A . . .*
10. γεγόνασι, str. perf. of γίγνομαι.

76

Phormio the Athenian wins a battle, 430 B.C.

Καὶ οἱ μὲν Πελοποννήσιοι ἐτάξαντο κύκλον τῶν νεῶν, τὰς
πρῴρας μὲν ἔξω, εἴσω δὲ τὰς πρύμνας, καὶ τὰ λεπτὰ πλοῖα ἃ

συνέπλει ἐντὸς ποιοῦνται, καὶ πέντε ναῦς τὰς ἄριστα πλεούσας,
ὅπως ἐκπλέοιεν διὰ βραχέος παραγιγνόμεναι, εἴ πη προσ-
πλέοιεν οἱ ἐναντίοι. οἱ δ᾽ Ἀθηναῖοι κατὰ μίαν ναῦν τεταγμένοι   5
περιέπλεον αὐτὰς κύκλῳ, καὶ συνῆγον ἐς ὀλίγον, ἐγγύτατα
παραπλέοντες, καὶ δόκησιν παρέχοντες ὡς αὐτίκα ἐμβαλοῦσι.
ὁ δὲ Φορμίων προειρήκει μὴ ἐπιχειρεῖν πρὶν ἂν αὐτὸς σημήνῃ.
ἤλπιζε γὰρ οὐ μενεῖν τὴν τάξιν αὐτῶν, ἀλλὰ συμπεσεῖσθαι
πρὸς ἀλλήλας τὰς ναῦς, καὶ τὰ πλοῖα ταραχὴν παρέξειν.   10

Thucydides, II. 84

l. 1. ἐτάξαντο κύκλον, *arranged a circle of ships.*
4. ἐκπλέοιεν, *sail out.* Notice these different compounds of πλέω.
διὰ βραχέος, διὰ + gen. neut. adj. *soon,* i.e. at a short interval.
παραγιγνόμεναι, *standing by they might quickly sail out.*
5. κατὰ μίαν ναῦν, *in a single line.*
8. προειρήκει, pluperf., *had given previous orders.*
σημήνῃ, see Syntax M and O3, p. 304-6.

77

Phormio (continued)

Ὡς δὲ τὸ πνεῦμα κατῄει ὅπερ εἰώθει γίγνεσθαι ἐπὶ τὴν ἔω,
αἱ νῆες τῶν Πελοποννησίων, ἐν ὀλίγῳ ἤδη οὖσαι, ὑπό τε τοῦ
ἀνέμου καὶ τῶν πλοίων ἐταράσσοντο, ναῦς δὲ νηὶ προσέπιπτε,
καὶ τοῖς κόντοις διωθοῦντο. βοῇ δ᾽ ἐχρῶντο καὶ πρὸς ἀλλήλους λοιδορίᾳ, ὥστε οὐδὲν κατακούειν οὔτε τῶν παραγγελ-   5
λομένων οὔτε τῶν κελευστῶν. καὶ τὰς κώπας ἀδύνατοι ἦσαν
ἐν κλυδωνίῳ ἀναφέρειν ὡς ὄντες ἄπειροι, ὥστε τὰς ναῦς τοῖς
κυβερνήταις ἀπειθεστέρας παρεῖχον. τότε δὴ σημαίνει ὁ

Φορμίων, καὶ οἱ ᾿Αθηναῖοι προσπεσόντες πρῶτον μὲν καταδύουσι
τῶν στρατηγίδων νεῶν μίαν, ἔπειτα δὲ πάσας ᾗ χωρήσειαν 10
διέφθειρον.

Thucydides, ii. 84

l. 1. κατῄει, *blew down* (the Gulf of Corinth) (Par. 81, p. 272).
  5. παραγγελλομένων, the order of the τριήραρχος.
  6. κελευστῶν. The κελευστής gave the time to the rowers. ὠόπ
    meant " easy ".
  7. ὡς ὄντες ἄπειροι, *being inexpert*.
  10. ᾗ χωρήσειαν, Syntax N2.

78

The chances of the sea

Ναυηγοῦ τάφος εἰμί· σὺ δὲ πλέε, καὶ γὰρ ὅθ᾽ ἡμεῖς
ὠλόμεθ᾽, αἱ λοιπαὶ νῆες ἐποντοπόρουν.

Anthologia Palatina, vii. 282

l. 2. ὠλόμεθ᾽, str. aor. mid. of ὄλλυμι, *destroy*. Passive meaning,
perished.

On a shipwrecked sailor

Ναυτίλε, μὴ πεύθου τίνος ἐνθάδε τύμβος ὅδ᾽ εἰμί,
ἀλλ᾽ αὐτὸς πόντου τύγχανε χρηστοτέρου.

Anthologia Palatina, vii. 350

l. 1. πεύθου, pres. imper. of πεύθομαι = πυνθάνομαι, *I enquire*.

79

The battle of Aegospotami, 404 B.C.

Οἱ δ᾽ ᾿Αθηναῖοι ἔπλευσαν εἰς Αἰγὸς ποταμούς, ἀντίον τῆς
Λαμψάκου. διέχει δ᾽ ὁ Ἑλλήσποντος ταύτῃ σταδίους εἰς

πεντεκαίδεκα, οἱ δ' Ἀθηναῖοι παρετάξαντο ὡς εἰς ναυμαχίαν.
ἐπεὶ δ' οὐκ ἀντανῆγε Λύσανδρος, καὶ τῆς ἡμέρας ὀψὲ ἦν,
ἀπέπλευσαν πάλιν πρὸς τοὺς Αἰγὸς ποταμούς. καὶ οὕτως 5
ἐποίησαν τέτταρας ἡμέρας. ἐπεὶ δ' ἦν ἡμέρα πεμπτή, εἶπεν
ὁ Λύσανδρος τοῖς κατασκόποις, ἐπὴν κατίδωσι τοὺς Ἀθηναίους ἐκβεβηκότας τῶν νεῶν, καὶ ἐσκεδασμένους κατὰ τὴν
Χερρόνησον, τὰ σιτία ὠνουμένους, τότε ἀποπλεῖν παρ' αὐτόν,
καὶ ἆραι ἀσπίδα κατὰ μέσον τοῦ πλοῦ. ταῦτα ἐποίησαν, 10
Λύσανδρος δ' εὐθὺς ἐσήμηνε, καὶ τὰς Ἀθηναίων ναῦς ἔλαβε
παρὰ τῇ γῇ.

Xenophon, *Hellenica*, II. i. 21

l. 7. ἐπὴν = ἐπεὶ + ἄν, *whenever they should see.* Syntax N1.
9. παρ' αὐτόν, *to his own place.*
10. ἆραι, aor. inf. of αἴρω, *raise.* 12. παρὰ τῇ γῇ, *beached.*

80

Duilius the Roman defeats the Carthaginians, 254 B.C.

Ὁ δὲ Γάϊος Δουίλιος, στρατηγὸς Ῥωμαῖος, πυθόμενος τοὺς
πολεμίους πορθεῖν τὴν Σικελίαν, ἐπιπλεῖ τῷ στόλῳ παντί.
συνιδόντες δ' οἱ Καρχηδόνιοι μετὰ χαρᾶς ἀνήγοντο, κατα-
φρονοῦντες τῆς ἀπειρίας τῶν Ῥωμαίων. ἅμα δὲ τῷ πλησιά-
ζειν, θεωροῦντες τοὺς κόρακας ἐν ταῖς τῶν πολεμίων πρώραις, 5
τέως μὲν ἠπόρουν, ἀλλ' ἐνέβαλον οἱ πρῶτοι πλέοντες. αἱ δὲ
σκάφαι συνεπλέκοντο, ἀεὶ δεδεμέναι τοῖς κόραξι, καὶ οἱ
Ῥωμαῖοι ἐπορεύοντο ἐπὶ τοῖς κόραξι, καὶ ἐμάχοντο ἐπὶ τοῖς
καταστρώμασι. οὕτως τὸ γενόμενον παραπλήσιον ἦν πεζο-
μαχίᾳ. τριάκοντα δὲ ναῦς Καρχηδόνιοι ἀπέβαλον. 10

Polybius, I. 23

l. 5. κόρακας, *the crows* : an invention like a grappling iron, *beaks.*
7. ἀεὶ δεδεμέναι, *held fast.* From δέω.

Throne room of the Palace of Minos at Cnossos in Crete

81

The island of Delos is purified 426 B.C.

Τοῦ δ' αὐτοῦ χειμῶνος, Δῆλον ἐκάθηραν οἱ Ἀθηναῖοι κατὰ
χρησμόν τινα. ὅσαι γὰρ θῆκαι ἦσαν ἐν Δήλῳ τῶν τεθνη-
κότων πάσας ἀνεῖλον, καὶ τὸ λοιπὸν προεῖπον μήτε ἐναποθνῄσκειν ἐν τῇ νήσῳ, μήτε ἐντίκτειν, ἀλλ' ἐς τὴν Ῥήνειαν δια-
κομίζεσθαι, ἀπέχει δὲ τῆς Δήλου ἡ Ῥήνεια πάνυ ὀλίγον. καὶ   5
τότε πρῶτον μετὰ τὰ καθάρσια ἐποίησαν οἱ Ἀθηναῖοι τὰ
Δήλια. ἦν δέ ποτε καὶ πάλαι σύνοδος ἐς τὴν Δῆλον τῶν
Ἰώνων μετὰ τῶν γυναικῶν καὶ παίδων, καὶ ἀγὼν ἐποιεῖτο καὶ
γυμνικὸς καὶ μουσικός.

Thucydides, III 104

l. 1. ἐκάθηραν, aor. of καθαίρω, *purify*: note double augment.
   3. προεῖπον μήτε ἐναποθνῄσκειν, syntax M., *they proclaimed that
   no-one....*

82

Crete, and her ruler Minos

Μίνως, παλαίτατος ἐκείνων οὓς ἴσμεν ναυτικὸν ἐκτήσατο,
καὶ τῆς Ἑλληνικῆς θαλάσσης ἐπὶ πλεῖστον ἐκράτησε, καὶ τῶν
Κυκλάδων νήσων ἦρξε. τοὺς δὲ λῃστὰς καθῄρει ἐκ τῆς
θαλάσσης, ἵνα αἱ πρόσοδοι μᾶλλον ἴοιεν αὐτῷ. οἱ γὰρ Ἕλληνες
πάλαι, ἐπειδὴ ἤρξαντο ἰέναι ναυσὶν ἐπ' ἀλλήλους, ἐτρά-   5
ποντο πρὸς λῃστείαν, καὶ προσπίπτοντες πόλεσιν ἀτειχίστοις
ἥρπαζον, καὶ τὸν πλεῖστον τοῦ βίου ἐντεῦθεν ἐποιοῦντο.

Thucydides, I. 4

83

Euboea is invaded by the Persians, 490 B.C.

Οἱ δὲ βάρβαροι, ὡς ἀπῆλθον ἐκ τῆς Δήλου, προσῖσχον πρὸς
τὰς νήσους, ἐντεῦθεν δ᾽ ὁμήρους τῶν νησιωτῶν παῖδας ἐλάμ-
βανον. Ἐρετριεῖς δέ, πυθόμενοι τὴν στρατιὰν τῶν Περσῶν
ἐφ᾽ αὑτοὺς ἐπιπλέουσαν, Ἀθηναίων ἐδέοντο βοηθεῖν, ἄλλοι
δὲ ἴδια κέρδη παρὰ τῶν Περσῶν προσδεχόμενοι προδοσίαν 5
παρεσκευάζοντο. οἱ δὲ Πέρσαι πλέοντες κατέσχον τὰς ναῦς
εἰς τόπους τινὰς τῆς Ἐρετρικῆς χώρας, οἱ δ᾽ Ἐρετριεῖς ἐντὸς
τῶν τειχῶν μένοντες οὐκ ἤθελον ἐκλιπεῖν τὴν πόλιν. προσ-
βολῆς δὲ γενομένης πρὸς τὰ τείχη ἔπεσον ἐπὶ ἓξ ἡμέρας
πολλοὶ ἀμφοτέρων, τῇ δ᾽ ἑβδόμῃ ἄνδρες τινες προύδοσαν τὴν 10
πόλιν τοῖς Πέρσαις, οἳ τὰ μὲν ἱερὰ κατέκαυσαν, τοὺς δ᾽ ἀνθρώπους ἠνδραπόδισαν.

Herodotus, VI. 99 (adapted)

l. 6. κατέσχον τὰς ναῦς, *put in with their ships.*

IX

LAND BATTLES AND SIEGES

Kneeling archer representing Heracles

84

Battle of Marathon, 490 B.C.

Μαχομένων ἐν τῷ Μαραθῶνι χρόνος ἐγένετο πολύς. καὶ
τὸ μὲν μέσον τοῦ στρατοπέδου ἐνίκων οἱ βάρβαροι, ᾗ Πέρσαι
αὐτοὶ τεταγμένοι ἦσαν, καὶ ῥήξαντες ἐδίωκον ἐς τὴν μεσόγαιαν·
τὸ δὲ κέρας ἑκάτερον ἐνίκων Ἀθηναῖοί τε καὶ Πλαταιεῖς.
νικῶντες δὲ τὸ μὲν τετραμμένον τῶν βαρβάρων φεύγειν εἴων, 5
τοῖς δὲ τὸ μέσον ῥήξασιν αὐτῶν, συναγαγόντες τὰ κέρατα
ἀμφότερα, ἐμάχοντο Ἀθηναῖοι, καὶ ἐνίκων. φεύγουσι δὲ τοῖς
Πέρσαις εἵποντο κόπτοντες, ἕως ἐπὶ τὴν θάλασσαν ἀφικό-
μενοι πῦρ τε ᾔτουν, καὶ ἐπελαμβάνοντο τῶν νεῶν. καὶ ἐν
τούτῳ τῷ πόνῳ ὁ πολέμαρχος Καλλίμαχος διαφθείρεται, ἀνὴρ 10
γενόμενος ἀγαθός· καὶ Κυνέγειρος ὁ Εὐφορίωνος ἐνταῦθα
ἐπιλαβόμενος τῶν ἀφλάστων νεὼς τὴν χεῖρα ἀποκοπεὶς
πελέκει πίπτει, ἄλλοι δ᾽ Ἀθηναίων πολλοί τε καὶ ὀνομαστοί.

Herodotus, VI. 113 (adapted)

l. 1. μαχομένων, *while they were fighting*, gen. abs.
  4. τὸ δὲ κέρας, adv., *on each side.* νικᾶν takes a cognate acc.
  5. τὸ τετραμμένον from τρέπω, *the routed portion.* εἴων from ἐῶ.
  6. τοῖς . . . ῥήξασιν, *with those who had broken through.* This
     dative is governed by ἐμάχοντο.
 12. τῶν ἀφλάστων, neut. plur., *the decorated stern.*
 12. τὴν χεῖρα ἀποκοπείς, retained acc. with pass. verb.

85

Battle of Tegea, 418 B.C.

Ἐπεὶ δὲ συνιέναι ἔμελλον ἤδη, ἐνταῦθα παραινέσεις καθ᾽

ἑκάστους ὑπὸ τῶν οἰκείων στρατηγῶν ἐγένοντο, Μαντινεῦσι
μὲν ὅτι ὑπὲρ τῆς πατρίδος ἡ μάχη ἔσται, καὶ ὑπὲρ ἀρχῆς ἢ
καὶ δουλείας, Ἀργείοις δ' ὑπὲρ τῆς παλαιᾶς ἡγεμονίας, τοῖς
δ' Ἀθηναίοις ὅτι ἐν Πελοποννήσῳ Λακεδαιμονίους νικήσαντες 5
τὴν ἀρχὴν μείζω καὶ βεβαιοτέραν ἕξουσι, Λακεδαιμονίοις δὲ
ὅτι ἔργων μελέτη πλέον σῴζει ἢ λόγων καλῶς ῥηθεῖσα
παραίνεσις. καὶ μετὰ ταῦτα ἡ σύνοδος ἦν, οἱ δ' Ἀργεῖοι καὶ οἱ
σύμμαχοι ἐντόνως καὶ μετ' ὀργῆς χωροῦντες, Λακεδαιμόνιοι δὲ
βραδέως, καὶ ὑπὸ αὐλητῶν πολλῶν, ἵνα ὁμαλῶς καὶ μετὰ 10
ῥυθμοῦ βαίνοντες προέλθοιεν, καὶ μὴ διασπασθείη αὐτοῖς ἡ
τάξις.

Thucydides, v. 69

l. 10. ὑπ' αὐλητῶν πολλῶν, to the sound of many flutes.

86

Battle of Tegea (continued)

Ἔδεισε δ' Ἆγις ὁ Λακεδαιμονίων βασιλεὺς μὴ κυκλωθῇ τὸ
εὐώνυμον αὐτοῦ. καὶ γὰρ αἱ στρατιαὶ ἐν ταῖς συνόδοις
ἐξωθεῖσθαι εἰώθασιν ἐπὶ τὰ δεξιὰ κέρατα· φοβούμενοι γὰρ δια-
φυλάσσουσι τὰ γυμνὰ ἕκαστος τῇ τοῦ ἐν δεξιᾷ παρατεταγμένου
ἀσπίδι· καὶ ἡγεῖται μὲν ὁ πρωτοστάτης τοῦ δεξιοῦ κέρως, 5
ἕπονται δὲ διὰ τὸν αὐτὸν φόβον καὶ οἱ ἄλλοι. δείσας οὖν τοῦτο
ὁ Ἆγις εἰς τὸ διάκενον δύο λόχους ἀπὸ τοῦ δεξιοῦ κέρως
παρήγγειλε παρελθεῖν καὶ πληρῶσαι, ἀλλ' ἐμπεσόντες εἰς τὸ
διάκενον ἔφθασαν οἱ Μαντινεῖς καὶ ἡσσῶντο οἱ Λακεδαιμόνιοι.
τῷ δ' ἄλλῳ κέρᾳ, καὶ μάλιστα τῷ μέσῳ, ᾗπερ ὁ Ἆγις ἦν, 10
προσπεσόντες τοῖς πολεμίοις ἔτρεψαν· τούτων γὰρ οἱ πολλοὶ
οὐκ ἐς χεῖρας ὑπέμειναν ἐλθεῖν, ἀλλ' ὡς ἐπῆσαν οἱ Λακε-

δαιμόνιοι εὐθὺς ἐνέδοσαν. ἡ μέντοι φυγὴ καὶ δίωξις οὐ μακρὰ
οὐδὲ βίαιος ἦν· οἱ γὰρ Λακεδαιμόνιοι, τρέψαντες τοὺς
πολεμίους, βραχείας ποιοῦνται τὰς διώξεις.

Thucydides, v. 69

l. 5. ἡγεῖται, sets up this movement, i.e. edging to the right.
   8. ἔφθασαν ἐμπέσοντες, got in their attack first. (Par. 97, 6, p.
291).

87

The battle of Leuctra, 371 B.C.

Πρώτη δ᾿ ἦν ἱππομαχία τῶν Λακεδαιμονίων πρὸς τοὺς
Θηβαίους· ἦν δὲ τὸ Θηβαίων ἱππικὸν μεμελετηκὸς διὰ τὸν
πρὸς Ὀρχομενίους πόλεμον, τοῖς δὲ Λακεδαιμονίοις κατ᾿
ἐκεῖνον τὸν χρόνον πονηρότατον ἦν τὸ ἱππικόν. τῆς δὲ
φάλαγγος τοῖς μὲν Λακεδαιμονίοις οὐ πλέον ἢ εἰς δώδεκα τὸ 5
βάθος, οἱ δὲ Θηβαῖοι οὐκ ἔλασσον ἢ ἐπὶ πεντήκοντα ἀσπίδων
συντεταγμένοι ἦσαν, λογιζόμενοι ὅτι, εἰ νικήσειαν τὸ περὶ τὸν
βασιλέα Κλεόμβροτον, τὸ ἄλλο πᾶν εὐχείρωτον ἂν εἴη. ἐπεὶ
δ᾿ ἤρξατο προχωρεῖν ὁ Κλεόμβροτος, οἱ ἱππεῖς αὐτοῦ ταχὺ
ἡσσῶντο καὶ φεύγοντες ἐνέπεσον τοῖς αὐτῶν ὁπλίταις, καὶ οἱ 10
μὲν περὶ τὸν βασιλέα τὸ πρῶτον ἐκράτουν, ἐπεὶ μέντοι ἀπέθανον
πολλοί, ἐνέκλιναν, τὸ μὲν δεξιὸν κέρας πρῶτον, ἔπειτα δὲ τὸ
εὐώνυμον. οἱ δὲ πολέμαρχοι ὁρῶντες ἁπάντων Λακεδαιμονίων
τεθνεῶτας ἐγγὺς χιλίους, ἔπεμψαν κήρυκα περὶ σπονδῶν. οἱ
δὲ Θηβαῖοι τοὺς νεκροὺς ὑποσπόνδους ἀπέδοσαν. 15

Xenophon, Hellenica, VI. 4, 10

l. 2. μεμελετηκός, in a state of training, from μελετάω.
   6. ἐπὶ πεντήκοντα ἀσπίδων, they were formed in a mass, 50 deep.

88

Dulce et decorum est pro patria mori

Ὃς δ᾽ αὖτ᾽ ἐν προμάχοισι πεσὼν φίλον ὤλεσε θυμόν,
ἄστυ τε καὶ λαοὺς καὶ πόλιν εὐκλεΐσας,
πολλὰ διὰ στέρνοιο καὶ ἀσπίδος ὀμφαλοέσσης
καὶ διὰ θώρηκος πρόσθεν ἐληλαμένος,
τὸν δ᾽ ὀλοφύρονται μὲν ὁμῶς νέοι ἠδὲ γέροντες,   5
ἀργαλέῳ τε πόθῳ πᾶσα κέκηδε πόλις.
καὶ τύμβος καὶ παῖδες ἐν ἀνθρώποις ἀρίσημοι
καὶ παίδων παῖδες καὶ γένος ἐξοπίσω.
οὐδέ ποτε κλέος ἐσθλὸν ἀπόλλυται, οὐδ᾽ ὄνομ᾽ αὐτοῦ
ἀλλ᾽ ὑπὸ γῆς περ ἐὼν γίγνεται ἀθάνατος,   10
ὅντιν᾽ ἀριστεύοντα μένοντα τε μαρνάμενόν τε
γῆς πέρι καὶ παίδων θοῦρος Ἄρης ὀλέσῃ.

Tyrtaeus : Hiller, Anth. Lyrica, p. 28

Tyrtaeus wrote for the Spartans in the seventh century. Elegiac poetry was originally written to a flute accompaniment. Cf. 85, where the Spartans march into battle to the sound of flutes at the battle of Tegea.

l. 1. αὖτ᾽ = αὖτε (αὖ + τε), *furthermore, however.*
    προμάχοισι, poetical for προμάχοις.
  3. στέρνοιο, uncontracted for στέρνου.
  4. ἐληλαμένος, perf. part. pass. of ἐλαύνω, *I smite (drive).*
 10. περ = καίπερ.   ἐὼν = ὤν.
 12. ὀλέσῃ, note poetic omission of ἄν, syntax N1, p. 306.
    περὶ accented πέρι if it follows its case.

89

A few Spartans fought many Persians

Μυριάσιν ποτε τῆδε τριηκοσίαις ἐμάχοντο
ἐκ Πελοποννάσου χιλιάδες τέτορες.

Simonides, Anthologia Palatina, VII. 248

l. 1. τριηκοσίαις = τριακοσίαις.
2. Πελοποννάσου = Πελοποννήσου. τέτορες : Doric for τέτταρες.

90

Far from home

Οἴδε ποτ' Αἰγαίοιο βαρύβρομον οἶδμα λιπόντες
Ἐκβατάνων πεδίῳ κείμεθα μεσσατίῳ.
Χαῖρε κλυτή ποτε πατρὶς Ἐρέτρια, χαίρετ' Ἀθῆναι
γείτονες Εὐβοίης, χαῖρε θάλασσα φίλη.

Anthologia Palatina, vii. 256

Eretria was sacked by Darius in 490 B.C., and some hundreds
of captives transported to the heart of Persia.

l. 1. οἴδε ποτ', trans. *we who once* . . .
2. μεσσατίῳ, poet. for μέσῳ.

91

The battle of Issus, 333 B.C.

Εὐθὺς δ' ἐν χερσὶν ἡ μάχη ἐγένετο, καὶ τρέπονται οἱ ἐν
ἀριστερῷ κέρᾳ τεταγμένοι τοῦ Περσικοῦ στρατεύματος· καὶ
ταύτῃ μὲν ἐνίκα Ἀλέξανδρος, οἱ δ' Ἕλληνες, οἱ μισθοφόροι οἱ
σὺν Δαρείῳ, ἐμβάλλουσι τοῖς Μακεδόσιν ᾗ μάλιστα διεσπαρ-
μένην αὐτοῖς τὴν φάλαγγα κατεῖδον. ἐν δὲ τούτῳ οἱ ἀπὸ τοῦ 5

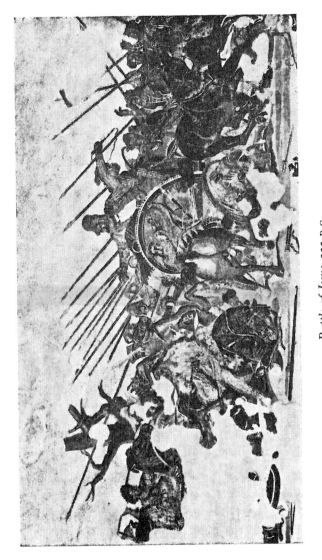

Battle of Issus, 333 B.C.

δεξιοῦ κέρως τῶν Μακεδόνων τῷ πονουμένῳ αὐτῶν βοη-
θοῦντες ἔκοπτον τοὺς Ἕλληνας. Δαρεῖος δ' ὡς αὐτῷ τὸ
κέρας τὸ ἀριστερὸν ἐφοβήθη, εὐθὺς ὡς εἶχεν ἐπὶ τοῦ ἅρματος
ἔφυγεν. καὶ ἐπεὶ δυσχωρίαις ἐνέτυχε τὸ ἅρμα ἀπολείπει καὶ
τὴν ἀσπίδα, αὐτὸς δὲ ἵππου ἐπιβὰς ἔφευγεν. τότε δὴ λαμπρὰ 10
καὶ ἐκ πάντων ἡ φυγὴ ἐγένετο. ἡ δὲ νὺξ ἐπιγενομένη ἀφείλετο
Δαρεῖον ὥστε μὴ ὑπ' Ἀλεξάνδρου ἁλῶναι.

Arrian, *Anabasis Alexandri*, II. 11

l. 5. ἐν δὲ τούτῳ, meanwhile.
8. ὡς εἶχεν, just as he was, without more ado.
12. ἁλῶναι, Par. 72, p. 241.

92

Issus (continued)

Ἀλέξανδρος δὲ τέως μὲν κατὰ κράτος ἐδίωξεν, ὡς δὲ
συνεσκόταζεν ἤδη, ἐς τὸ ἔμπαλιν ἐτράπετο. τὸ μέντοι ἅρμα
τοῦ Δαρείου ἔλαβε καὶ τὴν ἀσπίδα, τὸ δὲ στρατόπεδον τοῦ
Δαρείου ἐξ ἐφόδου ἑάλω. καὶ ἡ μήτηρ Δαρείου καὶ ἡ γυνὴ
καὶ παῖς νήπιος ἑάλωσαν. τῇ δ' ὑστεραίᾳ, καίπερ τετρω- 5
μένος τὸν μηρὸν Ἀλέξανδρος τοὺς τραυματίας συνέλεξε, καὶ
τοὺς νεκροὺς συναγαγὼν ἔθαψε μεγαλοπρεπῶς καὶ λόγῳ
ἐπεκόσμησε πάντας ὅσοι διαπρεπές τι εἰργασμένοι ἦσαν, καὶ
χρημάτων διαδόσει ἀξίως ἐτίμησεν.

Arrian, *Anabasis Alexandri*, II. 11–12

l. 1. κατὰ κράτος , with all his might.
4. ἐξ ἐφόδου, at the first assault. ἑάλω (p. 240).
5. τετρωμένος from τιτρώσκω, wounded.
6. τὸν μηρὸν, acc. of respect.
8. ὅσοι . . . ἦσαν, all who had achieved something notable.

93

The war-song of Hybrias the Cretan

Ἔστι μοι πλοῦτος μέγας δόρυ καὶ ξίφος
καὶ τὸ καλὸν λαισήιον, πρόβλημα χρωτός.
τούτῳ γὰρ ἀρῶ, τούτῳ θερίζω,
τούτῳ πατέω τὸν ἁδὺν οἶνον ἀπ' ἀμπέλω.
τοὶ δὲ μὴ τολμῶντ' ἔχειν δόρυ καὶ ξίφος,   5
καὶ τὸ καλὸν λαισήιον, πρόβλημα χρωτός,
πάντες γόνυ πεπτηῶτες ἐμὸν
πάντες χαμαί με προσκυνέονθ' ἅτε δεσπόταν
καὶ μέγαν βασιλῆα φωνέοντες.

Smyth, Greek Melic Poets, p. 153

Translated by Campbell :

> *My wealth's a burly spear and brand*
> *And a right good shield of hides untanned,*
> *   Which on my arm I buckle.*
> *With these I plough, I reap, I sow,*
> *With these I make the sweet vintage flow*
> *   And all around me truckle.*
> *But your wights that take no pride to wield*
> *A massy spear and well-made shield,*
> *   Nor joy to draw the sword,*
> *Oh, I bring those heartless, hapless drones*
> *Down in a trice on their marrow bones*
> *   To call me King and Lord.*

This poem is thought to have been written by a Cretan in the service of the Persian king, and is to be dated *c.* 500 B.C.

Note many Doric forms, α for η, ω for ου, uncontracted vowels, τολμῶντι for τολμῶσι, κ.τ.λ.

l. 7. πεπτηῶτες, perf. partic. of πτήσσω, *cowering at my knee.*

94

Siege of Troy, c. 1180 B.C.

Πάρις, ὁ καὶ ᾿Αλέξανδρος, πείθει τὴν ῾Ελένην ἀπελθεῖν μεθ᾿
αὐτοῦ, καὶ ἧκον εἰς Τροίαν. ᾿Αγαμέμνων δ᾿ ἀδελφὸς τοῦ
Μενελάου τοῦ ἀνδρὸς ῾Ελένης, στρατιὰν ἠθρόιζε, καὶ κατα-
κλείσας τοὺς Τρῶας ἐπολιόρκει. καὶ ἔμπροσθε τῶν νεῶν
ἃς ἀνείλκυσαν τεῖχος ποιοῦσι, καὶ τάφρον· γενομένης δὲ   5
μάχης οἱ Τρῶες τοὺς ᾿Αχαιοὺς εἰς τὸ τεῖχος διώκουσιν.
᾿Αχιλλεὺς δ᾿ ὁρῶν καιομένας τὰς ναῦς ἐκπέμπει Πάτροκλον.
τεθνηκότος δ᾿ ἐκείνου ῞Εκτορι αὐτὸς μάχεται, καὶ ῞Εκτορα
ἀποκτείνει. τῷ δὲ δεκάτῳ ἐνιαυτῷ εἷλον τὴν Τροίαν οἱ
῞Ελληνες, καὶ κατέσκαψαν.   10
                                        After Homer, *Iliad*
l. 5. ἀνείλκυσαν from ἀνέλκω.

95

Siege of Plataea, 429 B.C.

Οἱ δὲ Πελοποννήσιοι περιετείχιζον τὴν πόλιν κύκλῳ. καὶ
ἐπειδὴ πᾶν κατείργαστο, καταλιπόντες φύλακας ἀνεχώρησαν τῷ
στρατῷ. Πλαταιεῖς δὲ παῖδας μὲν καὶ γυναῖκας καὶ τοὺς
πρεσβυτάτους τε καὶ πλῆθος τὸ ἄχρηστον πρότερον ἐκόμισαν
ἐς τὰς ᾿Αθήνας, αὐτοὶ δὲ ἐπολιορκοῦντο τετρακόσιοι, ᾿Αθη-   5
ναίων δ᾿ ὀγδοήκοντα, γυναῖκες δὲ δέκα καὶ ἑκατὸν σιτοποιοί.
τοῦ δ᾿ ἐπιγιγνομένου ἔτους ἐξῆλθον ἄνδρες δώδεκα καὶ διακόσιοι νυκτί. καὶ γὰρ ἐτήρησαν νύκτα χειμέριον ὕδατι καὶ
ἅμα ἀσέληνον. καὶ προσθέντες κλίμακας τῷ τείχει ὑπερ-

Winged Victory of Samothrace

ἔβαινον, καὶ διέβησαν τὴν τάφρον, χαλεπῶς καὶ βιαίως,
κρύσταλλος γὰρ ἐπεπήγει ἐν αὐτῇ οὐ βέβαιος, καὶ ἐσώθησαν
εἰς τὰς Ἀθήνας.

Thucydides, III. 22

96

Siege of Syracuse, 414 B.C.

Ὁ δὲ Δημοσθένης, πείσας Νικίαν, τὴν ἐπιχείρησιν τῶν
Ἐπιπολῶν ποιεῖται, καὶ λανθάνουσι τοὺς φύλακας τῶν
Συρακοσίων ἀπὸ πρώτου ὕπνου, καὶ τὸ τείχισμα αἱροῦσιν.
οἱ δὲ διαφυγόντες ἀγγέλλουσι τὴν ἔφοδον τοῖς Συρακοσίοις οἳ
φύλακες ἦσαν, οἱ δ' ἐβοήθουν εὐθύς. καὶ ἐνταῦθα ἤδη ἐν 5
πολλῇ ἀπορίᾳ ἦσαν οἱ Ἀθηναῖοι, ἐν γὰρ νυκτομαχίᾳ πῶς ἄν
τις σαφῶς τι ᾔδει; ἦν μὲν γὰρ σελήνη, ἑώρων δ' οὕτως
ἀλλήλους ὡς ἐν σελήνῃ εἰκός ἂν εἴη, οὐκ ἐπιστάμενοι πρὸς ὅ
τι χρὴ χωρῆσαι.

Thucydides, VII. 43

97

Siege of Tyre, 332 B.C.

Καὶ μέγα ἔργον ἡ πολιορκία τῆς Τύρου ἐφαίνετο, νῆσος
γὰρ αὐτοῖς ἡ πόλις ἦν, καὶ τείχεσιν ὑψηλοῖς ἰσχυροτέρα
ἐγένετο, καὶ τὰ ἀπὸ θαλάττης πρὸς τῶν Τυρίων μᾶλλον
ἐφαίνετο, τῶν Περσῶν ἔτι θαλαττοκρατούντων. ὅμως δ'
ἔδοξεν Ἀλεξάνδρῳ χῶμα χῶσαι ἐκ τῆς ἠπείρου ἐπὶ τὴν 5
πόλιν. ἔστι δὲ πορθμὸς τεναγώδης τὸ χωρίον, καὶ τὰ μὲν

πρὸς τῇ ἠπείρῳ τῆς θαλάττης βραχέα καὶ πηλώδη, τὰ δὲ
πρὸς αὐτῇ τῇ πόλει, ὅπου τὸ βαθύτατον ἦν, τριῶν μάλιστα
ὀργυιῶν τὸ βάθος. ὡς δὲ τῷ βαθυτέρῳ ἐπλησίαζον οἱ Μακεδόνες, ἀπὸ τῶν τειχῶν τῶν ὑψηλῶν βαλλόμενοι ἐκακοπάθουν, 10
καὶ ταῖς τριήρεσιν ἄλλη καὶ ἄλλη τοῦ χώματος ἐπιπλέοντες
οἱ Τύριοι χαλεπὸν τὸ ἔργον τοῖς Μακεδόσιν ἐποίουν.

Arrian, *Anabasis Alexandri*, II. 18

l. 3. τὰ ἀπὸ θαλάττης . . . ἐφαίνετο, *and sea warfare seemed to favour
   the Tyrians more, for the Persians* . . .
  6. τὰ μὲν . . . τῆς θαλάττης, *the part of the sea.*
  11. ἄλλη καὶ ἄλλη, *on this side and on that.*

X

TRAVEL

Arkesilas of Cyrene

98

A Greek doctor goes to Susa, capital of Persia

Ἐν δὲ Σούσοις βασιλεὺς Δαρεῖος ἔκαμνε· ἐν γὰρ ἄγρᾳ ἀπο-
θρώσκων ἀφ᾽ ἵππου ἐστράφη τὸν πόδα· καὶ ἰσχυρότερον ἐστράφη,
ὁ γὰρ ἀστράγαλος ἐξεχώρησεν ἐκ τῶν ἄρθρων. πρῶτον μὲν
Αἰγυπτίοις ἐχρῆτο ἰατροῖς, οἱ δὲ στρεβλοῦντες καὶ βιάζοντες
τὸν πόδα, κακὸν μεῖζον εἰργάζοντο· ἐφ᾽ ἑπτὰ μὲν ἡμέρας καὶ 5
νύκτας ἀγρυπνίαις εἴχετο Δαρεῖος, τῇ δ᾽ ὀγδόῃ ἀκούσας τις
πρότερον ἐν Σάρδεσι τὴν τέχνην τοῦ Κροτωνιάτου Δημοκήδους
ἀγγέλλει τῷ Δαρείῳ. ὁ δ᾽ ἄγειν αὐτὸν ὡς τάχιστα παρ᾽ ἑαυτὸν
ἐκέλευσεν. καὶ Δαρεῖος ἠρώτα εἰ ἠπίστατο τὴν τέχνην· ὁ δὲ
Δημοκήδης ἠρνεῖτο, δείσας μὴ ἀληθεύσας τὸ παράπαν τῆς 10
Ἑλλάδος ἀπεστερημένος ᾖ. ἐπεὶ δὲ μάστιγας καὶ κέντρα
προσέφερον ἔφη φαύλως πως ἔχειν τὴν τέχνην. μετὰ δὲ τοῦτο,
Ἑλληνικοῖς χρώμενος ἰάσμασι, καὶ ἤπια μετὰ τὰ ἰσχυρὰ
προσάγων, ὕπνου λαγχάνειν Δαρεῖον ἐποίει, καὶ ἐν χρόνῳ
ὀλίγῳ ὑγιᾶ ἀπέδειξεν. 15

Herodotus, III. 129 (adapted)

l. 2. ἐστράφη τὸν πόδα, *he was twisted as to his foot*, i.e. *he sprained
his foot*. Retained acc. with pass. verb.
7. Κροτωνιάτου : from Croton in S. Italy.
10. δείσας μή, Syntax K, p. 302.
12. φαύλως πως ἔχειν τὴν τέχνην, *had some poor measure of skill*.

99

A Greek doctor (continued)

Ὁ δὲ Δημοκήδης οὗτος ἐκ Κρότωνος ἀφιγμένος Πολυκράτει
Σαμίων τυράννῳ ὡμίλησε. πατέρα γὰρ εἶχεν ἐν Κρότωνι
ὀργῇ χαλεπόν, καὶ οὐ δυνάμενος τοῦτο φέρειν ἀπέδρα εἰς
Αἴγιναν. καὶ ταχέως ὑπερεβάλετο τοὺς ἄλλους ἰατρούς. καὶ
δευτέρῳ ἔτει ταλάντου Αἰγινῆται μισθοῦνται, τρίτῳ δ᾽ ἔτει   5
Ἀθηναῖοι ἑκατὸν μνῶν, τετάρτῳ δ᾽ ἔτει Πολυκράτης, δοὺς
τάλαντον. οὕτως ἀφίκετο ἐς τὴν Σάμον. Ὀροίτης δέ, Πέρσης
ἀνήρ, Πολυκράτην ἀποκτείνας, εἶχε Δημοκήδην ἐν τοῖς
ἀνδραπόδοις. τότε δὴ ἐν Σούσοις Δαρεῖον ἰασάμενος οἶκον
μέγιστον εἶχε, καὶ πλὴν ἑνός, τοῦ ἐς Ἑλλάδα ἀπιέναι, πάντα   10
τὰ ἄλλα παρῆν. ἔπειτα Ἄτοσσαν, Δαρείου γυναῖκα, ἰασάμενος,
ταύτης ὑπουργούσης, κατῆλθεν ἐς τὴν Ἑλλάδα.

Herodotus, III. 129, etc. (adapted)

l. 3. ἀπέδρα, str. aor. of ἀποδιδράσκω, *run away*.
5. μισθοῦνται : note the existence of a National Health Service
in these states! τάλαντου=about £235. ταλάντου, gen. of
price.
6. μνῶν, from μνᾶ, *mina*. 60 μναῖ = 1 talent.
Polycrates made D. a present of a talent. The amount of the
annual salary that he paid him is not stated.

100

Amasis, King of Egypt, favours Greek traders

Ἐπ᾽ Ἀμάσιος δὲ βασιλέως λέγεται Αἴγυπτος μάλιστ᾽ εὐδαι-
μονῆσαι. φιλέλλην δὲ γενόμενος ὁ Ἄμασις ἄλλα τ᾽ ἠὐερ-
γέτησε τοὺς Ἕλληνας καὶ τοῖς ἀφιγμένοις ἐς Αἴγυπτον ἔδωκε

Ναύκρατιν πόλιν ἐνοικῆσαι. ἦν δὲ τὸ πάλαι μόνη ἡ Ναύκρατις
ἐμπόριον Αἰγύπτου· εἰ δέ τις ἐς ἄλλο τι στόμα τοῦ Νείλου 5
ἀφίκετο, ἐχρῆν ὀμόσαι μὴ ἕκοντα ἐλθεῖν, ἔπειτα δὲ τῇ νηὶ μετὰ
τοῦ φορτίου πλεῖν ἐς τὸ Κανωβικὸν στόμα, ἐκεῖ γὰρ ἦν ἡ
Ναύκρατις. ἔγημε δὲ Ἄμασις Ἑλληνίδα γυναῖκα ἐκ Κυρήνης.

Herodotus, II. 177 (adapted)

l. 2. ἄλλα τε... καὶ, *in other respects ... and also.*
4. μόνη ἡ Ναύκρατις, we should put μόνη with ἐμπόριον in English.

101

Foundation of the Greek city of Cyrene, c. 630 B.C.

Πολύμνηστος, ἀνὴρ τῶν Θηραίων δόκιμος, γυναῖκα ἔλαβε,
καὶ ἐγένετο αὐτῷ υἱὸς ἰσχόφωνος καὶ τραυλός· τούτῳ ὄνομα
ἦν Βάττος· ἐπεὶ δ' ἠνδρώθη, ἦλθεν εἰς Δελφοὺς περὶ τῆς
φωνῆς, ἐρωτῶντι δ' αὐτῷ ἡ Πυθία εἶπε τάδε·

Βάττ' ἐπὶ φωνὴν ἦλθες· ἄναξ δέ σε Φοῖβος Ἀπόλλων 5
ἐς Λιβύην πέμπει μηλοτρόφον, οἰκητῆρα.

ὁ δ' ἠμείβετο, Ὦναξ, ἐγὼ μὲν ἦλθον παρὰ σὲ περὶ τῆς
φωνῆς, σὺ δέ μοι ἄλλα ἀδύνατα θεσπίζεις.

ταῦτα λέγων οὐκ ἔπειθε τὸν θεὸν ἄλλα θεσπίζειν. μετὰ δὲ
ταῦτα τοῖς Θηραίοις ἀπεκρίνατο ὁ θεὸς Κυρήνην τῆς Λιβύης 10
οἰκίζοντας ἄμεινον πράξειν. πλεύσαντες οὖν πρῶτον μὲν
νῆσον ἐπὶ Λιβύῃ κειμένην ᾤκουν, ἑβδόμῳ δ' ἔτει οἱ Λίβυες
ἤγαγον αὐτοὺς εἰς τὴν καλλίστην τῶν χωρῶν, ἥπερ ἐστὶ πρὸς
τῇ νῦν Κυρήνῃ καλουμένῃ.

Herodotus, IV. 150 (adapted)

Sailing ships

102

Darius crosses the Ister (Danube) into Scythia, 512 B.C.

Δαρεῖος δ᾽ ὡς ἀφίκετο καὶ ὁ πεζὸς ἅμ᾽ αὐτῷ στρατὸς ἐπὶ
τὸν Ἴστρον, ἐνταῦθα διαβάντων πάντων ἐκέλευσε τοὺς Ἴωνας,
τὴν γέφυραν λύσαντας, ἕπεσθαι αὐτῷ· μελλόντων δὲ τῶν
Ἰώνων λύειν, Κώης ὁ Μυτιληναίων στρατηγὸς ἔλεξε Δαρείῳ
τάδε· Ὦ βασιλεῦ, ἐπὶ γῆν μέλλεις στρατεύεσθαι ἐν ᾗ οὔτ᾽ 5
ἄροτός ἐστιν οὔτε πόλις οἰκουμένη· φέροικοι γὰρ ὄντες ἱππο-
τοξόταί εἰσι, ζῶσι δ᾽ οὐκ ἀπ᾽ ἀρότου ἀλλ᾽ ἀπὸ κτηνῶν· σὺ νῦν
ἔα ταύτην τὴν γέφυραν ἑστάναι, φύλακας λιπὼν τούτους οἳ
ἔζευξαν αὐτήν. καὶ ἢν κατὰ νοῦν πράξωμεν εὑρόντες τοὺς
Σκύθας, ἤν τε μὴ εὑρεῖν δυνώμεθα, ἡ ἄφοδός ἐστιν ἀσφαλής. οὐ 10
γὰρ ἔδεισα μὴ ὑπὸ Σκυθῶν μάχῃ νικώμεθα, ἀλλὰ μή, οὐ
δυνάμενοι εὑρεῖν αὐτούς, πάθωμέν τι ἀλώμενοι.

Herodotus, IV. 97 (adapted)

l. 11. ἔδεισα, see Syntax K 2.

103

The Royal Road from Sardis to Susa

Ὁ δὲ Ξέρξης ἔπεμψεν ἐς Πέρσας ἀγγέλλων τὴν ἐν Σαλαμῖνι
συμφοράν. οὐδὲν δ᾽ ἐστὶν ὅ τι θᾶσσον παραγίγνεται τούτων
τῶν ἀγγέλων, λέγουσι γὰρ ὡς, ὁπόσων ἂν ἡμερῶν ᾖ ἡ πᾶσα
ὁδός, τοσοῦτοι ἵπποι τε καὶ ἄνδρες διεστᾶσι, κατὰ ἡμερησίαν
ὁδὸν ἑκάστην ἵππος τε καὶ ἀνὴρ τεταγμένος· οὓς οὔτε νιφετὸς 5
οὔτ᾽ ὄμβρος, οὔτε καῦμα οὔτε νὺξ κατείργει μὴ οὐ κατανύσαι
ὡς τάχιστα τὸν προκείμενον αὐτοῖς δρόμον. ὁ μὲν δὴ πρῶτος

δραμὼν παραδίδωσι τὰ ἀγγελθέντα τῷ δευτέρῳ, ὁ δὲ δεύτερος τῷ τρίτῳ, ὥσπερ ἐν Ἕλλησιν ἡ λαμπαδηφορία ἦν τῷ Ἡφαίστῳ ἐπιτελοῦσιν.˘ ἡ δὲ πρώτη περὶ Ξέρξου ἀγγελία, ὡς ἔχοι 10 Ἀθήνας, σφόδρα ἔτερψε τοὺς Πέρσας, ἡ δὲ δευτέρα τὸ ἀληθὲς ἤγγειλεν.

Herodotus, VIII. 98 (adapted)

l. 2. θᾶσσον, compar. of ταχύς.   τούτων τῶν, compar. gen.
    6. μὴ οὐ κατανύσαι : note the double neg., common with verbs of preventing.

104

Alexander receives the surrender of Porus, an Indian prince, 326 B.C.

Ἀλέξανδρος δ' οὐδὲ μετὰ τὴν μάχην τῷ Πώρῳ χαλεπὸς ἐγένετο, ἀλλ' ἄλλους ἐν μέρει ἔπεμπε καὶ δὴ καὶ Μερόην, ἄνδρα Ἰνδόν, ὅτι φίλον εἶναι ἐκ παλαιοῦ τῷ Πώρῳ ἔμαθε. Πῶρος δ' ὡς τὰ παρὰ τοῦ Μερόου ἤκουσεν, ἐπέστησε τὸν ἐλέφαντα καὶ κατέβη ἀπ' αὐτοῦ. τότε δὲ ἄγειν αὐτὸν ἐκέλευσε 5 παρ' Ἀλέξανδρον· Ἀλέξανδρος δ' ὡς προσελθόντα ἐπύθετο, προσιππεύσας πρὸ τῆς τάξεως μετ' ὀλίγων ἑταίρων ἀπαντᾷ τῷ Πώρῳ, καὶ ἐπιστήσας τὸν ἵππον, τὸ μέγεθος αὐτοῦ ἐθαύμαζε, (ἦν γὰρ ὑπὲρ πέντε πήχεις), καὶ τὸ κάλλος· καὶ οὐχ ὡς δεδου-λωμένος τῇ γνώμῃ ἐφαίνετο ὁ Πῶρος, ἀλλ' ὡς ἀνὴρ ἀγαθός, 10 ὑπὲρ τῆς βασιλείας πρὸς βασιλέα ἄλλον ἠγωνισμένος. ἔνθα Ἀλέξανδρος πρῶτος προσειπὼν αὐτὸν λέγειν ἐκέλευσεν ὅ τι ἑαυτῷ γενέσθαι ἐθέλοι. καὶ ἐκεῖνος, Βασιλικῶς μοι χρῆσαι, ὦ Ἀλέξανδρε.

Arrian, *Anabasis Alexandri*, V. 18

105

Alexander's army refuses to advance

Τὰ δὲ πέραν τοῦ Ὑφάσιος ποταμοῦ εὐδαίμονα ἔχειν τὴν
χώραν ἔλεγόν τινες, καὶ ἀνθρώπους ἀγαθοὺς καὶ γῆς ἐργάτας,
γενναίους δὲ τὰ πολέμια. ταῦτα δ᾽ ἐξαγγελλόμενα Ἀλέξ-
ανδρον μὲν παρώξυνε ἐς ἐπιθυμίαν τοῦ πρόσω ἰέναι, οἱ δὲ
Μακεδόνες ἐξέκαμνον ἤδη ταῖς γνώμαις. σύλλογος δ᾽ ἐγίγ- 5
νετο κατὰ τὸ στρατόπεδον καὶ ὀδυρόμενοι διισχυρίζοντο ὡς
οὐκ ἀκολουθήσουσιν, οὐδ᾽ ἢν Ἀλέξανδρος ἡγῆται· συγκαλέσας
δὲ τοὺς στρατηγοὺς ἔλεξεν, Ἆρα μεμπτοί εἰσιν ὑμῖν οἱ
μέχρι τούτου πόνοι καὶ ἐγὼ ἡγούμενος ; Ἰωνία γὰρ ἔχεται
καὶ Ἑλλήσποντος καὶ Αἴγυπτος καὶ Βαβυλών. τί ὀκνεῖτε καὶ 10
τὸν Ὕφασιν καὶ τὰ ἐπέκεινα τοῦ Ὑφάσιος προσθεῖναι τῇ
Μακεδόνων ἀρχῇ ; μετὰ δὲ ταῦτα ἐκφαίνει τῇ στρατιᾷ ὅτι
ἔδοξεν ὀπίσω ἰέναι. οἱ δὲ ἐβόων χαίροντες καὶ ἐδάκρυον οἱ
πολλοὶ αὐτῶν.

Arrian, *Anabasis Alexandri*, v. 25

l. 3. τὰ πολέμια, adv. acc.   Translate *in warfare*.

106

Britain described by Strabo the Geographer

Ἡ δὲ Βρεταννικὴ τρίγωνος μέν ἐστι τῷ σχήματι, παρα-
βέβληται δὲ τὸ μέγιστον αὐτῆς πλεῦρον τῇ Κελτικῇ. ἐστὶ
δ᾽ ἡ πλείστη τῆς νήσου πεδιὰς καὶ κατάδρυμος, πολλὰ δὲ καὶ
γεώλοφα τῶν χωρίων ἐστί· φέρει δὲ σῖτον καὶ βοσκήματα καὶ
ἄργυρον καὶ σίδηρον· ταῦτα δὲ ἐκκομίζεται ἐξ αὐτῆς, καὶ 5

δέρματα, καὶ ἀνδράποδα, καὶ κύνες εὐφυεῖς πρὸς τὰς κυνη-
γεσίας· Κέλτοι δὲ κυσὶ καὶ πρὸς τοὺς πολεμίους χρῶνται, τὰ
δ᾽ ἔθη τὰ μὲν ὅμοια τοῖς Κέλτοις, τὰ δὲ ἁπλούστερα, ὥστ᾽
ἐνίους γάλακτος μὲν εὐπορεῖν, τυροποιεῖν δὲ μή, ὑπὸ τῆς
ἀπειρίας. πρὸς δὲ τοὺς πολεμίους ἀπήναις χρῶνται τὸ πλέον. 10
ἔπομβροι δ᾽ εἰσὶν οἱ ἀέρες μᾶλλον ἢ νιφετώδεις· ὁμίχλη δὲ
κατέχει πολὺν χρόνον, ὥστε ἐπὶ τρεῖς μόνον ἢ τέτταρας ὥρας
ὁρᾶσθαι τὸν ἥλιον.

Strabo, 199

Strabo's dates are *c.* 63 B.C.–A.D. 21.

XI

FRIENDSHIP

Achilles binding up Patroclus' wounded arm

107

Theseus and Peirithous

Ἡ πρὸς Πειρίθοον φιλία Θησέως τοῦτον τὸν τρόπον ἐγένετο·
δόξαν εἶχεν ὁ Θησεὺς ἐπὶ ῥώμῃ καὶ ἀνδρείᾳ μεγίστην· βουλόμενος οὖν ὁ Πειρίθοος ἐξελέγξαι καὶ πεῖραν λαβεῖν, ἤλασε βοῦς
αὐτοῦ ἐκ Μαραθῶνος, καὶ πυθόμενος διώκειν ἐκεῖνον οὐκ
ἔψυγεν ἀλλ' ἀπήντησεν· ὡς δ' εἶδεν ἕτερος τὸν ἕτερον, ἐθαύ- 5
μασεν ἕκαστος τοῦ ἑτέρου τὸ κάλλος καὶ τὴν τόλμαν. καὶ
μάχης μὲν ἔσχοντο, Πειρίθοος δὲ πρότερος τὴν δεξιὰν προ-
τείνας ἐκέλευσεν αὐτὸν γενέσθαι δικαστὴν τῆς βοηλασίας,
ἑκὼν γὰρ ὑφέξειν ἣν ἂν ὁρίσῃ δίκην ἐκεῖνος. Θησεὺς δὲ τὴν
μὲν δίκην ἀφῆκεν, προὐκαλεῖτο δὲ φίλον καὶ σύμμαχον εἶναι. 10

Plutarch, *Theseus*

l. 7. ἔσχοντο, mid., *refrain, from.*
9. ἑκὼν ὑφέξειν, nom. and infin. after ἐκέλευσεν, Syntax F 1.

108

Achilles and Patroclus

Πάτροκλος υἱὸς ἦν Μενοιτίου, καὶ ἐν παιδιᾷ περὶ ἀστρα-
γάλων διενεχθεὶς παῖδ' ἀπέκτεινε, καὶ φυγὼν παρὰ Πηλεῖ
κατῴκει, καὶ Ἀχιλλεῖ ἑταῖρος γίγνεται. μετὰ δὲ τούτου ἦλθεν
ἐπ' Ἴλιον· ὡς δ' εἶδεν Ἀχιλλεὺς καιομένας τὰς ναῦς, πρότερον
ὀργισθεὶς πέμπει Πάτροκλον μετὰ τῶν Μυρμιδόνων, τοῖς 5
αὐτοῦ ὅπλοις ἐξοπλίσας· ἰδόντες δὲ Πάτροκλον οἱ Τρῶες,
καὶ νομίσαντες Ἀχιλλέα εἶναι, εἰς φυγὴν τρέπονται, κατα-

113

διώξας δ' αὐτοὺς ἐπὶ τὸ τεῖχος πολλοὺς ἀπέκτεινε, ἀλλ' ὑφ'
Ἕκτορος αὐτὸς ἀπέθανεν· μετὰ ταῦτα Ἀχιλλεὺς ἐξέρχεται
ἐπὶ τὸν πόλεμον, καὶ Ἕκτορα ἐν μονομαχίᾳ ἀποκτείνει. 10
θάπτων δὲ Πάτροκλον ἀγῶνα ἐπ' αὐτῷ τίθησι.

After Homer, *Iliad*, IX and XVI–XXIV

109

Love and the stars

Ἀστέρας εἰσαθρεῖς, Ἀστὴρ ἐμός· εἴθε γενοίμην
οὐρανός, ὡς πολλοῖς ὄμμασιν εἰς σὲ βλέπω.

Plato, *Anthologia Palatina*, VII. 669

Translated by A. C. Benson :

> *I watched thee gazing, O my star,*
> *Upon the starry skies afar.*
> *Ah, would that I the heaven might be,*
> *To gaze with myriad eyes on thee.*

Morning Star and Evening Star

Ἀστὴρ πρὶν μὲν ἔλαμπες ἐνὶ ζωοῖσιν ἑῶος,
νῦν δὲ θανὼν λάμπεις ἕσπερος ἐν φθιμένοις.

Plato, *Anthologia Palatina*, VII. 670

Translated by Shelley :

> *Thou wert the morning star among the living*
> *Ere thy fair light had fled.*
> *Now, having died, thou art as Hesperus, giving*
> *New splendour to the dead.*

110

Friendship not severed by death

Εἶπέ τις, Ἡράκλειτε, τεὸν μόρον, ἐς δέ με δάκρυ
ἤγαγεν, ἐμνήσθην δ' ὁσσάκις ἀμφότεροι
ἥλιον ἐν λέσχῃ κατεδύσαμεν, ἀλλὰ σὺ μέν που,
ξεῖν' Ἁλικαρνησσεῦ, τετραπάλαι σποδιή.
αἱ δὲ τεαὶ ζώουσιν ἀηδόνες, ἧσιν ὁ πάντων   5
ἁρπακτὴρ Ἀίδης οὐκ ἐπὶ χεῖρα βαλεῖ.

Callimachus, *Anthologia Palatina*, VII. 80

Translated by Cory :

They told me, Heracleitus, they told me you were dead :
They brought me bitter news to hear, and bitter tears to shed.
I wept as I remembered how often you and I
Had tired the sun with talking and sent him down to sky.

And now that thou art lying, my dear old Carian guest,
A handful of grey ashes, long, long ago at rest,
Still are thy pleasant voices, thy nightingales, awake,
For Death, he taketh all away, but these he cannot take.

l. 1. τεὸν = σόν, and line 5, τεαὶ = σαὶ.
2. ὁσσάκις for ὁσάκις. ἐμνήσθην, from μιμνήσκω.
4. ξεῖνος = ξένος. τετραπάλαι, *long ago*.
5. ζώουσι for ζῶσι. ἧσιν for αἷς.
6. ἐπὶ ... βαλεῖ : the compound ἐπιβαλεῖ is divided.
οὐκ ἐπιβαλεῖ χεῖρα = *will not lay his hand*.

Socrates

III

Socrates as described by Alcibiades

Ἐπεὶ στρατεία ἡμῖν, ἐμοὶ καὶ Σωκράτει, ἐγένετο ἐς Ποτί-
δαιαν, συνεσιτοῦμεν ἐκεῖ· πρῶτον μὲν οὖν τοῖς πόνοις οὐ μόνον
ἐμοῦ περιῆν ἀλλὰ καὶ τῶν ἄλλων ἁπάντων. καὶ ὁπότε ἀναγκασ-
θείημεν ἀσιτεῖν, οὐδὲν ἦσαν οἱ ἄλλοι πρὸς τὸ καρτερεῖν, καὶ
Σωκράτη μεθύοντα οὐδεὶς πώποθ᾽ ἑώρακεν ἀνθρώπων. ἔτι δὲ 5
ὅτε ἀπὸ Δηλίου φυγῇ ἀνεχώρει τὸ στρατόπεδον, ἐγὼ μὲν
ἐπορευόμην ἵππον ἔχων, Σωκράτης δ᾽ ὅπλα· καὶ ἐγὼ μὲν ἧττον
ἦν ἐν φόβῳ διὰ τὸ ἐφ᾽ ἵππου εἶναι, Σωκράτης δὲ καίπερ πεζὸς
ὢν ἠρέμα περιεσκόπει τούς τε φίλους καὶ τοὺς πολεμίους, καὶ
δῆλον ἦν, εἴ τις ἅψεται τούτου τοῦ ἀνδρός, ὅτι μάλ᾽ ἐρρω- 10
μένως ἀμυνεῖται.

Plato, *Symposium*, 219 E

II2

Orestes and Pylades

Μετὰ δὲ τὸν Ἀγαμέμνονος θάνατον, Ἠλέκτρα, μία τῶν
Ἀγαμέμνονος θυγατρῶν, τὸν ἀδελφὸν Ὀρέστην ἐκκλέπτει,
καὶ δίδωσι Στροφίῳ Φωκεῖ τρέφειν· ὁ δ᾽ αὐτὸν τρέφει μετὰ
Πυλάδου παιδὸς ἰδίου. ἀνδρωθεὶς δ᾽ Ὀρέστης εἰς Δελφοὺς
παραγίνεται, καὶ τὸν θεὸν ἐρωτᾷ εἰ χρὴ τοὺς ἀποκτείναντας 5
τὸν πατέρα μετελθεῖν. καὶ ἐπιτρέποντος τοῦ θεοῦ ἀπέρχεται
εἰς Μυκήνας μετὰ Πυλάδου, καὶ ἀποκτείνει τήν τε μητέρα καὶ
τὸν Αἴγισθον. μετὰ δ᾽ οὐ πολὺν χρόνον ὑπ᾽ Ἐρινύων
διωκόμενος εἰς Ἀθήνας παραγίνεται, καὶ κρίνεται ἐν Ἀρείῳ
πάγῳ· κριθεὶς δ᾽ ἀπολύεται. 10

Apollodorus, II. 24

113

The Sacred Band at Thebes

Τὸν δ' ἱερὸν λόχον, ὥς φασι, συνετάξατο Γοργίδας πρῶτος
ἐξ ἀνδρῶν ἐπιλέκτων τριακοσίων, οἷς ἡ πόλις αὐτῶν, Θῆβαι,
οἴκησιν καὶ δίαιταν ἐν τῇ Καδμείᾳ παρεῖχεν. ὁ δὲ λόχος ἐκ
φίλων συνέστη, καὶ τοῦτο θαυμαστὸν οὔκ ἐστιν· καὶ γὰρ
ἀπόντας τοὺς φίλους μᾶλλον αἰδούμεθα ἢ ἑτέρους παρόντας· 5
καί ποτε μέλλοντος πολεμίου δυοῖν φίλοιν τὸν ἕτερον ἀπο-
σφάττειν, ἐδεῖτο ὁ κείμενος διὰ τοῦ στέρνου διωθεῖν τὸ ξίφος,
ʽΌπως, ἔφη, ὁ φίλος μὴ καταισχυνθῇ ὁρῶν με νεκρόν, διὰ
νώτου τετρωμένον.

φίλτατοι δ' ἦσαν κατὰ τοὺς χρόνους τούτους ἀλλήλοις 10
Θηβαῖοι Ἐπαμεινώνδας καὶ Πελοπίδας.

Plutarch, Pelopidas, 18

l. 6. μέλλοντος . . . : <i>when an enemy was about to stab one of a pair
of friends.</i> 9. τετρωμένον, see τιτρώσκω.

114

Glaucus of Sparta and his friend from Miletus

Γλαῦκος ἤκουσεν ἄριστα περὶ δικαιοσύνης πάντων ὅσοι
τὴν Λακεδαίμονα τοῦτον τὸν χρόνον ᾤκουν· καὶ ἀνὴρ Μιλήσιος ἀφικόμενος ἐς Σπάρτην εἶπε πρὸς αὐτὸν τάδε· Εἰμὶ μὲν
Μιλήσιος, ἥκω δὲ σῆς, ὦ Γλαῦκε, δικαιοσύνης βουλόμενος
ἀπολαύειν, ἧς ἐστιν πολὺς ὁ λόγος ἐν Ἰωνίᾳ· καὶ ὅτι ἐπικίν- 5
δυνός ἐστιν ἡ Ἰωνία, ἔδοξέ μοι ἐξαργυροῦν τὰ ἡμίση πάσης
τῆς οὐσίας καὶ καταθέσθαι παρὰ σέ· εὖ γὰρ ἐπίσταμαι ὅτι
ἔσται παρὰ σοὶ σῶα. σὺ δὲ τὰ σύμβολα σῷζε ἔχων, ὅς δ'
ἂν ἔχων τὰ ἕτερα σύμβολα ἀφικνῆται, τούτῳ ἀποδώσεις.

χρόνου δὲ πολλοῦ διελθόντος ἦλθον εἰς τὴν Σπάρτην οἱ παῖδες 10
τοῦ καταθεμένου τὰ χρήματα, καὶ ἀποδεικνύντες τὰ σύμβολα
ἀπῄτουν. ὁ δὲ διωθεῖτο λέγων, Οὐ μέμνημαι τοῦ πράγματος,
ἀναμνησθεὶς δὲ ποιήσω πᾶν τὸ δίκαιον.

Herodotus, VI. 86 (adapted)

l. 8. σύμβολα, *tallies*: the halves of a coin which two ξένοι broke
between them, each party keeping one piece.

115

Glaucus (continued)

Οἱ μὲν οὖν Μιλήσιοι ἀπηλλάχθησαν ἀγανακτήσαντες, ὡς
ἐστερημένοι τῶν χρημάτων. Γλαῦκος δὲ εἰς Δελφοὺς
ἐπορεύετο· καὶ ἐρωτῶντι πότερον δεῖ τὰ χρήματα ἀποδιδόναι
ἠμείβετο ἡ Πυθία ὅτι μὴ ἀποδιδόντι αὐτίκα μὲν βέλτιον
ἔσται, μετέπειτα δὲ οὐ βέλτιον, ἐπεὶ Ὅρκου παῖς διώκων 5
κολάζει τοὺς ἁμαρτάνοντας. ταῦτ' ἀκούσας ὁ Γλαῦκος
συγγνώμην τοῦ θεοῦ παρῃτεῖτο διὰ τὰ ῥηθέντα· ἡ δὲ Πυθία
ἔφη τὸ πειρᾶσθαι τοῦ θεοῦ καὶ τὸ ποιεῖν ἴσον δύνασθαι.
Γλαῦκος μὲν ἀποδίδωσι τοῖς ξένοις τὰ χρήματα, ἐξέπλησε δ'
ὁ θεὸς ἃ προειρήκει, καὶ ἡ γενεὰ Γλαύκου πρόρριζος ἐκ- 10
τέτριπται ἐκ Σπάρτης.

Herodotus, VI. 86 (adapted)

l. 1. ἀπηλλάχθησαν, *were got rid of.* 5. Ὅρκου, *of an oath.*
8. ἴσον δύνασθαι, *were of equal importance.*

116

Damon and Phintias

Ὁ μὲν Φιντίας κατηγορεῖτο πρὸς Διονύσιον τὸν Συρακοσίων
τύραννον ὅτι ἐπεβούλευεν αὐτῷ, καὶ ἔδει ἀποθνήσκειν τὸν

Φιντίαν. ὁ δ᾽ ἠξίου τὸ λοιπὸν τῆς ἡμέρας μέρος δίδοσθαι ἵνα
τά τε καθ᾽ ἑαυτὸν καὶ κατὰ Δάμωνα εὐτρεπίζῃ, συνεβίωσαν
γὰρ οἱ ἄνδρες οὗτοι, καὶ ἐκοινώνουν ἁπάντων. Εἰ δὲ ταῦτα 5
ἐάσεις, ἔφη, ἐγγυητὴν καταστήσω τὸν Δάμωνα τῆς ἐμῆς
τότε παρουσίας. Διονύσιος οὖν μεταπεμψάμενος τὸν Δάμωνα,
ὡς ἐγγυητὴν ἐδέξατο, ἐφ᾽ ᾧ τε μενεῖ αὐτοῦ. καὶ οἱ περὶ
τὸν Διονύσιον ἔσκωπτον τὸν Δάμωνα ὡς μέλλοντα ἐγκατα-
λείπεσθαι. ὄντος δ᾽ ἡλίου περὶ δυσμάς, ἧκεν ὁ Φιντίας ὡς 10
ἀποθανούμενος. ᾔτησε δ᾽ ὁ Διονύσιος τρίτος εἰς τὴν φιλίαν
αὐτῶν εἰσελθεῖν ἐᾶσθαι.

Iamblichus, Life of Pythagoras, 33. 234

l. 4. τὰ καθ᾽ ἑαυτόν, his own concerns.

117

Alexander and Clitus

Κλεῖτος, φίλος καὶ σύντροφος τῷ ᾽Αλεξάνδρῳ, ὅμως
ἤχθετο ἐκείνῳ ὅτι τοὺς τρόπους πρὸς τὸ βάρβαρον μετέβαλε,
καὶ τοὺς τῶν κολάκων λόγους ἤκουσε. τότε δὲ ὑπὸ τοῦ οἴνου
οὐκ εἴα ᾽Αλέξανδρον εἰς τὰ θεῖα ὑβρίζειν, οὔτε τὰ τῶν πάλαι
ἀνδρῶν ὡς φαῦλα ἀποδεικνύναι. οὐ γὰρ ᾽Αλεξάνδρου μόνου 5
εἶναι τὰ ἔργα, ἀλλὰ πολλῶν Μακεδόνων. καὶ τέλος ὠνείδισεν
αὐτῷ ὅτι πρὸς ἑαυτοῦ Κλείτου ἐσώθη ἐν τῇ ἐπὶ Γρανικῷ
μάχῃ· καὶ τὴν δεξιὰν ἀνατείνας, Αὕτη σε ἡ χείρ, ἔφη, ὦ
᾽Αλέξανδρε, ἐν τῷ τότε ἔσωσε. καὶ ᾽Αλέξανδρος, λόγχην
παρὰ σωματοφύλακός τινος ἁρπάσας, ἀποκτείνει αὐτόν. 10

Arrian, Anabasis Alexandri, iv. 8

XII

GREAT MEN

Pericles

118

Aristides, c. 530-468 B.C.

Ἤδη δ' ὁ δῆμος ἐπὶ τῇ Μαραθῶνι μάχῃ μέγα φρονῶν ἤχθετο τοῖς ὄνομα καὶ δόξαν ὑπὲρ τοὺς πολλοὺς ἔχουσι, καὶ συνελθόντες εἰς ἄστυ πανταχόθεν, ἐξοστρακίζουσι τὸν Ἀριστείδην φθόνῳ τῆς δόξης, ὡς δ' ἔλεγον φόβῳ τυραννίδος. ὁ δ' ἐξοστρακισμὸς ἦν μετανάστασις ἐτῶν δέκα· ἦν δὲ τοιοῦτο τὸ 5 γενόμενον. ὄστρακον λαβὼν ἕκαστος γράφει ὃν ἐβούλετο μεταστῆσαι τῶν πολιτῶν, φέρει δὲ εἰς ἕνα τόπον τῆς ἀγορᾶς. οἱ δ' ἄρχοντες διηρίθμουν τὸ σύμπαν τῶν ὀστράκων πλῆθος· εἰ γὰρ ἐξακισχιλίων ἐλάττονες οἱ γράψαντες ἦσαν, ἀτελὴς ἦν ὁ ἐξοστρακισμός. γραφομένων οὖν τότε τῶν ὀστράκων, λέγεταί 10 τινα τῶν ἀγραμμάτων δόντα τῷ Ἀριστείδῃ τὸ ὄστρακον, ὡς ἑνὶ τῶν τυχόντων, παρακαλεῖν ὅπως Ἀριστείδην ἐγγράφοι. τοῦ δὲ θαυμάσαντος, καὶ πυθομένου μή τι κακὸν αὐτὸν Ἀριστείδης πεποίηκεν, Οὐδέν, εἶπεν, οὐδὲ γιγνώσκω τὸν ἄνθρωπον, ἀλλ' ἐνοχλοῦμαι πανταχοῦ τὸν Δίκαιον ἀκούων. ἀπεκρίνατο μὲν 15 οὐδὲν ὁ Ἀριστείδης, ἀλλ' ἐνέγραψε τὸ ὄνομα τῷ ὀστράκῳ.

Plutarch, *Aristides*, VII

l. 10. λέγεταί τινα, *it is said that one.*
  11. ὡς ἑνὶ τῶν τυχόντων, *as to a casual person.*

119

Themistocles, c. 514–449 B.C.

Εὐρυβιάδης μὲν τὴν ἡγεμονίαν τῶν νεῶν εἶχε διὰ τὸ τῆς
Σπάρτης ἀξίωμα, μαλακὸς δὲ περὶ τὸν κίνδυνον ὢν ἐβούλετο
πλεῖν ἐπὶ τὸν ἰσθμόν. ὁ δὲ Θεμιστοκλῆς ἀντέλεγεν. τότε δὴ
Εὐρυβιάδου πρὸς αὐτὸν εἰπόντος Ὦ Θεμιστόκλεις, ἐν τοῖς
ἀγῶσι τοὺς προεξισταμένους πατάσσουσιν, Ναί, ἔφη ὁ 5
Θεμιστοκλῆς, ἀλλὰ τοὺς ἀπολειφθέντας οὐ στεφανοῦσιν.
ἐπεὶ δὲ τὴν βακτηρίαν ἐπῆρεν ὡς πατάξων, ὁ Θεμιστοκλῆς
ἔφη, Πάταξον μέν, ἄκουσον δέ. εἰπόντος δέ τινος ὡς ἀνὴρ
ἄπολις οὐκ ὀρθῶς διδάσκει τοὺς ἔχοντας πόλιν καταλιπεῖν καὶ
προέσθαι τὰς πατρίδας, ὁ Θεμιστοκλῆς, Ἡμεῖς τοι, ἔφη, ὦ 10
πονηρέ, τὰς μὲν οἰκίας καὶ τείχη καταλελοίπαμεν, οὐκ
ἀξιοῦντες ἀψύχων ἕνεκα δουλεύειν, πόλις δ' ἡμῖν ἐστι μεγίστη
τῶν Ἑλληνίδων, αἱ διακόσιαι τριήρεις. σὺ δή, εἰ μενεῖς αὐτοῦ,
μένων ἀνὴρ γενήσει ἀγαθός· εἰ δὲ μή, ἀναστρέψεις τὴν
Ἑλλάδα. τὸ πᾶν ἡμῖν τοῦ πολέμου φέρουσιν αἱ νῆες. ἀλλ' 15
ἐμοὶ πείθου. ἢν δὲ ταῦτα μὴ ποιήσῃς, ἡμεῖς μέν, ὡς ἔχομεν,
εἰς Ἰταλίαν μέλλομεν ἀποπλεῖν. ὑμεῖς δὲ συμμάχων τοιούτων
στερηθέντες μεμνήσεσθε τῶν ἐμῶν λόγων.

Herodotus, VIII. 59 (adapted)

l. 10. προέσθαι from προίημι, mid. *abandon.*
15. τὸ πᾶν . . . φέρουσι, *carry the whole burden.*
16. ὡς ἔχομεν, *without more ado.*

120

Pericles, c. 500–429 B.C.

Ὃ δὲ πλείστην μὲν ἡδονὴν τοῖς Ἀθηναίοις, μεγίστην δὲ τοῖς
ἄλλοις ἔκπληξιν παρεῖχεν, καὶ ἔτι νῦν τῇ Ἑλλάδι μαρτυρεῖ
περὶ τῆς παλαιᾶς δυνάμεως τῆς πόλεως, ἦν ἡ τῶν ἀναθημάτων
κατασκευή. καὶ διὰ τοῦτο διέβαλλον μὲν αὐτὸν οἱ ἐχθροί,
ἐδίδασκε δὲ τὸν δῆμον ὁ Περικλῆς ὅτι τῶν χρημάτων τῶν 5
ἀναλωθέντων οὐκ ὀφείλουσι τοῖς συμμάχοις λόγον· καὶ γὰρ
ἐπολέμησεν ἡ πόλις ὑπὲρ τῶν συμμάχων, καὶ τοὺς βαρβάρους
ἠμύνετο· οἱ δὲ σύμμαχοι οὐχ ἵππον, οὐ ναῦν, οὐχ ὁπλίτην,
ἀλλὰ χρήματα μόνον ἐτέλουν. τὰ δὲ χρήματα οὔκ ἐστι τῶν
διδόντων, ἀλλὰ τῶν λαμβανόντων, ἐὰν παρέχωσι τοῦτ᾽ ἀνθ᾽ οὗ 10
λαμβάνουσι.

Plutarch, *Pericles*, XII

l. 6. ἀναλωθέντων, spent, from ἀναλίσκω.   λόγον, account.
   10. ἀνθ᾽ οὗ, in payment of which.

121

Plato, c. 427–347 B.C.

Δίων μὲν ἐγγενὴς ἦν τῷ Διονυσίῳ τῷ Συρακοσίων
τυράννῳ· ἤλπιζε δὲ τὸν Πλάτωνα ἐλθόντα ἐς Συρακούσας
ἀφαιρήσειν τὸ δεσποτικὸν τῆς τυραννίδος, καὶ νόμιμον ἄρχοντα
τὸν Διονύσιον καταστήσειν. ὁ τοίνυν Πλάτων εἰς Σικελίαν
ἀφικόμενος τὸ μὲν πρῶτον θαυμαστῆς ἐτύγχανε φιλοφροσύνης 5
καὶ τιμῆς. καὶ γὰρ ἄρμα βασιλικὸν παρέστη αὐτῷ καταβάντι
τῆς τριήρους, καὶ θυσίαν ἔθυσε Διονύσιος, ὡς δι᾽ εὐτύχημά τι.
ἅπαντες δὲ πρὸς λόγους καὶ φιλοσοφίαν ἐτράποντο, καὶ μέγα
τι πλῆθος ἦν τῶν γεωμετρούντων.

Plutarch, *Dion*, XII

Demosthenes

122

Plato (continued)

ἀλλὰ μετ' οὐ πολὺν χρόνον ἐλοιδόρουν τὸν Δίωνα, λέγοντες
ὅτι κατεπᾷδε Διονύσιον τῷ Πλάτωνος λόγῳ, ἔνιοι δὲ ἐδυσ-
χέραινον ὅτι Ἀθηναῖοι πρότερον μὲν ναυτικαῖς καὶ πεζικαῖς
δυνάμεσι πλεύσαντες εἰς Σικελίαν ἀπώλοντο, νῦν δὲ δι' ἑνὸς
σοφιστοῦ (τὸν Πλάτωνα λέγοντες) καταλύσουσι τὴν Διονυσίου   5
ἀρχήν, πείσαντες αὐτὸν τοὺς δορυφόρους καὶ τὰς τριήρεις
ἀποπέμπειν, καὶ διὰ γεωμετρίας εὐδαίμονα γενέσθαι. ἐκ δὲ
τούτων πρῶτον μὲν ὑποψία, ἔπειτα δ' ὀργὴ ἐγένετο τῷ
Διονυσίῳ. καὶ τὸν μὲν Δίωνα πρὸς τὴν θάλατταν ἀπαγαγὼν
ἐνέθηκεν ἀκατίῳ καὶ τὸν Πλάτωνα ἀποπέμπει.   10

Plutarch, *Dion*

l. 8. ἐγένετο τῷ Δ., came over D.

123

Demosthenes, c. 385–322 B.C.

Τὸν δὲ Δημοσθένην πυθόμενος ἱκέτην ἐν τῷ ἱερῷ τοῦ
Ποσειδῶνος ἐν Καλαυρίᾳ τῇ νήσῳ καθίζεσθαι, διαπλεύσας ὁ
Ἀρχίας ἔπειθεν ἀναστάντα βαδίζειν μεθ' αὑτοῦ λέγων ὅτι
βίαιον πείσεται οὐδέν. ὁ δὲ Δημοσθένης ἐτύγχανεν ὄψιν
ἑωρακὼς ἐν ὕπνῳ ἐκείνης τῆς νυκτός. ἐδόκει γὰρ ἀνταγω-   5
νίζεσθαι τῷ Ἀρχίᾳ τραγῳδίαν ὑποκρινόμενος, ὃς ὑποκρίτης
πρότερον ἦν, νῦν δὲ τὰ Μακεδόνων ἐφρόνει. διὸ τοῦ Ἀρχίου
πολλὰ καὶ φιλάνθρωπα εἰπόντος, ὁ Δημοσθένης ἀναβλέψας,
Ὦ Ἀρχία, ἔφη, οὔτε ὑποκρινόμενός μ' ἔπεισάς πώποτε,
οὔτε νῦν πείσεις ἐπαγγελλόμενος. ἀρξαμένου δ' ἀπειλεῖν τοῦ   10
Ἀρχίου, Μικρὸν ἐπίσχες, ἔφη, ὅπως ἐπιστέλλω τι τοῖς οἴκοι.

καὶ λαβὼν δέλτους, ὡς γράψειν μέλλων, τῷ στόματι τὸν
κάλαμον προσήνεγκεν, καὶ ἔδακνε, ὥσπερ ἐν τῷ διανοεῖσθαι
καὶ γράφειν εἰώθει. αἰσθόμενος δ᾽ ὅτι τὸ ἐν τῷ καλάμῳ φάρμακον εἰργάζετο διαβλέψας πρὸς τὸν Ἀρχίαν, Οὐκ ἂν 15
φθάνοις, ἔφη, ὑποκρινόμενος τὸν ἐκ τῆς τραγῳδίας Κρέοντα,
καὶ τὸ σῶμα τοῦτο ῥίπτων ἄταφον. ταῦτ᾽ εἰπὼν ἄφηκε τὴν
ψυχήν.

Plutarch, *Demosthenes*

l. 2. Καλαυρία, an island off Troezen in the Peloponnese.
   5. ἀνταγωνίζεσθαι, *compete against.*
   7. τὰ Μακεδόνων ἐφρόνει, *was a Macedonian sympathiser.*
   9. ἔπεισας, *you never convinced me.*   15. εἰργάζετο, *was working.*
   οὐκ ἂν φθάνοις, *you could not be too soon in acting Creon....*
   Creon in Sophocles' *Antigone* refuses to bury Polyneices.

XIII

LOVE OF COUNTRY

Mourning Athena

Codrus gives his life for Athens

Ἀθηναίοις καὶ Πελοποννησίοις πόλεμος ἦν, ὁ δὲ θεὸς ἔφη
νικήσειν Ἀθηναίους ἐὰν ὁ βασιλεὺς αὐτῶν ἀποθάνη ὑπ' ἀνδρὸς
Πελοποννησίου. ἦν δὲ τότε τῶν Ἀθηναίων βασιλεὺς Κόδρος.
τοῖς οὖν πολεμίοις, εἰδόσι ταῦτα, παρήγγειλεν ὁ στρατηγὸς
αὐτῶν ἐν ταῖς μάχαις ἀπέχεσθαι Κόδρου· ὁ δὲ Κόδρος (ἦν 5
γὰρ ἑσπέρα) ἐσθῆτα φρύγανα συλλέγοντος ἀνδρὸς λαβών, τοῦ
στρατοπέδου ἐξελθὼν ἔτεμνε τὴν ὕλην. ἔτυχον δὲ καὶ Πελοποννήσιοι ἄνδρες κατ' αὐτὸ τοῦτο, τὸν φρυγανισμόν, ἥκοντες.
τούτοις μάχεται Κόδρος, καὶ τὸ δρέπανον αὐτοῦ ἔτρωσέ τινα
αὐτῶν. οἱ δ' ἀποκτείνουσιν αὐτὸν τοῖς δρεπάνοις· τηνικαῦτα 10
οἱ Ἀθηναῖοι, ὡς τοῦ χρησμοῦ τετελεσμένου, πλείονι θυμῷ
μαχόμενοι ἐνίκησαν.

Lycurgus (the Orator), *in Leocratem*, 84

l. 8. κατ' αὐτὸ τοῦτο, *for this same reason.*

Thermopylae, 480 B.C.

Οἱ δ' ἐν Θερμοπύλαις Ἕλληνες, ἐπειδὴ πέλας ἐγένοντο οἱ
Πέρσαι, ἐβουλεύοντο ἐς Ἰσθμὸν ἀναχωρεῖν. Λεωνίδας δὲ
Σπάρτης βασιλεὺς αὐτοῦ μένειν ἐψηφίζετο. ἔπεμπε δὲ Ξέρξης
κατάσκοπον ὀψόμενον ὁπόσοι τ' εἰσὶ καὶ ὅ τι ποιοῦσιν. ὁ δὲ

προσιὼν πρὸς τὸ στρατόπεδον τοὺς μὲν ἑώρα τῶν ἀνδρῶν 5
γυμναζομένους, τοὺς δὲ τὰς κόμας κτενιζομένους. ὁ δὲ
Ξέρξης, ἀπορῶν ὅ τι ἐσήμαινε τοῦτο, Δημάρατον ἄνδρα
Σπαρτιάτην ἠρώτα· ὁ δὲ ἀπεκρίνατο, Οἱ ἄνδρες οὗτοι μαχέ-
σονται ἡμῖν περὶ τῆς εἰσόδου· νόμος γὰρ αὐτοῖς ἐστίν, ἐπειδὰν
μέλλωσι κινδυνεύειν τῇ ψυχῇ, τότε τὰς κεφαλὰς κοσμεῖσθαι. 10
σφόδρα δ' ἄπιστα τῷ Ξέρξῃ ἐφαίνετο τὰ λεγόμενα. καὶ προσ-
ελθόντων τῶν βαρβάρων, οἱ ἡγεμόνες αὐτῶν ἐρράπιζον πάντ'
ἄνδρα, ἐς τὸ πρόσω ἐποτρύνοντες. οἱ δ' Ἕλληνες ἐπιστάμενοι
τὸν μέλλοντα ἔσεσθαι θάνατον ἐκ τῶν περιϊόντων τὸ ὄρος,
ἐπεδείκνυντο ὅσην ἔχουσι ῥώμην τοῖς βαρβάροις. καὶ τὰ μὲν 15
δόρατα τοῖς πλείστοις κατεαγότα ἦν, οἱ δὲ τοῖς ξίφεσι διεργά-
ζοντο τοὺς Πέρσας. καὶ Λεωνίδας ἐν τούτῳ πίπτει, ἀνὴρ
γενόμενος ἄριστος· οἱ δ' ἄλλοι ἀνεχώρουν ἐς τὸ στενὸν τῆς
εἰσόδου, καὶ ἵζοντο ἐπὶ τὸν κολωνόν, ὅπου νῦν ὁ λίθινος λέων
ἕστηκεν ἐπὶ Λεωνίδᾳ, καὶ πάντες ὑπὸ τῶν βαρβάρων 20
διεφθάρησαν.

Herodotus, VII. 224 (adapted)

l. 14. τῶν περιϊόντων, those led by the traitor along the secret path
to encircle the Spartans.

126

On the Spartan dead at Thermopylae

Ὦ ξεῖν' ἀγγέλλειν Λακεδαιμονίοις ὅτι τῇδε
κείμεθα τοῖς κείνοις ῥήμασι πειθόμενοι.

Simonides

l. 1. ἀγγέλλειν, infin. for imper.

127

Into Battle : the Greek war-cry at Salamis

Ὦ παῖδες Ἑλλήνων ἴτε
ἐλευθεροῦτε πατρίδ᾽, ἐλευθεροῦτε δέ
παῖδας, γυναῖκας, θεῶν τε πατρῴων ἕδη,
θήκας τε προγόνων, νῦν ὑπὲρ πάντων ἀγών.

Aeschylus, Persae, 402–5

128

Pericles praises the Athenian dead

Ὅταν μεγάλη δόξῃ εἶναι ἡ πόλις, χρὴ ἐνθυμεῖσθαι ὅτι
τολμῶντες, καὶ γιγνώσκοντες τὰ δέοντα, ἄνδρες τοῦτ᾽ ἐκτήσαντο.
κοινῇ γὰρ τὰ σώματα διδόντες, ἰδίᾳ τὸν ἀγήρων ἔπαινον ἐλάμ-
βανον, καὶ τὸν τάφον ἐπισημότατον ἔχουσιν οὐκ ἐν ᾧ κεῖνται,
ἀλλ᾽ ἐν ᾧ ἡ δόξα αὐτῶν ἀείμνηστος καταλείπεται. ἀνδρῶν 5
γὰρ ἐπιφανῶν πᾶσα γῆ τάφος· καὶ τοῦτο σημαίνει οὐ
στηλῶν μόνον ἐν τῇ οἰκείᾳ γῇ ἐπιγραφή, ἀλλὰ καὶ ἐν τῇ μὴ
προσηκούσῃ ἄγραφος μνήμη.

Thucydides, II. 43

This speech was delivered in memory of men who died abroad,
and for whom a cenotaph (κενὸς τάφος) was erected. The
sentiment here is like that of Rupert Brooke's sonnet, which
begins :

> *If I should die, think only this of me,*
> *That there's some corner of a foreign field*
> *That is for ever England.*

l. 2. τὰ δέοντα, *one's duty.*   8. προσήκειν, here = *belong.*

Attic stele

129

Demosthenes describes his call to arms against Philip

Ἑσπέρα μὲν γὰρ ἦν, ἧκε δ᾽ ἀγγέλλων τις ὡς Ἐλάτεια
κατείληπται. τῇ δ᾽ ὑστεραίᾳ οἱ πρυτάνεις ἐκάλουν τὴν
βουλὴν εἰς τὸ βουλευτήριον, ὑμεῖς δ᾽ εἰς τὴν ἐκκλησίαν
ἐπορεύεσθε. καὶ ἠρώτα ὁ κῆρυξ, Τίς ἀγορεύειν βούλεται ;
καὶ πολλάκις τοῦ κήρυκος ἐρωτῶντος ἀνίστατο οὐδείς. 5
ἀνίστατ᾽ οὐδείς, ἁπάντων μὲν τῶν στρατηγῶν παρόντων,
ἁπάντων δὲ τῶν ῥητόρων, καλούσης δὲ τῆς πατρίδος τῇ κοινῇ
φωνῇ τὸν μέλλοντα ἐρεῖν ὑπὲρ σωτηρίας. τέλος δ᾽ ἐγὼ
παρελθὼν ἔφην· Τί οὖν βούλεται Φίλιππος, καὶ τίνος ἕνεκα
τὴν Ἐλάτειαν συνείληφε ; πλησίον δύναμιν δείξας τοὺς μὲν 10
ἑαυτοῦ φίλους θρασεῖς ποιῆσαι βούλεται, τοὺς δ᾽ ἐναντιου-
μένους καταπλῆξαι. τί οὖν φημὶ δεῖν ; πρῶτον μὲν τὸν
παρόντα καταλῦσαι φόβον, ἔπειτα Ἐλευσῖνάδε ἐξελθόντας
τοὺς ἐν ἡλικίᾳ, δεῖξαι πᾶσιν ὑμᾶς ἐν τοῖς ὅπλοις ὄντας, ἵνα
τοῖς ἐν Θήβαις φρονοῦσι τὰ ἡμέτερα ἐξῇ παρρησιάζεσθαι 15
ὑπὲρ τῶν δικαίων.

Demosthenes, de Corona, 169

l. 2. κατείληπται, perf. pass. of καταλαμβάνω, *capture.*
πρυτάνεις, *presiding officers.*
3. βουλή, *Council.*
15. τοῖς φρονοῦσι τὰ ἡμέτερα, *those that sympathise with us.*
ἐξῇ from ἔξεστι.

130

On the Athenian dead at Plataea

Εἰ τὸ καλῶς θνῄσκειν ἀρέτης μέρος ἐστὶ μέγιστον
ἡμῖν ἐκ πάντων τοῦτ᾽ ἀπένειμε Τύχη.
Ἑλλάδι γὰρ σπεύσαντες ἐλευθερίαν περιθεῖναι
κείμεθ᾽ ἀγηράντῳ χρώμενοι εὐλογίᾳ.

Simonides

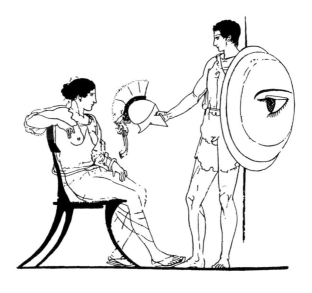

XIV
PEACE

" My Peace I leave with you "

Ταῦτα λελάληκα ὑμῖν παρ' ὑμῖν μένων·
ὁ δὲ Παράκλητος, τὸ πνεῦμα τὸ ἅγιον, ὃ πέμψει ὁ πατὴρ
ἐν τῷ ὀνόματί μου, ἐκεῖνος ὑμᾶς διδάξει πάντα, καὶ ὑπομνήσει
ὑμᾶς πάντα ἃ εἶπον ὑμῖν.

εἰρήνην ἀφίημι ὑμῖν, εἰρήνην τὴν ἐμὴν δέδωκα ὑμῖν, οὐ   5
καθὼς ὁ κόσμος δίδωσιν, ἐγὼ δίδωμι ὑμῖν. μὴ ταρασσέσθω
ὑμῶν ἡ καρδία, μηδὲ δειλιάτω.

St. John's Gospel, XIV. 25-7

τέλος δεδωκώς, Χριστέ, σοὶ χάριν φέρω.

Thank God, that's done!

Written by the scribe of the Medicean MS. when he had copied out the seven plays of Aeschylus.

THE ALPHABET

THE Greeks learnt the use of writing from the Phoenicians, probably about the ninth century. They adopted the consonantal Semitic alphabet of twenty-two letters, taking four of these to represent the vowel sounds A, E, I, O, and adding a letter for U. Later the long and short vowel sounds of E and O were distinguished, and symbols added for the double letters Φ, X, Ψ.

There were many local variations in the forms of the letters used. Athens officially adopted the Ionic alphabet in 403 B.C. That is the alphabet we use for our Greek texts. The Latin alphabet, which is also our alphabet, was derived from the Western type of Greek alphabet, either through the Greek colonies in Southern Italy and Sicily or through the Etruscans. Hence its resemblance to the Greek alphabet.

Attic, the dialect of Athens and its state Attica, is by convention the dialect on which the study of Greek grammar is based. It is the dialect used by

the historians	Thucydides and Xenophon
the orator	Demosthenes
the philosopher	Plato
the tragedians	Aeschylus, Sophocles, Euripides
the comedian	Aristophanes

Evolution of the left-to-right Greek Alphabets from the right-to-left Phoenician Alphabet

PHOENICIAN	GREEK		
Right to Left	Right to Left	Left to Right	
		EASTERN	WESTERN
aleph	alpha		
beth	beta		
gimel	gamma		
daleth	delta		
he	epsilon		
waw	digamma		
zayin	zeta		
cheth	eta		
teth	theta		
yod	iota		
kaph	kappa		
lamed	lambda		
men	mu		
nun	nu		
samekh	xi		exchanged with chi
ayin	omicron		
pe	pi		
tsade	san		
qoph	koppa		Latin Q
resh	rho		
shin	sigma		
tau	tau		
	upsilon		Latin V for U
	xi		
	phi		
	chi		exchanged with ψ
	psi		
	omega		

Note the resemblance of Western Greek letters to Roman letters. The alphabet reached Rome either through the Greek colonies in S. Italy such as Cumae, or through the Etruscans. A Western Greek type of alphabet was in use both in the colonies of the Campanian coast and with the Etruscans.

Letters		English Equivalent	Names
A	α	a	alpha
B	β	b	beta
Γ	γ	g	gamma
Δ	δ	d	delta
E	ε	e	epsīlon
Z	ζ	z	zēta
H	η	ē	ēta
Θ	θ	th	thēta
I	ι	i	iota
K	κ	k	kappa
Λ	λ	l	lambda
M	μ	m	mū
N	ν	n	nū
Ξ	ξ	x	xī
O	o	o	omīcron
Π	π	p	pī
P	ρ	r	rho
Σ	σ	s	sigma
T	τ	t	ṭau
Y	υ	u	upsīlon
Φ	φ	ph	phī
X	χ	ch	chī
Ψ	ψ	ps	psi
Ω	ω	ō	ōmega

Every initial vowel carries a breathing sign.

‘ represents an aspirate and is called a *rough breathing*, as ἥν.

’ represents absence of aspirate and is called a *smooth breathing*, as ἤν.

Diphthongs carry the breathing on the second vowel, as αὐ.

Initial ρ carries the rough breathing, ῥ. Hence the spelling of Greek derivatives such as *rhythm* and *rheumatism*. Double ρ in a word is usually written ῤῥ, as ἐῤῥει.

The sign σ is used for any sigma except a final one, for which we write
ς, as σεσωσμένος.

ι after long α, η, ω, is written under that letter as ᾳ η ῳ, and called
iota subscript. With capitals, however, it stands after the letter, e.g.
μούσῃ, but *ΜΟΥΣΗΙ.*

Stops

Full stop .   semicolon or colon   ·   comma   ,   question mark   ;

Pronunciation

> ā and ă as Latin   *fāmă.*
> η and ε as Latin   *rēgĕ* (ablative of *rex*).
> ī and ĭ as Latin   *tībĭa.*
> o and ω as Latin   *dŏlō* (ablative of *dolus*).
> ῡ and ῠ as French   *sûr* and *du.*
> αι, ει, οι, υι marking the sound of both vowels.
> αυ as English   *lout.*
> ου as English   *loot.*
> ευ as English   *feud.*

Pronounce consonants in the same way as the English equivalents given
in the alphabet table.

Consonants

ν, ρ, and ς are the only consonants which can end a Greek word.
Exceptions. ἐκ (*out of*), οὐκ (*not*), and οὐχ (*not*). ξ and ψ count as a
final ς.
Consonants are grouped as follows :

Gutturals	γ	κ	χ	σσ[1]
Labials	β	π	φ	ππ
Dentals	δ	τ	θ	ντ
Liquids	λ	μ	ν	ρ

Consonant changes

> Guttural   + σ = ξ
> Labial   + σ = ψ

γ before a guttural is nasalised, e.g. ἄγγελος, cf. *angel*; ἄγκῡρα, cf. *anchor.*

> ν before κ   γ   χ   ξ changes to γ.
> ν before β   π   φ   μ changes to μ.
> ν before λ   or   ρ changes to λ or ρ.

---

[1] In later Attic written ττ.

These changes are clearly shown in verbs compounded with prepositions.

Examples. ἐν + γράφω = ἐγγράφω.

ἐν + βαίνω = ἐμβαίνω.

ἐν + πορεύομαι = ἐμπορεύομαι.

συν + λέγω = συλλέγω.

συν + ῥέω = συρρέω.

Preposition ἐκ *out of* becomes ἐξ before a vowel.
οὐ *not* becomes οὐκ before a vowel, οὐχ before an aspirated vowel.
For other consonant changes see consonant stem verbs, pp. 230–4.

Vowels

Elision. A short final vowel is commonly dropped if the next word begins with a vowel. The place of the elided letter is taken by an apostrophe. This is especially common with prepositions.

Examples. δι᾽ ἐμοῦ   for   διὰ ἐμοῦ.

ἐφ᾽ ἡμῶν   for   ἐπὶ ἡμῶν.

ν, called ν ἐφελκυστικόν,[1] can be added to ε and ι of many 3rd person verbal endings, and to dative plural 3rd declension, to avoid *hiatus* or elision ; e.g. λύουσιν for λύουσι.

Never elide: (1) περί and πρό.

(2) ι of dative singular and plural 3rd declension.

(3) Final υ.

(4) Monosyllables except those in ε, as σε, τε, etc.

(5) Conjunction ὅτι : ὅτ᾽ or ὅθ᾽ represents ὅτε, *when.*

The augment ε, the mark of a secondary tense in the indicative, is sometimes prodelided in verse.

οὐδ᾽ ἱκόμην ἔγωγ᾽ ἄν εἰ σὺ μὴ ᾽κάλεις (for ἐκάλεις).

I should not have come if you were not calling.

---

[1] ν " dragged after," or suffixed.

Read :

ἄλφα, βῆτα, γάμμα, δέλτα,
ἒ ψιλόν, ζῆτα, ἦτα, θῆτα, ἰῶτα,
κάππα, λάμβδα, μῦ, νῦ, ξῖ, ὂ μῑκρόν,
πῖ, ῥῶ, σίγμα, ταῦ, ῦ ψῑλόν,
φῖ, χῖ, ψῖ, ὢ μέγα.

ἐγώ εἰμι τὸ "Αλφα καὶ τὸ "Ω, ἀρχὴ καὶ τέλος, λέγει Κύριος ὁ Θεός.
Rev. 1. 8.
" I am Alpha and Omega, the beginning and the ending, saith the
Lord."

ἡ 'Ιλιὰς καὶ ἡ 'Οδυσσεία.   ὁ "Ομηρος.

Μῆνιν ἄειδε, θεά, Πηληϊάδεω 'Αχιλῆος
οὐλομένην, ἣ μυρί' 'Αχαιοῖς ἄλγε' ἔθηκεν.
                                    Homer, *Iliad*, I. 1–2.

"Ανδρα μοι ἔννεπε, Μοῦσα, πολύτροπον ὃς μάλα πολλὰ
πλάγχθη ἐπεὶ Τροίης ἱερὸν πτολίεθρον ἔπερσεν.
                                    Homer, *Odyssey*, I. 1–2.

ἕπτα πόλεις διερίζουσιν περὶ ῥίζαν 'Ομήρου,
Σμύρνα 'Ρόδος Κολοφὼν Σαλαμὶν "Ιος "Αργος 'Αθῆναι.

τυφλὸς ἀνήρ, οἰκεῖ δὲ Χίῳ ἔνι παιπαλοέσσῃ
τοῦ πᾶσαι μετόπισθεν ἀριστεύσουσιν ἀοιδαί.
                              Homeric Hymn to Delian Apollo

Θουκυδίδης Ξενοφῶν Δημοσθένης Πλάτων.
'Αισχύλος Σοφοκλῆς 'Ευριπίδης 'Αριστοφάνης.

ὠὸπ ὄπ ὠὸπ ὄπ.   βρεκεκεκὲξ κοὰξ κοάξ, βρεκεκεκὲξ κοὰξ κοάξ.
                                    Aristophanes, *Frogs*

INTRODUCTORY EXERCISES
AND
GRAMMAR

ALPHA

1st declension nouns, masculine and feminine (Pars. 1–2, p. 175).
Definite article, ὁ, ἡ, τό (Par. 3).
Verbs (active). Present and imperfect indicative of -ω verbs. P. 206.
Present and imperfect indicative of verb *to be*. P. 268.

		Present	*Imperfect*	
Singular	1.	λύω *I loose*	ἔλυον	*I was loosing*
	2.	λύεις	ἔλυες	
	3.	λύει	ἔλυε	
Plural	1.	λύομεν	ἐλύομεν	
	2.	λύετε	ἐλύετε	
	3.	λύουσι(ν)	ἔλυον	

ἐ- prefixed in the imperfect is called the AUGMENT (Par. 54).

Singular	1.	εἰμί *I am*	1.	ἦν *I was*
	2.	εἶ	2.	ἦσθα
	3.	ἐστίν	3.	ἦν
Plural	1.	ἐσμέν	1.	ἦμεν
	2.	ἐστέ	2.	ἦτε
	3.	εἰσί(ν)	3.	ἦσαν

VOCABULARY

Nouns

Feminine	*Masculine*
ἡ ἀγορά, *the market-place*	ὁ κριτής, *the judge*
ἡ ᾿Αθηνᾶ, *Athena*, alpha throughout	ὁ ναύτης, *the sailor*
ἡ ἅμαξα, *the waggon*	ὁ νεανίας, *the young man*
ἡ ἐκκλησία, *the assembly*	ὁ ποιητής, *the poet*
ἡ θάλασσα, *the sea*	ὁ πολίτης, *the citizen*
ἡ θύρα, *the door*	ὁ Σπαρτιάτης, *the Spartan*
ἡ κώμη, *the village*	ὁ στρατιώτης, *the soldier*
ἡ μάχη, *the battle*	
ἡ νίκη, *the victory*	
ἡ οἰκία, *the house*	
ἡ πύλη, *the gate*	
ἡ τιμή, *honour*	
ἡ χώρα, *the land*	

Verbs

Stems in ι or υ	*Consonant stems*
θύω, *I sacrifice.*	διώκω, *I pursue.*
κλείω, *I shut.*	πέμπω, *I send.*
λύω, *I loose.*	φεύγω, *I flee.*
παιδεύω, *I teach.*	

Both groups are conjugated like λύω in present and imperfect.

Prepositions

Accusative	*Genitive*	*Dative*
εἰς, *into.*	ἐκ, *out of.*	ἐν, *in.*
διά, *on account of.*	πρό, *in front of.*	

Particles, Adverbs

ἔπειτα, *next, then.*

δέ, *and, but,* or simply a connective.

μέν . . . δέ mark an apposition or contrast. They come between the article and its noun, or, if there is no article, after the words themselves. μέν and δέ cannot stand after οὐ.

ὁ μέν . . . , *the one.*	ὁ δέ . . . , *the other.*
οἱ μέν, . . . , *some.*	οἱ δέ . . . , *others.*

καί, *and, also.*

οὐ, *not.* Write οὐκ before a vowel, οὐχ before an aspirated vowel.

A

1. ἐν τῇ θαλάσσῃ οἱ ναῦται παιδεύουσι τοὺς νεανίας.

2. οὔκ εἰσιν ἅμαξαι ἐν τῇ χώρᾳ διὰ τὴν μάχην.

3. ἔθυον ἐν ταῖς κώμαις τῇ Ἀθηνᾷ πρὸ τῆς ἐκκλησίας.

4. τὸν μὲν στρατιώτην ὁ κριτὴς ἔλυε, τὸν δὲ ναύτην οὔ.

5. οὐκ ἐπέμπομεν τὰς ἁμάξας ἐκ τῆς ἀγορᾶς.

6. οἱ μὲν ποιηταί εἰσιν ἐν τῇ ἀγορᾷ πρὸ τῆς οἰκίας, οἱ δὲ ναῦται φεύγουσιν.

7. τοὺς μὲν λύουσι, τοὺς δὲ διώκουσιν.

8. οἱ μὲν Σπαρτιᾶται φεύγουσιν, οἱ δὲ πολῖται διώκουσιν. διώκουσι δ᾽ ἐκ τῆς ἀγορᾶς εἰς τὰς οἰκίας, καὶ κλείουσι τὰς θύρας καὶ τὰς πύλας. ἔπειτα τῇ Ἀθηνᾷ θύουσι διὰ τὴν νίκην καὶ τὴν τιμήν.

a

1. The Spartan is escaping from the land.
2. You were not teaching the assembly.
3. Some were fleeing, others pursuing.
4. The soldiers are setting the young men free because of Athena.
5. He is chasing the sailors into the market-place.
6. The judges were in the assembly, but the soldiers were not.
7. We were sending the carts into the village.

8. The soldiers were in pursuit of the Spartans, but they (οἱ δὲ) took refuge in the house, and were closing the doors because of the soldiers. Thereupon the judge offered a sacrifice to Athena before the gates.

The English words are not exactly as given in the vocabulary. Think of synonymous words and expressions.

BETA

2nd declension nouns, masculine, feminine and neuter (Par. 4, p. 178).
Verbs (active).   Future indicative of -ω verbs.

Future

Singular.   1. λύσω,   *I shall loose.*
            2. λύσεις.
            3. λύσει.

Plural.   1. λύσομεν.
          2. λύσετε.
          3. λύσουσιν.

Conjugate like λύω all verbs with stem in ι or υ.

Consonant stems

Gutturals κ, γ, χ, σσ, σκ combine with σ to form ξ.
Example.   πράσσω, future πράξω.   (Par. 64).

Labials π, β, φ, πτ combine with σ to form ψ.
Example.   πέμπω, future πέμψω.   (Par. 65).

A possessive genitive stands between the article and the noun.
Example.   οἱ τῶν Σπαρτιατῶν στρατιῶται.

The Spartans' soldiers, the soldiers of the Spartans.

A possessive dative is often used with the verb *to be*.
Example. ἐστὶν οἰκία τῷ κριτῇ. *The judge has a house.*

The article is not used with the predicate.
Example. ἐστὶ ναύτης. *He is a soldier.*

A neuter plural subject takes a singular verb.
Example. τὰ ὅπλα ἐστὶν ἐν τῇ ἀγορᾷ.
The weapons are in the market-place.

VOCABULARY
Nouns

Masculine	Feminine	Neuter
ὁ Ἀθηναῖος, Athenian	ἡ ἤπειρος, mainland	τὸ δῶρον, gift.
ὁ δοῦλος, slave.	ἡ θεός, goddess.	τὸ ἔργον, deed.
ὁ ἥλιος, sun.	ἡ νῆσος, island.	τὰ ὅπλα, plur., arms,
ὁ θεός, god.	ἡ νόσος, disease.	weapons.
ὁ ἵππος, horse.	ἡ ὁδός, road.	τὸ πεδίον, plain.
ὁ λόγος, word.		τὸ πλοῖον, boat.
ὁ πολέμιος, enemy.		τὸ στρατόπεδον, camp.
ὁ πόλεμος, war.		
ὁ ποταμός, river.		
ὁ Πέρσης, 1. Persian.	ἡ σελήνη, 1. moon.	
ὁ στρατηγός, general.		

Verbs
κωλύω, prevent.
παίω, strike.
πιστεύω, with dat., trust.
πράσσω, do.

Particles
ἀλλά, but.
γάρ, for.   Cannot stand first in its clause.
λόγῳ μέν ... ἔργῳ δέ, contrast words with facts.

B
1. οἱ τῶν δούλων ἵπποι ἦσαν ἐν τῷ στρατοπέδῳ.
2. τὰ τοῦ στρατηγοῦ δῶρά ἐστιν ἐν τῇ νήσῳ.

3. ἐστὶ δῶρα τῷ στρατηγῷ.

4. φεύγουσιν ἐκ τῆς τῶν Περσῶν χώρας διὰ τὴν νόσον.

5. λόγῳ μὲν οἱ νεανίαι πιστεύουσι τοῖς Πέρσαις, ἔργῳ δὲ πολέμιοί εἰσιν.

6. κωλύσει ὁ θεὸς τὰ τοῦ πολέμου ἔργα.

7. οἱ στρατιῶται πέμψουσι τοὺς δούλους ἐκ τῆς νήσου εἰς τὴν ἤπειρον διὰ τὸν πόλεμον. οὐ γὰρ πράσσουσι τὰ τοῦ πολέμου ἔργα.

8. τῷ μὲν ἡλίῳ θύσει, τῇ δὲ σελήνῃ οὔ· θεὸς γάρ ἐστιν ὁ ἥλιος.

9. στρατιώτας ἔπεμπεν, ἀλλ᾽ οὐκ ἐκώλυε τὸν πόλεμον. οἱ γὰρ πολῖται οὐκ ἐπίστευον τῷ στρατηγῷ.

10. οὐ πιστεύσει τοῖς τῶν πολεμίων λόγοις ἀλλὰ τοῖς ἔργοις ὁ στρατηγός, καὶ διώκει τοὺς Πέρσας ἐν τῷ πεδίῳ. καὶ παίσουσιν οἱ μὲν τῶν Ἀθηναίων στρατιῶται τοὺς τῶν Περσῶν ναύτας, οἱ δὲ ναῦται τοὺς στρατιώτας πρὸ τῶν πλοίων ἐν τῇ ὁδῷ.

β

1. The soldiers have [1] horses, but the sailors have not.[2]

2. The Persians are fleeing from the island because of the plague.

3. The general pursues the enemy into the Athenians' camp.

4. The battle was on the plain in front of the river.

5. They are citizens in name, but in fact they are enemies.

6. The boats are in the river, but they will not prevent the war.

7. I shall sacrifice to the goddess on account of the victory.

8. The sun is a god, the moon is not.[2]

9. The Athenian sailors were smiting the Persian soldiers in the battle. The Athenians will gain the victory,[1] for the Persians are fleeing to their ships.

10. Sailors do not put their trust in horses, for there are ships in the river ; but slaves will not perform the deeds of war.

The words of the English should not always be literally translated.

GAMMA

3rd declension nouns, consonant stems (Paragraphs 5–11).
Verbs (active). Aorist indicative of -ω verbs.

---

[1] Possessive dative with verb *to be*.
[2] μέν and δέ cannot stand after οὐ. See Ex. A4.

Aorist = ἀόριστος, *undefined*. Denotes an event merely as taking place in the past.

Imperfect denotes continuance in the past.

Perfect denotes completion in the past.

The aorist, like the English preterite, is the commonest past tense.

STEMS IN ι OR υ AS λύω

Singular. 1. ἔλυσα.
2. ἔλυσας.
3. ἔλυσε.

Plural. 1. ἐλύσαμεν.
2. ἐλύσατε.
3. ἔλυσαν.

Guttural stems form ξ, as for future (Par. 64).

διώκω, *pursue*, aor. ἐδίωξα.

λέγω, *say*, aor. ἔλεξα.

Labial stems form ψ (Par. 65).

πέμπω, *send*, aor. ἔπεμψα.

Dental stems in τ, δ, θ, ζ, drop the dental before σ (Par. 66).

σῴζω, *save*, fut. σώσω, aor. ἔσωσα.

Present infinitive active. Add -ειν to present stem.

Examples. λύω, infin. λύειν. διώκω, infin. διώκειν.

VOCABULARY

Nouns

Nom. sing.	Gen. sing.	Dat. pl.	Meaning
ὁ ἀγών	τοῦ ἀγῶνος	τοῖς ἀγῶσι	*contest*
ὁ γέρων	τοῦ γέροντος	τοῖς γέρουσι	*old man*
ὁ γίγας	τοῦ γίγαντος	τοῖς γίγασι	*giant*
ὁ δαίμων	τοῦ δαίμονος	τοῖς δαίμοσι	*god*
ἡ Ἑλλάς	τῆς Ἑλλάδος	—	*Greece*
ὁ Ἕλλην	τοῦ Ἕλληνος	τοῖς Ἕλλησι	*Greek*
ὁ ἡγεμών	τοῦ ἡγεμόνος	τοῖς ἡγεμόσι	*leader*
ὁ κῆρυξ	τοῦ κήρυκος	τοῖς κήρυξι	*herald*
ὁ λέων	τοῦ λέοντος	τοῖς λέουσι	*lion*
ὁ λιμήν	τοῦ λιμένος	τοῖς λιμέσι	*harbour*
ὁ παῖς	τοῦ παιδός	τοῖς παισί	*boy, child*
ἡ πατρίς	τῆς πατρίδος	ταῖς πατρίσι	*native land*
ὁ ῥήτωρ	τοῦ ῥήτορος	τοῖς ῥήτορσι	*orator*

ἡ σάλπιγξ	τῆς σάλπιγγος	ταῖς σάλπιγξι	*trumpet*
τὸ σῶμα	τοῦ σώματος	τοῖς σώμασι	*body*
τὸ τείχισμα	τοῦ τειχίσματος	τοῖς τειχίσμασι	*fortification*
ἡ φάλαγξ	τῆς φάλαγγος	ταῖς φάλαγξι	*phalanx*
ὁ φύλαξ	τοῦ φύλακος	τοῖς φύλαξι	*guard*

Verbs

Initial α, ε and η become η when augmented.

ἀκούω, aor. ἤκουσα, *hear*, with gen. of source of sound.[1]

ἄρχω, aor. ἦρξα, *rule*, with gen.

βουλεύω, aor. ἐβούλευσα, *take counsel.*

ἐθέλω, aor. ἠθέλησα irreg., *be willing.*

ἐρίζω, aor. ἤρισα, *compete, strive*, with dat.

ἡσυχάζω, aor. ἡσύχασα, *keep quiet.*

προσβάλλω, irreg. (Par. 68), *attack*, with dat.   Imperf. προσέβαλλον.

τειχίζω, aor. ἐτείχισα, *build, fortify.*

Prepositions

περί + gen., *about, for, concerning.*

πρός + acc., *against, to, towards.*

Adverbs, etc.

δίς, *twice.*

ἐπεί, *when.*

νῦν, *now.*

οὖν, *accordingly, therefore*, stands second.

οὕτω, οὕτως, *thus.*

ποτε, *once, formerly.*

A qualifying prepositional phrase stands between article and noun.

Example.   οἱ ἐν τῇ νήσῳ στρατιῶται.   *The soldiers on the island.*

Γ

1. οἱ φύλακες οὐκ ἔλυσαν τοὺς λέοντας.

2. τοὺς τῶν Ἑλλήνων ῥήτορας ἔπεμψαν οἱ κήρυκες ἐκ τοῦ στρατοπέδου, καὶ ἐτείχιζον τὴν νῆσον.

3. οἱ γέροντες βουλεύσουσι περὶ τῆς Ἑλλάδος ἐν ταῖς τῶν Ἑλλήνων
νήσοις.

---

[1] Often acc. of thing, gen. of person.

4. τὰ τῶν νεανιῶν σώματα οὐκ ἦν ἐν τῷ λιμένι.

5. οἱ δαίμονες ἤριζον τοῖς γίγασιν ἐν τῷ ἀγῶνι.

6. οἱ παῖδες ἔλυσαν τοὺς ποιμένας, ἀλλ᾽ οὐκ ἔπεμψαν εἰς τὴν πατρίδα.

7. ὁ ἡγεμὼν οὐκ ἤθελεν ἄρχειν τῶν Ἑλλήνων.

8. δὶς παῖδες οἱ γέροντες· οὕτως ἔλεξεν ὁ ποιητής.

9. οὐκ ἐπίστευσαν οἱ ἡγεμόνες τοῖς τοῦ ποιητοῦ λόγοις, ἀλλὰ τοῖς πολεμίοις προσέβαλλον.

10. οἱ τῆς φάλαγγος στρατιῶται ἡσύχαζον, ἐπεὶ δὲ τῆς σάλπιγγος ἤκουσαν ἤθελον προσβάλλειν τοῖς τειχίσμασι. ἔλεξε δ᾽ ὁ ἡγεμών, Νῦν περὶ τῆς πατρίδος ὁ ἀγών. καὶ οὕτω τὴν πατρίδα ἔσωσαν, τὴν Ἑλλάδα.

γ

1. There are lions in the goddess's house.
2. The old man was a boy once, and a citizen of Greece.
3. The Greeks were fortifying the harbour and the road.
4. The soldiers in the assembly [1] kept quiet, for they were reluctant [2] to trust the old men.
5. For the sons of Greece, their native land was at stake. [2]
6. The Greeks will save Greece by their bodies, not by fortifications.
7. The soldiers were attacking the phalanx, for they had heard (aorist) the herald's trumpet.
8. The citizens are attacking the fortifications and the sailors the camp.
9. The lions are not willing to keep quiet in the market-place.
10. At the sound of the trumpet the Greeks would not remain inactive, since [3] their country was at stake. They kept attacking [4] the harbour road and the fortifications, and victory and honour fell to the Greeks. Thus they saved their country in the fight, but not their leader.

DELTA

3rd declension neuters in -ος (Par. 12).
3rd declension vowel stems (Paragraphs 13–18).
Proper names (Par. 23). No help is given in the vocabulary with proper names that decline according to the rules on p. 187.
The article is often used with proper names.

[1] "The in the assembly soldiers." [2] Can be rendered by the words already learnt. [3] Use γάρ explanatory. [4] Imperfect for repeated action.

Words given in the prescribed grammar sections will no longer be given in the special vocabularies for each exercise.

VOCABULARY

ὁ ἀνδριάς, -άντος, 3. *statue.*
τὸ βάθος, -ους, 3. *depth.*
τὸ δρᾶμα, -ατος, 3. *play.*
τὸ ναυτικόν, 2. *fleet.*
τὸ πέζον, 2. *army.*
τὸ ὄρος, -ους, 3. *mountain.*
τὸ τεῖχος, -ους, 3. *wall.*
τὸ τέλος, -ους, 3. *end.*
τὸ ὕψος, -ους, 3. *height.*

Proper Names

ὁ Ἀχαιός, -α, -ον, The Achaean.
ὁ Αἰσχύλος.
ὁ Ἀπόλλων, -ωνος.
ὁ Δαρεῖος.
ὁ Δημοσθένης.
ὁ Δωριεύς, The Dorian.
ὁ Εὐριπίδης.
ὁ Θεμιστοκλῆς.
ὁ Θησεύς.
ἡ Καλυψώ.
ἡ Λητώ.
ὁ Μαραθών, -ῶνος.
ὁ Μιλτιάδης.
ὁ Ξέρξης.
ὁ Πειραιεύς.
ὁ Περικλῆς.
ἡ Σαλαμίς, -ῖνος.
ἡ Σαπφώ.
ὁ Σοφοκλῆς.
ὁ Σωκράτης.

κατασκάπτω, αορ. κατέσκαψε, *destroy, pull down.*
κελεύω, *give orders, command.*
οὔτε . . . οὔτε, *neither . . . nor.* τέλος adv., *at last.*

ἐν + dative denotes *place where*, e.g. ἐν Σαλαμῖνι, *at Salamis.*
Exception. Names of Attic demes,[1] e.g. Μαραθῶνι, *at Marathon.*

Δ

1. τὸ τοῦ τείχους ὕψος καὶ τὸ τοῦ ποταμοῦ βάθος ἐκώλυσε τοὺς στρατιώτας.

2. οἱ Δωριῆς κατασκάψουσι τὰ τοῦ Πειραιῶς τείχη καὶ τὰ τῆς πόλεως τειχίσματα.

3. ἐν τῇ μὲν θαλάσσῃ εἰσὶν ἰχθύες, ἐν δὲ τῷ ποταμῷ καὶ ἐγχέλεις.

---

[1] Parishes.

4. τῷ Θεμιστοκλεῖ αἱ νῆες ἦσαν τείχη.

5. εἰσὶν ἀνδριάντες ἐν τῇ τοῦ Περικλέους πόλει.

6. ἤκουσας τὰ τοῦ Αἰσχύλου δράματα καὶ τὰ τοῦ Σοφοκλέους καὶ τὰ τοῦ Εὐριπίδου, ἀλλ᾽ οὐκ ἀκούεις τὰ τῆς Σαπφοῦς· οὐ γὰρ ἔγραψε δράματα.

7. ὦ Ζεῦ βασιλεῦ, ἔσωσας τὰς τῆς Ἀθηνᾶς [1] ναῦς ἐν Σαλαμῖνι, καὶ ἦν ἡ νίκη τοῖς Ἀθηναίοις· τέλος δὲ οὔτε νῆες οὔτε τείχη ἔσωσαν τὴν τῆς Ἀθηνᾶς καὶ τοῦ Θησέως πόλιν.

8. Αἰσχύλος ἔγραψε τὸ δρᾶμα τὸ περὶ Ξέρξου βασιλέως,[2] καὶ περὶ τῆς ἐν Σαλαμῖνι μάχης. οὔκ ἐστι δρᾶμα περὶ Μιλτιάδου καὶ Δαρείου καὶ περὶ τῆς Μαραθῶνι νίκης.

δ

1. He gave the king orders to save the cities of the Greeks.

2. There are no lions now in the mountains of Greece.

3. We did not pull down the city, nor the city walls, nor the fortifications of the harbour.

4. The depth of the sea saved the fishes and eels.

5. The Dorians were sacrificing to Heracles on the mountain, while the Athenians (sacrificed) to Theseus in the city.

6. O Apollo, son of Zeus and Leto, you will command Zeus to save the ships of the citizens and the statues of the gods.

7. They wanted [3] to hear about Xerxes, Miltiades and Themistocles, but not about Euripides, Socrates and Demosthenes.

8. Odysseus, leader of the Achaeans, was not in his ship, but on the island of Calypso.

9. The army of Darius attacked the Athenians, but the Persians did not win the victory. For the goddess saved the Athenians at the battle of Marathon.

EPSILON

3rd declension irregular nouns (Paragraphs 19–22).
1st and 2nd declension adjectives (Paragraphs 24–6).

[1] Ἀθηνᾶ retains α throughout.
[2] The Persian king was generally Βασιλεύς without the article.
[3] ἐθέλω, (see Γ Vocabulary).

ἀνδρεῖος, *brave.*
ἄξιος, w. gen., *worthy.*
καλός, *beautiful, honourable.*
ὀλίγος, *small, few.*
λίθινος, *made of stone* (λίθος).
ξύλινος, *made of wood* (ξύλον).
φίλος, *dear.*
ἡ δύναμις, -εως, *power.*
δή adds emphasis, *indeed.*
καὶ δὴ καί, *and moreover.*
ὅμως, *nevertheless.*
ὑπέρ, prep. w. gen., *on behalf of.*
οὐ μόνον ... ἀλλὰ καί ... , *not only ... but also.*
ἆρα μή, expects negative answer, *surely ... not.* Latin *num.*
ἆρ’ οὐ, expects affirmative answer. Latin *nonne.*
δεῖ, impersonal verb, *must, should, ought.* Used with acc. and infin.
or infin. alone.
εἶναι, pres. infin. of εἰμί, *to be.*

E

Ὦ ἄνδρες πολῖται, οὐ μόνον ὑπὲρ τῆς πόλεως ἀλλὰ καὶ ὑπὲρ παίδων καὶ
γυναικῶν ἐστι νῦν ὁ ἀγών. καὶ ἐν τῇ Μαραθῶνι μάχῃ ὀλίγοι μὲν ἦσαν οἱ
πατέρες ὑμῶν, ἀνδρεῖοι δέ. τότε δὴ τοῖς πατράσιν ὑμῶν [1] οἱ Πέρσαι προσέβαλλον, πολλοὶ πρὸς ὀλίγους, καὶ ὅμως ἡ νίκη οὐκ ἦν τοῖς πολλοῖς ἀλλὰ
τοῖς ἀνδρείοις : οὕτω δὴ οἱ πατέρες τὴν φίλην πατρίδα ἔσωσαν. ἆρ’ οὐκ
ἀνδρεῖοι υἱεῖς ἐστέ, τῶν φίλων πατέρων καὶ τῆς καλῆς πόλεως ἄξιοι ; δεῖ
γὰρ ἀεὶ τὸν υἱὸν ἄξιον εἶναι τοῦ πατρός. νῦν δὴ αἱ νῆες ὑμῶν εἰσι τείχη
τῇ πόλει, οὐ λίθινα ἀλλὰ ξύλινα. ὁ γὰρ θεὸς ξυλίνοις τείχεσι, ταῖς δὴ ναυσί,
πιστεύειν τὸν Θεμιστοκλέα ἐκέλευσεν. οὕτως οὖν αἱ νῆες καὶ δὴ καὶ οἱ
ἀνδρεῖοι ναῦται τὴν τῶν πολεμίων δύναμιν κωλύσουσιν.

ε

The city of Athena is fair, and the deeds of the Athenians must be in
keeping with their city. Now indeed our dear country is at stake. Are
you not now, O citizens, though greatly outnumbered, not only checking
the power of the King of Persia but also saving your wives and children?
You must be brave, and worthy of your fathers. For once, at Salamis,
your [1] fathers saved not only their city but Greece as well. Great was
Xerxes' fleet, but the ships of the Athenians were not great. None the

---

[1] ὑμῶν, *of you, your.* Not between noun and article.

less it was not walls of stone but walls of wood, and above all brave men, that saved the city of the goddess. Therefore the city of Themistocles will always trust her ships and her sailors.

Render possessive adjectives, e.g. *her, their*, by the definite article.

ZETA

3rd declension adjectives (Paragraphs 27–30).
Participles : present and aorist active (Par. 31).
The article can be used with a participle to form a substantive ; e.g. οἱ διώκοντες, *the pursuers, those who pursue*.

The article, without a noun, but accompanying an adverb or preposi-tional phrase, can be used demonstratively, e.g. οἱ νῦν, *men of the present day*; οἱ ἐν τῇ πόλει, *those in the city*. With a neuter adjective it represents a noun ; e.g. τὸ ἀληθές, *truth*.

VOCABULARY

ἀληθής, *true*.	βαθύς, *deep*.
ἀσθενής, *weak*.	βαρύς, *heavy, deep* (of sound).
ἀσφαλής, *safe*.	εὐρύς, *broad*.
αὐθάδης, *headstrong*.	ἡδύς, *sweet*.
εὐγενής, *noble*.	ταχύς, *swift*.
ψευδής, *false*.	
μακρός, *long*.	
μικρός, *small*.	

πᾶς, πᾶσα, πᾶν, *every, all*. Does not come between article and noun. πάντες οἱ πολῖται, *all the citizens*.

ἦλθον, *came*. This is a strong aorist, i.e. one with different stem from the present, and endings -ον, -ες, -ε, etc., as imperfect (Par. 68).

ἄρχων, -οντος, *ruler, archon*.	βλάπτω ἔβλαψα, *hurt*.
ἡ φωνή, *voice*.	δουλεύω, *be a slave*.

Z

1. δεῖ τὴν ὁδὸν εὐρεῖαν εἶναι.
2. ἤκουσα τοῦ αὐθάδους ἄρχοντος τοὺς ψευδεῖς λόγους.

3. οἱ εὐγενεῖς πατέρες παιδεύουσι τοὺς μικροὺς υἱοὺς ἐν τῇ μεγάλῃ πόλει.

4. αἱ ταχεῖαι νῆες ἦλθον εἰς τὸν εὐρὺν λιμένα.

5. ἐκώλυον τοὺς τὰ μακρὰ τείχη κατασκάπτοντας.

6. οὐ δεῖ τοὺς ἀσθενεῖς ἄρχειν τῆς πόλεως.

7. οὐ πιστεύω πᾶσι τοῖς ναύταις· οὐ γὰρ ἀεὶ τὸ ἀληθὲς λέγουσιν.

8. ἐδίωκον τοὺς τὴν θεὸν βλάψαντας εἰς τὴν θάλασσαν.

9. οἱ τοῦ σώφρονος βασιλέως λόγοι σαφεῖς ἦσαν καὶ ἀληθεῖς.

10. ἆρα μὴ σῶφρόν ἐστιν τὸ ψευδὲς [1] ἀεὶ λέγειν;

ζ

1. The river was deep and the harbour wide.

2. The woman's voice was sweet, while the man's was deep.

3. All the citizens trusted the orator's lying words.

4. Those in the ship were not trusting the noble general.

5. The children were heavy for the weak women.

6. They will pull down all the fortifications and the long walls.

7. The swift dogs were chasing the little children, but they will not hurt (them) for they are weak.

8. They came into a harbour, wide and safe for ships.

9. We shall not trust the king, for he tells lies.

10. Surely it is not right for all women to rule their husbands?

ETA

Comparison of adjectives (Paragraphs 33–9).

Perfect and pluperfect active of λύω (p. 208). Reduplication (Paragraphs 55–9).

Look up these tenses also for consonant stems (pp. 230–234).

Active participles of λύω and consonant stems (p. 192).

Active infinitives of λύω and consonant stems (pp. 207–9 and 231–3).

Infinitives and participles of εἰμί (Par. 79).

Vocabulary. No fresh words except the adjectives used for examples of comparatives (Paragraphs 33–9). ´

---

[1] Common in plur., τὰ ψευδῆ.

Comparison : ἤ, *than*, corresponds to Latin *quam*. The two words compared are both in the same case. μᾶλλον ἤ, *rather than*.

With a comparative adjective in nominative or accusative the genitive [1] of comparison can be used instead of ἤ.

Examples (1) ὁ βασιλεὺς σοφώτερός ἐστιν ἢ ὁ ἡγεμών.

(2) ὁ βασιλεὺς σοφώτερός ἐστι τοῦ ἡγεμόνος.

The king is wiser than the leader.

Participles and infinitives : Tenses of these are considered in their relation to the main verb, i.e. present, past, future, with reference to the time of the main verb.

H

1. ἄμεινόν ἐστι διώκειν ἢ φεύγειν.

2. αἱ γυναῖκες ἀξιώτεραι εἰσι τῶν παίδων, ἀλλ' ἀφρονέστεραι τῶν ἀνδρῶν.

3. ὀρθοτάτη ἐστὶν ἡ ὁδὸς καὶ χρησιμωτάτη τοῖς στρατιώταις.

4. τὰ τῶν νεανιῶν δῶρά ἐστι βαρύτατα, τὰ δὲ τοῦ βασιλέως μέγιστα.

5. τὸ ὕδωρ ταῖς μὲν γυναιξὶν ἄριστόν ἐστι, τοῖς δ' ἀνδράσι κάκιστον.

6. οἱ τοῦ ῥήτορος λόγοι ἀκριβέστεροι ἦσαν ἢ οἱ τοῦ ποιητοῦ.

7. εὐηθέστατόν ἐστι τὰ ψευδῆ λέγειν.

8. ἄμεινόν ἐστι κάλλιστον εἶναι ἢ αἴσχιστον.

9 τοὺς ἐχθροὺς ναύτας πεπαιδεύκαμεν.

10. οἱ δεδουλευκότες σοφώτεροί εἰσιν ἢ εὐδαιμονέστεροί.[2]

11. διώξαντες τοὺς πολεμίους ἡσύχαζον.

12. γεγράφαμεν πολλὰ τῷ βασιλεῖ ἀλλὰ πλείω τοῖς ἄρχουσιν.

η

1. We shall hurt those-who-hurt (aor. partic.) the little boy.

2. It was wiser to have written.

3. The river is deeper, but the harbour is wider.

4. The king's sons are fairer than those of the judge.

---

[1] Cf. Latin comparative ablative.

[2] Note double comparative, a Latin idiom also.

5. It is wiser to speak the truth rather than falsehood.

6. The fortifications of the Peiraeus are greater than the wall.

7. He had injured the ugliest slaves.

8. Better to be a slave than to flee.

9. It is easier for those who have been slaves to tell lies.

10. There is no hope for those in servitude.

11. The soldiers are handsomer than the sailors, but the poets are the handsomest of all.[1]

12. The dog is swift, the horse swifter, but Achilles (use δέ) swiftest of all.

THETA

Formation and comparison of adverbs (Paragraphs 40–2).

Middle and passive of λύω : indicative, infinitives, participles (pp. 210–217).

The middle voice denotes the interest of the doer in the action, i.e. he acts for or on himself, or causes an action to be done in his interest.

Examples.

λούω, *I wash.*	λούομαι, *I bathe.*
λύω, *I loose.*	λύομαι, *I ransom.*
δανείζω, *I lend.*	δανείζομαι, *I get myself lent, borrow.*

Many verbs are found only in the middle : e.g. μάχομαι, *fight.*

The passive voice is used as in Latin. Only the future and aorist passive differ in form from the corresponding tenses of the middle voice.

The **instrument** with a passive verb is rendered by the dative.

The **agent** with a passive verb is rendered by ὑπό + genitive.

παίεται τῷ πελέκει, *he is being struck with the axe.*

παίεται ὑπὸ τοῦ δούλου, *he is being struck by the slave.*

The GENITIVE ABSOLUTE is used with noun and participle unconnected with the main verb, like ablative absolute in Latin.   Par. 98.

VOCABULARY

βούλομαι, *wish, be willing* (see Verb Table, p. 314).

μάχομαι, *fight* (p. 316).

παύω, active, *stop.*   παύομαι, mid., *cease* : often with participle, or gen.

---

[1] No article.

φέρω, active, *bear, bring.* φέρομαι, mid., *win.*
τὸ ἱερόν, 2. *temple.*
ἡ νύξ, νυκτός, 3. *night.*
ὁ πέπλος, 2. *robe.*
ἤδη, adv., *already.*
οὐκέτι, adv., *no longer.*

Θ

1. κλείσας τὰς πύλας τὴν πόλιν ἔσωσεν.
2. ἆρ’ οὐ βούλεσθε μάχεσθαι καὶ τοῖς Πέρσαις προσβάλλειν ;
3. μείζω καὶ πλείω δῶρα εἰς τὸ τῆς Ἀθηνᾶς ἱερὸν ἔφερον.
4. ὁ διώκων ὑπὸ τῶν φευγόντων διωχθήσεται.
5. ἡ νὺξ ταχέως τὴν μάχην ἔπαυσε, νίκην φέρουσα τοῖς Ἀθηναίοις.
6. ἆρ’ οὐχ ἡ μάχη ταχέως παύσεται ; ἤδη γὰρ οἱ ἱππῆς διώκοντες ἐπαύσαντο, ὀλίγοι ὄντες πρὸς πλέονας.
7. οὐ δεῖ λύεσθαι τοὺς δούλους. οἱ γὰρ λυθέντες οὐκέτι ἐν μάχῃ ἀνδρεῖοι ἔσονται.
8. ὁ πέπλος λουθήσεται ὡς βέλτιστα ἐν τῷ τοῦ ποταμοῦ ὕδατι ὑπὸ τῆς τοῦ βασιλέως θυγατρός.
9. πολλαὶ γυναῖκες ἐλούοντο ἐν τῇ θαλάσσῃ.
10. ἄμεινόν ἐστι τῷ βασιλεῖ ἢ τῷ ποιητῇ πολλὰ καὶ καλὰ δῶρα φέρεσθαι.

θ

1. Being greatly outnumbered they ceased fighting.
2. Hindered by the general, they were no longer fighting bravely.
3. The soldiers were chased into the sea by the Persians.
4. I am winning more gifts than the general.
5. The children will be saved [1] as quickly as possible by the women.
6. As the cavalry charge (genitive abs.) the slaves fight more bravely.
7. We shall loose the horses and ransom the cavalry.
8. It is best to save those freed by the enemy.
9. The mothers will wash the goddess's robe, but it is not right for the king's daughter to wash Odysseus.
10. As they are so brave, the Athenians are willing to attack the enemies' ships as soon as possible.[2]

---

[1] σῴζω makes pass. σωθήσομαι and ἐσώθην.   [2] Par. 42.

IOTA

Contracted verbs in α, ε, ο in active, middle, and passive, of indicative, infinitive, and participles (pp. 218–229).

δηλόω, *show.*
δουλόω, *enslave.*
ἐλευθερόω, *set free.*
νικάω, *conquer.*
ὁράω, *see* (see Par. 71).
ποιέω, *do.*
εὖ ποιεῖν + acc., *do good to.*
κακὰ ποιεῖν + acc., *do harm to.*
πολεμέω, *fight.*
τιμάω, *honour.*
φιλέω, *love.*

Forms that can contract must be contracted, though the uncontracted form is given here in the vocabulary.

αὔριον, adv., *to-morrow.*
σήμερον, adv., *to-day.*
χθές, adv., *yesterday.*
ἀπό, prep. w. gen., *from.*
ὑπέρ, w. gen., *for the sake of, over.*
οὔποτε, *never.*

Participles often correspond idiomatically to relative clauses in English (Par. 97).

I

1. οἱ τοὺς πολίτας δουλοῦντες οὐ φιλοῦνται.

2. ἀεὶ ἐτίμων τοὺς τὴν πόλιν φιλοῦντας.

3. ἀνδρείως πολεμοῦντες τοὺς Πέρσας ἐνίκων.

4. οἱ Ἀθηναῖοι ἠλευθέρωσαν τὴν Ἑλλάδα ἀπὸ τῶν Περσῶν.

5. τῶν πολεμίων ἀνδρείως πολεμησάντων, ἡ νίκη ἦν ὅμως τοῖς Ἕλλησιν.

6. χθὲς τὸ ἱερὸν τοῖς ξένοις ἐδηλοῦμεν, σήμερον τῷ βασιλεῖ δηλοῦμεν, αὔριον ταῖς γυναιξὶ δηλώσομεν.

7. φιλεῖτε τοὺς ἐν μάχῃ τετιμημένους.

8. ὁ στρατηγὸς ὁρᾷ τοὺς ναύτας ὑπὲρ τῆς πατρίδος μαχομένους.

9. ἄμεινόν ἐστι νικᾶν ἢ νικᾶσθαι.
10. ἀεὶ φιλοῦμεν τοὺς εὖ ποιοῦντας τὴν πατρίδα.

ι

1. We are enslaving those who do harm to their country.
2. Greece is being freed from the enemy by the Athenians.
3. Those who love truth are honoured by the citizens.
4. Those who have been conquered in battle are never honoured.
5. The king is enslaving the vanquished.
6. Those who are defeated to-day will conquer to-morrow.
7. Brave fighters will be honoured by the king.
8. He was made general by the Athenians.
9. It is not right to enslave the citizens.
10. The gods who see everything do not wish to be seen by men.

KAPPA

Verbs with Dental Stems : indicative, infinitive, participle (Par. 66).
Verbs with Liquid Stems : indicative, infinitive, participle (Par. 67).
Note contracted futures (as ποιῶ pres.).
Demonstrative pronouns οὗτος, *this*; ὅδε, *this*; ἐκεῖνος, *that* (Par. 45) ; οὗτος and ἐκεῖνος often stand alone as 3rd person pronouns.

VOCABULARY

DENTAL STEMS

κομίζω, *carry.*
νομίζω, *think, consider.*
θεοὺς νομίζειν, *believe in the gods.*
πείθω, *persuade* ;
  mid. and pass. + dat., *obey.*
πορίζω, *provide.*
ὑβρίζω, *insult.*

LIQUID STEMS

ἀγγέλλω, *announce.*
κρίνω, *judge, decide.*
νέμω, *assign*, mid., *possess, inhabit.*

Ἀττική, ἡ, 1. *Attica* (γῆ, *land* understood).
δίκη, ἡ, 1. *lawsuit, case.*
ἄνθρωπος, ὁ (or ἡ), 2. *man, human being, homo* : ἀνήρ corresponds to Latin *vir.*

Κ

1. οὗτοι οἱ ἄνθρωποι τὴν Ἀττικὴν πάλαι ἐνείμαντο.
2. ἐκεῖνοι οἱ δοῦλοι κομιοῦσι πολλὰ καὶ μεγάλα δῶρα τῷ βασιλεῖ.
3. οὔποτε τοῦτον ὑβριοῦμεν· θεὸν γὰρ νομίζομεν.
4. ὑπὸ τοῦ Σωκράτους πεισθέντες οἱ νεανίαι τοὺς τῆς πόλεως θεοὺς οὐκέτι ἐνόμισαν.
5. οὐχ ὑβρίσθησαν ἐκεῖνοι τοῖς τοῦδε τοῦ ξένου λόγοις.
6. τοῦτο μὲν ἀληθὲς εἶναι νομίζει, ἐκεῖνο δ’ οὔ.
7. ἡ μὲν πόλις τούτους τοὺς θεοὺς νομίζει, ὁ δὲ Σωκράτης οὐκ ἐνόμιζε.
8. οὔποτε πείσουσι τὸν δοῦλον ταῦτα τῷ ἄρχοντι ἀγγέλλειν.
9. τήνδε τὴν νίκην ἀγγείλαντες ὑπὸ τῶν πολιτῶν ἐτιμήθησαν.
10. πᾶσαι αἱ δίκαι σήμερον ἤδη κεκριμέναι εἰσίν.

κ

1. Under the persuasion of the citizens he will decide the case.
2. These young men will no longer believe in the city's gods. Can Socrates have prevailed upon them?
3. All these (things [1]) were provided for the general by the magistrates.[2]
4. They have never been insulted by those children.
5. I shall never be persuaded to stop fighting.
6. Socrates was considered the wisest of all the Athenians.
7. We shall announce this victory to all the citizens in the marketplace.
8. Attica was long ago inhabited by these men.
9. This case has already been settled by the judges.
10. They did not consider this news [3] to be true.

LAMBDA

Strong or 2nd Aorists, Perfects, and Future Passives (Paragraphs 68–70).
Common verbs with several stems (Par. 71).
2nd Aorist Paradigms for reference (Par. 72, pp. 240–245).

[1] Omit. Use neut. plur. of demonstrative.
[2] οἱ ἄρχοντες.   [3] Use a neut. plur. participle.

The aorist participle represents time that is past, relatively to the main verb. λιπόντες τὴν πόλιν ἀπῆλθον. *They left the city and went away.*
The aorist infinitive represents momentary action.
The present infinitive represents continuous or repeated action.
Note, however, that in accusative and infinitive constructions tense usages correspond to those of the indicative.

VOCABULARY

ἀντέχω, *hold out.* See ἔχω, p. 315.
ἀποθνήσκω, *die, be killed* (Par. 71, ἀποκτείνω).
ἀποκτείνω, *kill* (Par. 71).
ἐλπίζω, *hope.*
ἐξέρχομαι, *go out* (Par. 71).
καθαιρῶ (εω), *destroy* (Par. 71).
καθορῶ (αω), *see* Par. 71.
καταλαμβάνω, *seize, capture* (Par. 68).
λείπω, *leave* (see p. 316).
πλέον ποιῶ, *succeed.*
φεύγω, *flee* (see p. 317).

ἡμέρα, ἡ, 1. *day.*
ἔνδον, *within.*
λάθρᾳ, *secretly.*
ὅσον οὐ, *almost.*
οὐδέ, adv. *nor, not even.*
πανταχόθεν, *from all sides.*
Dative denotes time when.

Λ

ταύτῃ δὲ τῇ ἡμέρᾳ οἱ πολέμιοι τὴν πόλιν κατέλαβον. οἱ γὰρ ἔνδον πολῖται, πανταχόθεν προσβαλόντων τῶν πολεμίων, οὐκέτι ἀντέσχον. λιπόντες οὖν τοὺς παῖδας καὶ τὰς γυναῖκας λάθρᾳ ἐξῆλθον, ἐλπίζοντες δὴ οὕτως φεύξεσθαι καὶ μὴ (negative)[1] ἀποθανεῖσθαι ὑπὸ τῶν προσβαλλόντων. ἀλλ᾽ οὐ πλέον ἐποίησαν οὐδὲ ἔφυγον. οἱ γὰρ πολέμιοι κατεῖδον ἐξερχομένους, καὶ λαβόντες ἀπέκτειναν ὅσον οὐ πάντας. καὶ ἀποθανόντων τῶν πολιτῶν ῥᾳδίως τὰ τῆς πόλεως τείχη καθεῖλον.

λ

The enemy attacked the city from all sides, for they were anxious to capture and destroy it as soon as possible. But all the citizens secretly

[1] Verbs of hoping take fut. infin. Negative μή.

fled. For they saw the enemy attacking, and by their resistance they met with no success. But after going out they were almost all captured and killed by their attackers. Thus the enemy after destroying the city captured those within.[1]

MU

2nd Aorist Paradigms (Par. 72, pp. 240–245).
Declinable numerals (Par. 44).
Pronouns (Paragraphs 46–50).
Positions of pronouns (Paragraphs 94 and 95).

Note. εἶπον τάδε : *they spoke as follows,* points forward.
ταῦτα εἶπον : *these were the words they spoke,* points back.

Time during—accusative. Time within—genitive. Time when—dative.

ἀπό compounded with verbs usually means *away,* as ἀποβαίνω and ἀπέρχομαι, *go away.*

Vocabulary. See the grammar sections referred to above, and general vocabulary.

M

1. γνοὺς τοῦτο ὁ ἐμὸς πατὴρ ἐμοὶ πείθεται.
2. ἐβίω τρία ἔτη καὶ τρεῖς ἡμέρας· πλείω δὲ χρόνον ζῆν [2] οὐκ ἐβούλετο.
3. ἡμᾶς ἰδόντες οἱ παῖδες αὐτοῦ τάδε εἶπον.
4. τρεῖς γυναῖκας νυκτὸς ἐρχομένας εἶδον.
5. ἐγὼ μὲν ἓν δῶρον ἤνεγκον, σὺ δὲ ἤνεγκας τέσσαρα.
6. ταῦτα εἰποῦσα ἀπέβη· πλέον γὰρ εἰπεῖν οὐκ ἐβούλετο.
7. οὐδεὶς πείσεται τῇδε τῇ γυναικί· ψευδῆ γὰρ εἰποῦσα ἑάλω.
8. δεῖ σοφὸν ἄνδρα γνῶναι ἑαυτόν, καὶ τοὺς ἑαυτοῦ φίλους.
9. τί ἰδόντες οὕτω ταχέως ἀπέβησαν ; ἆρα μὴ αὐτοὺς ἀποκτενοῦσι ;
10. παῖδάς τινας καὶ μίαν γυναῖκα καὶ ἕνα ἄνδρα ἐν τῇ ἡμετέρᾳ οἰκίᾳ κατεῖδον τεθνηκότας.

μ

1. I do not want to see you.
2. After these words they went away.
3. Fairer women we do not wish to see.

---

[1] Article + adverb.   [2] Slightly irregular. See footnote, p. 242.

4. No-one was killed on that day, but many were captured (use ἁλίσκομαι, Par. 72).

5. After going out of the city they spoke as follows.

6. With these words she killed herself.

7. Knowing the enemy to outnumber them they went away.

8. My father and her son fled on seeing your daughter.

9. Who saw my mother?

10. My father died in the night, his mother is dying to-day, and to-morrow our children will die.

NU

Use of article; predicative and attributive position of pronouns, adjectives, etc. (Paragraphs 93–5).
Interrogative and indefinite pronouns (Par. 50).
Participles, absolute construction and impersonal verbs (Paragraphs 97–9).

VOCABULARY

Impersonal verbs given in Pars. 98 and 99.
μένω, v. *remain* (as νέμω, par. 67).
Ἀθῆναι αἱ, 1. *Athens.*
δόξα ἡ, 1. *reputation.*
ἐπιτήδεια τά, pl. adj., *provisions.*
μέρος τό, 3. *part.*
ξίφος τό, 3. *sword.*
σῖτος ὁ, 2. *food.*
στρατόπεδον τό, 2. *camp.*
χρόνος ὁ, 2. *time.* πολὺν χρόνον, *for a long time.*
πάντι σθένει, *with all one's might.* The only use of this noun in Attic prose.
τοιοῦτος τοιαύτη τοιοῦτο, dem. pron., *of such a kind, so great.* Latin *talis.* Declines like οὗτος but with no additional τ.
ἔξω, adv., *outside.*
οἴκαδε, *homewards, home,* motion towards.
πρῶτον μέν ... ἔπειτα δέ, *First ... next.*

διά τι, *why? on account of what?*
ἐπί, prep. (see p. 280).

N

1. αὐτὸς ὁ βασιλεὺς τὰ αὐτὰ δῶρα ἔλαβεν.

2. πρῶτον μὲν τοὺς αὐτοῦ παῖδας ἀπέκτεινεν, ἔπειτα δὲ αὐτὸν τῷ αὐτῷ ξίφει. οὐκέτι γὰρ ἔμελεν αὐτῷ τῆς πόλεως.

3. οἱ μὲν οἴκαδ' ἀπῆλθον, οἱ δὲ ἔφυγον εἰς τὴν πόλιν τὴν ἐπὶ τῷ ὄρει· μένουσι δέ τινες ἐν ταῖς ναυσίν.

4. σίτου οὐκέτ' ὄντος οἱ τεθνηκότες σήμερον εὐδαιμονέστεροί εἰσι τῶν ζώντων.

5. ἡ Ἀττικὴ μέρος τι τῆς Ἑλλάδος ἐστιν.

6. εὖ παρασχὸν τὴν πόλιν ἑλεῖν, ἔδοξε τοῖς Λακεδαιμονίοις παντὶ σθένει τοῖς τείχεσι προσβαλεῖν.

7. οὐκ ἐξὸν εἰς τὴν οἰκίαν εἰσελθεῖν ἐχρῆν ἡμᾶς ἔξω μένειν.

8. οὐ πρέπει ἀνδρὶ τοιούτῳ τὰ ψευδῆ λέγειν.

9. καίπερ πάντων σοφώτατος ὤν, ὅμως οὐκ ἐβούλετο ὁ Σόλων ἐν τῇ ἑαυτοῦ πατρίδι μένειν.

10. διὰ τί χρὴ τοὺς πολίτας τὰς οἰκίας λιπόντας ἐξελθεῖν, τὰ ἐπιτήδεια μεθ' αὑτῶν εἰς τὸ στρατόπεδον λαβόντας ;

ν

1. He saved his wife, but not your children.

2. Who is wiser than my father?   Not even Socrates himself.

3. The one they killed, the other they made their leader.

4. It is not seemly for such a man to enslave the living and insult the dead.

5. Some have come,[1] wanting to see the king.   But as it is impossible to see him they have gone home.

6. Why is it fitting for us to obey a woman of that kind?

7. As they had to stay a long time the citizens decided (ἔδοξε) to bring their provisions into the camp.

8. I care nothing for the living, nor even for the dead.

9. On the orders of the Spartans the Athenians destroyed the fortifications of Athens and the walls of the Piraeus.

10. The Spartans decided to attack Athens with all their might, for they had no concern for the reputation of the Athenians.

[1] Par. 71.

XI

Syntax A to G (pp. 294–301). Negatives (par. 100, p. 293).
Imperative, subjunctive, optative of λύω, consonant stems, contracted verbs, strong aor. verbs (pp. 206–245).

ἐξελαύνω, *drive out.* See ἐλαύνω (p. 315).
γίγνομαι, *become, be, happen.* See p. 314.
ὀλιγωρῶ(εω) + gen., *despise.*
τοίνυν, τοιγαροῦν, *therefore.*

Ξ

1. εἶπον ὅτι τῆς μητρὸς οὐκ ὀλιγωροίην.
2. τὸν μὲν θεὸν φιλεῖτε, τὸν δὲ βασιλέα τιμᾶτε. μήποτε φιλεῖτε τοὺς κακούς.
3. εἰ γὰρ μὴ ἔλεξέ μοι ὅτι ἡ μήτηρ μου τέθνηκεν.
4. ἔγνωσαν τοὺς Πέρσας ἥξοντας.
5. εἶπεν ὅτι ἴδοι τὸν κύνα.
6. ἤγγειλαν ὅτι οἱ πολέμιοι πλείους εἰσὶν ἡμῶν.

τί εἴπωμεν τῷ ξένῳ ; εἴπατε αὐτῷ ὅτι σήμερον τὴν ἡμετέραν πατρίδα ἐκ τῶν βαρβάρων λύσομεν. εἰ γὰρ αὐτὸς βούλοιτο[1] μεθ᾽ ἡμῶν μάχεσθαι ἵνα τοὺς βαρβάρους νικῶμεν καὶ ἐλεύθεροι γενοίμεθα. μήποτε ὀλιγωρεῖτε τῶν πολεμίων μηδὲ σήμερον ὑμᾶς κακοὺς ὄντας δηλώσητε. μάχεσθε τοίνυν ἵνα τοὺς Πέρσας ἐκ τῆς Ἀττικῆς ἐξελάσητε. λέγει γὰρ Βασιλεὺς ὅτι πᾶσαν τὴν Ἑλλάδα δουλώσει, καὶ δὴ καὶ ἐλπίζει τοῦτο ποιήσειν. ἀλλὰ νῦν, ὦ ἄνδρες πολῖται, ἐν τῇδε τῇ μάχῃ ἐλαύνωμεν τοὺς βαρβάρους εἰς τὴν θάλασσαν. μὴ φύγητε, ἀλλ᾽ ὡς ἀνδράσι πρέπει μάχεσθε. εἰ γὰρ ὑφ᾽ ἡμῶν ἡ Ἑλλὰς ἐλευθέρα γένοιτο. καὶ πολὺν χρόνον δεῖ πολεμεῖν ἵνα μὴ δοῦλοι γενώμεθα.

ξ

1. Do not now despise your mother.
2. He knew that the enemy had not gone away.
3. They said that I did not want to go home.
4. They did this in order that I might not want to go home.
5. He saw the woman, but he did not say he had seen her.
6. We shall announce that the enemy outnumber us.

[1] Optative belongs to secondary, subjunctive to primary sequence system.

" Do you want to save your country and to stop fighting? Your fathers fought bravely for a long time in order to drive out the enemy and save the city of the goddess. You must therefore also (καί) drive the barbarians out of your land, so as to become free, as Athenians should be. I tell you all that although you are far [1] fewer, yet you will overcome the Persians." These were the general's words. But the orator replied that the Athenians would not obey a man of that type. If only Themistocles himself were willing to become their general, so that all might fight as bravely as possible for their country!

OMICRON

Syntax H (p. 302).
ἵστημι, all inflexions (pp. 246–251).

N.B.—1st aor. act. and mid. is *transitive* ;
  2nd aor. act. and perf. act. are *intransitive.*
Prepositions compounded with verbs (pp. 278–283).
Relative pronouns (Par. 51).

VOCABULARY

Transitive Tenses	Intransitive Tenses
	ἀνθίσταμαι, *resist*, with dative.
ἀφίστημι, *cause to revolt.*	ἀφίσταμαι, *revolt.* ἀπο + gen. or gen. alone, *from* ; ὑπὸ + gen., *at instigation of.*
καθίστημι, *cause, appoint, bring to.*	καθίσταμαι, *be caused, appointed; come to, arise.*
μεθίστημι, *change.*	μεθίσταμαι, *be changed, change* intr.
ἵστημι, *set up, place, appoint.*	ἵσταμαι, *stand, be placed.*
ἱστάναι τινὰ χαλκοῦν [2]	
Set up a bronze statue to ...	

For other words see general vocabulary.

O

1. ὁ Ἱστιαῖος πάντας τοὺς Ἴωνας ἀπὸ τῶν Περσῶν ἀπέστησε.
2. πᾶσα ἡ Ἰωνία ὑπὸ τοῦ Ἱστιαίου τῶν Περσῶν ἀπέστη.

---

[1] πολλῷ, *by much.*   [2] Par. 26, adjectives in -ους.

3. οὐ χρὴ τοῖς τῶν ἀρχόντων βουλεύμασιν ἀνθίστασθαι.

4. εἰς δημοκρατίαν τὴν πόλιν μεθίστωμεν.

5. Φειδίας χρυσοῦν τὸν Δία ἔστησεν Ὀλυμπίασιν ἐν τῷ τοῦ Διὸς ἱερῷ.

6. ὁ Περικλῆς χαλκοῦς ἔστη Ἀθήνησι.

7. ἐκείνη ἡ συμφορὰ εἰς φόβον κατεστήσατο τοὺς Ἀθηναίους.

ἀφισταμένων τῶν συμμάχων οἱ Ἀθηναῖοι οὐκέτι οἷοι τ᾽ ἦσαν τοῖς Λακεδαιμονίοις ἀνθίστασθαι· αἴτιοι δὴ ἦσαν αὐτοὶ οἱ Ἀθηναῖοι, τὴν συμμαχίαν εἰς
ἀρχὴν μεταστήσαντες· οὕτως γὰρ τοὺς συμμάχους ἀφ᾽ αὑτῶν ἀπέστησαν.
οἱ δὲ Λακεδαιμόνιοι μετὰ τὴν ἐν Αἰγὸς ποταμοῖς νίκην ἄλλους ἄρχοντας
τοῖς Ἀθηναίοις κατέστησαν ὥστε ἡ πόλις ἐκ δημοκρατίας εἰς ὀλιγαρχίαν
μετέστη. ἀλλ᾽ οὐ πολλῷ ὕστερον δημαγωγοί τινες καθιστάμενοι, τοὺς
ὀλίγους ἐξέβαλον ἵνα τὴν πόλιν εἰς δημοκρατίαν αὖθις μεθίσταιεν

o

1. All the Ionians revolted at the instigation of Histiaeus.
2. If only this city had never resisted the Persians!
3. They will set up leaders in all the cities of Greece.
4. The city changed from democracy to oligarchy.
5. A bronze statue of the goddess stands in her own temple.
6. They will set up a golden statue of Zeus at Olympia.
7. After the disaster at Aegospotami the Athenians became afraid.

All the allies abandoned the cause of the Athenians, with the result that
they no longer resisted the Spartans. For the Athenians by changing the
alliance into an empire had turned their allies to enmity (ἔχθρα). But
after being conquered at Aegospotami other rulers were appointed, who
changed the city into an oligarchy. But soon afterwards they set up
popular leaders again, with the result that the city revolted against the
Spartans.

PI

Syntax K–O (pp. 302–307).
τίθημι, δίδωμι, δείκνυμι, ἵημι (pp. 250–267).
Interrogative and demonstrative words (Paragraphs 88–91).

VOCABULARY

ἀνατίθημι, *set up, dedicate.*
προστίθημι, *add.* In middle, *join oneself to.*
ἀποδίδωμι, *give away, give back.*
ἀποδίδομαι, *sell.*
ἐνδίδωμι, *give in, surrender,* with or without object.
παραδίδωμι, *hand over.*
προδίδωμι, *betray.*
προδότης, ὁ, 1. *traitor.*
ἀνοίγνυμι, *open* (p. 314).
ἀπόλλυμι, *destroy, lose ; perish* (intrans. tenses). See ὄλλυμι (p. 316).
κατάγνυμι, aor. κατέαξα, *break.*
ἀφίημι, *let go.*
ἐφίεμαι, *desire,* + gen.
φοβοῦμαι, (εο), *fear.* See p. 302.

The following verbs take a participle construction : (p. 291).

διατελέω, *continue,* fut. διατελῶ, aor. διετέλεσα.
λανθάνω, *escape notice, not be seen* (Par. 97, 6).
τυγχάνω, *happen* (Par. 97, 6).

Example. ἔτυχον πολεμοῦντες, *they happened to be fighting.*

Π

1. ἀπέδοτο τὰ αὑτοῦ κτήματα ἵνα ἀνδριάντα τῇ θεῷ ἀναθείη.
2. τὴν πόλιν καὶ τοὺς φίλους τοῖς πολεμίοις προὔδωκε.¹
3. ἀνοίξαντες τὰς πύλας πάντα τὰ ὅπλα τοῖς πολεμίοις παρέδοσαν.
4. ἐὰν τὸ ξίφος καταγνύῃς μὴ σαυτὸν ἐνδῷς.
5. οὐκ ἐφοβοῦντο παραδοῦναι παῖδας καὶ γυναῖκας, ἵνα φεύγοντες λάθοιεν.
6. οὐκ ἐφοβούμην μὴ τοὺς προδότας ἀφεῖεν. πολλοὶ γὰρ σύμμαχοι ἡμῖν προσέθεντο.
7. πᾶς τις κτημάτων ἐφίεται.
8. οὐκ οἴκαδ' ἀποβήσομαι πρὶν ἂν τὰς βοῦς ἀποδῶμαι.
9. ἐφοβούμην μὴ ἡ μητὴρ ἀπόλωλεν. ἔτυχε γὰρ νοσοῦσα.
10. ἐὰν νικῶμεν, τοὺς συμμάχους ἀφήσομεν.

¹ Note contraction of augment.

π

1. The king dedicated this gift in the temple.

2. Give me your hand that we may escape without being seen.

3. If ever he broke his sword he would continue fighting.

4. I was afraid that he might betray the city.

5. He happened to lose his way, so that he could no longer see in what direction he was going.

6. They joined [1] their allies so as not to surrender.

7. I did not go home till I had shown him the way.

8. Do not surrender the city till you have saved the women and children.

9. I did not know how many ships had joined [1] the Persian fleet.

10. When ever I happened to win I offered up the weapons in the temple.

RHO

Syntax P–S (pp. 308–13).

Compare wishes, indefinite construction, conditionals, potentials and concessives (Syntax D, N, P, R, S).

οἶδα, *know* (Par. 73 and Syntax F 3, p. 300).

Other -μι verbs (Paragraphs 79–85).

Note. φημί, *say*, introducing indirect speech always takes nominative or accusative and infinitive construction (Par. 96). It is also used parenthetically after two or three words, like *inquit*, *said he*, giving the actual words spoken.

οὔ φημι, like *nego*, translates *I say . . . not . . .*

Example. οὔ φημι ἐκεῖνον εἰδέναι.
    I say that he does not know.

ἐπίσταμαι : with participle, *know* (F 3, p. 300) ;
        with infinitive, *know how to.*

ἐρωτῶ, (αω), *ask* (p. 315).

πειρῶμαι, (αο), fut. πειράσομαι, aor. ἐπειράθην, *try.* Note pure alpha.

P

Ποῦ κεῖνται οἱ τεθνηκότες ; ἦ [2] δ' ὅς. Μαραθῶνι, ἐν τῷ πεδίῳ, ἦν δ' ἐγώ. Πόσοι εἰσίν ; Τοσοῦτοι ὥστε μὴ ἀριθμεῖσθαι δύνασθαι. Ποῖ, ἔφη,

---

[1] Use προστίθημι, mid.   [2] Par. 80.

ἴασιν οἱ Πέρσαι ; Φασὶν οἴκαδ' ἀπιέναι, ἔφην, ὡς τάχιστα δύνανται. τίς οἶδεν εἰ αὖθις κατίασιν ; Οὔ φημι αὐτοὺς οἵους τ' εἶναι κατελθεῖν. ἐπίστανται γὰρ πολλῷ ἀνδρειοτέρους ὄντας τοὺς ἐλευθέρους τῶν δούλων, καὶ τοῦτ' εἰδότες αὖθις προσβάλλειν οὐ πειράσονται. "Ομως, ἔφη, εἰ οὐδὲν ποιοῦντες καθήμεθα, κατεῖσι Βασιλεύς, καὶ τὸν Ἱππίαν μεθ' αὐτοῦ κατάξει. ἆρ' οὐκ εὖ ἴσμεν τοῦτο ; πολλάκις ἐπειράθην πείθειν ὑμᾶς τὴν ῥαθυμίαν ἀφιέναι. οἱ δὲ πολέμιοι ἤδη φασὶν ἡμᾶς οὐδὲν ποιοῦντας οἴκοι καθῆσθαι· εἰ πρὸ τῆς μάχης μηδὲν ἐποιήσαμεν, τὴν Ἑλλάδα οὐκ ἂν ἐσώσαμεν. εἰ δὲ τῶν Περσῶν ὀλιγωροῦμεν οὐ σοφοί ἐσμεν. εἰ τοὺς Πέρσας μὴ ἐνικήσαμεν οὐ νῦν ἀσφαλεῖς ἂν ἦμεν· ἐὰν οἱ Πέρσαι οἴκαδ' ἀπίωσιν οὔποτ' αὖθις κατίασιν. ἀλλ' ὡς ἐμοὶ δοκεῖ, εἰ νῦν ἡμῖν ἀνθίσταιντο, (ὃ μὴ γένοιτο) ἡ νίκη αὐτοῖς οὐκ ἂν εἴη. εἰδότες οὖν τοὺς ἀνδρειοτέρους νικήσοντας, ὑπὲρ πατρίδος μαχώμεθα.

ρ

If he had asked where the dead were I should have said that they lay at Marathon. So many died on that day that I am not able to count them. If the Persians will go home we shall be safe. But if we knew they were so many we should not have resisted them. But as things are,[1] knowing that we are greatly outnumbered, even (καί) now if they should resist we would drive them out of Greece. But if we were to despise the enemy and suffer defeat, Greece would never again become free. Let us not therefore sit idle at home, but continue to fight bravely, and would that victory might be ours. It is certainly best to attempt to hold out against the enemy, and this we have always endeavoured to do. Let us therefore with all speed lay aside our inactivity. For it does not become men who fought at Marathon.

[1] οὕτως ἐχόντων τῶν πραγμάτων.

NOUNS

1. First declension

A. FEMININES. These are of three types. The singulars show variations. The plurals are the same for all three types.

I. Pure Alpha Stems
Nominative is in -α preceded by ε or ι or ρ. α is kept in all case endings of the singular.

II. Impure Alpha Stems
Nominative is in -α preceded by any consonant except ρ. α is changed to η for genitive and dative singular.

III. Eta Stems
Nominative is in -η.
η is kept in all case endings of the singular.

		I Pure Alpha	II Impure Alpha	III Eta
SING.	N.V.	χώρα *land*	θάλασσα *sea*	ἀρχή *rule or beginning*
	A.	χώραν	θάλασσαν	ἀρχήν
	G.	χώρας	θαλάσσης	ἀρχῆς
	D.	χώρᾳ	θαλάσσῃ	ἀρχῇ
DUAL	N.V.A.	χώρα	θαλάσσα	ἀρχά
	G.D.	χώραιν	θαλάσσαιν	ἀρχαῖν
PLUR.	N.V.	χῶραι	θάλασσαι	ἀρχαί
	A.	χώρας	θαλάσσας	ἀρχάς
	G.	χωρῶν	θαλασσῶν	ἀρχῶν
	D.	χώραις	θαλάσσαις	ἀρχαῖς

175

2. First declension

B. MASCULINES

These are of two types, corresponding to I. Pure Alpha and III. Eta feminine types.

Genitive singular of all 1st declension masculines is -ου.

Dual and plural are the same as for feminines.

I. Pure Alpha Stems

Nominative in -ας preceded by a vowel.

α is kept in all case endings of singular, *except genitive singular*, which ends in -ου as in 2nd declension.

III. Eta Stems

Nominative in -ης preceded by a consonant.

η is kept in all case endings of singular, *except genitive singular*, which ends in -ου.

Vocative usually -α.

		I Pure Alpha	III Eta
SING.	N.	νεανίας, *young man*	ναύτης, *sailor*
	V.	νεανία	ναῦτα
	A.	νεανίαν	ναύτην
	G.	νεανίου	ναύτου
	D.	νεανίᾳ	ναύτῃ
DUAL	N.V.A.	νεανία	ναύτα
	G.D.	νεανίαιν	ναύταιν
PLUR.	N.V.	νεανίαι	ναῦται
	A.	νεανίας	ναύτας
	G.	νεανιῶν	ναυτῶν
	D.	νεανίαις	ναύταις

First declension masculine nouns are mostly occupational names, as κριτής, *a judge* ; ταμίας, *a steward*.

3. The definite article

The definite article is used in Greek mainly in the same way as " the " in English (Par. 93). It is fully declined in all three genders in singular, dual and plural. The feminine forms are like the 1st declension *eta*-stems. The masculine and neuter forms are like the 2nd declension. Duals are 2nd declension in all three genders.

		M.	F.	N.
SING.	N.	ὁ	ἡ	τό
	A.	τόν	τήν	τό
	G.	τοῦ	τῆς	τοῦ
	D.	τῷ	τῇ	τῷ
DUAL	N.A.	τώ	τώ	τώ
	G.D.	τοῖν	τοῖν	τοῖν
PLUR.	N.	οἱ	αἱ	τά
	A.	τούς	τάς	τά
	G.	τῶν	τῶν	τῶν
	D.	τοῖς	ταῖς	τοῖς

Henceforward all nouns are declined with the article to ensure the observation of the gender.

4. Second declension

A. MASCULINES

Nominative in -ος. Stem in -ο.

FEMININES

A few exceptions of identical form with the masculine.

B. NEUTERS

Nominative in -ον. Stem in -ο.
These differ from the masculine only in the nominative and vocative singular and plural, and in the accusative plural.

		Masc.		Fem.		Neuter
SING.	N.	ὁ λόγος, *word*	ἡ	νόσος, *disease*	τό	ἔργον, *deed*
	V.	λόγε [1]		νόσε		ἔργον
	A.	τὸν λόγον	τὴν	νόσον	τό	ἔργον
	G.	τοῦ λόγου	τῆς	νόσου	τοῦ	ἔργου
	D.	τῷ λόγῳ	τῇ	νόσῳ	τῷ	ἔργῳ
DUAL	N.V.A.	τὼ λόγω	τὼ	νόσω	τὼ	ἔργω
	G.D.	τοῖν λόγοιν	τοῖν	νόσοιν	τοῖν	ἔργοιν
PLUR.	N.V.	οἱ λόγοι	αἱ	νόσοι	τὰ	ἔργα
	A.	τοὺς λόγους	τὰς	νόσους	τὰ	ἔργα
	G.	τῶν λόγων	τῶν	νόσων	τῶν	ἔργων
	D.	τοῖς λόγοις	ταῖς	νόσοις	τοῖς	ἔργοις

Nouns in -ως. The rare so-called Attic declension substitutes ω for ο. ω and υ cannot stand together and υ drops out. ω and ι are written ῳ.

Example. νεώς, *a temple.*

Sing. N.V. νεώς   A. νεών   G. νεώ   D. νεῴ
Dual. N.V.A. νεώ   G.D. νεῴν
Plur. N.V. νεῴ   A. νεώς   G. νεών.   D. νεῴς

5. Third declension

There are two main groups in this declension

                  A. CONSONANT STEMS
                  B. VOWEL STEMS

6. A. Consonant stems

These present little difficulty once the *stem*, clearly shown in the oblique cases,[2] is known. It is therefore essential to learn each noun with its genitive.

Example. ὁ φύλαξ, genitive τοῦ φύλακ-ος, gives stem φυλακ-

Nominative singular and dative plural show some apparent irregularities, as in these cases σ of the ending comes up against the stem consonant. The rules for the modification of consonants will explain these. (pp. 142-3.)

Example. Nominative singular φύλαξ represents φύλακ-ς.

---

[1] The article is not used with the vocative.
[2] Accusative, genitive, and dative.

Example. SING. N.V. ὁ   φύλαξ, *guard* (guttural stem)
             A.   τὸν   φύλακα
             G.   τοῦ   φύλακος
             D.   τῷ   φύλακι

       DUAL   N.V.A.   τὼ   φύλακε
              G.D.   τοῖν   φυλάκοιν

       PLUR.   N.V.   οἱ   φύλακες
              A.   τοὺς   φύλακας
              G.   τῶν   φυλάκων
              D.   τοῖς   φύλαξι(ν)

7. Guttural stems κ, κτ, γ, γγ, χ.

Any stem guttural, meeting σ of nominative singular or dative plural, combines with it to form ξ.

Nom. sing.	Gen. sing.	Dat. plur.	Meaning
ὁ κῆρυξ	τοῦ κήρυκος	τοῖς κήρυξι,	herald
ἡ νύξ	τῆς νυκτός	ταῖς νυξί,	night
ἡ φλόξ	τῆς φλογός	ταῖς φλοξί,	flame
ἡ φάλαγξ	τῆς φάλαγγος	ταῖς φάλαγξι,	phalanx, infantry array
ὁ ὄνυξ	τοῦ ὄνυχος	τοῖς ὄνυξι,	nail, hoof

8. Labial stems β, π.

Any stem labial, meeting σ of nominative singular or dative plural, combines with it to form ψ.

ἡ φλέψ	τῆς φλεβός	ταῖς φλεψί, vein
ὁ γύψ	τοῦ γυπός	τοῖς γυψί, vulture

9. Dental stems δ, τ, θ, ντ.

Stem dentals are dropped before a σ. *Example.* λαμπάδς becomes λαμπάς.

Nom. sing.	Gen. sing.	Dat. plur.	Meaning
ὁ παῖς	τοῦ παιδός	τοῖς παισί,	child, boy
ὁ ἔρως	τοῦ ἔρωτος	τοῖς ἔρωσι,	love
τὸ σῶμα	τοῦ σώματος	τοῖς σώμασι,	body
ὁ ἀνδριάς	τοῦ ἀνδριάντος	τοῖς ἀνδριᾶσι,	statue

Feminine abstract nouns in -της.

Example. ἡ δικαιότης, τῆς δικαιότητος, *justice.*   Many abstract nouns from adjectives in -ος are formed in this way.

Feminines in -ις or -ίς.

Feminines in -ις unaccented have accusative -ιν as

ἡ ἔρις	ἔριν	ἔριδος	ἔριδι,	*strife,*	dat. pl.	ἔρισι
ἡ χάρις	χάριν	χάριτος	χάριτι,	*grace,*	dat. pl.	χάρισι

But, if accented -ίς, accusative is normal, as

| ἡ πατρίς | πατρίδα | πατρίδος | πατρίδι, | *country,* | dat. pl. | πατρίσι |
| ἡ ἐλπίς | ἐλπίδα | ἐλπίδος | ἐλπίδι, | *hope,* | dat. pl. | ἐλπίσι |

Neuter verbal nouns in -μα.

Example. τὸ ἀδίκημα, τοῦ ἀδικήματος, *a sin*; from ἀδικεῖν, *to sin.* Many neuter nouns are thus formed from verb stem + -μα to denote the result of the verb.

Stems in -οντ.

Nominative singular -ων, dative plural -ουσι (cf. Participles, Par. 31).

ὁ γέρων	τοῦ γέροντος	τοῖς γέρουσι, *old man*
ὁ λέων	τοῦ λέοντος	τοῖς λέουσι, *lion*

10. Liquid stems ν.

Stems in ν lengthen ο or ε for nominative and drop σ, making ων or -ην. ν is dropped before -σι of dative plural.

Nom. sing.	Gen. sing.	Dat. plur.	meaning
ὁ ποιμήν	τοῦ ποιμένος	τοῖς ποιμέσι,	*shepherd*
ὁ Ἕλλην	τοῦ Ἕλληνος	τοῖς Ἕλλησι,	*Greek*
ὁ δαίμων	τοῦ δαίμονος	τοῖς δαίμοσι,	*god, divinity*
ὁ ἀγών	τοῦ ἀγῶνος	τοῖς ἀγῶσι,	*contest*

Note. The vowel of the nominative singular is no indication of whether the stem vowel is ω or ο, η or ε. Each individual word must be learnt separately with its genitive. Nominative -ων needs particular care as it can represent

-ων	-οντος	like	λέων,	*lion*
-ων	-ωνος	like	ἀγών,	*contest*
-ων	-ονος	like	δαίμων,	*god*

11. Liquid stems ρ.

Stems in ρ, like ν stems, lengthen ο or ε for nominative singular and drop σ. For dative plural ρ and σι stand side by side making -ρσι. Stem vowel must be learnt for each individual word.

Nom. sing.	Gen. sing.	Dat. plur.	meaning
ὁ θήρ	τοῦ θηρός	τοῖς θηρσί	wild beast
ὁ ἀστήρ	τοῦ ἀστέρος	τοῖς ἀστράσι [1],	star
ὁ ῥήτωρ	τοῦ ῥήτορος	τοῖς ῥήτορσι,	orator
ὁ φώρ	τοῦ φωρός	τοῖς φωρσί,	thief

Irregular

ὁ μάρτυς	τοῦ μάρτυρος	τοῖς μάρτυσι,	witness

Vocatives of liquid stems in ν and ρ.
Same as nominative, if final syllable of nominative is accented.

Example.   Nom. ποιμήν, Voc. ποιμήν.
Same as stem vowel, if final syllable of nominative is unaccented.

Example.   Nom. δαίμων, Voc. δαῖμον.

Exceptions.
Nom. σωτήρ, Gen. σωτῆρος, *saviour* ; Voc. σῶτερ.
Nom. Ἀπόλλων, Gen. Ἀπόλλωνος, *Apollo* ; Voc. Ἄπολλον.
Nom. Ποσειδῶν, Gen. Ποσειδῶνος, *Poseidon* ; Voc. Πόσειδον.

12. Neuters with nominative -ος.

This is an important group. Owing to contraction the endings are different from all other consonant stems. Many of these neuter nouns denote quality, as βάρος, *heaviness* (Par. 28). Carefully distinguish them from 2nd declension masculines.[2]

	SING.	DUAL	PLURAL
N.V.	τὸ μέρος, *part*	τὼ μέρει	τὰ μέρη
A.	τὸ μέρος		τὰ μερη
G.	τοῦ μέρους	τοῖν μέροιν	τῶν μερῶν
D.	τῷ μέρει		τοῖς μέρεσι(ν)

---

[1] Irregular (cf. πατήρ, Par. 20).
[2] Cf. opus, operis, 3rd n. in Latin.

13. B. Vowel stems

There are four main types :

    I. Nominative in -ις, genitive -εως.
   II. Nominative in -υς, genitive -υος.
  III. Nominative in -υς, genitive -εως.
  IV. Nominative in -ευς, genitive -εως.

14. Nominative in -ις.   Mostly feminine.

	SING.		DUAL	PLUR.
N.	ἡ	πόλις, *city*	τὼ πόλει	αἱ πόλεις
V.		πόλι		
A.	τὴν	πόλιν		τὰς πόλεις
G.	τῆς	πόλεως	τοῖν πολέοιν	τῶν πόλεων
D.	τῇ	πόλει		ταῖς πόλεσι(ν)

The majority of these nouns end in -σις or -τις.[1] They are derived from verbs and denote the *action* of the verb. Compare the neuters in -μα (Par. 9) which denote the *result* of the verb.

Examples.   μιμεῖσθαι, *to imitate*
               ἡ μίμησις, *the act of imitation*
               τὸ μίμημα, *the actual copy*

15. II. Nominative in -υς, genitive -υος.

Includes all nouns in -υς except the four of type III.

	SING.		DUAL	PLUR.
N.	ὁ	ἰχθύς, *fish*	τὼ ἰχθύε	οἱ ἰχθύες or ἰχθῦς
V.		ἰχθύ		
A.	τὸν	ἰχθύν		τοὺς ἰχθῦς
G.	τοῦ	ἰχθύος	τοῖν ἰχθύοιν	τῶν ἰχθύων
D.	τῷ	ἰχθύι		τοῖς ἰχθύσι(ν)

ΙΧΘΥΣ, the early Christian symbol of the fish, was an acrostic for

Ἰησοῦς	Jesus
Χριστός	Christ
Θεοῦ	of God
Υἱός	Son
Σωτήρ	Saviour

[1] The accent stands as far back as possible (cf. Par. 9, fem. in -ις.).

16. III. Nominative in -υς, genitive -εως

These exactly follow πόλις, except that -υς, -υ, -υν replace -ις, -ι, -ιν in the singular. There are four only :

ὁ πρέσβυς, *old man,* plur. *ambassadors*
ὁ πῆχυς,   *fore-arm, cubit*
ὁ πέλεκυς, *axe*
ὁ ἔγχελυς, *eel.*   Singular like II ἰχθύς, plur. like I πόλις and III πρέσβυς.

	SING.	DUAL	PLUR.
N.	ὁ πρέσβυς	τὼ πρέσβει	οἱ πρέσβεις
V.	πρέσβυ		πρέσβεις
A.	τὸν πρέσβυν		τοὺς πρέσβεις
G.	τοῦ πρέσβεως	τοῖν πρεσβέοιν	τῶν πρέσβεων
D.	τῷ πρέσβει		τοῖς πρέσβεσι(ν)

Group with these the neuter :

τὸ ἄστυ, *town*	τὰ ἄστη
τοῦ ἄστεως	τῶν ἄστεων
τῷ ἄστει	τοῖς ἄστεσιν

17. IV. Nominative in -ευς, all masculine

SING.	N.	ὁ	βασιλεύς, *king*
	V.		βασιλεῦ
	A.	τὸν	βασιλέα
	G.	τοῦ	βασιλέως
	D.	τῷ	βασιλεῖ
DUAL	N.V.A.	τὼ	βασιλεῖ
	G.D.	τοῖν	βασιλέοιν
PLUR.	N.V.	οἱ	βασιλῆς or βασιλεῖς
	A.	τοὺς	βασιλέας
	G.	τῶν	βασιλέων
	D.	τοῖς	βασιλεῦσι(ν)

Nouns of this group are *either* from verbs and denote agency :

e.g. as ἱππεύς, *a rider* ;

or they denote local origin,

e.g. Ἐρετριεύς, *an Eretrian.*

18. Three important irregular nouns with vowel stems

	SINGULAR		SINGULAR		SINGULAR
N.	ὁ or ἡ βοῦς, *ox or cow*		ἡ γραῦς, *old woman*		ἡ ναῦς, *ship*
V.	βοῦ		γραῦ		ναῦ
A.	τὴν βοῦν		τὴν γραῦν		τὴν ναῦν
G.	τῆς βοός		τῆς γραός		τῆς νεώς
D.	τῇ βοΐ		τῇ γραΐ		τῇ νηΐ

	DUAL		DUAL		DUAL
N.V.A.	τὼ βόε		τὼ γρᾶε		τὼ νῆε
G.D.	τοῖν βοοῖν		τοῖν γραοῖν		τοῖν νεοῖν

	PLURAL		PLURAL		PLURAL
N.V.	αἱ βόες		αἱ γρᾶες		αἱ νῆες
A.	τὰς βοῦς		τὰς γραῦς		τὰς ναῦς
G.	τῶν βοῶν		τῶν γραῶν		τῶν νεῶν
D.	ταῖς βουσί(ν)		ταῖς γραυσί(ν)		ταῖς ναυσί(ν)

19. Common irregular nouns

SING.	N.	ὁ	ἀνήρ, *man*	ἡ	γυνή, *woman*
	V.		ἄνερ		γύναι
	A.	τὸν	ἄνδρα	τὴν	γυναῖκα
	G.	τοῦ	ἀνδρός	τῆς	γυναικός
	D.	τῷ	ἀνδρί	τῇ	γυναικί
DUAL	N.V.A.	τὼ	ἄνδρε	τὼ	γυναῖκε
	G.D.	τοῖν	ἀνδροῖν	τοῖν	γυναικοῖν
PLUR.	N.V.	οἱ	ἄνδρες	αἱ	γυναῖκες
	A.	τοὺς	ἄνδρας	τὰς	γυναῖκας
	G.	τῶν	ἀνδρῶν	τῶν	γυναικῶν
	D.	τοῖς	ἀνδράσιν	ταῖς	γυναιξί(ν)

ὁ κύων, *the dog*, voc. κύον ;

then regularly from stem κυν-, κύνα, κυνός, κυνί ;

plur. κύνες, κύνας, κυνῶν, κυσί(ν).

20. ὁ πατήρ, *father*; ἡ μήτηρ, *mother*; ἡ θυγάτηρ, *daughter*, are declined exactly alike. Note dropping of ε in genitive and dative singular and in dative plural.

SING.	N.	ὁ	πατήρ, *father*
	V.		πάτερ
	A.	τὸν	πατέρα
	G.	τοῦ	πατρός
	D.	τῷ	πατρί
DUAL	N.V.A.	τὼ	πατέρε
	G.D.	τοῖν	πατέροιν
PLUR.	N.V.	οἱ	πατέρες
	A.	τοὺς	πατέρας
	G.	τῶν	πατέρων
	D.	τοῖς	πατράσι(ν)

Like πατήρ is declined also ἡ γαστήρ, *belly*.

21. ὁ υἱός, *son*, has both 2nd and 3rd declension forms.

		2nd		3rd	
SING.	N.	ὁ	υἱός	—	
	V.		υἱέ	—	
	A.	τὸν	υἱόν	—	
	G.	τοῦ	υἱοῦ	τοῦ	υἱέος
	D.	τῷ	υἱῷ	τῷ	υἱεῖ
DUAL	N.V.A.	τὼ	υἱώ	τὼ	υἱεῖ
	G.D.	τοῖν	υἱοῖν	τοῖν	υἱέοιν
PLUR.	N.V.	οἱ	υἱοί	οἱ	υἱεῖς
	A.	τοὺς	υἱούς	τοὺς	υἱεῖς
	G.	τῶν	υἱῶν	τῶν	υἱέων
	D.	τοῖς	υἱοῖς	τοῖς	υἱέσι(ν)

Both 2nd and 3rd declension forms are sometimes spelt without the *iota*, as ὁ ὑός, τοῦ ὑέος, etc.

22. Parts of the body

Hand : ἡ χείρ, τῆς χειρός, etc., regular from stem χειρ-, has two irregular forms, dative dual and plural, χεροῖν [1] and χερσί.

Foot : ὁ πούς, τοῦ ποδός, τοῖς ποσί, regular from stem ποδ- except for nominative singular.

Knee : τὸ γόνυ, τοῦ γόνατος, τοῖς γόνασι. Stem γονατ-.

Hair : ἡ θρίξ, τρίχα, τριχός, τριχί, τρίχες, τρίχας, τριχῶν, θριξί. Stem τριχ-. In nominative singular and dative plural, where χ and σ combine to join ξ, the ousted aspirate reappears in the previous syllable, turning τ to θ.[2]

Nose : ἡ ῥίς, τῆς ῥινός, ταῖς ῥισί, regular from stem ῥιν-.

Ear : τὸ οὖς, τοῦ ὠτός, τὰ ὦτα, τοῖς ὠσί, regular from stem ὠτ- except for nominative and accusative singular.

Mouth : τὸ στόμα, τοῦ στόματος, τὰ στόματα, τοῖς στόμασι, regular dental stem στοματ- like ἀδίκημα (Par. 9).

Tooth : ὁ ὀδούς, τοῦ ὀδόντος, οἱ ὀδόντες, τοῖς ὀδοῦσι, regular from stem -οντ- except for nominative singular.

		Fire	and	*Water*
SING.	N.V.A.	τὸ πῦρ		τὸ ὕδωρ
	G.	τοῦ πυρός		τοῦ ὕδατος
	D.	τῷ πυρί		τῷ ὕδατι
PLUR.	N.V.A.	τὰ πυρά		τὰ ὕδατα
	G.	τῶν πυρῶν		τῶν ὑδάτων
	D.	τοῖς πυροῖς [3]		τοῖς ὕδασι(ν)

[1] Common for obvious reasons. Other forms from stem χερ- are frequent in poetry.

[2] Cf. τρέφω fut. θρέψω (p. 317).   [3] 2nd declension in plural.

23. Proper names
MASCULINES
Masculine names in -ος are 2nd declension.
Masculine names in -ης are 1st declension like ναύτης (Par. 2).
Vocative is in -η except for national names.

Examples.

N. Ξέρξης   V. Ξέρξη   A. Ξέρξην   G. Ξέρξου   D. Ξέρξη
N. Πέρσης   V. Πέρσα   A. Πέρσην   G. Πέρσου   D. Πέρση

Exceptions. To the 3rd declension belong masculine names compounded with the neuter nouns: γένος, *race*; κράτος, *power*; μένος, *might*; νεῖκος, *strife*; σθένος, *strength*; τέλος, *perfection*.

    Example. N. Σωκράτης
                V. Σώκρατες
                A. Σωκράτη
                G. Σωκράτους
                D. Σωκράτει

Also compounds of κλεός, *glory*. These contract from -κλεής.

    Example. N. Περικλῆς
                V. Περίκλεις
                A. Περικλέα
                G. Περικλέους
                D. Περικλεῖ

Proper nouns in -ευς decline like βασιλεύς. *Example*: Ὀδυσσεύς, Ἀχιλλεύς (see Par. 17).
-ευς after a vowel as Πειραιεύς. These often drop ε in acc. and gen. sing., and in plur. *Example*: Πειραιᾶ, Πειραιῶς. Δωριᾶς, Δωριῶν.
For other 3rd declension proper nouns the stem must be known.
N.B. Ζεύς: voc. Ζεῦ, acc. Δία, gen. Διός, dat. Διί.

FEMININES
Most are 1st declension -α or -η.
There is a group of feminine 3rd declension names in -ω.

    Example. N. Σαπφώ
                V. Σαπφοῖ
                A. Σαπφώ
                G. Σαπφοῦς
                D. Σαπφοῖ

Similarly Ἰώ, Καλυψώ, Λητώ, and others.

24. Adjectives, 1st and 2nd declension

Many adjectives form masculine and neuter like 2nd declension nouns, and feminine like 1st declension nouns. (Cf. *bonus, bona, bonum* in Latin.) The feminines vary between pure alpha (type I) and eta (type III), according to whether the letter before the ending is

ϵ or ι or ρ, which produces pure alpha,

or a consonant other than ρ which produces η.

The regular comparative and superlative endings show this principle clearly.

Positive

	M.	F.	N.	
	δίκαιος	δικαία	δίκαιον	*just*

Comparative

	δικαιότερος	δικαιοτέρα	δικαιότερον	*more just*

Superlative

	δικαιότατος	δικαιοτάτη	δικαιότατον	*most just*

	δίκαιος, *just*			σόφος, *wise*		
	SINGULAR			SINGULAR		
	M.	F.	N.	M.	F.	F.
M.	δίκαιος	δικαία	δίκαιον, *just*	σοφός	σοφή	σοφόν, *wise*
V.	δίκαιε	δικαία	δίκαιον	σοφέ	σοφή	σοφόν
A.	δίκαιον	δικαίαν	δίκαιον	σοφόν	σοφήν	σοφόν
G.	δικαίου	δικαίας	δικαίου	σοφοῦ	σοφῆς	σοφοῦ
D.	δικαίῳ	δικαίᾳ	δικαίῳ	σοφῷ	σοφῇ	σοφῷ
	DUAL			DUAL		
N.V.A.	δικαίω	δικαία	δικαίω	σοφώ	σοφά	σοφώ
G.D.	δικαίοιν	δικαίαιν	δικαίοιν	σοφοῖν	σοφαῖν	σοφοῖν
	PLURAL			PLURAL		
N.V.	δίκαιοι	δίκαιαι	δίκαια	σοφοί	σοφαί	σοφά
A.	δικαίους	δικαίας	δίκαια	σοφούς	σοφάς	σοφά
G.	δικαίων	δικαίων	δικαίων	σοφῶν	σοφῶν	σοφῶν
D.	δικαίοις	δικαίαις	δικαίοις	σοφοῖς	σοφαῖς	σοφοῖς

25. Some adjectives in -os are two-termination only, masculine and feminine being alike. To this group belong compound adjectives. Many are compounds of

εὐ-, *well*, as εὔδοξος -ον, *well-reputed, famous.*
δυσ-, *difficult*, as δύσκριτος -ον, *hard to judge.*
ἀ- or ἀν- negative [1] (Latin *in-*) as ἄδικος -ον, *unjust.*

			M.F.	N.
Example.	SING.	N.	εὔδοξος	εὔδοξον
		V.	εὔδοξε	εὔδοξον
		A.	εὔδοξον	
		G.	εὐδόξου, etc.	

26. Two important irregular adjectives, πολύς, *much, many* ; μέγας, *great*

	SINGULAR			SINGULAR		
	M.	F.	N.	M.	F.	N.
N.	πολύς	πολλή	πολύ	μέγας	μεγάλη	μέγα
V.	πολύς	πολλή	πολύ	μεγάλε	μεγάλη	μέγα
A.	πολύν	πολλήν	πολύ	μέγαν	μεγάλην	μέγα
G.	πολλοῦ	πολλῆς	πολλοῦ	μεγάλου	μεγάλης	μεγάλου
D.	πολλῷ	πολλῇ	πολλῷ	μεγάλῳ	μεγάλῃ	μεγάλῳ

	DUAL			DUAL		
N.V.A.	—	—	—	μεγάλω	μεγάλα	μεγάλω
G.D.	—	—	—	μεγάλοιν	μεγάλαιν	μεγάλοιν

	PLURAL			PLURAL		
N.V.	πολλοί	πολλαί	πολλά	μεγάλοι	μεγάλαι	μεγάλα
A.	πολλούς	πολλάς	πολλά	μεγάλους	μεγάλας	μεγάλα
G.	πολλῶν	πολλῶν	πολλῶν	μεγάλων	μεγάλων	μεγάλων
D.	πολλοῖς	πολλαῖς	πολλοῖς	μεγάλοις	μεγάλαις	μεγάλοις

Adjectives in -οῦς, -ῆ or -ᾶ, -οῦν, mostly denoting metals, have dropped or contracted ε.

Example : χρυσοῦς, χρυσῆ, χρυσοῦν, *golden*
  ἀργυροῦς, ἀργυρᾶ, ἀργυροῦν, *silver.*

The only differences of ending are in nom. and acc. sing where εο contracts to ου.

[1] Called *alpha privative.*

27. Third declension adjectives

I. Adjectives from 3rd declension only. Endings -ων -ον and -ης -ες.
Masculine and feminine have the same forms throughout.
Neuter differs only in nominative and accusative of singular and plural

		M.F.	N.	M.F.	N.
SING.	N.	σώφρων	σῶφρον *wise*	σαφής	σαφές *clear*
	V.	σῶφρον		σαφές	
	A.	σώφρονα	σῶφρον	σαφῆ	σαφές
	G.	σώφρονος		σαφοῦς	
	D.	σώφρονι		σαφεῖ	
DUAL	N.V.A.	σώφρονε		σαφεῖ	
	G.D.	σωφρόνοιν		σαφοῖν	
PLUR.	N.V.	σώφρονες	σώφρονα	σαφεῖς	σαφῆ
	A.	σώφρονας	σώφρονα	σαφεῖς	σαφῆ
	G.	σωφρόνων		σαφῶν	
	D.	σώφροσι(ν)		σαφέσι(ν)	

28. II. Adjectives from 3rd and 1st declension.

(1) Stems in -υ, as ἡδύς, *sweet*.

		M.	F.	N.
SING.	N.	ἡδύς	ἡδεῖα	ἡδύ
	V.	ἡδύ	ἡδεῖα	ἡδύ
	A.	ἡδύν	ἡδεῖαν	ἡδύ
	G.	ἡδέος	ἡδείας	ἡδέος
	D.	ἡδεῖ	ἡδείᾳ	ἡδεῖ
DUAL	N.V.A.	ἡδεῖ	ἡδεία	ἡδεῖ
	G.D.	ἡδέοιν	ἡδείαιν	ἡδέοιν
PLUR.	N.V.	ἡδεῖς	ἡδεῖαι	ἡδέα
	A.	ἡδεῖς	ἡδείας	ἡδέα
	G.	ἡδέων	ἡδειῶν	ἡδέων
	D.	ἡδέσι(ν)	ἡδείαις	ἡδέσι(ν)

Many of these adjectives have corresponding neuter nouns of quality
(Par. 12).

Example. βαρύς, βαρεῖα, βαρύ, *heavy*; τὸ βάρος, *weight*.
ταχύς, ταχεῖα, ταχύ, *swift*; τὸ τάχος, *speed*.

29. (2) Stems in -ν-. Note impure alpha (Par. 1) of feminines.

		M.	F.	N.
SING.	N.	μέλας	μέλαινα	μέλαν, *black*
	V.	μέλαν	μέλαινα	μέλαν
	A.	μέλανα	μέλαιναν	μέλαν
	G.	μέλανος	μελαίνης	μέλανος, etc.
	also	τάλας	τάλαινα	τάλαν, *wretched*
and	N.	τέρην	τέρεινα	τέρεν, *tender*
	V.	τέρεν	τέρεινα	τέρεν
	A.	τέρενα	τέρειναν	τέρεν, etc.

30. Stems in -ντ- with feminine impure alpha (Par. 9 and 31).

		M.	F.	N.
	N.V.	ἑκών	ἑκοῦσα	ἑκόν, *willing*
	A.	ἑκόντα	ἑκοῦσαν	ἑκόν
	G.	ἑκόντος	ἑκούσης	ἑκόντος, etc.
	Dat. pl.	ἑκοῦσι(ν)	ἑκούσαις	ἑκοῦσι(ν)
and		ἄκων	ἄκουσα	ἆκον, *unwilling*
SING.	N.V.	πᾶς	πᾶσα	πᾶν, *every, all, whole*
	A.	πάντα	πᾶσαν	πᾶν
	G.	παντός	πασῆς	παντός
	D.	παντί	πασῇ	παντί
		NO DUAL		
PLUR.	N.V.	πάντες	πᾶσαι	πάντα
	A.	πάντας	πάσας	πάντα
	G.	πάντων	πασῶν	πάντων
	D.	πᾶσι(ν)	πάσαις	πᾶσι(ν)

and its compounds ἅπας and σύμπας, *all*. (Syntax, Par. 93, *a*).

31. Participles

Greek verbs have participles for four tenses of each voice. These are fully declined in each gender like adjectives.

-ω verbs, Active.

Active	Pres.	λύων	λύουσα	λῦον	(Par. 30)
	Fut.	λύσων	λύσουσα	λῦσον	(Par. 30)
	Aor.	λύσας	λύσασα	λῦσαν	(Par. 30)
	Perf.	λελυκώς	λελυκυῖα	λελυκός	(Pars. 9 and 24)
		λελυκότα	λελυκυῖαν	λελυκός, etc.	
Mid. and Pres.		λυόμενος	λυομένη	λυόμενον	(Par. 24)
Passive Perf.		λελυμένος	-η	-ον	
Middle Fut.		λυσόμενος	-η	-ον	
	Aor.	λυσάμενος	-η	-ον	
Passive Fut.		λυθησόμενος	-η	-ον	
	Aor. N.	λυθείς	λυθεῖσα	λυθέν	(Par. 9)
	A.	λυθέντα	λυθεῖσαν	λυθέν	
	G.	λυθέντος	λυθείσης	λυθέντος, etc.	
	D. Pl.	λυθεῖσι(ν)	λυθείσαις	λυθεῖσι(ν)	

32. Participles of -μι verbs (see pp. 246–277).

εἰμί	Pres. N.	ὤν	οὖσα	ὄν	
	G.	ὄντος			like λύων
εἶμι	Pres. N.	ἰών	ἰοῦσα	ἰόν	
	G.	ἰόντος			

τίθημι	Pres. N.	τιθείς	τιθεῖσα	τιθέν	like λυθείς Aor. Pass.
	Aor. N.	θείς	θεῖσα	θέν	

ἵστημι	Pres. N.	ἱστάς	ἱστᾶσα	ἱστάν	like πᾶς (Par. 30)
	Aor. N.	στάς	στᾶσα	στάν	

δίδωμι	Pres. N.	διδούς	διδοῦσα	διδόν	
	G.	διδόντος, etc.			
	D. Pl.	διδοῦσι(ν)	διδούσαις	διδοῦσι(ν)	
	Aor. N.	δούς	δοῦσα	δόν	

δείκνυμι	Pres. N.	δεικνύς	δεικνῦσα	δεικνύν	
	G.	δεικνύντος	δεικνύσης	δεικνύντος	
	D. Pl.	δεικνῦσι(ν)	δεικνύσαις	δεικνῦσι(ν)	

33. Comparison of adjectives

Most adjectives add -τερος, -τερα, -τερον to stem for comparative,
-τατος, -τατη, -τατον to stem for superlative.

Comparative has feminine in pure α, superlative in η.

Examples of comparison :

κοῦφος, *light*, stem κουφο- makes κουφότερος, κουφότατος.
βαρύς, *heavy*, stem βαρυ- makes βαρύτερος, βαρύτατος.
σαφής, *clear*, stem σαφεσ- makes σαφέστερος, σαφέστατος.

Note. With second declension adjectives if the *last syllable but one* [1] *scans short*, o of the stem is changed to ω.

Example. ἄξιος, *worthy*, ἀξιώτερος, ἀξιώτατος.

This prevents four short syllables coming one after the other.

Examples of regular comparison of 2nd declension adjectives :

ἄδικος	ἀδικώτερος	ἀδικώτατος,	*unjust*
δίκαιος	δικαιότερος	δικαιότατος,	*just*
ἕτοιμος	ἑτοιμότερος	ἑτοιμότατος,	*ready*
κοινός	κοινότερος	κοινότατος,	*common*
ὀρθός [2]	ὀρθότερος	ὀρθότατος,	*right, straight*
ὅσιος,	ὁσιώτερος	ὁσιώτατος,	*holy*
σεμνός [2]	σεμνότερος	σεμνότατος,	*solemn, holy*
χρήσιμος	χρησιμώτερος	χρησιμώτατος,	*useful*

34. Third declension adjectives in -ων add -εστερος to stem -ον-, as
εὐδαίμων, *happy*, εὐδαιμονέστερος, εὐδαιμονέστατος.

Examples of regular comparison of adjectives in -υς, -ων and -ης :

ἀκριβής	ἀκριβέστερος	ἀκριβέστατος,	*accurate*
ἄφρων	ἀφρονέστερος	ἀφρονέστατος,	*witless*
βαθύς	βαθύτερος	βαθύτατος,	*deep*
ἐπιστήμων	ἐπιστημονέστερος	ἐπιστημονέστατος,	*wise*
εὐήθης	εὐηθέστερος	εὐηθέστατος,	*foolish*
μνήμων	μνημονέστερος	μνημονέστατος,	*mindful*
ὀξύς	ὀξύτερος	ὀξύτατος,	*sharp*

[1] Termed *penult.*
[2] A short vowel before two consonants scans long, as ὀρθός and σεμνός.

35. These few important adjectives add -ιων -ιστος to the stem. Some are slightly irregular in other ways.

αἰσχρός	αἰσχίων	αἴσχιστος, *ugly, base*
ἐχθρός	ἐχθίων	ἔχθιστος, *hostile*
ἡδύς	ἡδίων	ἥδιστος, *sweet*
καλός	καλλίων [1]	κάλλιστος, *beautiful*
μέγας	μείζων	μέγιστος, *great*
ῥᾴδιος	ῥᾴων	ῥᾷστος, *easy*
ταχύς	θάσσων [2]	τάχιστος, *swift*

36. Declension of comparatives in -ιων and -ων.

	SINGULAR		DUAL		PLURAL	
	M.F.	N.	M.F.N.		M.F.	N.
N.V.	μείζων	μεῖζον	N.V.A. μείζονε	N.V.	{ μείζονες { μείζους	{ μείζονα { μείζω
A.	{ μείζονα { μείζω	μεῖζον		A.	{ μείζονας { μείζους	{ μείζονα { μείζω
G.	μείζονος		G.D. μειζόνοιν	G.	μειζόνων	
D.	μείζονι			D.	μείζοσι(ν)	

Only comparatives show these alternative contracted forms. They are not found in adjectives like σώφρων (Par. 27).

37. Irregular comparison, often with different stems.

ἀγαθός	ἀμείνων *better*	ἄριστος *best*
good	βελτίων	βέλτιστος
	κρείσσων *stronger*	κράτιστος *strongest*
κακός	κακίων	κάκιστος
bad	χείρων	χείριστος
μικρός	μικρότερος	μικρότατος
small	ἐλάσσων	ἐλάχιστος
ὀλίγος	ἐλάσσων	ἐλάχιστος
little, plur. *few*		ὀλίγιστος
πολύς	πλείων	πλεῖστος
much, plur. *many*		

---

[1] Note doubling of λ, as in the noun τὸ κάλλος, *beauty.*

[2] See on θρίξ (Par. 22).

38. Irregular comparative forms, but from the same stem :

γεραιός	γεραίτερος	γεραίτατος,	old
εὔνους [1]	εὐνούστερος	εὐνούστατος,	kindly
ἴσος	ἰσαίτερος	ἰσαίτατος,	equal
μέσος	μεσαίτερος	μεσαίτατος,	middle
παλαιός	παλαίτερος	παλαίτατος,	ancient
πένης [2]	πενέστερος	πενέστατος,	poor
φίλος	—	φίλτατος,	dear

39. Comparison may also be made by μᾶλλον, *more* and μάλιστα, *most*, with the positive adjective.

Example.

φιλος *dear*	μᾶλλον φίλος *more dear,*	μάλιστα φίλος *most dear,*
	dearer.	dearest.

Note also πάνυ, *altogether*, with positive adjectives and adverbs, as πάνυ πονηρός, *very bad*.

40. Adverbs

The normal adverbial ending is -ως.
To form adverbs from adjectives :

Change final ν of masculine genitive plural to ς.

This rule holds good for all declensions and endings.

Examples.

Nom. sing.		Gen. plur. masc.	Adverb	
δίκαιος,	just	δικαίων	δικαίως,	justly
ἡδύς,	sweet	ἡδέων	ἡδέως,	sweetly
πᾶς,	all	πάντων	πάντως,	altogether
σαφής,	clear	σαφῶν	σαφῶς,	clearly
σοφός,	wise	σοφῶν	σοφῶς,	wisely
σώφρων,	prudent	σωφρόνων	σωφρόνως,	prudently

Note. πολύ,   *much*   ὀλίγον, *little*   μόνον,   *only*
These are neuter accusative singular adjectives used adverbially.

---

[1] εὔνοος contracted.
[2] Genitive πένητος, dental stem (cf. Par. 9).

41. Comparative adverbial ending is   -τερον.
    Superlative   ,,   ,,   ,,   ,,   -τατα.
Comparative adverbs are supplied by the *neuter accusative,* SINGULAR of the comparative adjective. *Example* : σοφώτερον, *more wisely.*

Superlative adverbs are supplied by the *neuter accusative* PLURAL of the superlative adjective. *Example* : σοφώτατα, *most wisely.*

Examples.

δικαίως *justly*	δικαιότερον *more justly*	δικαιότατα *most justly*
σαφῶς *clearly*	σαφέστερον *more clearly*	σαφέστατα *most clearly*
σωφρόνως *prudently*	σωφρονέστερον *more prudently*	σωφρονέστατα *most prudently*
ἡδέως *sweetly*	ἥδιον *more sweetly*	ἥδιστα *most sweetly*
κακῶς *badly*	κάκιον *worse*	κάκιστα *worst, most badly*
εὖ, *well* (adverb for ἀγαθός)	ἄμεινον βέλτιον *better*	ἄριστα βέλτιστα *best*

The following has no corresponding adjective :

μάλα *very*	μᾶλλον *more*	μάλιστα *most*

42. Comparative and superlative are also used, as in Latin, both with adjectives and adverbs, to denote excess of a quantity.

    Example.   σοφώτερον, *too wise, too wisely* ;
                 σοφώτατα, *very wise, very wisely.*

    IDIOM.   ὡς   with any superlative adverb.
              ὡς   τάχιστα, *as quickly as possible (quam celerrime).*
              ὡς   βέλτιστα, *as well as possible.*

    also   ἐπεὶ τάχιστα, *as soon as . . .*

43. Numerals

There are three kinds of numerals, cardinal, ordinal and adverbial.[1]
Of cardinal numbers these only decline :
1–4.
All hundreds after 100 (compounds of -κόσιοι).
All thousands (compounds of -χίλιοι).
All tens of thousands (compounds of -μύριοι).
Ordinal numbers are all 2nd and 1st declension adjectives.

Symbol		Cardinal	Ordinal	Adverb
1	α΄	εἷς, μία, ἕν, one	πρῶτος, first -η, -ον	ἅπαξ, once
2	β΄	δύο, two	δεύτερος, second -α, -ον	δίς, twice
3	γ΄	τρεῖς, τρία, three	τρίτος, third -η, -ον	τρίς, three times
4	δ΄	τέσσαρες, -α, four	τέταρτος, fourth	τετράκις, four times
5	ε΄	πέντε	πέμπτος	πεντάκις
6	ς΄ [2]	ἕξ	ἕκτος	ἑξάκις
7	ζ΄	ἕπτα	ἕβδομος	ἑπτάκις
8	η΄	ὀκτω	ὄγδοος -η, -ον	ὀκτάκις
9	θ΄	ἐννέα	ἔνατος	ἐνάκις
10	ι΄	δέκα	δέκατος	δεκάκις
11	ια΄	ἕνδεκα	ἑνδέκατος	ἑνδεκάκις
12	ιβ΄	δώδεκα	δωδέκατος	δωδεκάκις
13	ιγ΄	τρεῖς καὶ δέκα	τρίτος καὶ δέκατος	—
14	ιδ΄	τέσσαρες καὶ δέκα	τέταρτος καὶ δέκατος	—
15	ιε΄	πεντεκαίδεκα	πέμπτος καὶ δέκατος	—
16	ις΄	ἑκκαίδεκα	ἕκτος καὶ δέκατος	—
17	ιζ΄	ἑπτακαίδεκα	ἕβδομος καὶ δέκατος	—
18	ιη΄	ὀκτωκαίδεκα	ὄγδοος καὶ δέκατος	—
19	ιθ΄	ἐννεακαίδεκα	ἔνατος καὶ δέκατος	—
20	κ΄	εἴκοσι	εἰκοστός	εἰκοσάκις
21	κα΄	εἷς καὶ εἴκοσι, εἴκοσι εἷς	πρῶτος καὶ εἰκοστός	—
30	λ΄	τριάκοντα	τριακοστός	τριακοντάκις
40	μ΄	τεσσαράκοντα	τεσσαρακοστός	τεσσαρακοντάκις

[1] Greek, unlike Latin, has no distributives.
[2] This sign represents Vau, the obsolete digamma.

Symbol		Cardinal	Ordinal	Adverb
50	ν′	πεντήκοντα	πεντηκοστός	πεντηκοντάκις
60	ξ′	ἑξήκοντα	ἑξηκοστός	ἑξηκοντάκις
70	ο′	ἑβδομήκοντα	ἑβδομηκοστός	ἑβδομηκοντάκις
80	π′	ὀγδοήκοντα	ὀγδοηκοστός	ὀγδοηκοντάκις
90	ϙ′ [1]	ἐνενήκοντα	ἐνενηκοστός	ἐνενηκοντάκις
100	ρ′	ἑκατόν	ἑκατοστός	ἑκατοντάκις
200	σ′	διακόσιοι, -αι, -α	διακοσιοστός	διακοσιάκις
300	τ′	τριακόσιοι, -αι, -α	τριακοσιοστός	—
400	υ′	τετρακόσιοι, -αι, -α	τετρακοσιοστός	—
500	φ′	πεντακόσιοι, -αι, -α	πεντακοσιοστός	—
600	χ′	ἑξακόσιοι, -αι, -α	ἑξακοσιοστός	—
700	ψ′	ἑπτακόσιοι, -αι, -α	ἑπτακοσιοστός	—
800	ω′	ὀκτακόσιοι, -αι, -α	ὀκτακοσιοστός	—
900	ϡ′ [2]	ἐνακόσιοι, -αι, -α	ἐνακοσιοστός	—
1,000	͵α	χίλιοι, -αι, -α	χιλιοστός	χιλιάκις
2,000	͵β	δισχίλιοι, -αι, -α	δισχιλιοστός	—
3,000	͵γ	τρισχίλιοι, -αι, -α	τρισχιλιοστός	—
10,000	͵ι	μύριοι, -αι, -α	μυριοστός	μυριάκις
20,000	͵κ	δισμύριοι, -αι, -α	—	—
37	λζ′	τριάκοντα ἕπτα		
		τριάκοντα καὶ ἕπτα		
		ἕπτα καὶ τριάκοντα		

473　νογ′　τετρακόσιοι, -αι, -α ἑβδομήκοντα τρεῖς, τρία

1,004　͵αδ′ [3]　χίλιοι, -αι -α καὶ τέσσαρες, -α

Note. μύριοι, **ten thousand.**

μυρίοι, **innumerable.**　Also used in singular for *countless.*

[1] ϙ is *koppa,* which corresponds to Q and is not found in Attic.　It often represents the initial of Κόρινθος on coins.

[2] ϡ is *sampi,* or *san,* a form of sigma.

[3] The Greek and Roman systems of numeration do not represent units, tens, etc., in the number of figures employed.

44. Numbers 1 to 4, whenever they occur, decline as follows :

		M.	F.	N.			M.F.N.
SING.	N.V.	εἷς	μία	ἕν, *one*	DUAL	N.V.A.	δύο, *two*
	A.	ἕνα	μίαν	ἕν			
	G.	ἑνός	μίας	ἑνός		G.D.	δυοῖν
	D.	ἑνί	μιᾷ	ἑνί			

Like εἷς are declined

οὐδείς οὐδεμία οὐδέν and μηδείς μηδεμία μηδέν, *no-one.*

		M.F.	N.	M.F.	N.
PLUR.	N.V.	τρεῖς	τρία, *three*	τέσσαρες [1]	τέσσαρα, *four*
	A.	τρεῖς	τρία	τέσσαρας	τέσσαρα
	G.	τριῶν		τεσσάρων	
	D.	τρισί(ν)		τέσσαρσι(ν)	

45. I. Demonstrative pronouns

οὗτος, *this,* Latin *hic.* τοιοῦτος, *of such a kind,* Latin *talis.*
ὅδε,   *this,* Latin *is.*   τοσοῦτος, *so great,* Latin *tantus.*
ἐκεῖνος, *that,* Latin *ille.*

		M.	F.	N.
SING.	N.V.	οὗτος	αὕτη	τοῦτο, *this*
	A.	τοῦτον	ταύτην	τοῦτο
	G.	τούτου	ταύτης	τούτου
	D.	τούτῳ	ταύτῃ	τούτῳ
DUAL	N.V.A.	τούτω	τούτω	τούτω
	G.D.	τούτοιν	τούτοιν	τούτοιν
PLUR.	N.V.	οὗτοι	αὗται	ταῦτα
	A.	τούτους	ταύτας	ταῦτα
	G.	τούτων	τούτων	τούτων
	D.	τούτοις	ταύταις	τούτοις

οὗτος. o or ω in the second syllable give o in the first syllable.
α or η in the second syllable give α in the first syllable.
When the article has no initial τ neither has οὗτος.

[1] Often written τέτταρες, ττ being the later Attic form of σσ.

Similarly, but without inserting τ :

τοιοῦτος, τοιαύτη, τοιοῦτο, *of such a kind*, Latin *talis*.
τοσοῦτος, τοσαύτη, τοσοῦτο, *so great*, plur. *so many*, Latin *tantus*.

ὅδε, ἥδε, τόδε, *this*, Latin *is*, *ea*, *id* declines exactly like the article (Par. 3) with -δε attached.

ἐκεῖνος, ἐκείνη, ἐκεῖνο, *that*, Latin *ille*, declines like a regular 2nd and 1st declension adjective, except for nominative and accusative singular of neuter which are in -o instead of -ον.

These three demonstrative pronouns when they qualify a noun are always used *with the article*, but never stand between the article and the noun (Syntax, Par. 94). *Example :* οὗτος ὁ ἀνήρ, τῇδε τῇ γυναικί, τὸ τεῖχος ἐκεῖνο (less common).

46. II. Personal pronouns, 1st and 2nd person

SING.	N.V.	ἐγώ,	*I*	σύ, *thou*	
	A.	ἐμέ or με		σέ	
	G.	ἐμοῦ or μου		σοῦ	
	D.	ἐμοί or μοι		σοί	
DUAL	N.V.A.	νώ		σφώ	
	G.D.	νῷν		σφῷν	
PLUR.	N.V.	ἡμεῖς,	*we*	ὑμεῖς, *you*	
	A.	ἡμᾶς		ὑμᾶς	
	G.	ἡμῶν		ὑμῶν	
	D.	ἡμῖν		ὑμῖν	

47. 3rd person, *he, she, it, they*

The nominatives, if expressed apart from the verbal endings, are rendered by the demonstratives οὗτος, ἐκεῖνος or ὅδε in the appropriate gender and number. The oblique cases are taken from αὐτός -η -ο. The nominative of αὐτός means *self* (see Syntax, Par. 94).

		M.	F.	N.
SING.	A.	αὐτόν, *him*	αὐτήν, *her*	αὐτό, *it*
	G.	αὐτοῦ	αὐτῆς	αὐτοῦ
	D.	αὐτῷ	αὐτῇ	αὐτῷ
DUAL	A.	αὐτώ	αὐτώ	αὐτώ
	G.D.	αὐτοῖν	αὐτοῖν	αὐτοῖν
PLUR.	A.	αὐτούς, *them*	αὐτάς, *them*	αὐτά, *them*
	G.	αὐτῶν	αὐτῶν	αὐτῶν
	D.	αὐτοῖς	αὐταῖς	αὐτοῖς

48. III. Reflexive pronouns

Reflexives are used when the subject of the sentence reappears in another case. They have no nominative [1] (cf. Latin, *se, sui, sibi, se*).

	SINGULAR		PLURAL
1st Person.	A. ἐμαυτόν, ἐμαυτήν,	A.	ἡμᾶς αὐτούς or αὐτάς.
	G. ἐμαυτοῦ, etc.	G.	ἡμῶν αὐτῶν, etc.
	myself		*ourselves*
2nd Person.	A. σεαυτόν, σεαυτήν,	A.	ὑμᾶς αὐτούς or αὐτάς.
	G. σεαυτοῦ, etc.	G.	ὑμῶν αὐτῶν, etc.
	(often contracted to σαυτόν)		*yourselves*
	thyself		
3rd Person.	A. ἑαυτόν, ἑαυτήν, ἑαυτό	A.	ἑαυτούς, ἑαυτάς, ἑαυτά,
	G. ἑαυτοῦ, etc.	or	αὐτούς, αὐτάς, etc.
	(often contracted to αὑτόν, etc.)		*themselves* [2]
	himself, herself, itself		

49. IV. Possessive pronouns

These exist for 1st and 2nd persons only, and agree like adjectives (cf. Latin *meus, noster*, etc).

	SINGULAR	PLURAL
1st Person.	ἐμός, ἐμή, ἐμόν, etc.	ἡμέτερος, ἡμετέρα, ἡμέτερον, etc.
	my	*our*
2nd Person.	σός, σή, σόν, etc.	ὑμέτερος, ὑμετέρα, ὑμέτερον, etc.
	thy	*your*
3rd Person.	αὐτοῦ,[3] *of him, his*	αὐτῶν,[3] *of them, their*
	αὐτῆς, *of her, her*	
	Cf. Latin *eius*	

[1] See Par. 47 on αὐτός.
[2] σφᾶς αὐτούς, σφῶν αὐτῶν, σφίσιν αὐτοῖς, also occur.
[3] Cf. Paragraphs 47 and 94.

50. V. Interrogative pronoun

τίς, τί, *who? what?*
Always accented on the *iota*.

VI. Indefinite pronoun

τις, τι, *anyone, some, a.*
Never accented on the *iota*.
Follows the word it refers to.
ἀνήρ τις, *a man, some man.*

		M.F.		N.	M.F.		N.
SING.	N.	τίς		τί	τις		τι
	A.	τίνα		τί	τινά		τι
	G.	τίνος	or	τοῦ	τινός	or	τοῦ
	D.	τίνι	or	τῷ	τινί	or	τῳ
DUAL	N.A.	τίνε			τινέ		
	G.D.	τίνοιν			τινοῖν		
PLUR.	N.	τίνες		τίνα	τινές		τινά
	A.	τίνας		τίνα	τινάς		τινά
	G.		τίνων			τινῶν	
	D.		τίσι			τισί	

51. VII. Relative pronouns

ὅς, ἥ, ὅ, *who, which, what.*

Declines almost like the article, only with rough breathing instead of τ.

Note.   ἥ, οἵ, αἵ of relative are *accented,*
                 ἡ, οἱ, αἱ of article are *unaccented.*

ὅστις, *whoever* (indefinite).

	M.			F.		N.		
SING.	ὅστις			ἥτις		ὅ τι		
	ὅντινα			ἥντινα		ὅ τι		
	οὗτινος	or	ὅτου	ἧστινος		οὗτινος	or	ὅτου
	ᾧτινι	or	ὅτῳ	ἧτινι		ᾧτινι	or	ὅτῳ
DUAL	ὥτινε			ὥτινε		ὥτινε		
	οἷντινοιν			or		ὅτοιν		
PLUR.	οἵτινες			αἵτινες		ἅτινα	or	ἅττα
	οὕστινας			ἅστινας		ἅτινα		ἅττα
	ὧντινων	or	ὅτων	ὧντινων		ὧντινων	or	ὅτων
	οἷστισι	or	ὅτοις	αἷστισι		οἷστισι	or	ὅτοις

VERBS

52. Greek verbs, in addition to the full inflexions of the Latin verb, have

(1) **2nd and 3rd person** dual throughout.

(2) An **aorist tense** [1] in all moods.

(3) An **optative mood,** used for wishes, potentiality, and many subordinate clauses in secondary sequence.

(4) A **middle voice,** sometimes conveying the interest of the doer in the action, sometimes with reflexive meaning.

(5) **Infinitives** and **participles** with present future aorist and perfect forms in active middle and passive voices.

The **imperfect** and **pluperfect** tenses exist only in the **indicative.**

53. Primary tenses include present, future and perfect, and the whole subjunctive mood.[2]

Secondary tenses include imperfect, aorist, and pluperfect and the whole optative mood.[3]

Primary and secondary tenses show some differences of termination.

	Primary	Secondary
3rd pers. plur. active	-σι	-ν
3rd pers. sing. and plur. mid. and pass.	-ται	-το
2nd and 3rd pers. dual active	-σθον, -σθον	-σθον, -σθην

54. The augment

The two main **secondary** tenses, *imperfect* and *aorist*, prefix **in the indicative** ἐ to the verb stem. This is called the augment.

Example.   Pres. λύω   Imperf. ἔλυον   Aor. ἔλυσα, *loose*

An initial ρ is doubled.

Example.   Pres. ῥίπτω   Imperf. ἔρριπτον, *throw*

An initial vowel is lengthened to form the augment.

α and ε become η,   ι ο υ become ι ω̄ ῡ

Example.   Pres. ἄγω   Imperf. ἦγον,   *lead*
              οἰκτείρω   ᾤκτειρον, *pity*

Augment by addition of ε is called *syllabic augment.*
Augment by lengthening of initial vowel is called *temporal augment.*

---

[1] ἀόριστος, *undefined,* i.e. past indefinite.   [2] Present, aorist, and perfect subjunctive.
[3] Present aorist and perfect optative.   The future optative is very rare.

55. Reduplication

Perfects of all moods reduplicate as follows :

(a) Verbs with a single initial consonant prefix *that consonant* + ε to the verb stem. Include with single consonants a *mute* + *liquid* as

βλ	βρ	γλ	γρ	δρ	θλ	θρ	κλ	κρ	κν
πρ	πλ	πν	τλ	τρ	φλ	φρ	χλ	χρ	

Example. Pres. λύω   Perf. λέλυκα,   *loose*
               παύω   πέπαυκα, *stop*
               κλείω   κέκλεικα, *shut*
               κρούω   κέκρουκα, *strike*

(b) Verbs beginning with an *aspirated consonant* prefix the *unaspirated* form of the consonant + ε.

Example. Pres. θύω   Perf. τέθυκα,   *sacrifice*
               φύω   πέφυκα,   *bring forth*
               χράω   κέχρηκα, *give an oracle*

56.

(c) *Augment instead of reduplication* is used in verbs beginning with :

(1) A vowel or diphthong.
(2) A double consonant (ζ, ξ, ψ).
(3) Two consonants other than those given just above, in Par. 55, (a).

Example. Pres. ὁρμάω   Perf. ὥρμηκα,   *rush*
               μνημονεύω   ἐμνημόνευκα, *remind*

57.

Pluperfect[1] *indicative* adds *augment to reduplication* where possible.

Pres. λύω	Aor. ἔλυσα	Perf. λέλυκα	Plup. ἐλελύκη,	*loose*
στερέω	ἐστέρησα	ἐστέρηκα	ἐστερήκη,	*deprive*
οἰκέω	ᾤκησα	ᾤκηκα	ᾠκήκη,	*dwell*

58.

Verbs compounded with a preposition augment and reduplicate *after* the preposition.

Example. Pres. προσβάλλω   Imperf. προσέβαλλον, *attack*

Prepositions, except περί and πρό, drop a final vowel before the augment.

Example. Pres. ἀποβάλλω   Imperf. ἀπέβαλλον, *throw away*
               περιβάλλω   περιέβαλλον, *surround*

---

[1] Pluperfect is not common, and is always formed regularly from perfect.

Chief prepositions compounded with verbs :

ἀνά	εἰς		κατά	πρός
ἀπό	ἐκ	(ἐξ before a vowel)	μετά	συν (συμ before a labial

ανά   εἰς   κατά   πρός
ἀπό   ἐκ   (ἐξ before a vowel)   μετά   συν (συμ before a labial
                                                  συγ before a guttural[1]
                                                  συλ before a liquid)[3]

ἀντί   ἐν   (ἐμ before a labial [1]   παρά   ὑπέρ
            ἐγ before a guttural
            ἐλ before a liquid)[3]

διά   ἐπί   περί   ὑπό

Look out for, and remember to remove, inserted augments or reduplication in looking up such forms as

κατεκύλινδον	from	κατακυλίνδω,	*roll down*
συνέχαιρον	from	συγχαίρω,	*rejoice with*
ἀπελελύκη	from	ἀπολύω,	*release*
ἐξέκλησα	from	ἐκκλείω,	*shut out*

59. Examples of augment and reduplication

In order to emphasise the rules for their formation, these are not grouped according to type.

Pres.	Aor.	Perf.	Pluperf.	Meaning
ἀδικέω	ἠδίκησα	ἠδίκηκα	ἠδικήκη,	*wrong*
ἀπαιτέω	ἀπήτησα	ἀπήτηκα	ἀπητήκη,	*demand*
ἐκπέμπω	ἐξέπεμψα	ἐκπέπομφα [2]	ἐξεπεπόμφη,	*send out*
θηρεύω	ἐθήρευσα	τεθήρευκα	ἐτεθηρεύκη,	*hunt*
ἱκετεύω	ἱκέτευσα	ἱκέτευκα	ἱκετεύκη,	*entreat*
κελεύω	ἐκέλευσα	κεκέλευκα	ἐκεκελεύκη,	*command*
κρούω	ἔκρουσα	κέκρουκα	ἐκεκρούκη,	*knock*
ὀρθόω	ὤρθωσα	ὤρθωκα	ὠρθώκη,	*set straight*
παύω	ἔπαυσα	πέπαυκα	ἐπεπαύκη,	*check*
στρατεύω	ἐστράτευσα	ἐστράτευκα	ἐστρατεύκη,	*serve as soldier*
ὑβρίζω	ὕβρισα	ὕβρικα	ὑβρίκη,	*insult*
φιλέω	ἐφίλησα	πεφίληκα	ἐπεφιλήκη,	*love*

Reduplication of perfect is used in **all moods**.
Augment is used only in **indicative**.
Augment + reduplication is used only for **pluperfect indicative**.
Augment *pro reduplicatione* is used in **all moods**.

[1] See consonant changes (p. 142).   [2] Slightly irregular.   [3] λ or ρ.

60. I. Verbs in -ω

A **Uncontracted** : stem in ι or υ.

λύω, *I loose,*

Active

		Indicative	Imperative	Subjunctive
Present	S. 1	λύω	—	λύω
λύω, *I loose,*	2	λύεις	λῦε	λύῃς
am loosing	3	λύει	λυέτω	λύῃ
	D. 2	λύετον	λυέτον	λύητον
	3	λύετον	λυέτων	λύητον
	P. 1	λύομεν	—	λύωμεν
	2	λύετε	λύετε	λύητε
	3	λύουσι(ν)	λυόντων	λύωσι(ν)

Imperfect	S. 1	ἔλυον
ἔλυον, *I was*	2	ἔλυες
loosing	3	ἔλυε
	D. 2	ἐλύετον
	3	ἐλυέτην
	P. 1	ἐλύομεν
	2	ἐλύετε
	3	ἔλυον

Future	S. 1	λύσω
λύσω, *I shall*	2	λύσεις
loose	3	λύσει
Note charac-	D. 2	λύσετον
teristic -σ-	3	λύσετον
	P. 1	λύσομεν
	2	λύσετε
	3	λύσουσι(ν)

Active

Optative	Infinitive	Participle
S. 1 λύοιμι	λύειν	λύων λύουσα λῦον
2 λύοις		λύοντα,[1] etc.
3 λύοι		
D. 1 λύοιτον		
3 λυοίτην		
P. 1 λύοιμεν		
2 λύοιτε		
3 λύοιεν		

S. 1 λύσοιμι [2]	λύσειν	λύσων [1] λύσουσα λῦσον
2 λύσοις		λύσοντα, etc.
3 λύσοι		
D. 2 λύσοιτον		
3 λυσοίτην		
P. 1 λύσοιμεν		
2 λύσοιτε		
3 λύσοιεν		

[1] See Par. 31.   [2] Fut. opt. is only found in indirect speech.   Syntax F 2.

Verbs in -ω

A **Uncontracted** : stem in ι or υ.

Active

			Indicative	Imperative	Subjunctive
Aorist	S.	1	ἔλυσα	—	λύσω
ἔλυσα, *I loosed*		2	ἔλυσας	λῦσον	λύσῃς
Note character-		3	ἔλυσε	λυσάτω	λύσῃ
istic -σα-	D.	2	ἐλύσατον	λύσατον	λύσητον
		3	ἐλυσάτην	λυσάτων	λύσητον
	P.	1	ἐλύσαμεν	—	λύσωμεν
		2	ἐλύσατε	λύσατε	λύσητε
		3	ἔλυσαν	λυσάντων	λύσωσι(ν)

Perfect	S.	1	λέλυκα	—	λελύκω
λέλυκα, *I have*		2	λέλυκας	λέλυκε	λελύκῃς
loosed		3	λέλυκε(ν)	λελυκέτω	λελύκῃ
Note charac-	D.	2	λελύκατον	λελύκετον	λελύκητον
teristic -κ-		3	λελύκατον	λελυκέτων	λελύκητον
	P.	1	λελύκαμεν	—	λελύκωμεν
		2	λελύκατε	λελύκετε	λελύκητε
		3	λελύκασι(ν)	λελυκόντων	λελύκωσι(ν)

Pluperfect	S.	1	ἐλελύκη
ἐλελύκη, *I had*		2	ἐλελύκης
loosed		3	ἐλελύκει
	D.	2	ἐλελύκετον
		3	ἐλελυκέτην
	P.	1	ἐλελύκεμεν
		2	ἐλελύκετε
		3	ἐλελύκεσαν

Active

Optative [1]	Infinitive	Participle
S. 1 λύσαιμι	λῦσαι	λύσας λύσασα λῦσαν,
2 λύσειας		λύσαντα,[2] etc.
3 λύσειε		
D. 2 λύσαιτον		
3 λυσαίτην		
P. 1 λύσαιμεν		
2 λύσαιτε		
3 λύσειαν		

S. 1 λελύκοιμι	λελυκέναι	λελυκώς [2] -κυῖα -κός
2 λελύκοις		λελυκότα, etc.
3 λελύκοι		
D. 2 λελύκοιτον		
3 λελυκοίτην		
P. 1 λελύκοιμεν		
2 λελύκοιτε		
3 λελύκοιεν		

[1] Aor. Opt. has also 2nd and 3rd sing. λύσαις, λύσαι and 3rd plur. λύσαιεν.
[2] See Par. 31.

Verbs in -ω
Uncontracted : stem in ι or υ.

Middle and passive

			Indicative	Imperative	Subjunctive
Present	S.	1	λύομαι	—	λύωμαι
λύομαι		2	λύει	λύου	λύῃ
Mid. *I loose for*		3	λύεται	λυέσθω	λύηται
myself	D.	2	λύεσθον	λύεσθον	λύησθον
Pass. *I am*		3	λύεσθον	λυέσθων	λύησθον
being loosed	P.	1	λυόμεθα	—	λυώμεθα
		2	λύεσθε	λύεσθε	λύησθε
		3	λύονται	λυέσθων	λύωνται

Imperfect	S.	1	ἐλυόμην
ἐλυόμην		2	ἐλύου
Mid. *I was*		3	ἐλύετο
loosing for	D.	2	ἐλύεσθον
myself		3	ἐλυέσθην
Pass. *I was*	P.	1	ἐλυόμεθα
being loosed		2	ἐλύεσθε
		3	ἐλύοντο

Middle and passive

		Optative	Infinitive	Participle
S.	1	λυοίμην	λύεσθαι	λυόμενος -η -ον
	2	λύοιο		
	3	λύοιτο		
D.	2	λύοισθον		
	3	λυοίσθην		
P.	1	λυοίμεθα		
	2	λύοισθε		
	3	λύοιντο		

Verbs in -ω
Uncontracted : stem in ι or υ

Middle only

		Indicative	Imperative	Subjunctive
Future	S. 1	λύσομαι	—	
λύσομαι	2	λύσει		
Mid. *I shall*	3	λύσεται		
loose for myself D.	2	λύσεσθον		
Note character-	3	λύσεσθον		
istic -σ-	P. 1	λυσόμεθα		
	2	λύσεσθε		
	3	λύσονται		

Aorist	S. 1	ἐλυσάμην	—	λύσωμαι
ἐλυσάμην	2	ἐλύσω	λῦσαι	λύσῃ
Mid. *I loosed*	3	ἐλύσατο	λυσάσθω	λύσηται
for myself D.	2	ἐλύσασθον	λύσασθον	λύσησθον
Note charac-	3	ἐλυσάσθην	λυσάσθων	λύσησθον
teristic -σα-	P. 1	ἐλυσάμεθα	—	λυσώμεθα
	2	ἐλύσασθε	λύσασθε	λύσησθε
	3	ἐλύσαντο	λυσάσθων	λύσωνται

Middle only

Optative [1]	Infinitive	Participle
S. 1 λυσοίμην	λύσεσθαι	λυσόμενος -η -ον
2 λύσοιο		
3 λύσοιτο		
D. 2 λύσοισθον		
3 λυσοίσθην		
P. 1 λυσοίμεθα		
2 λύσοισθε		
3 λύσοιντο		

S. 1 λυσαίμην	λύσασθαι	λυσάμενος, -η -ον
2 λύσαιο		
3 λύσαιτο		
D. 2 λύσαισθον		
3 λυσαίσθην		
P. 1 λυσαίμεθα		
2 λύσαισθε		
3 λύσαιντο		

[1] Fut. opt. is only found in indirect speech and even then is generally replaced by fut. indic.

Verbs in -ω
Uncontracted : stem in ι or υ

Passive only

			Indicative	Imperative	Subjunctive
Future	S.	1	λυθήσομαι		
λυθήσομαι		2	λυθήσει		
Pass. *I shall be*		3	λυθήσεται		
loosed	D.	2	λυθήσεσθον		
Note charac-		3	λυθήσεσθον		
teristic -θησ-	P.	1	λυθησόμεθα		
		2	λυθήσεσθε		
		3	λυθήσονται		

Aorist	S.	1	ἐλύθην	—	λυθῶ
ἐλύθην		2	ἐλύθης	λύθητι	λυθῇς
Pass. *I was*		3	ἐλύθη	λυθήτω	λυθῇ
loosed	D.	2	ἐλύθητον	λύθητον	λυθῆτον
Note charac-		3	ἐλυθήτην	λυθήτων	λυθῆτον
teristic -θη-	P.	1	ἐλύθημεν	—	λυθῶμεν
		2	ἐλύθητε	λύθητε	λυθῆτε
		3	ἐλύθησαν	λυθέντων	λυθῶσι(ν)

Passive only

Optative [1]	Infinitive	Participle
S. 1 λυθησοίμην	λυθήσεσθαι	λυθησόμενος -η -ον
2 λυθήσοιο		
3 λυθήσοιτο		
D. 2 λυθήσοισθον		
3 λυθησοίσθην		
P. 1 λυθησοίμεθα		
2 λυθήσοισθε		
3 λυθήσοιντο		

S. 1 λυθείην	λυθῆναι	λυθείς [2] λυθεῖσα λυθέν
2 λυθείης		λυθέντα, etc.
3 λυθείη		
D. 2 λυθεῖτον		
3 λυθείτην		
P. 1 λυθεῖμεν		
2 λυθεῖτε		
3 λυθεῖεν		

[1] Fut. opt. is only found in indirect speech and even then is usually replaced by fut. indic.

[2] See Par. 31.

Verbs in -ω
Uncontracted : stem in ι or υ

Middle and passive

			Indicative	Imperative	Subjunctive
Perfect	S.	1	λέλυμαι	—	λελυμένος ὦ
λέλυμαι		2	λέλυσαι	λέλυσο	λελυμένος ᾖς
Mid. *I have*		3	λέλυται	λελύσθω	λελυμένος ᾖ
loosed for myself	D.	2	λέλυσθον	λέλυσθον	λελυμένω ἦτον
Pass. *I have*		3	λέλυσθον	λελύσθων	λελυμένω ἦτον
been loosed	P.	1	λελύμεθα	—	λελυμένοι ὦμεν
		2	λέλυσθε	λέλυσθε	λελυμένοι ἦτε
		3	λέλυνται	λελύσθων	λελυμένοι ὦσι(ν)

Pluperfect	S.	1	ἐλελύμην
ἐλελύμην		2	ἐλέλυσο
Mid. *I had*		3	ἐλέλυτο
loosed for	D.	2	ἐλέλυσθον
myself		3	ἐλελύσθην
Pass. *I had*	P.	1	ἐλελύμεθα
been loosed		2	ἐλέλυσθε
		3	ἐλέλυντο

Middle and passive

Optative		Infinitive	Participle
S. 1	λελυμένος εἴην	λελύσθαι	λελυμένος -η -ον
2	λελυμένος εἴης		
3	λελυμένος εἴη		
D. 2	λελυμένω εἶτον		
3	λελυμένω εἴτην		
P. 1	λελυμένοι εἶμεν		
2	λελυμένοι εἶτε		
3	λελυμένοι εἶεν		

61. Verbs in -ω

B 1. **Contracted** : stem in α as τιμάω, *I honour*.

Active

			Indicative	Imperative	Subjunctive [1]
Present	S.	1	τιμῶ	—	τιμῶ
		2	τιμᾷς	τίμα	τιμᾷς
		3	τιμᾷ	τιμάτω	τιμᾷ
	D.	2	τιμᾶτον	τιμᾶτον	τιμᾶτον
		3	τιμᾶτον	τιμάτων	τιμᾶτον
	P.	1	τιμῶμεν	—	τιμῶμεν
		2	τιμᾶτε	τιμᾶτε	τιμᾶτε
		3	τιμῶσι	τιμώντων	τιμῶσι

Imperfect	S.	1	ἐτίμων	
		2	ἐτίμας	$α + ε$ or $η = \bar{α}$
		3	ἐτίμα	
	D.	2	ἐτιμᾶτον	$α + ει$ or $η = ᾳ$
		3	ἐτιμάτην	
	P.	1	ἐτιμῶμεν	$α + o$ or $ου$ or $ω = ω$
		2	ἐτιμᾶτε	
		3	ἐτίμων	$α + οι$ $= ῳ$

Future		τιμήσω		
Aorist	As	ἐτίμησα	τίμησον	τιμήσω
Perfect	λύω	τετίμηκα	τετίμηκε	τετιμήκω
Pluperfect		ἐτετιμήκη		

[1] Present indicative and present subjunctive are identical in α verbs, as α contracts to ᾱ with ε or η.

Verbs in -ω

Active

	Optative [1]	Infinitive	Participle
S. 1	τιμῴην	τιμᾶν	τιμῶν τιμῶσα τιμῶν
2	τιμῴης	(No *iota*	τιμῶντα, etc.
3	τιμῴη	*subscript*)	
D. 2	τιμῷτον		
3	τιμῴτην		
P. 1	τιμῷμεν·		
2	τιμῷτε		
3	τιμῷεν		

Future	τιμήσοιμι	τιμήσειν	τιμήσων -σουσα -σον
Aorist	τιμήσαιμι	τιμῆσαι	τιμήσας -σασα -σαν
Perfect	τετιμήκοιμι	τετιμηκέναι	τετιμηκώς -κυῖα -κός

---

[1] Notice this different type of optative, formed of α + -οίην, -οίης, -οίη, etc. It is found also with aor. pass. (-θείην, -θείης, - θείη) of all verbs, and with -μι verbs in pres. and aor. optat. act.

Verbs in -ω

B 1. **Contracted Verbs :** stem in α.

Middle and passive

			Indicative	Imperative	Subjunctive [1]
Present	S.	1	τιμῶμαι	—	τιμῶμαι
		2	τιμᾷ	τιμῶ	τιμᾷ
		3	τιμᾶται	τιμάσθω	τιμᾶται
	D.	2	τιμᾶσθον	τιμᾶσθον	τιμᾶσθον
		3	τιμᾶσθον	τιμάσθων	τιμᾶσθον
	P.	1	τιμώμεθα	—	τιμώμεθα
		2	τιμᾶσθε	τιμᾶσθε	τιμᾶσθε
		3	τιμῶνται	τιμάσθων	τιμῶνται

Imperfect	S.	1	ἐτιμώμην
		2	ἐτιμῶ
		3	ἐτιμᾶτο
	D.	2	ἐτιμᾶσθον
		3	ἐτιμάσθην
	P.	1	ἐτιμώμεθα
		2	ἐτιμᾶσθε
		3	ἐτιμῶντο

$α + ε$	or	$η = α$
$α + ει$	or	$η = ᾳ$
$α + o$ or $ου$ or $ω = ω$		
$α + οι$		$= ῳ$

Fut. Mid.	τιμήσομαι		
Fut. Pass.	τιμηθήσομαι		
Aorist Mid.	ἐτιμησάμην	τίμησαι	τιμήσωμαι
Aorist Pass.	ἐτιμήθην	τιμήθητι	τιμηθῶ
Perf. Mid. and Pass.	τετίμημαι	τετίμησο	τετιμημένος ὦ
Plup. Mid. and Pass.	ἐτετιμήμην		

[1] Same as pres. indic.   Why?

Verbs in -ω

Middle and passive

	Optative	Infinitive	Participle
S. 1	τιμώμην	τιμᾶσθαι	τιμώμενος -η -ον
2	τιμῷο		
3	τιμῷτο		
D. 2	τιμῷσθον		
3	τιμῴσθην		
P. 1	τιμῴμεθα		
2	τιμῷσθε		
3	τιμῷντο		

Future Mid.	τιμησοίμην	τιμήσεσθαι	τιμησόμενος
Future Pass.	τιμηθησοίμην	τιμηθήσεσθαι	τιμηθησόμενος
Aorist Mid.	τιμησαίμην	τιμήσασθαι	τιμησάμενος
Aorist Pass.	τιμηθείην	τιμηθῆναι	τιμηθείς
Perf. Mid. and Pass.	τετιμημένος εἴην	τετιμῆσθαι	τετιμημένος

62. Verbs in -ω
B 2. **Contracted :** stem in ε as ποιέω, *I do.*

Active

		Indicative	Imperative	Subjunctive
Present	S. 1	ποιῶ	—	ποιῶ
	2	ποιεῖς	ποίει	ποιῇς
	3	ποιεῖ	ποιείτω	ποιῇ
	D. 2	ποιεῖτον	ποιεῖτον	ποιῆτον
	3	ποιεῖτον	ποιείτων	ποιῆτον
	P. 1	ποιοῦμεν	—	ποιῶμεν
	2	ποιεῖτε	ποιεῖτε	ποιῆτε
	3	ποιοῦσι(ν)	ποιούντων	ποιῶσι(ν)

Imperfect	S. 1	ἐποίουν
	2	ἐποίεις
	3	ἐποίει
	D. 2	ἐποιεῖτον
	3	ἐποιείτην
	P. 1	ἐποιοῦμεν
	2	ἐποιεῖτε
	3	ἐποίουν

Future	ποιήσω		
Aorist	ἐποίησα	ποίησον	ποιήσω
Perfect	πεποίηκα	πεποίηκε	πεποιήκω
Pluperfect	ἐπεποιήκη		

Verbs in -ω

Active

	Optative	Infinitive	Participle
S. 1	ποιοίην	ποιεῖν	ποιῶν ποιοῦσα ποιοῦν
2	ποιοίης		ποιοῦντα, etc.
3	ποιοίη		
D. 2	ποιοῖτον		
3	ποιοίτην		
P. 1	ποιοῖμεν		
2	ποιοῖτε		
3	ποιοῖεν		

$\epsilon + \epsilon = \epsilon\iota$

$\epsilon + o = ov$

ϵ before any long vowel or diphthong disappears.

Disyllabic verbs contract only $\epsilon\epsilon$ and $\epsilon\epsilon\iota$, as πλέω, πλεῖς, πλεῖ, πλέομεν, etc. *I sail.* *Exception*: δέω, *I bind*, contracted throughout.

Future	ποιήσοιμι	ποιήσειν	ποιήσων
Aorist	ποιήσαιμι	ποιῆσαι	ποιήσας
Perfect	πεποιήκοιμι	πεποιηκέναι	πεποιηκώς

Verbs in -ω

B 2. **Contracted :** stem in ε.

Middle and passive

			Indicative	Imperative	Subjunctive
Present	S.	1	ποιοῦμαι	—	ποιῶμαι
		2	ποιεῖ	ποιοῦ	ποιῇ
		3	ποιεῖται	ποιείσθω	ποιῆται
	D.	2	ποιεῖσθον	ποιεῖσθον	ποιῆσθον
		3	ποιεῖσθον	ποιείσθων	ποιῆσθον
	P.	1	ποιούμεθα	—	ποιώμεθα
		2	ποιεῖσθε	ποιεῖσθε	ποιῆσθε
		3	ποιοῦνται	ποιείσθων	ποιῶνται
Imperfect	S.	1	ἐποιούμην		
		2	ἐποιοῦ		
		3	ἐποιεῖτο		
	D.	2	ἐποιεῖσθον		
		3	ἐποιείσθην		
	P.	1	ἐποιούμεθα		
		2	ἐποιεῖσθε		
		3	ἐποιοῦντο		

	Indicative	Imperative	Subjunctive
Future Mid.	ποιήσομαι		
Future Pass.	ποιηθήσομαι		
Aorist Mid.	ἐποιησάμην	ποίησαι	ποιήσωμαι
Aorist Pass.	ἐποιήθην	ποιήθητι	ποιηθῶ
Perf. Mid. and Pass.	πεποίημαι	πεποίησο	πεποιημένος ὦ
Plup. Mid. and Pass.	ἐπεποιήμην		

Verbs in -ω

Middle and passive

		Optative	Infinitive	Participle
S.	1	ποιοίμην	ποιεῖσθαι	ποιούμενος -η -ον
	2	ποιοῖο		
	3	ποιοῖτο		
D.	2	ποιοῖσθον		
	3	ποιοίσθην		
P.	1	ποιοίμεθα		
	2	ποιοῖσθε		
	3	ποιοῖντο		

$\epsilon + \epsilon = \epsilon\iota$

$\epsilon + o = ov$

ϵ before any long vowel or diphthong disappears.

Future Mid.	ποιησοίμην	ποιήσεσθαι	ποιησόμενος
Future Pass.	ποιηθησοίμην	ποιηθήσεσθαι	ποιηθησόμενος
Aorist Mid.	ποιησαίμην	ποιήσασθαι	ποιησάμενος
Aorist Pass.	ποιηθείην	ποιηθῆναι	ποιηθείς
Perf. Mid. and Pass.	πεποιημένος εἴην	πεποιῆσθαι	πεποιημένος

63. Verbs in -ω

B 3. **Contracted** : stem in o as δηλόω, *I show*.

Active

			Indicative	Imperative	Subjunctive
Present	S.	1	δηλῶ	—	δηλῶ [1]
		2	δηλοῖς	δήλου	δηλοῖς
		3	δηλοῖ	δηλούτω	δηλοῖ
	D.	2	δηλοῦτον	δηλοῦτον	δηλῶτον
		3	δηλοῦτον	δηλούτων	δηλῶτον
	P.	1	δηλοῦμεν	—	δηλῶμεν
		2	δηλοῦτε	δηλοῦτε	δηλῶτε
		3	δηλοῦσι(ν)	δηλούντων	δηλῶσι(ν)

Imperfect	S.	1	ἐδήλουν
		2	ἐδήλους
		3	ἐδήλου
	D.	2	ἐδηλοῦτον
		3	ἐδηλούτην
	P.	1	ἐδηλοῦμεν
		2	ἐδηλοῖτε
		3	ἐδήλουν

o + ε or o or ου	=	ου
o + η or ω	=	ω
o + ει or η or οι	=	οι

Future	δηλώσω		
Aorist	ἐδήλωσα	δήλωσον	δηλώσω
Perfect	δεδήλωκα	δεδήλωκε	δεδηλώκω
Pluperfect	ἐδεδηλώκη		

[1] Contracted from δηλόω, δηλόῃς, δηλόῃ, δηλόητον, δηλόητον, δηλόωμεν, δηλόητε δηλόωσι. See rules.

Verbs in -ω

Active

		Optative	Infinitive	Participle
S.	1	δηλοίην	δηλοῦν	δηλῶν δηλοῦσα δηλοῦν
	2	δηλοίης	(No *iota*	δηλοῦντα, etc.
	3	δηλοίη	*subscript*)	
D.	2	δηλοῖτον		
	3	δηλοίτην		
P.	1	δηλοῖμεν		
	2	δηλοῖτε		
	3	δηλοῖεν		

Future	δηλώσοιμι	δηλώσειν	δηλώσων
Aorist	δηλώσαιμι	δηλῶσαι	δηλώσας
Perfect	δεδηλώκοιμι	δεδηλωκέναι	δεδηλωκώς

Verbs in -ω

B 3. **Contracted** : stem in o.

Middle and passive

		Indicative	Imperative	Subjunctive
Present	S. 1	δηλοῦμαι	—	δηλῶμαι
	2	δηλοῖ	δηλοῦ	δηλοῖ [1]
	3	δηλοῦται	δηλούσθω	δηλῶται
	D. 2	δηλοῦσθον	δηλοῦσθον	δηλῶσθον
	3	δηλοῦσθον	δηλούσθων	δηλῶσθον
	P. 1	δηλούμεθα	—	δηλώμεθα
	2	δηλοῦσθε	δηλοῦσθε	δηλῶσθε
	3	δηλοῦνται	δηλούσθων	δηλῶνται

Imperfect	S. 1	ἐδηλούμην
	2	ἐδηλοῦ
	3	ἐδηλοῦτο
	D. 2	ἐδηλοῦσθον
	3	ἐδηλούσθην
	P. 1	ἐδηλούμεθα
	2	ἐδηλοῦσθε
	3	ἐδηλοῦντο

o + ε or o or ου = ου
o + η or ω = ω
o + ει or η or οι = οι

Future Mid.	δηλώσομαι		
Future Pass.	δηλωθήσομαι		
Aorist Mid.	ἐδηλωσάμην	δήλωσαι	δηλώσωμαι
Aorist Pass.	ἐδηλώθην	δηλώθητι	δηλωθῶ
Perf. Mid. and Pass.	δεδήλωμαι	δεδήλωσο	δεδηλωμένος ὦ
Plup. Mid. and Pass.	ἐδεδηλώμην		

[1] Contracted from δηλόῃ. In pres. indic. mid. δηλοῖ represents δηλόει.

Verbs in -ω

Middle and passive

	Optative	Infinitive	Participle
S. 1	δηλοίμην	δηλοῦσθαι	δηλούμενος -η -ον
2	δηλοῖο		
3	δηλοῖτο		
D. 2	δηλοῖσθον		
3	δηλοίσθην		
P. 1	δηλοίμεθα		
2	δηλοῖσθε		
3	δηλοῖντο		

Future Mid.	δηλωσοίμην	δηλώσεσθαι	δηλωσόμενος
Future Pass.	δηλωθησοίμην	δηλωθήσεσθαι	δηλωθησόμενος
Aorist Mid.	δηλωσαίμην	δηλώσασθαι	δηλωσάμενος
Aorist Pass.	δηλωθείην	δηλωθῆναι	δηλωθείς
Perf. Mid. and Pass.	δεδηλωμένος εἴην	δεδηλῶσθαι	δεδηλωμένος

64. Verbs in -ω

C 1. Consonant stems : **Guttural**, κ, γ, χ, σκ, σσ (ττ).

Guttural + σ combines to form ξ.

```
      „     + κ      „      „      χ.
      „  before τ  becomes     κ.
      „     „   θ      „         χ.
      „     „   μ      „         γ.
```

Example. πράσσω, *I do.* Perfect, Mid. and Pass.

S.		D.		P.	
1.	πέπραγμαι			1.	περπάγμεθα
2.	πέπραξαι	2.	πέπραχθον [2]	2.	πέπραχθε [2]
3.	πέπρακται	3.	πέπραχθον	3.	πεπραγμένοι εἰσίν [1]

Apart from these consonant changes the tense endings are like those of λύω ; e.g. Aor. Act. ἔπραξα, ἔπραξας, ἔπραξε, etc.

Example. πράσσω, *I do, make, fare.*

Active

	Indicative	Imperative	Subjunctive
Present	πράσσω	πρᾶσσε	πράσσω
Imperfect	ἔπρασσον		
Future	πράξω		
Aorist	ἔπραξα	πρᾶξον	πράξω
Perfect	πέπραχα	πέπραχε	πεπράχω
Pluperfect	ἐπεπράχη		

Middle and passive

	Indicative	Imperative	Subjunctive
Pres. Mid and Pass.	πράσσομαι	πράσσου	πράσσωμαι
Imperf. Mid. and Pass.	ἐπρασσόμην		
Future Mid.	πράξομαι		
Future Pass.	πραχθήσομαι		
Aorist Mid.	ἐπραξάμην	πρᾶξαι	πράξωμαι
Aorist Pass.	ἐπράχθην	πράχθητι	πραχθῶ
Perf. Mid. and Pass.	πέπραγμαι [3]	πέπραξο	πεπραγμένος ὦ
		πεπράχθω, etc.	
Plup. Mid. and Pass.	ἐπεπράγμην		

[1] Note compound, to avoid three consecutive consonants which -νται ending would give.

[2] σ omitted between χ and θ.   [3] See above for full inflection.

Verbs in -ω

Active

	Optative	Infinitive	Participle
Present	πράσσοιμι	πράσσειν	πράσσων
Future	πράξοιμι	πράξειν	πράξων
Aorist	πράξαιμι	πρᾶξαι	πράξας
Perfect	πεπράχοιμι	πεπραχέναι	πεπραχώς

Middle and passive

	Optative	Infinitive	Participle
Pres. Mid.	πρασσοίμην	πράσσεσθαι	πρασσόμενος
Fut. Mid.	πραξοίμην	πράξεσθαι	πραξόμενος
Fut. Pass.	πραχθησοίμην	πραχθήσεσθαι	πραχθησόμενος
Aor. Mid.	πραξαίμην	πράξασθαι	πραξάμενος
Aor. Pass.	πραχθείην	πραχθῆναι	πραχθείς
Perf. Mid. and Pass.	πεπραγμένος εἴην	πέπραχθαι [1]	πεπραγμένος

[1] σ omitted between χ and θ.

65. Verbs in -ω

C 2. Consonant stems : **Labial,** $\pi, \beta, \phi, \pi\tau$.

Labial $+\sigma$ combines to form ψ.
    ,, $+\kappa$,,   ,,   ,, ϕ.
    ,, before τ becomes π.
    ,,   ,, θ ,, ϕ.
    ,,   ,, μ ,, μ.

Example. βλάπτω, *I injure.* Perfect, Mid. and Pass.

S. 1. βέβλαμμαι   D.   P. 1. βεβλάμμεθα
   2. βέβλαψαι   2. βέβλαφθον   2. βέβλαφθε
   3. βέβλαπται   3. βέβλαφθον   3. βεβλαμμένοι εἰσίν

The indicative paradigm only is given below. Other moods are formed regularly, and correspond to the equivalent indicative tense. The imperfect is as for λύω, as it has vowel endings. Contrast contracted verbs.

INDICATIVE

	Pres.	Fut.	Aor.	Perf.
Active	βλάπτω	βλάψω	ἔβλαψα	βέβλαφα
Middle	βλάπτομαι	βλάψομαι	ἐβλαψάμην	βέβλαμμαι
Passive	βλάπτομαι	βλαφθήσομαι	ἐβλάφθην	βέβλαμμαι

66. Verbs in -ω

C 3. Consonant Stems : **Dentals,** $\tau, \delta, \theta, \zeta$.

Dental before σ disappears.
    ,,   ,, κ ,,
    ,,   ,, μ becomes σ.
    ,,   ,, τ ,, σ.
    ,,   ,, θ ,, σ.

Example. πείθω, *I persuade.* Perfect, Mid. and Pass.

S. 1. πέπεισμαι   D.   P. 1. πεπείσμεθα
   2. πέπεισαι   2. πέπεισθον   2. πέπεισθε [1]
   3. πέπεισται   3. πέπεισθον   3. πεπεισμένοι εἰσίν

[1] In consonant verbs -σθον, -σθε and -σθαι endings are treated as -θον, -θε and -θαι. See perf. mid. and pass. indic., imper., and infin.

Stems in -ιζω, if the verb contains more than two syllables, form futures active and middle by dropping σ and contracting -εω and -εομαι throughout like ποιέω (p. 222).

Example. νομίζω, *I consider*, fut. indic. νομιῶ, νομιεῖς, νομιεῖ, νομιοῦμεν, etc. fut. optat. νομιοίην, fut. infin. act. νομιεῖν, fut. infin. mid. νομιεῖσθαι.

INDICATIVE

	Pres.	Fut.	Aor.	Perf.
Active	πείθω, *I persuade*	πείσω	ἔπεισα	πέπεικα
	κομίζω, *I carry*	κομιῶ, -εῖς, etc.	ἐκόμισα	κεκόμικα
Middle	πείθομαι	πείσομαι	—	πέπεισμαι
	κομίζομαι	κομιοῦμαι	ἐκομισάμην	κεκόμισμαι
Passive	πείθομαι	πεισθήσομαι	ἐπείσθην	πέπεισμαι
	κομίζομαι	κομισθήσομαι	ἐκομίσθην	κεκόμισμαι

67. Verbs in -ω

C 4. Consonant stems : **Liquids,** λ, ρ, μ, ν.
Liquids do not form futures or aorists in σ.
Future active and middle are in -εω and -εομαι contracted.
λλ becomes λ. *Example.* στέλλω, *I send* ; future στελῶ.
The stem vowel is often shortened.
Example. φθείρω, *I destroy.*

Future paradigm :

active	φθερῶ	φθεροίην	φθερεῖν	φθερῶν, -οῦσα, -οῦν
middle	φθεροῦμαι	φθεροίμην	φθερεῖσθαι	φθερούμενος

Aorist active and middle : usual endings, but without σ.

Example. ἔνειμα, ἔνειμας, ἔνειμε, etc.

A short stem vowel in present is lengthened.

Example. νέμω, *I distribute.* Aor. ἔνειμα.

Aor. Act. paradigm : ἔνειμα, νεῖμον, νείμω, νείμαιμι, νεῖμαι, νείμας, -ασα, -αν.

Perfect. Often with stem variation.
λ and ρ stand unaltered before perfect endings, active and middle.
μ and ν often insert η before perfect endings.

Examples. μένω, *I remain*, μεμένηκα, νέμω, *I distribute*, νενέμηκα.

ν is sometimes dropped.

Example. κρίνω, *I judge* : κέκρικα, κέκριμαι.

Verbs in -ω (*continued*)

C 4. Consonant stems : **Liquids,** λ, ρ, μ, ν.

	Present	Future	Aorist	Perfect
Act.	ἀγγέλλω, *announce*	ἀγγελῶ, -εῖς, εῖ,	ἤγγειλα	ἤγγελκα
Mid.	ἀγγέλλομαι	ἀγγελοῦμαι	ἠγγειλάμην	ἤγγελμαι
Pass.	ἀγγέλλομαι	ἀγγελθήσομαι	ἠγγέλθην	ἤγγελμαι
Act.	σπείρω, *sow*	σπερῶ (-εω)	ἔσπειρα	ἔσπαρκα
Mid.	σπείρομαι	σπεροῦμαι	ἐσπειράμην	ἔσπαρμαι
Pass.	σπείρομαι	σπαρήσομαι [1]	ἐσπάρην [1]	ἔσπαρμαι
Act.	νέμω, *allot*	νεμῶ (-εω)	ἔνειμα	νενέμηκα
Mid.	νέμομαι	νεμοῦμαι	ἐνειμάμην	νενέμημαι
Pass.	νέμομαι	νεμηθήσομαι	ἐνεμήθην	νενέμημαι
Act.	κρίνω, *judge*	κρινῶ (-εω)	ἔκρινα	κέκρικα
Mid.	κρίνομαι	κρινοῦμαι	ἐκρινάμην	κέκριμαι
Pass.	κρίνομαι	κριθήσομαι	ἐκρίθην	κέκριμαι

68. Strong or second aorist

Some verbs, few in number but of common occurrence, form what is called a strong or second aorist, in active and middle voice. This tense, which takes the place of a weak or first (-σα) aorist in those verbs which possess it,[2] is formed from

a different stem from the present + imperfect endings in the indicative,

+ present endings in the other moods.

Example. βάλλω, *I throw.* Aor. ἔβαλον.

			Active			**Middle**
2nd Aorist	S.	1.	ἔβαλον	S.	1.	ἐβαλόμην
Indicative		2.	ἔβαλες		2.	ἐβάλου
		3.	ἔβαλε		3.	ἐβάλετο
	Pl.	1.	ἐβάλομεν	Pl.	1.	ἐβαλόμεθα
		2.	ἐβάλετε		2.	ἐβάλεσθε
		3.	ἔβαλον		3.	ἐβάλοντο

[1] (Par. 70).   [2] A few verbs have both, e.g. πείθω, ἔπεισα and ἔπιθον (poetic).

Example. βάλλω, *I throw.*

Active

Present	Ind. βάλλω	Imp. βάλλε	Subj. βάλλω
	Opt. βάλλοιμι	Inf. βάλλειν	Part. βάλλων

Imperfect   ἔβαλλον

Future [1]	Ind. βαλῶ		
	Opt. βαλοίην	Inf. βαλεῖν	Part. βαλῶν -οῦσα -οῦν βαλοῦντα, etc.

2nd Aorist	Ind. ἔβαλον	Imp. βάλε	Subj. βάλω
	Opt. βάλοιμι	Inf. βαλεῖν	Part. βαλών -οῦσα -όν βαλόντα, etc.

Middle

Present	Ind. βάλλομαι	Imp. βάλλου	Subj. βάλλωμαι
	Opt. βαλλοίμην	Inf. βάλλεσθαι	Part. βαλλόμενος
Imperfect	Ind. ἐβαλλόμην		

Future [1]	Ind. βαλοῦμαι		
	Opt. βαλοίμην βαλοῖο, etc.	Inf. βαλεῖσθαι	Part. βαλούμενος

2nd Aorist	Ind. ἐβαλόμην	Imp. βαλοῦ	Subj. βάλωμαι
	Opt. βαλοίμην βάλοιο βάλοιτο, etc.	Inf. βαλέσθαι	Part. βαλόμενος

[1] Contracted ε throughout.

Example. λαμβάνω, *I take.*

Active

Present	Ind. λαμβάνω	Imp. λάμβανε	Subj. λαμβάνω
	Opt. λαμβάνοιμι	Inf. λαμβάνειν	Part. λαμβάνων

Imperfect	ἐλάμβανον		

Future	Ind. λήψομαι, mid.		
(irreg.)	Opt. ληψοίμην	Inf. λήψεσθαι	Part. ληψόμενος

2nd Aorist	Ind. ἔλαβον	Imp. λαβέ	Subj. λάβω
	Opt. λάβοιμι	Inf. λαβεῖν	Part. λαβών -οῦσα -όν
			λαβόντα, etc.

Middle

Present	Ind. λαμβάνομαι	Imp. λαμβάνου	Subj. λαμβάνωμαι
	Opt. λαμβανοίμην	Inf. λαμβάνεσθαι	Part. λαμβανόμενος

Imperfect	ἐλαμβανόμην		

2nd Aorist	Ind. ἐλαβόμην	Inf. λαβοῦ	Subj. λάβωμαι
	Opt. λαβοίμην	Inf. λαβέσθαι	Part. λαβόμενος

69. Strong or second perfect active

These forms occur in some verbs, sometimes in addition to the weak forms. The endings are like those of weak perfects, only without κ or equivalent consonant, and sometimes with modification of the stem vowel. Often the strong perfect has intransitive sense.

Present	Weak Perfect	Strong Perfect
πράσσω, I do, I fare	πέπραχα, I have done (trans.)	πέπραγα, I have fared (intrans.)
ἀπόλλυμι, I destroy	ἀπολώλεκα, I have destroyed (trans.)	ἀπόλωλα, I have perished (intrans.)
διαφθείρω, I corrupt, destroy	διέφθαρκα, I have corrupted (trans.)	διέφθορα (generally transitive)

70. Strong or second future and aorist passive.

The endings for these are the same as for the equivalent weak tenses, only without θ. Sometimes there is vowel modification.

Fut. pass. adds -ήσομαι, -ήσει, -ήσεται, etc.

Aor. pass. adds -ην, -ης, -η, etc.

Both weak and strong aorist passives are found in a few verbs, often with no difference of meaning, occasionally alternative future passives also.

Examples. βλάπτω, I injure. ζεύγνυμι, I yoke. κλέπτω, I steal. διαφθείρω, I destroy. τρέπω, I turn.

Wk. fut. pass.	Wk. aor. passive	Str. fut. pass.	Str. aor. pass.
—	ἐβλάφθην	βλαβήσομαι	ἐβλάβην
—	ἐζεύχθην	ζυγήσομαι	ἐζύγην
κλεφθήσομαι	ἐκλέφθην	—	ἐκλάπην
διαφθεροῦμαι [1]	—	διαφθαρήσομαι	διεφθάρην
τρέψομαι [1]	ἐτρέφθην	—	ἐτράπην

2nd Aorist passive paradigm

τρέπω, Ind. ἐτράπην Imp. τράπητι Subj. τραπῶ
I turn. Opt. τραπείην Inf. τραπῆναι Part. τραπείς, -εῖσα, -έν, τραπέντα, etc.

[1] Middle with passive meaning.

71. Common verbs using several stems

Active

Pres.	Fut.	Aor.	Perf.
αἱρέω, *I take,* mid. *choose*	αἱρήσω	εἷλον	ᾕρηκα
ἀποκτείνω, *I kill*	ἀποκτενῶ (-εω)	ἀπέκτεινα	ἀπέκτονα
ἔρχομαι, *I go*	εἶμι [1] ἤξω	ἦλθον	ἐλήλυθα or ἥκω, *I come*
ἐσθίω, *I eat*	ἔδομαι	ἔφαγον	ἐδήδοκα
ζάω,[2] *I live*	βιώσομαι	ἐβίων [2]	βεβίωκα
λέγω, ἀγορεύω *I say*	λέξω or ἐρῶ (-εω)	εἶπον	εἴρηκα
ὁράω,[3] *I see*	ὄψομαι	εἶδον	ἑώρακα ὄπωπα (poetic)
τρέχω, *I run*	δραμοῦμαι	ἔδραμον	δεδράμηκα
φέρω, *I bear*	οἴσω	ἤνεγκον [2]	ἐνήνοχα
φέρομαι, mid. *I win*	οἴσομαι	ἠνεγκάμην	ἐνήνεγμαι

[1] See Par. 81.   [2] See Par. 72, p. 242-4.
[3] Imperf. ἑώρων with double augment.

Passive

Aor.	Perf.
ἑάλων or ᾑρέθην	ᾕρημαι
ἀπέθανον [1] *I die*, used as pass. of *kill*	τέθνηκα
ἠδέσθην	ἐδήδεσμαι
	βεβίωμαι
ἐλέχθην ἐρρήθην	εἴρημαι
ὤφθην [2]	ἑώραμαι ὦμμαι
ἠνέχθην	ἐνήνεγμαι

---

[1] From ἀποθνῄσκω, fut. ἀποθανοῦμαι, *die.*
[2] Fut. pass. ὀφθήσομαι.

72. Some second aorist paradigms

Note the difference between indicative and other moods, caused by the removal of the augment. εἶπον is for ἔειπον, hence the apparent retention of the augment in the other moods, e.g. εἰπεῖν. Contrast εἷλον, infinitive ἑλεῖν.

The aorist indicative is given in full where it is irregular. Otherwise it is as ἔβαλον (Par. 68), i.e. 2nd aorist stem + imperfect endings.

εἶπον and ἤνεγκον have an admixture of forms of -α 1st aorist type.

ἑάλων, ἔβην, ἐβίων and ἔγνων are -μι type 2nd aorists (cf. ἔστην, Par. 74).

Verb			Indic.	Imper.	Subjunc.
αἱρῶ (εω), *I take*			εἷλον	ἕλε	ἑλῶ
					-ῇς
					-ῇ
ἁλίσκομαι, *I am*	S.	1	ἑάλων, *I was caught*		ἁλῶ
caught		2	ἑάλως		ἁλῷς
		3	ἑάλω		ἁλῷ
	D.	4	ἑάλωτον		ἁλῶτον
		3	ἑαλώτην		ἁλῶτον
	P.	1	ἑάλωμεν		ἁλῶμεν
		2	ἑάλωτε		ἁλῶτε
		3	ἑάλωσαν		ἁλῶσι(ν)
ἀποθνῄσκω, *I die*			ἀπέθανον	ἀπόθανε	ἀποθάνω
-βαίνω,[1] *I go*	S.	1	ἔβην	—	βῶ
		2	ἔβης	βῆθι	βῇς
		3	ἔβη	βήτω	βῇ, etc.
	D.	2	ἔβητον	βῆτον	
		3	ἐβήτην	βήτων	
	P.	1	ἔβημεν	—	
		2	ἔβητε	βῆτε	
		3	ἔβησαν	βάντων	

[1] Usually compounded with a preposition, as ἀποβαίνω, *I go away*.

	Optat.	Infin.	Partic.
	ἕλοιμι	ἑλεῖν	ἑλών -οῦσα -όν ἑλόντα, etc.

		Optat.	Infin.	Partic.
S.	1	ἁλοίην	ἁλῶναι	ἁλούς -οῦσα -όν
	2	ἁλοίης		ἁλόντα, etc.
	3	ἁλοίη		
D.	2	ἅλοιτον		
	3	ἁλοίτην		
P.	1	ἅλοιμεν		
	2	ἅλοιτε		
	3	ἅλοιεν		

	Optat.	Infin.	Partic.
	ἀποθάνοιμι	ἀποθανεῖν	ἀποθανών -οῦσα -όν ἀποθανόντα, etc.

		Optat.	Infin.	Partic.
S.	1	βαίην	βῆναι	βάς βᾶσα βάν
	2	βαίης		βάντα, etc.
	3	βαίη, etc.		
D.	2			
	3			
P.	1			
	2			
	3			

Second aorist paradigms (*continued*)

Verb			Indic.	Imper.	Subjunc.
γιγνώσκω,	Aor. S.	1	ἔγνων	—	γνῶ
I get to know		2	ἔγνως	γνῶθι	γνῷς
		3	ἔγνω	γνώτω	γνῷ
	D.	2	ἔγνωτον	γνῶτον	γνῶτον
		3	ἐγνώτην	γνώτων	γνῶτον
	P.	1	ἔγνωμεν	—	γνῶμεν
		2	ἔγνωτε	γνῶτε	γνῶτε
		3	ἔγνωσαν	γνόντων	γνῶσι(ν)
ἔρχομαι, *I come*		Aor.	ἦλθον	ἐλθέ	ἔλθω -ῃς -ῃ
ζάω [1]	Contracts S.	1	ζῶ Aor. ἐβίων	βιῶθι	βιῶ
I live	Present	2	ζῇς ἐβίως	as γνῶθι	as γνῶ
		3	ζῇ ἐβίω		
	D.	2	ζῆτον ἐβίωτον		
		3	ζῆτον ἐβιώτην		
	P.	1	ζῶμεν ἐβίωμεν		
		2	ζῆτε ἐβίωτε		
		3	ζῶσιν ἐβίωσαν		
λέγω, *I say*	Aor. S.	1	εἶπον	—	εἴπω
		2	εἶπας	εἰπέ	-ῃς
		3	εἶπε	εἰπάτω	-ῃ
	D.	2	εἴπατον	εἴπατον	
		3	εἰπάτην	εἰπάτων	
	P.	1	εἴπομεν	—	
		2	εἴπατε	εἴπατε	
		3	εἶπον	εἰπόντων	
ὁρῶ (αω), *I see*		Aor.	εἶδον	—	ἴδω
				ἰδέ	-ῃς
				ἰδέτω	-ῃ
				ἰδέτον	
				ἰδέτων	
				—	
				ἰδέτε	
				ἰδόντων	

---

[1] Present infinitive ζῆν. Others in -αω that contract η instead of α are διψάω, *I thirst* ; πεινάω, *I hunger* ; χράω, *I give oracles* ; and χράομαι, *I use*.

		Optat.	Infin.	Partic.
S.	1	γνοίην,	γνῶναι	γνούς, γνοῦσα, γνόν
	2	etc		γνόντα, etc.
	3			
D.	2			
	3			
P.	1			
	2			
	3			
		ἔλθοιμι	ἐλθεῖν	ἐλθών -οῦσα -όν
				ἐλθόντα, etc.
S.	1	βιῴην, as	βιῶναι	βιούς βιοῦσα βιόν
	2	τιμῴην		βιόντα, etc.
	3			
D.	2			
	3			
P.	1			
	2			
	3			
S.	1	εἴποιμι	εἰπεῖν	εἰπών -οῦσα -όν
	2			εἰπόντα, etc.
	3			
D.	2			
	3			
P.	1			
	2			
	3			
		ἴδοιμι	ἰδεῖν	ἰδών -οῦσα -όν
				ἰδόντα, etc.

Second aorist paradigms (continued)

Verb				Indicative	Imperative	Subjunctive
φέρω,	Aor.	S.	1	ἤνεγκον [1]	—	ἐνέγκω
I bear			2	ἤνεγκας	ἔνεγκε	
			3	ἤνεγκε(ν)	ἐνεγκάτω, etc.	
		D.	2	ἠνέγκατον		
			3	ἠνεγκάτην		
		P.	1	ἠνέγκαμεν		
			2	ἠνέγκατε		
			3	ἤνεγκαν		

[1] Mostly 1st Aorist endings without σ.

73. Irregular verb

οἶδα, *I know*. This is a 2nd perfect and pluperfect form from the same root as εἶδον, *I saw*. It is used with present meaning (cf. Latin *cognovi*). Compare with εἰμί, *I am* (Par. 79), and εἶμι, *I shall go* (Par. 81), both of which it resembles.

Verb			Indicative	Imperative	Subjunctive
Perfect,	S.	1	οἶδα	—	εἰδῶ
I know		2	οἶσθα	ἴσθι	εἰδῇς
		3	οἶδε(ν)	ἴστω	εἰδῇ
	D.	2	ἴστον	ἴστον	εἰδῆτον
		3	ἴστον	ἴστων	εἰδῆτον
	P.	1	ἴσμεν	—	εἰδῶμεν
		2	ἴστε	ἴστε	εἰδῆτε
		3	ἴσασι(ν)	ἴστων	εἰδῶσι(ν)
Pluperfect,	S.	1	ᾔδη		
I knew		2	ᾔδησθα		
		3	ᾔδει		
	D.	2	ᾖστον		
		3	ᾔστην		
	P.	1	ᾖσμεν		
		2	ᾖστε		
		3	ᾔδεσαν or ᾖσαν		
Future			εἴσομαι		

	Optative	Infinitive	Participle
S. 1	ἐνέγκαιμι	ἐνεγκεῖν ¹	ἐνεγκών -οῦσα -όν ¹
2	ἐνέγκαις		ἐνεγκόντα, etc.
3	ἐνέγκαι, etc.		
D. 2			
3			
P. 1			
2			
3			

¹ 2nd Aorist forms.

Irregular verb (*continued*)

	Optative	Infinitive	Participle
S. 1	εἰδείην	εἰδέναι	εἰδώς, εἰδυῖα εἰδός
2	εἰδείης		εἰδότα, etc.
3	εἰδείη		
D. 2	εἰδεῖτον		
3	εἰδείτην		
P. 1	εἰδεῖμεν		
2	εἰδεῖτε		
3	εἰδεῖεν		

εἰσοίμην   εἴσεσθαι   εἰσόμενος

74. II. Verbs in -μι

1. ἵστημι, stem -στα-, *I make to stand.*

Active

		Indicative	Imperative	Subjunctive
Present	S. 1	ἵστημι	—	ἱστῶ
I make to stand	2	ἵστης	ἵστη	ἱστῇς
(trans.)	3	ἵστησι(ν)	ἱστάτω	ἱστῇ
	D. 2	ἵστατον	ἵστατον	ἱστῆτον
	3	ἵστατον	ἱστάτων	ἱστῆτον
	P. 1	ἵσταμεν	—	ἱστῶμεν
	2	ἵστατε	ἵστατε	ἱστῆτε
	3	ἱστᾶσι(ν)	ἱστάντων	ἱστῶσι(ν)

Imperfect	S. 1	ἵστην
I was making	2	ἵστης
to stand (trans.)	3	ἵστη
	D. 2	ἵστατον
	3	ἱστάτην
	P. 1	ἵσταμεν
	2	ἵστατε
	3	ἵστασαν

Future. *I shall make to*	στήσω
stand (trans.)	

Weak Aorist. *I made*	ἔστησα	στῆσον	στήσω
to stand (trans.)			

Strong Aorist	S. 1	ἔστην	—	στῶ
I stood (intrans.)	2	ἔστης	στῆθι	στῇς
	3	ἔστη	στήτω	στῇ
	D. 2	ἔστητον	στῆτον	στῆτον
	3	ἐστήτην	στήτων	στῆτον
	P. 1	ἔστημεν	—	στῶμεν
	2	ἔστητε	στῆτε	στῆτε
	3	ἔστησαν	στάντων	στῶσι(ν)
		(as wk. aorist)		

Active

	Optative	Infinitive	Participle
S. 1	ἱσταίην	ἱστάναι	ἱστάς, ἱστᾶσα, ἱστάν,
2	ἱσταίης		ἱστάντα, etc.
3	ἱσταίη		
D. 2	ἱσταῖτον		
3	ἱσταίτην		
P. 1	ἱσταῖμεν		
2	ἱσταῖτε		
3	ἱσταῖεν		

	στήσοιμι	στήσειν	στήσων
	στήσαιμι	στῆσαι	στήσας
S. 1	σταίην	στῆναι	στάς, στᾶσα, στάν,
2	σταίης		στάντα, etc.
3	σταίη		
D. 2	σταῖτον		
3	σταίτην		
P. 1	σταῖμεν		
2	σταῖτε		
3	σταῖεν		

Verbs in -μι

1. ἵστημι, stem -στα-.

Active

			Indicative	Imperative	Subjunctive
Perfect. *I am*					
standing (intrans.) (1st)	S.	1	ἕστηκα	(1) ἕστηκε, etc.	(1) ἑστήκω, etc.
Note breathing. Also		2	ἕστηκας		
alternative forms.		3	ἕστηκε		
(2nd)	D.	2	ἕστατον	(2) ἕσταθι, etc.	(2) ἕστω, etc.
		3	ἕστατον	ἑστάτω, etc.	
	P.	1	ἕσταμεν		
		2	ἕστατε		
		3	ἑστᾶσιν		

Pluperf. *I was stand-*   εἱστήκη
ing (intrans.)
Note rough breathing.

Middle and passive

Present. *I stand*	S.	1	ἵσταμαι	—	ἱστῶμαι
(intrans.)		2	ἵστασαι	ἵστασο	ἱστῇ
		3	ἵσταται	ἱστάσθω	ἱστῆται
	D.	2	ἵστασθον	ἵστασθον	ἱστῆσθον
		3	ἵστασθον	ἱστάσθων	ἱστῆσθον
	P.	1	ἱστάμεθα	—	ἱστώμεθα
		2	ἵστασθε	ἵστασθε	ἱστῆσθε
		3	ἵστανται	ἱστάσθων	ἱστῶνται
Imperfect. *I was*	S.	1	ἱστάμην		
standing (intrans.)		2	ἵστασο		
		3	ἵστατο		
	D.	2	ἵστασθον		
		3	ἱστάσθην		
	P.	1	ἱστάμεθα		
		2	ἵστασθε		
		3	ἵσταντο		

Future Middle. *I shall*   στήσομαι
stand (intrans.)

Aorist Middle. *I set up*   ἐστησάμην   στῆσαι   στήσωμαι
(trans.)   στησάσθω, etc.

Active

Optative	Infinitive	Participle
(1) ἑστήκοιμι, etc.	(1) ἑστηκέναι	(1) ἑστηκώς -κυῖα -κός ἑστηκότα, etc.
(2) ἑσταίην, etc.	(2) ἑστάναι	(2) ἑστώς ἑστῶσα ἑστός ἑστῶτα, etc.

Middle and passive

S. 1	ἱσταίμην	ἵστασθαι	ἱστάμενος -η -ον
2	ἱσταῖο		
3	ἱσταῖτο		
D. 2	ἱσταῖσθον		
3	ἱσταίσθην		
P. 1	ἱσταίμεθα		
2	ἱσταῖσθε		
3	ἱσταῖντο		

στησοίμην	στήσεσθαι	στησόμενος -η -ον
στησαίμην	στήσασθαι	στησάμενος -η -ον

Verbs in -μι

Middle and passive

	Indicative	Imperative	Subjunctive
Perf. Mid. and Pass. *I have been set up* (pass.)	ἕσταμαι	ἕστασο	
Future Passive. *I shall be set up*	σταθήσομαι		
Aorist Passive. *I was set up*	ἐστάθην	στάθητι	σταθῶ

Note which tenses are transitive—*set, cause to stand,*
and which are intransitive—*stand, be set up.*
Active. All TRANSITIVE save STRONG AORIST, PERFECT, AND PLUPERFECT.
Middle and Passive. None transitive save AORIST MIDDLE.

TRANSITIVE

Note Aorists have ἐ. Perfects have ἑ.

Act.	Pres.	*I cause to stand*	ἵστημι
	Fut.	*I shall cause to stand*	στήσω
	Imperf.	*I was causing to stand*	ἵστην
	Wk. Aor.	*I caused to stand*	ἔστησα
Mid.	,, ,,		ἐστησάμην

INTRANSITIVE

Act.	Str. Aor.	*I stood*	ἔστην
	Perfect	*I am standing*	ἔστηκα
	Pluperf.	*I was standing*	εἱστήκη
Mid. Fut.		⎰ *I shall stand,*	στήσομαι
Pass. Fut.		⎱ *be set up*	σταθήσομαι
	Pres.	*I stand, am set up*	ἵσταμαι
	Imperf.	*I was standing*	ἱστάμην
	Aor.	*I stood, was set up*	ἐστάθην
	Perf.	*I have stood, been set up*	ἕσταμαι

75. II 2. τίθημι, *I place* ; stem -θε-.

Active

Present			Indicative	Imperative	Subjunctive
	S.	1	τίθημι	—	τιθῶ
		2	τίθης	τίθει	τιθῇς
		3	τίθησι(ν)	τίθετο	τιθῇ
	D.	2	τίθετον	τίθετον	τιθῆτον
		3	τίθετον	τιθέτων	τιθῆτον
	P.	1	τίθεμεν		τιθῶμεν
		2	τίθετε	τίθετε	τιθῆτε
		3	τιθέασι(ν)	τιθέντων	τιθῶσι(ν)

Middle and passive

Optative	Infinitive	Participle
	ἑστάσθαι	ἑσταμένος -η -ον
σταθησοίμην	σταθήσεσθαι	σταθησόμενος
σταθείην	σταθῆναι	σταθείς -θεῖσα, -θέν σταθέντα, etc.

Active

		Optative	Infinitive	Participle
S.	1	τιθείην	τιθέναι	τιθείς τιθεῖσα τιθέν
	2	τιθείης		τιθέντα, etc.
	3	τιθείη		
D.	2	τιθεῖτον		
	3	τιθείτην		
P.	1	τιθεῖμεν		
	2	τιθεῖτε		
	3	τιθεῖεν		

Verbs in -μι.

2. τίθημι, stem -θε-.

Active

			Indicative	Imperative	Subjunctive
Imperfect	S.	1	ἐτίθην		
		2	ἐτίθεις		
		3	ἐτίθει		
	D.	2	ἐτίθετον		
		3	ἐτιθέτην		
	P.	1	ἐτίθεμεν		
		2	ἐτίθετε		
		3	ἐτίθεσαν		
Future			θήσω		
Aorist	S.	1	ἔθηκα [1]	—	θῶ
		2	ἔθηκας	θές	θῇς
		3	ἔθηκε(ν)	θέτω	θῇ
	D.	2	ἔθετον	θέτον	θῆτον
		3	ἐθέτην	θέτων	θῆτον
	P.	1	ἔθεμεν	—	θῶμεν
		2	ἔθετε	θέτε	θῆτε
		3	ἔθεσαν or	θέντων	θῶσι(ν)
			ἔθηκαν [2]		
Perfect			τέθηκα	τέθηκε	τεθήκω
Pluperfect			ἐτεθήκη		

Middle and passive

			Indicative	Imperative	Subjunctive
Present	S.	1	τίθεμαι	—	τιθῶμαι
Mid. and Pass.		2	τίθεσαι	τίθεσο	τιθῇ
		3	τίθεται	τιθέσθω	τιθῆται
	D.	2	τίθεσθον	τίθεσθον	τιθῆσθον
		3	τίθεσθον	τιθέσθων	τιθῆσθον
	P.	1	τιθέμεθα	—	τιθώμεθα
		2	τίθεσθε	τίθεσθε	τιθῆσθε
		3	τίθενται	τιθέσθων	τιθῶνται

[1] Sing. aor. indic. is irregular 1st Aor. Dual and plur. aor. indic., and all other moods of aorist are 2nd Aor. forms.

[2] Alternative 1st Aor. form.

Active

Optative	Infinitive	Participle

		θήσοιμι	θήσειν	θήσων -ουσα -ον
				θήσοντα, etc.
S.	1	θείην	θεῖναι	θείς θεῖσα θέν
	2	θείης		θέντα, etc.
	3	θείη		
D.	2	θεῖτον		
	3	θείτην		
P.	1	θεῖμεν		
	2	θεῖτε		
	3	θεῖεν		
		τεθήκοιμι	τεθηκέναι	τεθηκώς -κυῖα -κός
				τεθηκότα, etc.

Middle and passive

S.	1	τιθείμην	τίθεσθαι	τιθέμενος -η -ον
	2	τιθεῖο		
	3	τιθεῖτο		
D.	2	τιθεῖσθον		
	3	τιθείσθην		
P.	1	τιθείμεθα		
	2	τιθεῖσθε		
	5	τιθεῖντο		

Verbs in -μι

2. τίθημι, stem -θε-.

Middle and passive

			Indicative	Imperative	Subjunctive
Imperfect	S.	1	ἐτιθέμην		
		2	ἐτίθεσο		
		3	ἐτίθετο		
	D.	2	ἐτίθεσθον		
		3	ἐτιθέσθην		
	P.	1	ἐτιθέμεθα		
		2	ἐτίθεσθε		
		3	ἐτίθεντο		

Middle

Future middle			θήσομαι		
Aorist middle	S.	1	ἐθέμην	—	θῶμαι
		2	ἔθου	θοῦ	θῇ
		3	ἔθετο	θέσθω	θῆται
	D.	2	ἔθεσθον	θέσθον	θῆσθον
		3	ἐθέσθην	θέσθων	θησθον
	P.	1	ἐθέμεθα	—	θώμεθα
		2	ἔθεσθε	θέσθε	θῆσθε
		3	ἔθεντο	θέσθων	θῶνται
Perfect			τέθειμαι	τέθεισο	τεθειμένος ὦ

Passive

Future		τεθήσομαι		
Aorist		ἐτέθην	τέθητι	τεθῶ
Perfect	Use	κεῖμαι *I lie*	κεῖσο	κείμενος ὦ

Middle and passive

Optative   Infinitive   Participle

Middle

θησοίμην   θήσεσθαι   θησόμενος -η -ον

S. 1 θείμην   θέσθαι   θέμενος -η -ον
  2 θεῖο
  3 θεῖτο
D. 2 θεῖσθον
  3 θείσθην
P. 1 θείμεθα
  2 θεῖσθε
  3 θεῖντο

τεθειμένος εἴη   τεθεῖσθαι   τεθειμένος

Passive

τεθησοίμην   τεθήσεσθαι   τεθησόμενος

τεθείην   τεθῆναι   τεθείς -θεῖσα -θέν
                   τεθέντα, etc.
κείμενος εἴη   κεῖσθαι   κείμενος

Verbs in -μι

76. II 3. δίδωμι, *I give*, stem -δο-.

Active

		Indicative	Imperative	Subjunctive
Present	S. 1	δίδωμι	—	διδῶ
	2	δίδως	δίδου	διδῷς
	3	δίδωσι(ν)	διδότω	διδῷ
	D. 2	δίδοτον	δίδοτον	διδῶτον
	3	δίδοτον	διδότων	διδῶτον
	P. 1	δίδομεν	—	διδῶμεν
	2	δίδοτε	δίδοτε	διδῶτε
	3	διδόασι(ν)	διδόντων	διδῶσι(ν)
Imperfect	S. 1	ἐδίδουν		
	2	ἐδίδους		
	3	ἐδίδου		
	D. 2	ἐδίδοτον		
	3	ἐδιδότην		
	P. 1	ἐδίδομεν		
	2	ἐδίδοτε		
	3	ἐδίδοσαν		
Future		δώσω		
Aorist	S. 1	ἔδωκα [1]	—	δῶ
	2	ἔδωκας	δός	δῷς
	3	ἔδωκε(ν)	δότω	δῷ
	D. 2	ἔδοτον	δότον	δῶτον
	3	ἐδότην	δότων	δῶτον
	P. 1	ἔδομεν	—	δῶμεν
	2	ἔδοτε	δότε	δῶτε
	3	ἔδοσαν	δόντων	δῶσι(ν)
Perfect		δέδωκα	δέδωκε	δεδώκω
Pluperfect		ἐδεδώκη		

[1] Dual and plur. aorist indic. and all aorists of other moods are 2nd Aorist. Sing aor. indic. is irregular 1st. Aor. Cf. τίθημι and ἵημι.

Active

		Optative	Infinitive	Participle
S.	1	διδοίην	διδόναι	διδούς διδοῦσα διδόν
	2	διδοίης		διδόντα, etc.
	3	διδοίη		
D.	2	διδοῖτον		
	3	διδοίτην		
P.	1	διδοῖμεν		
	2	διδοῖτε		
	3	διδοῖεν		

		δώσοιμι	δώσειν	δώσων
S.	1	δοίην	δοῦναι	δούς δοῦσα δόν
	2	δοίης		δόντα etc.
	3	δοίη		
D.	2	δοῖτον		
	3	δοίτην		
P.	1	δοῖμεν		
	2	δοῖτε		
	3	δοῖεν		
		δεδώκοιμι	δεδωκέναι	δεδωκώς

Verbs in μι

3. δίδωμι, stem -δο-.

Middle and passive

			Indicative	Imperative	Subjunctive
Present	S.	1	δίδομαι	—	διδῶμαι
		2	δίδοσαι	δίδοσο	διδῷ
		3	δίδοται	διδόσθω	διδῶται
	D.	2	δίδοσθον	δίδοσθον	διδῶσθον
		3	δίδοσθον	διδόσθων	διδῶσθον
	P.	1	διδόμεθα	—	διδώμεθα
		2	δίδοσθε	δίδοσθε	διδῶσθε
		3	δίδονται	διδόσθων	διδῶνται
Imperfect	S	1	ἐδιδόμην		
		2	ἐδίδοσο		
		3	ἐδίδοτο		
	D.	2	ἐδίδοσθον		
		3	ἐδιδόσθην		
	P.	1	ἐδιδόμεθα		
		2	ἐδίδοσθε		
		3	ἐδίδοντο		

Middle

Future			δώσομαι		
Aorist (2nd)	S.	1	ἐδόμην	—	δῶμαι
		2	ἔδου	δοῦ	δῷ
		3	ἔδοτο	δόσθω	δῶται
	D.	2	ἔδοσθον	δόσθον	δῶσθον
		3	ἐδόσθην	δόσθων	δῶσθον
	P.	1	ἐδόμεθα	—	δώμεθα
		2	ἔδοσθε	δόσθε	δῶσθε
		3	ἔδοντο	δόσθων	δῶνται

Passive

Future			δοθήσομαι		
Aorist			ἐδόθην	δόθητι	δοθῶ

Middle and passive

		Optative	Infinitive	Participle
S.	1	διδοίμην	δίδοσθαι	διδόμενος -η -ον
	2	διδοῖο		
	3	διδοῖτο		
D.	2	διδοῖσθον		
	3	διδοίσθην		
P.	1	διδοίμεθα		
	2	διδοῖσθε		
	3	διδοῖντο		

Middle

		δωσοίμην	δώσεσθαι	δωσόμενος
S.	1	δοίμην	δόσθαι	δόμενος
	2	δοῖο		
	3	δοῖτο		
D.	2	δοῖσθον		
	3	δοίσθην		
P.	1	δοίμεθα		
	2	δοῖσθε		
	3	δοῖντο		

Passive

δοθησοίμην	δοθήσεσθαι	δοθησόμενος
δοθείην	δοθῆναι	δοθείς -θεῖσα -θέν

Verbs in -μι

3. δίδωμι, stem -δο-.

Middle and passive

	Indicative	Imperative	Subjunctive
Perfect	δέδομαι	δέδοσο	
Pluperfect	ἐδεδόμην		

77. II 4. δείκνυμι, *I show*, stem δεικ- ; present stem δεικνυ-.

Active

			Indicative	Imperative	Subjunctive
Present	S.	1	δείκνυμι	—	δεικνύω
		2	δείκνυς	δείκνυ	δεικνύῃς
		3	δείκνυσι(ν)	δεικνύτω	δεικνύῃ
	D.	2	δείκνυτον	δείκνυτον	δεικνύητον
		3	δείκνυτον	δεικνύτων	δεικνύητον
	P.	1	δείκνυμεν	—	δεικνύωμεν
		2	δείκνυτε	δείκνυτε	δεικνύητε
		3	δεικνύασι(ν)	δεικνύντων	δεικνύωσι(ν)
Imperfect	S.	1	ἐδείκνυν		
		2	ἐδείκνυς		
		3	ἐδείκνυ		
	D.	2	ἐδείκνυτον		
		3	ἐδεικνύτην		
	P.	1	ἐδείκνυμεν		
		2	ἐδείκνυτε		
		3	ἐδείκνυσαν		
Future			δείξω [1]		
Aorist			ἔδειξα [1]	δεῖξον	δείξω
Perfect			δέδειχα [1]	δέδειχε	δεδείχω
Pluperfect			ἐδεδείχη		

[1] According to rules for guttural consonant stems (Par. 64).

Middle and passive

Optative	Infinitive	Participle
	δεδόσθαι	δεδομένος

Active

		Optative	Infinitive	Participle
S.	1	δεικνύοιμι [2]	δεικνύναι	δεικνύς, -νῦσα, -νύν,
	2	δεικνύοις		δεικνύντα, etc.
	3	δεικνύοι		
D.	2	δεικνύοιτον		
	3	δεικνυοίτην		
P.	1	δεικνύοιμεν		
	2	δεικνύοιτε		
	3	δεικνύοιεν		

δείξοιμι	δείξειν	δείξων
δείξαιμι	δεῖξαι	δείξας
δεδείχοιμι	δεδειχέναι	δεδειχώς

[2] Same type of optat. as λύω. Cf. other -μι verbs and contracted verbs.

Verbs in μι

4. δείκνυμι, stem δεικ- ; present stem δεικνυ-.

Middle and passive

		Indicative	Imperative	Subjunctive
Present	S. 1	δείκνυμαι	—	δεικνύωμαι
	2	δείκνυσαι	δείκνυσο	δεικνύῃ
	3	δείκνυται	δεικνύσθω	δεικνύηται
	D. 2	δείκνυσθον	δείκνυσθον	δεικνύησθον
	3	δείκνυσθον	δεικνύσθων	δεικνύησθον
	P. 1	δεικνύμεθα	—	δεικνυώμεθα
	2	δείκνυσθε	δείκνυσθε	δεικνύησθε
	3	δείκνυνται	δεικνύσθων	δεικνύωνται
Imperfect	S. 1	ἐδεικνύμην		
	2	ἐδείκνυσο		
	3	ἐδείκνυτο		
	D. 2	ἐδείκνυσθον		
	3	ἐδεικνύσθην		
	P. 1	ἐδεικνύμεθα		
	2	ἐδείκνυσθε		
	3	ἐδείκνυντο		

Middle

| Future | δείξομαι | | |
| Aorist | ἐδειξάμην [1] | δεῖξαι | δείξωμαι |

Passive

| Future | δειχθήσομαι | | |
| Aorist | ἐδείχθην [1] | δείχθητι | δειχθῶ |

Middle and passive

| Perfect | δέδειγμαι [1] | δέδειξο |
| Pluperfect | ἐδεδείγμην |

[1] According to rules for guttural stem δεικ- (Par. 64).

Middle and passive

		Optative	Infinitive	Participle
S.	1	δεικνυοίμην	δείκνυσθαι	δεικνύμενος -η -ον
	2	δεικνύοιο		
	3	δεικνύοιτο		
D.	2	δεικνύοισθον		
	3	δεικνυοίσθην		
P.	1	δεικνυοίμεθα		
	2	δεικνύοισθε		
	3	δεικνύοιντο		

Middle

δειξοίμην	δείξεσθαι	δειξόμενος
δειξαίμην	δείξασθαι	δειξάμενος

Passive

δειχθησοίμην	δειχθήσεσθαι	δειχθησόμενος
δειχθείην	δειχθῆναι	δειχθείς

Middle and passive

δεδείχθαι	δεδειγμένος

78. Verbs in -μι (*continued*)

No other verbs exactly follow ἵστημι, τίθημι or δίδωμι, except ἵημι, which corresponds almost entirely to τίθημι.

πίμπλημι, *I fill*; πίμπρημι, *I burn*, follow ἵστημι only. in present and imperfect.

Future and Aorist πλήσω, ἔπλησα and πρήσω, ἔπρησα (note weak Aorists).

For ὀνίνημι, *I benefit*, see Liddell and Scott's Lexicon.

-νυμι verbs having, like δείκνυμι, -μι forms only in present and imperfect are fairly numerous. See verb table, p. 314-7.

ἵημι, *I send, let go* ; stem ἑ.

Conjugates like τίθημι with τ and θ omitted.

ἑε- contracts to εἷ- as εἵμην from ἑέμην (cf. ἐθέμην).

Note aspirate throughout.

This verb is usually compounded with a preposition.

Active

		Indicative	Imperative	Subjunctive
Present	S. 1	ἵημι	—	ἱῶ
	2	ἵης	ἵει	ἱῇς
	3	ἵησι(ν)	ἱέτω	ἱῇ
	D. 2	ἵετον	ἵετον	ἱῆτον
	3	ἵετον	ἱέτων	ἱῆτον
	P. 1	ἵεμεν	—	ἱῶμεν
	2	ἵετε	ἵετε	ἱῆτε
	3	ἱᾶσιν [1]	ἱέντων	ἱῶσι(ν)
Imperfect	S. 1	ἵην		
	2	ἵεις		
	3	ἵει		
	D. 2	ἵετον		
	3	ἱέτην		
	P. 1	ἵεμεν		
	2	ἵετε		
	3	ἵεσαν		
Future		ἥσω		

[1] Cf. τιθέασι.

Active

		Optative	Infinitive	Participle
S.	1	ἱείην	ἱέναι	ἱείς, ἱεῖσα, ἱέν,
	2	ἱείης		ἱέντα, etc.
	3	ἱείη		
D.	2	ἱεῖτον		
	3	ἱείτην		
P.	1	ἱεῖμεν		
	2	ἱεῖτε		
	3	ἱεῖεν		

ἥσοιμι   ἥσειν   ἥσων

Verbs in -μι, ἵημι

Active

			Indicative	Imperative	Subjunctive
Aorist	S.	1	ἧκα	—	ὧ
		2	ἧκας	ἕς	ᾗς
		3	ἧκε	ἕτω	ᾗ
	D.	2	εἷτον	ἕτον	ἧτον
		3	εἵτην	ἕτων	ἧτον
	P.	1	εἷμεν	—	ὧμεν
		2	εἷτε	ἕτε	ἧτε
		3	εἷσαν or ἧκαν	ἕντων	ὧσι(ν)
Perfect			εἷκα	εἷκε	εἵκω
Pluperfect			εἵκη		

Middle and passive (as τίθεμαι)

			Indicative	Imperative	Subjunctive
Present	S.	1	ἵεμαι	—	ἱῶμαι
		2	ἵεσαι	ἵεσο	ἱῇ
		3	ἵεται, etc.	ἱέσθω, etc.	ἱῆται, etc.
Imperfect	S.	1	ἱέμην		
		2	ἵεσο		
		3	ἵετο, etc.		

Middle

			Indicative	Imperative	Subjunctive
Future			ἥσομαι		
Aorist	S.	1	εἵμην	—	ὧμαι
		2	εἷσο [1]	οὗ	ᾗ
		3	εἷτο	ἔσθω	ἧται
	D.	2	εἷσθον	ἔσθον	ἧσθον
		3	εἵσθην	ἔσθων	ἧσθον
	P.	1	εἵμεθα	—	ὥμεθα
		2	εἷσθε	ἔσθε	ἧσθε
		3	εἷντο	ἔσθων	ὧνται

Passive

			Indicative	Imperative	Subjunctive
Future			ἐθήσομαι		
Aorist			εἵθην [2]	ἕθητι	ἐθῶ

Middle and passive

	Indicative	Imperative
Perfect	εἷμαι	εἷσο
Pluperfect	εἵμην	

[1] Cf. ἕθου.   [2] ἐ-εθην contracted.

Active

		Optative	Infinitive	Participle
S.	1	εἴην	εἶναι	εἰς εἶσα ἔν
	2	εἴης		ἔντα, ctc.
	3	εἴη		
D.	2	εἶτον		
	3	εἴτην		
P.	1	εἶμεν		
	2	εἶτε		
	3	εἶεν		
		εἴκοιμι	εἰκέναι	εἰκώς

Middle and passive (ao τίθεμαι)

S.	1	ἱείμην	ἵεσθαι	ἱέμενος
	2	ἱεῖο		
	3	ἱεῖτο, etc.		

Middle

		ἡσοίμην	ἤσεσθαι	ἡσόμενος
S.	1	εἴμην	ἔσθαι	ἔμενος
	2	εἶο		
	3	εἶτο		
D.	2	εἶσθον		
	3	εἴσθην		
P.	1	εἴμεθα		
	2	εἶσθε		
	3	εἶντο		

Passive

	ἐθησοίμην	ἐθήσεσθαι	ἐθησόμενος
	ἐθείην	ἐθῆναι	ἐθείς, ἐθεῖσα, ἐθέν, ἐθέντα, etc.

Middle and passive

	εἶσθαι	εἱμένος

79. Irregular verbs in -μι

εἰμί, *I am.* Distinguish from εἶμι, *I shall go* (Par. 81).

		Indicative	Imperative	Subjunctive
Present	S. 1	εἰμί	—	ὦ
I am, etc.	2	εἶ	ἴσθι	ᾖς
	3	ἐστί(ν)	ἔστω	ᾖ
	D. 2	ἐστόν	ἔστον	ἦτον
	3	ἐστόν	ἔστων	ἦτον
	P. 1	ἐσμέν	—	ὦμεν
	2	ἐστέ	ἔστε	ἦτε
	3	εἰσί(ν)	ὄντων	ὦσι(ν)

Imperfect	S. 1	ἦ or ἦν
I was, etc.	2	ἦσθα
	3	ἦν
	D. 2	ἦστον
	3	ἤστην
	P. 1	ἦμεν
	2	ἦτε
	3	ἦσαν

Future	S. 1	ἔσομαι
I shall be, etc.	2	ἔσει
	3	ἔσται
	D. 2	ἔσεσθον
	3	ἔσεσθον
	P. 1	ἐσόμεθα
	2	ἔσεσθε
	3	ἔσονται

No other tenses occur.

		Optative	Infinitive	Participle
S.	1	εἴην	εἶναι	ὤν, οὖσα, ὄν,
	2	εἴης		ὄντα. etc.
	3	εἴη		
D.	2	εἶτον		
	3	εἴτην		
P.	1	εἶμεν		
	2	εἶτε		
	5	εἶεν		

S.	1	ἐσοίμην	ἔσεσθαι	ἐσόμενος
	2	ἔσοιο		
	3	ἔσοιτο		
D.	2	ἔσοισθον		
	3	ἐσοίσθην		
P.	1	ἐσοίμεθα		
	2	ἔσοισθε		
	3	ἔσοιντο		

80. Irregular verbs in -μι (*continued*)

φημί, *I say.*

			Indicative	Imperative	Subjunctive
Present	S.	1	φημί	—	φῶ
		2	φῇς	φάθι	φῇς
		3	φησί(ν)	φάτω	φῇ
	D.	2	φατόν	φάτον	φῆτον
		3	φατόν	φάτων	φῆτον
	P.	1	φαμέν	—	φῶμεν
		2	φατέ	φάτε	φῆτε
		3	φασίν	φάντων	φῶσι(ν)
Imperfect	S.	1	ἔφην		
		2	ἔφησθα		
		3	ἔφη		
	D.	2	ἔφατον		
		3	ἐφάτην		
	P.	1	ἔφαμεν		
		2	ἔφατε		
		3	ἔφασαν		
Future			φήσω		
Aorist			ἔφησα	φῆσον	φήσω

Note.—ἦ δ' ὅς, *said he*, and ἦν δ' ἐγώ, *said I*, from a verb ἠμί like φημί, are common in Attic. They are used parenthetically, like *inquit* in Latin, with the actual words of the speaker. ἠμί, *I say*, is found in Aristophanes. No other forms of this verb occur.

81. εἶμι, *I shall go* (present with future sense)

			Indicative	Imperative	Subjunctive
Present. *I shall*	S.	1	εἶμι	—	ἴω
go, etc.		2	εἶ	ἴθι	ἴῃς
		3	εἶσι(ν)	ἴτω	ἴῃ
	D.	2	ἴτον	ἴτον	ἴητον
		3	ἴτον	ἴτων	ἴητον
	P.	1	ἴμεν	—	ἴωμεν
		2	ἴτε	ἴτε	ἴητε
		3	ἴασι(ν)	ἰόντων	ἴωσι(ν)

		Optative	Infinitive	Participle
S.	1	φαίην	φάναι	φάς,[1] φᾶσα, φάν,
	2	φαίης		φάντα, etc.
	3	φαίη		
D.	2	φαῖτον		
	3	φαίτην		
P.	1	φαῖμεν		
	2	φαῖτε		
	3	φαῖεν		

Optative	Infinitive	Participle
φήσοιμι	φήσειν	φήσων
φήσαιμι	φῆσαι	φήσας

		Optative	Infinitive	Participle
S.	1	ἴοιμι	ἰέναι	ἰών, ἰοῦσα, ἰόν,
	2	ἴοις		ἰόντα, etc.
	3	ἴοι		
D.	2	ἴοιτον		
	3	ἰοίτην		
P.	1	ἴοιμεν		
	2	ἴοιτε		
	3	ἴοιεν		

[1] φάσκων is often used in Attic.

[continued overleaf]

Irregular verbs in -μι (*continued*).   εἶμι, *I shall go.*

			Indicative	Imperative	Subjunctive
Imperfect [1]	S.	1	ᾖα		
I was going,		2	ᾔεισθα		
I went, etc.		3	ᾔει		
	D. 2		ᾖτον		
		3	ᾔτην		
	P.	1	ᾖμεν		
		2	ᾖτε		
		3	ᾖσαν or ᾔεσαν		

Other tenses are supplied from ἔρχομαι (Par. 71).

For οἶδα, *I know*, see Par. 73.

82. κάθημαι, *I sit* (ἧμαι poetical), sometimes *sit idle*

			Indicative	Imperative	Subjunctive
Present	S.	1	κάθημαι	—	καθῶμαι
		2	κάθησαι	κάθησο	καθῇ
		3	κάθηται	καθήσθω	καθῆται
	D.	2	κάθησθον	κάθησθον	καθῆσθον
		3	κάθησθον	καθήσθων	καθῆσθον
	P.	1	καθήμεθα	—	καθώμεθα
		2	κάθησθε	κάθησθε	καθῆσθε
		3	κάθηνται	καθήσθων	καθῶνται
Imperfect	S.	1	ἐκαθήμην [2]		
		2	ἐκάθησο		
		3	ἐκάθητο		
	D.	2	ἐκάθησθον		
		3	ἐκαθήσθην		
	P.	1	ἐκαθήμεθα		
		2	ἐκάθησθε		
		3	ἐκάθηντο		
Future			καθεδοῦμαι [3]		

[1] Note *iota subscript* throughout, which distinguishes it from imperf. of εἰμί, *I am.* Cf. imperf. of οἶδα, par. 73.

[2] Also found without additional augment—καθήμην, etc.

[3] From καθίζομαι.

		Optative	Infinitive	Participle
S.	1	καθοίμην	καθῆσθαι	καθήμενος
	2	καθοῖο		
	3	καθοῖτο		
D.	2	καθοῖσθον		
	3	καθοίσθην		
P.	1	καθοίμεθα		
	2	καθοῖσθε		
	3	καθοῖντο		

καθεδοίμην	καθεδεῖσθαι	καθεδούμενος

83. Irregular verbs in -μι (continued)

κεῖμαι, *I lie*

		Indicative	Imperative	Subjunctive
Present	S. 1	κεῖμαι	—	Not found
	2	κεῖσαι	κεῖσο	
	3	κεῖται	κείσθω	
	D. 2	κεῖσθον	κεῖσθον	
	3	κεῖσθον	κείσθων	
	P. 1	κείμεθα	—	
	2	κεῖσθε	κεῖσθε	
	3	κεῖνται	κείσθων	

Imperfect	S. 1	ἐκείμην
	2	ἔκεισο
	3	ἔκειτο
	D. 2	ἔκεισθον
	3	ἐκείσθην
	P. 1	ἐκείμεθα
	2	ἔκεισθε
	3	ἔκειντο

Future	κείσομαι

Note that κάθημαι and κεῖμαι are *middle* -μι verbs, not *perfect* forms.

84. Similarly ἐπίσταμαι, *I understand, know*

	Indicative	Imperative	Subjunctive
Present	ἐπίσταμαι	ἐπίστασο	ἐπίστωμαι
Imperfect	ἠπιστάμην		
Future	ἐπιστήσομαι		
Aorist	ἠπιστήθην	ἐπιστήθητι	ἐπιστηθητῶ

Optative	Infinitive	Participle
Not found	κεῖσθαι	κείμενος
	κείσεσθαι	κεισόμενος

Optative	Infinitive	Participle
ἐπισταίμην	ἐπίστασθαι	ἐπιστάμενος
ἐπιστησοίμην	ἐπιστήσεσθαι	ἐπιστησόμενος
ἐπιστηθείην	ἐπιστηθῆναι	ἐπιστηθείς

Irregular verbs in -μι (*continued*)

85. δύναμαι, *I am able*, (middle -μι form)

Present			Indicative	Imperative	Subjunctive
	S.	1	δύναμαι	—	δύνωμαι
		2	δύνασαι	δύνασο	δύνῃ
		3	δύναται	δυνάσθω	δύνηται
	D.	2	δύνασθον	δύνασθον	δύνησθον
		3	δύνασθον	δυνάσθων	δύνησθον
	P.	1	δυνάμεθα	—	δυνώμεθα
		2	δύνασθε	δύνασθε	δύνησθε
		3	δύνανται	δυνάσθων	δύνωνται

Imperfect			
	S.	1	ἐδυνάμην [1]
		2	ἐδύνασο
		3	ἐδύνατο
	D.	2	ἐδύνασθον
		3	ἐδυνάσθην
	P.	1	ἐδυνάμεθα
		2	ἐδύνασθε
		3	ἐδύναντο

Future	δυνήσομαι		
Aorist	ἐδυνήθην [1]	δυνήθητι	δυνηθῶ
Perfect	δεδύνημαι	δεδύνησο	

[1] Sometimes augmented η as ἠδυνάμην or ἠδυνήθην.

	Optative	Infinitive	Participle
S. 1	δυναίμην	δύνασθαι	δυνάμενος
2	δύναιο		
3	δύναιτο		
D. 2	δύναισθον		
3	δυναίσθην		
P. 1	δυναίμεθα		
2	δύναισθε		
3	δύναιντο		

δυνησοίμην	δυνήσεσθαι	δυνησόμενος
δυνηθείην	δυνηθῆναι	δυνηθείς
	δεδυνάσθαι	δεδυναμένος

86. Prepositions

Greek prepositions are used to define more exactly the following case usages:
ACCUSATIVE for *motion to*, GENITIVE for *motion from*, DATIVE for *position at*.
Their case uses can be classified as follows:

Acc. only	Gen. only	Dat. only
ἀνά	ἀντί	ἐν
εἰς	ἀπό	σύν
	ἐκ	
	πρό	

Acc. and Gen.	Acc. Gen. and Dat.
διά	ἐπί
κατά	παρά
μετά	περί
ὑπέρ	πρός
	ὑπό

Prepositions are also compounded with verbs to modify their meaning.
Example. ἔρχομαι, *I go*; ἀπέρχομαι, *I go away*, (ἀπό + ἔρχομαι).

Table of main prepositional meanings and uses

Preposition	Accusative	Genitive	Dative	Compounded
ἀνά, *up*	ἀνὰ ποταμόν *upstream*			*up, back, again*
ἀντί, *instead of*		χρυσὸς ἀντὶ χαλκοῦ *gold instead of bronze*		*against, instead*

Prepositions (*continued*)

Preposition	Accusative	Genitive	Dative	Compounded
ἀπό, *from,* *away from* used of place, time, cause		ἀπὸ τῆς γῆς *from the land* ἀπ᾽ ἐκείνου τοῦ χρόνου, *from that time*		*away from, back, in return*
ἀπ᾽, before a vowel ἀφ᾽, before an aspirated vowel				
διά, acc., *on account of,* gen. *through, by means of*	δι᾽ ἄγγελον *on account of a messenger* διὰ τοῦτο, *therefore*	δι᾽ ἀγγέλου *by means of a messenger* διὰ πολλοῦ *after a long time (or distance)*		*thoroughly, apart*
δι᾽, before a vowel				
εἰς, (or ἐς) of place, *into* of time, *up to*	εἰς τὴν πόλιν *to or into the city* εἰς ἀεί, *for ever*			*into*

Prepositions (*continued*)

Preposition	Accusative	Genitive	Dative	Compounded
ἐκ, of place, *from, out of* of time, *since, from*		ἐκ τῆς πόλεως *out of the city* ἐκ τούτου *from this time, after this*		*out of, away from*
ἐξ, before a vowel				
ἐν, of place *in* of time			ἐν τῇ πόλει *in the city* ἐν τῷ θέρει *in the summer*	*in* *at*
ἐπί, *upon or at* acc. *to, towards* gen. *at, in the time of* dat. *at or on* ἐπ᾽ before a vowel ἐφ᾽ before an aspirated vowel	ἐπὶ τοὺς πολεμίους *against the enemy*	ἐφ᾽ ἵππου *on horseback* ἐφ᾽ ἡμῶν *in our time*	ἐπὶ θαλάσσῃ *at the sea* ἐπὶ τούτοις *on these terms* ἐφ᾽ ἡμῖν *in our power*	*upon, towards, against*

Preposition—*(continued)*

Preposition	Accusative	Genitive	Dative	Compounded
κατά, acc. (1) *down*, opp. of ἀνά (2) *according to*, opp. of παρά gen. *down from, against* κατ᾽ before a vowel καθ᾽ before an aspirate	κατὰ ποταμόν *down stream* κατὰ Λούκαν *according to St. Luke* καθ᾽ ἡμέραν *daily*	κατ᾽ ὀρῶν *down from the mountains* κατὰ Φιλίππου *against Philip*		*down, against* Sometimes adds transitive force
μετά, acc. *after* gen. *with* μετ᾽ before a vowel μεθ᾽ before an aspirate	μετὰ ταῦτα *after this* μετὰ τὸν πόλεμον *after the war*	μεθ᾽ ἡμῶν *with us*		*sharing (σύν more common) change*
παρά acc. *to, alongside, contrary to* gen. *from* dat. *at* παρ᾽ before vowels	παρὰ τὸν βασιλέα *to the king* παρὰ τοὺς νόμους *contrary to the laws* (opp. κατά + acc.)	παρὰ τοῦ βασιλέως *from the king*	παρὰ τῷ βασιλεῖ *at the king's side*	*alongside amiss*

Prepositions (*continued*)

Preposition	Accusative	Genitive	Dative	Compounded
περί acc. time, *around* place, *about* number gen. *concerning* *for the sake of* *of value* Unchanged before vowels	περὶ τὴν πόλιν *round the city* περὶ μέσας νύκτας *about midnight* περὶ ἑκατόν *about a hundred* οἱ περὶ τὸν Πλάτωνα *Plato's followers*	περὶ τούτου *concerning this matter* περὶ τῆς πατρίδος *for one's country* περὶ πολλοῦ ποιεῖσθαι *to value highly*		*round,* *exceedingly*
πρό, *before* place time preference Contracts with augment, e.g. προὔβαινον for προ-έ-βαινον		πρὸ τοῦ τείχους *in front of the wall* πρὸ τοῦ πολέμου *before the war* πρὸ τούτου *rather than this*		*before,* *in front of,* *in preference to*
πρός acc. *to, towards, against* gen. *from the direction of, in the interests of, by, by* (oath) dat. *at, in addition to*	πρὸς τοὺς πολίτας *against the citizens* πρὸς τί; *why?* πρὸς τὸν Βορρᾶν *Northward*	πρὸς τῆς θαλάσσης *From the sea (seawards)*[1] πρὸς τῶν θεῶν *by the gods!* πρὸς τῶν πολεμίων *in the enemies' interests* (cf. *e re publica*) *by the e.*	πρὸς τῇ πόλει *at the city* πρὸς τούτοις *In addition to this*	*against, towards,* *near,* *in addition*

[1] Estimating *from* instead of *to* the point viewed. Cf. Latin *a dextra* = on the right.

Prepositions (continued)

Preposition	Accusative	Genitive	Dative	Compounded
σύν, with (poetical for μετά + gen.) (sometimes ξύν)			σὺν φίλῳ with a friend. Usually μετά in prose. σὺν θεοῖς with the gods' help	Association
ὑπέρ acc. over, beyond gen. over, on behalf of	ὑπὲρ τὴν θάλασσαν beyond the sea ὑπὲρ δύναμιν beyond one's power	ὑπὲρ τῆς κεφαλῆς over one's head ὑπὲρ τῆς πατρίδος for one's country's sake		over, beyond, excess
ὑπό acc. under (motion towards) gen. by (of human agent) dat. under (position), of subjection	ὑπὸ νύκτα at nightfall (sub noctem)	ὑπὸ τοῦ βασιλέως by the king (agent, as ab + ablative in Latin)	ὑπὸ τῷ τείχει under the wall ὑπὸ τοῖς Πέρσαις subjected to the Persians, under the Persians' rule	under, secretly, slightly (cf. sub)

87. Adverbs used as prepositions

With genitive

ἄνευ, *without*	ἄνευ ἐλπίδος, *without hope*
ἐγγύς, *near*	ἐγγὺς τοῦ ποταμοῦ, *near the river*
εἴσω, *within*	εἴσω τοῦ τείχους, *inside the wall*
ἐντός, *inside*	ἐντός τοῦ τείχους, *inside the wall*
ἐκτός, *outside*	ἐκτὸς τοῦ τείχους, *outside the wall*
ἕνεκα, *on account of,* *for the sake of,* *as far as concerns* Often follows its case	ἕνεκα τῆς πατρίδος, *for one's country's sake* ἐμοῦ ἕνεκα, *as far as I am concerned*
μεταξύ,[1] *between*	μεταξὺ τοῦ πολέμου, *in the middle of the war*
μεχρί, *until*	μεχρὶ τούτου, *up till now*
	μεχρὶ τῆς νυκτός, *till nightfall*
πλήν, *except*	πλὴν ὅπλων, *except for their weapons*

With dative.

ἅμα, *at the same time as (simul).*	ἅμα τῷ ἦρι,[2] *at the return of spring*

[1] Often adverbially with participles. μεταξὺ δειπνοῦντες *in the midst of their dinner.*

[2] τὸ ἔαρ, τοῦ ἦρος, τῷ ἦρι, *spring.*

88. Pronouns and adjectives

In the following tables are given four corresponding types of words :

(1) Direct interrogative,[1]
(2) Indirect interrogative,
(3) Relative,
(4) Demonstrative.

INTERROGATIVE		RELATIVE	DEMONSTRATIVE
Direct	Indirect		
τίς	ὅστις, *who?*	ὅς, *who*	οὗτος (Par. 45)
	(Par. 51)	ὅστις, *whoever*	ὅδε, *this*
	Latin *quis*	(Par. 51)	ἐκεῖνος, *that*
		Latin *qui, qui-*	
		cumque	
πόσος -η -ον	ὁπόσος -η -ον	ὅσος (*as great*) *as*	τοσοῦτος,[2] *so*
	how large?		*great*
	Latin *quantus*	Latin *quantus*	Latin *tantus*
πόσοι -αι -α	ὁπόσοι -αι -α,	ὅσοι (*as many*) *as*	τοσοῦτοι,[2] *so many*
	how many?		
	Latin *quot*	Latin *quot*	Latin *tot*
ποῖος -α -ον	ὁποῖος -α -ον,	οἷος (*such*) *as*	τοιοῦτος,[2] *such*
	of what kind?		τοιόσδε [3]
	Latin *qualis*	Latin *qualis*	Latin *talis*
πότερος-α-ον	ὁπότερος -α -ον,	ὁπότερος, *which-*	ὁ ἕτερος, **the one**
	which of the two?	*ever of the two*	(*or the other*)
	Latin *uter*	Latin *uter*	Latin *alter*

[1] *Direct* interrogatives often introduce *indirect* questions in Greek, but never the converse.

[2] Declined like οὗτος, omitting the initial in (τ)οῦτο, etc.

[3] Declined τοιόσδε, τοιάδε, τοιόνδε, etc.

89. Adverbs

INTERROGATIVE		RELATIVE	DEMONSTRATIVE
Direct	Indirect		
ποῦ	ὅπου, *where?*	ὅπου, *where*	ἐκεῖ, *there*
	usually ποῦ	Latin *ubi*	Latin *illic*
	Latin *ubi*		ἐνταῦθα, αὐτοῦ
			ἐνθάδε, *here*
			Latin *hic*
ποῖ	ὅποι, *whither?*	ὅποι, *whither*	ἐκεῖσε, *thither*
	Latin *quo*	Latin *quo*	Latin *eo*
πόθεν	ὁπόθεν, *whence?*	ὅθεν, *whence*	ἐκεῖθεν, *thence*
	Latin *unde*	Latin *unde*	Latin *illinc, inde*
			ἐνθένδε, *hence*
			Latin *hinc, inde*
πότε	ὁπότε, *when?*	ὅτε, *when*	τότε, *then*
	Latin *quando*	Latin *quo tempore*	Latin *tum, tunc*
πῶς	ὅπως, *how?*	ὡς, ὅπως, *as*	οὕτω(ς), *thus*
	Latin *quo modo*	Latin *ut*	ὧδε, Latin *sic*

90. Direct questions (see Syntax B, p. 294)

These are introduced by :

(1) Any direct interrogative word from column 1 of preceding table.

(2) ἆρα = Latin *-ne*, for an open question.

ἆρ’ οὐ = Latin *nonne*, expecting answer Yes.

ἆρα μή = Latin *num*, expecting answer No.

(3) Alternative questions, πότερον . . . ἤ . . .

Latin *utrum . . . an . . .*

91. Indirect questions (see Syntax L, p. 304)

These are introduced by :

(1) Any Direct or Indirect interrogative word from columns 1 or 2 of preceding table.

(2) εἰ = *whether, if* (Latin *num*).

(3) Alternative questions : πότερον . . . ἤ . . .

εἰ . . . ἤ . . .

92. Particles

Greek is rich in particles and connecting words. Many of them express shades of meaning that can only be learnt by observation. Here are some of the commonest. Those asterisked never stand first in a clause.

ἀλλά, *but*

ἄλλως τε καί, *especially*

ἄρα,* *then* (of realisation)

αὖ, *again, moreover*

γάρ,* *for*

γε,* emphasises previous word, or the sentence

γοῦν,* *at any rate*

δέ,* *but, and*, connection

δή,* *indeed*

καί, *and, also, even*

καίτοι, *and yet*

μέντοι,* *however*

μέν * . . . δέ,* for contrast

οὐδέ, *nor, and not, not ever*

οὐ μόνον . . . ἀλλὰ καί . . . *not only . . . but also*

οὔτε . . . οὔτε *neither . . . nor*

οὖν,* *therefore,*

οὐκοῦν, *therefore, accordingly*

οὔκουν, *not therefore* (negative)

που,* *I suppose*

τοίνυν,* *therefore*

ὡς, *as, as though*

ὥσπερ, *as if*

ὥστε, *and so* (with indic.)

SYNTAX

93. The article. ὁ, ἡ, τό, *the,* used mainly as in English.

Abstract nouns normally, and proper nouns sometimes, take the article. ἡ ἀρετή, *virtue ;* ὁ Δημοσθένης.

(*a*) Qualifying words or phrases come between the article and its noun. This is called the *attributive position,* as opposed to the *predicative position,* outside the article and its noun.

πᾶς, *all* ; ὅλος, *whole* ; μέσος, *the middle of,*[1] take predicative position.

Attributive position	Predicative position
ἡ καλὴ πόλις, *the fair city*	ἡ πόλις καλή (ἐστιν), καλὴ ἡ πόλις *the city is fair*
ἡ τῶν Ἀθηναίων πόλις, *the Athenians' city*	ἡ πόλις τῶν Ἀθηναίων ἐστίν, *The city is the Athenians'*
ἡ ἄνω πόλις, *the city above*	ἡ πόλις ἄνω ἐστίν, *The city is above*
ἡ ἐπὶ τῷ ποταμῷ πόλις, *the city on the river*	ἐπὶ τῷ ποταμῷ ἐστιν ἡ πόλις, *the city is on the river*
ἡ μέση πόλις, *the city in the middle*	ἐν μέσῃ τῇ πόλει, *in the middle of the city*

Note.—Adverbs and prepositional phrases can be attached to nouns in a way that is quite impossible in Latin.

Occasionally the article is repeated with the epithet.

> ἡ πόλις ἡ καλή, *the fair city.*
> ἡ πόλις ἡ ἐπὶ τῷ ποταμῷ, *the city on the river.*

(*b*) The article is *never used* with a noun or adjective forming part of the *predicate.* ὁ ἐμὸς πατήρ ἐστι στρατιώτης, *my father is a soldier.*

(*c*) Some other uses of the article :

ὁ δέ, οἱ δέ, τὰ δέ, etc., are used as pronouns of reference at the beginning of a sentence. " *But he,*" etc.

πάντες Ξενοφῶντα παρεκάλουν· ὁ δέ... *All called upon X. ; but he ...*
ὁ μέν... ὁ δέ, *the one ... the other,* to point a contrast.

τὸν μὲν γὰρ ἡγοῦμαι σοφόν, τῷ δ' ἥδομαι, *I count the one wise, in the other I delight.*

οἱ μέν... οἱ δέ, *some ... others* (Latin *alii ... alii*).

οἱ *the men,* τὰ *the things,* as οἱ νῦν, *men of the present day ;* τὰ τῆς πόλεως, *the affairs of the city,* with nouns omitted.

---

[1] With μέσος this corresponds to a difference of meaning.

288

(*d*) The article is commonly used with participles and neuter adjectives to form a substantive.

οἱ τεθνηκότες, *the dead.* τὸ πρέπον (partic.), *seemliness.* τὸ ἄπρεπες (adj.), *unseemliness.*

So, too, a neuter singular article, in any case, with an infinitive : τὸ ἀγανακτεῖν, *resentment* ; τῷ ἀγανακτεῖν, *by resentment.*

τίς οἶδεν εἰ τὸ ζῆν μέν ἐστι κατθανεῖν, *Who knows if life be death?* [1]

94. Pronouns

Some take the attributive, some the predicative, position with the article.

ATTRIBUTIVE	PREDICATIVE
1. Possessive adjectives.	1. Genitive of pronoun.
ἐμός, *my*	ἐμοῦ, μου, *of me, my, mine*
σός, *thy*	σοῦ, *your, yours*
ἡμέτερος, *our*	αὐτοῦ, αὐτῆς, *his, her, hers*
ὑμέτερος, *your*	ἡμῶν, *our, ours*
For 3rd pers., see gen. of pronoun opposite.	ὑμῶν, *your, yours*
	αὐτῶν, *their, theirs*
Examples.	*Examples.*
ὁ ἐμὸς πατήρ, *my father*	ὁ πατὴρ ἐμοῦ, *my father*
ἡ ὑμετέρα μήτηρ, *your mother*	ἡ μήτηρ αὐτῶν, *their mother*
2. Reflexives for possessive.	2. Demonstrative pronouns.
ἐμαυτοῦ, *of myself, my own*	ὅδε, ἥδε, τόδε, *this* (looks forward : ἔλεξε τάδε, *he spoke as follows*)
σεαυτοῦ, *your own*	
ἑαυτοῦ or αὐτοῦ, *his own*	
ἑαυτῆς or αὐτῆς, *her own*	οὗτος, αὕτη, τοῦτο *this* (looks back : ταῦτα ἔλεξε, *these were his words*).
ἡμῶν αὐτῶν, *our own*	
ὑμῶν αὐτῶν, *your own*	
ἑαυτῶν or αὐτῶν, *their own*	ἐκεῖνος, ἐκείνη, ἐκεῖνο, *that*
Examples.	*Examples.*
ὁ ἐμαυτοῦ πατήρ, *my own father*	τάδε τὰ πράγματα, *these things*
τὸν αὐτοῦ πατέρα, *his own father*	αὕτη ἡ πόλις, *this city*
	ἐκεῖνος ὁ ἀνήρ, *that man*

[1] Observe absence of article with predicative κατθανεῖν (καταθανεῖν syncopated).

ATTRIBUTIVE	PREDICATIVE
Demonstratives for possessive :	
ἡ τούτου πόλις, *this man's city*	cf. οὗτος ὁ ἀνήρ, *this man*
οἱ ἐκείνων παῖδες, *their children*	

3. αὐτός, αὐτή, αὐτό, *the same*   αὐτός, αὐτή, αὐτό, *self*, intensive

Examples.   *Examples.*

ὁ αὐτὸς ἀνήρ, *the same man*	αὐτὸς ὁ βασιλεύς, *the king himself*
τὴν αὐτὴν πόλιν, *the same city*	αὐτῆς τῆς πόλεως, *of the city itself*
τοῦ αὐτοῦ ἔτους, *the same year*	τὸ ἔθνος αὐτό, *the race itself*

95. Interrogative and indefinite pronouns

Distinguish   τίς, *who?*   and   τις, *a certain*
               τί, *what?*   and   τι, *a certain*   by the accent.

τις and τι sometimes correspond to the indefinite article *an* in English :

ἡ Ἑλλάς ἐστι μέρος τι τῆς Εὐρώπης
Greece is a part of Europe

96. Cases

Nominative.   The subject and the complement of the subject.

Note that *nominative* is used with infinitive if the main verb and the infinitive have one and the same subject :

οὐκ ἔφη αὐτός,   ἀλλ᾽ ἐκεῖνον,   στρατηγὸν εἶναι
        se   eum
He said that not himself but the other man was general

The same rule applies to ὥστε + infinitive (consecutive)
                      and to πρίν + infinitive meaning *before*.

Accusative   Object case
Direct object.
Two objects, person and thing, with some verbs, e.g. *asking*, etc.
Internal limitation, repeating and defining an idea contained in the verb. Ὀλύμπια νικᾶν. *To win at the Olympic games.*
Accusative of specification. καλὴ τὸ εἶδος, *beautiful in appearance*
Duration of time.
Distance and measurement.
Accusative absolute with impersonal verbs.

Genitive Possession⎱ Latin genitive
          Partitive ⎰

          Separation from, origin⎤
          Comparison   ⎪
          Time within which   ⎬ Latin ablative
          Price or value   ⎪
          Genitive absolute   ⎦

          Exclamatory : οἴμοι τῶν δραχμῶν, *alas! the money!*

Dative   Indirect object   ⎤
          Dative of person interested ⎬ Latin dative
          Possession   ⎦

          Instrument ⎤
          Time when   ⎬ Latin ablative
          Place where [1]⎦

97. Participles

Participles are used much more freely in Greek than in Latin, as there
are participles corresponding to any **present, future, aorist, or perfect,**
in **active, middle, or passive,** that is in use in the indicative of a verb.

1. Relative.   Article with participle.

> οἱ πολῖται οἱ ὑπὲρ τῆς πατρίδος τεθνηκότες
> *Those citizens who have died for their country*

2. Temporal.   πολεμοῦντες, *when they were fighting*

3. Causal.   βουλόμενος τοῦτο ποιεῖν, *as I wanted to do this*
   ἅτε, ὡς and participle : *inasmuch as, seeing that*
   ἅτε παῖς ὤν, *being but a child*
   ὡς στρατηγῶν, *in his capacity as general*

4. Concessive, with καίπερ or καί, *although.*   Negative οὐ.
   καίπερ οὐκέτι βασιλεύων, *although no longer king*

5. Conditional.   A participle often represents an *if* clause.   Negative μή.
   μὴ νικήσας δίκας δώσω, *If I do not win I shall pay the penalty*

6. τυγχάνω, *happen,* λανθάνω, *escape notice,* φθάνω, *forestall,* διατελέω,
   continue, take a participle
   ἔτυχε νοσῶν, *he happened to be ill,* λάθε βιώσας, *live unnoticed*

[1] (usually with preposition)

98. Absolute construction

GENITIVE ABSOLUTE

This is used in Greek like the Ablative absolute in Latin.

A noun, that stands in no relation to the construction of the main verb, is used in the genitive case, with participle in agreement, to express attendant circumstances. The existence of *active* aorist participles makes this construction more freely available than in Latin.

Example.

'Εμοῦ θανόντος γαῖα μιχθήτω πυρί
On my death let earth be confounded with fire

ACCUSATIVE ABSOLUTE

With impersonal verbs (Par. 99) the *neuter accusative singular* of the participle is used for the absolute construction.

ἀδύνατον ὄν,	*as it was impossible*	from ἀδύνατον εἶναι
δέον,	*it being necessary*	from δεῖ
δόξαν (aor.),	*as it was decided, thought best*	from δοκεῖ
ἐξόν,	*since it is allowed*	from ἔξεστι
παρασχόν, often	*an opportunity being given*	from παρέχει
εὖ παρασχόν,		
παρόν,	*as it is possible*	from πάρεστι
προσῆκον,	*as it was (or is) right*	from προσήκει
συμφέρον,	*as it is expedient*	from συμφέρει

99. Impersonal verbs

There are some very common verbs of this type. They take either accusative or dative of the person, and an infinitive, present or aorist.

Accusative and infinitive

δεῖ, fut. δεήσει, aor. ἐδέησε⎫
χρή, imperf. ἐχρῆν, or χρῆν ⎬ *it is necessary (should, must, ought)*

Example.

σοφωτέρους γὰρ χρὴ βροτῶν[1] εἶναι θεούς
The gods must be wiser than men

---

[1] Comparative genitive.

Dative and infinitive

δοκεῖ, aor. ἔδοξε, *it seems good*

ἔξεστι, *it is possible, I may*

λυσιτελεῖ, *it is profitable*

πάρεστι, *it is possible, I can*

πρέπει, *it behoves, I should, ought*

προσήκει, *it concerns, it befits*

συμφέρει, *it is expedient*

Example.   τοιαῦθ' ἑλέσθαι σοι πάρεστιν ἐξ ἐμοῦ
Such things you may choose to take [1] *from me*

Dative of person with genitive of thing (instead of infinitive)

μέλει, fut. μελήσει, aor. ἐμέλησε, *to care for, be concerned with*

μεταμέλει, *repent*

μέτεστι, *have a share in*

Example.   ἐμοὶ δ' ἔλασσον Ζηνὸς ἢ μηδὲν μέλει
I care less than nothing for Zeus [2]

100. Negatives.   There are two negatives, οὐ and μή.
Each has its corresponding compound negative, as
οὐδείς and μηδείς *no-one*, οὐκέτι and μηκέτι *no longer*.

Οὐ is used with indicative.

> with optative and infinitive in *indirect speech.*
> with optative in *apodosis* of *conditionals.*
> with *potential* optatives.

Exception.   εἰ even with indicative always takes μή.

μή is used with imperative, subjunctive, optative, infinitive.

> with participles and infinitives for *generic* or *indefinite* sense.

Exceptions.   Optative and infinitive in indirect speech take οὐ.

> Optative for apodosis of conditionals and potential optative
> take οὐ.

A negative followed by a *simple* negative becomes affirmative.
οὐδεὶς ὃς οὐκ ἐκεῖν' ὀνειδιεῖ τάχα.   *Everyone will soon blame these acts.*

A negative followed by a *compound* negative is strengthened in negation.
βροτῶν λόγον οὐκ ἔσχεν οὐδένα.   *Of mortals he had no thought at all.*

Exception.   οὐ μή with future indicative or aorist subjunct. is an emphatic
denial for the future.

οὐ μὴ παύσωμαι φιλοσοφῶν.   *Never shall I cease philosophising.*

---

[1] Middle of αἱρέω.

[2] Cf. οὐδὲν τούτων τῷ Γαλλίωνι ἔμελεν, " *Gallio cared for none of these things.*"

SYNTAX OF CLAUSES

Main Clauses

A. Statements

Indicative in appropriate tense.   Negative οὐ.

B. Questions

1. *Indicative*, after interrogative word.[1]   οὐ for affirmative, μή for negative answer.

2. ἆρα [2] = Latin *-ne.*

3. ἆρ᾽ οὐ = Latin *nonne.*

4. ἆρα μή = Latin *num.*

5. *Subjunctive* for Deliberative (1st person) questions.   Negative μή.

[1] See Par. 88-90.
[2] Distinguish ἄρα, a particle of inference, *then.*

C. Commands

1. 1st Person.   *Subjunctive*, present or aorist.   Negative μή.

2. 2nd and 3rd Person.   Positive.   *Imperative* present or aorist.

3a. 2nd and 3rd Person.   Negative.   *Imperative*, present only, for general prohibitions.   Negative μή.

3b. *Subjunctive*, aorist only, for particular prohibitions.   Negative μή.

Main Clauses

A. Statements

μόνος θεῶν ὁ θάνατος οὐ δώρων ἐρᾷ
Alone of gods, death does not love gifts

B. Questions

1. τί δῆτ' ἐμοὶ ζῆν ἡδύ, πρὸς τί χρὴ βλέπειν ;
    Why indeed to me is life sweet?   Towards what shall I look?

2. ἆρ' εὐτυχεῖς οὖν σοῖς γάμοις ἢ δυστυχεῖς ;
    Are you happy therefore in your marriage, or unhappy?

3. ἆρ' [1] οὐκ ἄμεινον ἢ σὺ τἀν Θήβαις φρονῶ ;
    Do I not plan better than you the affairs in Thebes?

4. σοὶ δ' ἆρα μὴ τῆς μητρός, ὦ τέκνον, μέλει ;
    Do you not then care for your mother, O child?

5. εἴπω τι δῆτα κἄλλ', ἵν' ὀργίζῃ πλέον ;
    Shall I then tell other things, that you may rage the more?

    [1] μάτην ἄρ' ἡμεῖς, ὡς ἔοικεν, ἥκομεν. *In vain then, as it seems, have we come.*

C. Commands

1. κούφως φέρωμεν τὰς παρεστώσας τύχας
    Let us bear lightly the fortunes around us

2. χαλᾶτε κλῇδας ὡς τάχιστα πρόσπολοι
    Loose the bolts as quickly as you can, attendants

3a. μηδένα νομίζετ' εὐτυχεῖν πρὶν ἂν θάνῃ
    Count no man happy till he be dead.

3b. ὦ τέκνον, ὅρκους μηδαμῶς ἀτιμάσῃς
    O child, in no way dishonour your vows!

D. **Wishes**

1. For the future. *Optative*, with or without εἴθε or εἰ γάρ, *if only.*
Negative μή.
Compare conditionals, P 2.

2. For the present.
   (a) *Imperfect indicative*, with εἴθε or εἰ γάρ, *if only.* Negative μή.
   Cf. Conditionals, P 4 ;
or   (b) ὤφελον [1] -ες -ε (*I ought, you ought,* etc.) with *present infinitive.*
   Negative μή. Sometimes with εἴθε or εἰ γάρ.

   [1] Strong aorist of ὀφείλω, *I owe.* Distinguish ὠφελέω (regular), *I help.*

3. For the past.
   (a) *Aorist indicative*, with εἴθε or εἰ γάρ, *if only.* Negative μή.
   Cf. Conditionals, P 5 ;
or   (b) ὤφελον (see D 2) *with aorist infinitive*, sometimes introduced by
   εἴθε, εἰ γάρ or ὡς, *how.* Negative μή.

E. **Conjunctions with indicative**

The following take the same tense of the *indicative* as would be used
in a main clause. Negative οὐ.

After,	ἐπειδή,	*Since,* of cause	ἐπεί, ὅτι, ὡς,
	ἀφ' οὗ, ἐξ οὗ (*since* of time)	of time	ἀφ' οὗ, ἐξ οὗ
As	ὡς (distinguish ὧς, *thus*)	*When,*	ἐπεί, ἐπειδή, ὅτε, (relative)
Because,	ὅτι, διότι	*While,*	ἕως (*as long as*)

D. **Wishes**

Future

1.   εἰ γὰρ γενοίμην, τέκνον, ἀντὶ σοῦ νεκρός
Would I might become, child, in your place, a dead man!

σωτήρ θ' ἵκοιτο καὶ νόσου παυστήριος
May he come as saviour and stayer of the plague!

σοφὴν δὲ μισῶ. μὴ γὰρ ἔν γ' ἐμοῖς δόμοις
εἴη φρονοῦσα πλεῖον ἢ γυναῖκα χρή
*I hate a clever woman. May there not, at any rate, in my house
be one wiser than a woman should be!*

Present

2a.   εἴθ' εἶχες, ὦ τεκοῦσα, βελτίους φρένας
Would that you had, O mother, better wits!

2b.   εἴθ' ὤφελ' ἀνὴρ τῶνδε μηδὲν εἰδέναι
Would that the man knew nothing of these things!

    [1] ὡς τοῖς θανοῦσι πλοῦτος οὐδὲν ὠφελεῖ.   *Since wealth is no help to the dead.*

Past

3a.   εἴθ' ηὕρομέν σ' Ἄδμητε μὴ λυπούμενον
Would we had found you, Admetus, not sorrowing!

3b.   τὴν Σκῦρον οἴμοι μήποτ' ὤφελον λιπεῖν
Alas, would I had never left Scyrus!

    or,

    I should never have left Scyrus!

E. **Conjunctions with indicative**

ἐπεὶ δὲ πολλῶν δακρύων εἶχεν κόρον ...
But when she had her fill of much weeping ...

ἕως δ' ἔτ' ἔμφρων εἰμί, κηρύσσω φίλοις ...
As long as I am still sane, I declare to my friends ...

Subordinate Clauses
F. Indirect statement
There are two constructions after verbs of *saying* and *thinking.*

1. *Accusative* and *infinitive.*   Negative οὐ.
   If the speaker is also the subject of the infinitive (cf. *dixit se*)
   nominative and *infinitive* is used.
   The tense of the infinitive is the same as the corresponding indicative
   tense used in the speaker's *actual words.*   Present infinitive represents
   also imperfect indicative.
   φημί, *I say*, always takes the infinitive construction.   οὔ φημι is
   used like *nego* for *I say that . . . not . . .*

   ἐλπίζω, *I hope* ⎫
   ὄμνυμι, *I swear* ⎬ often take *future* infinitive.   Negative
   ὑπισχνοῦμαι(εο), *I promise* ⎭   μή.

2. ὅτι or ὡς (*that*) with *indicative* in Primary Sequence,
                      with *optative or indicative* in Secondary Sequence.
   Negative οὐ.
   Persons as in English.
   Tense used is that of the speaker's *actual words.*
   λέγω and εἶπον, *I say, said*, prefer this construction.

   Relative and other subordinate clauses in indirect speech take the same
   construction as ὅτι, i.e.

   > Primary sequence—*indicative.*
   > Secondary sequence—*optative or indicative.*

   Secondary tenses are kept in the indicative and not changed into
   optative.

EXAMPLES

F. Indirect statement

1. Infinitive construction

   1. ἔφη στρατηγὸν Νικίαν εἶναι Κλέων
Cleon said that Nicias was general

     στρατηγὸς εἶναι Νικίας αὐτός γ’ ἔφη
Nicias said that he was general himself

     οὐδένα γὰρ οἶμαι δαιμόνων εἶναι κακόν
For I think that none of the gods is evil

     οὔ φημ’ Ὀρέστην σ’ ἐνδίκως ἀνδρηλατεῖν
I say that you do not justly banish Orestes

     ὄμνυμι σεμνὴν Ἄρτεμιν Διὸς κόρην
     μηδὲν κακῶν σῶν ἐς φάος δείξειν ποτε
I swear by holy Artemis, daughter of Zeus,
that I will never display any of your ills to the light

2. ὅτι or ὡς construction

     ἄγγελλε δ’ ὡς ὄλωλεν Ἀργείας ὕπο γυναικός
Tell that he has perished by the hand of an Argive woman. Actual
words, ὄλωλεν, *he has perished*

     ἦλθε γάρ τις ἄγγελος λέγων
     ὡς οὐκέτ’ ἐν γῇ τῇδ’ ἀναστρέψοι[1] πόδα
     Ἱππόλυτος.
Some messenger came, telling that no longer in this land would Hippo-
lytus turn his step. Actual words ἀναστρέψει, *will turn*, which could
also stand here by the Graphic Construction, i.e. indicative for
optative in secondary sequence.

     [1]The only use of fut. opt. is for fut. indic. in *or. obl.*

F 3. Verbs of **knowing and perceiving**

These usually take a *participle* instead of infinitive or ὅτι construction. This participle agrees with the subject or object of the main verb according to the sense. Several verbs of perceiving take a genitive.

G. Final clauses

There are three constructions. The first is much the commonest.

1. ἵνα, ὅπως or ὡς, *so that, so as to, in order that.*
   + *Subjunctive* in Primary Sequence.
   + *Optative* or *Subjunctive* in Secondary Sequence.

   Negative μή.
   Negative final clauses are often introduced by μή alone.

2. *Future participle*, agreeing with subject or object of main verb.
   Negative οὐ.
   Sometimes introduced by ὡς, often to express alleged purpose.

3. ὅστις, relative + *future indicative* after Primary or Secondary verb.
   It is used like final *qui* in Latin.
   Negative μή.

EXAMPLES301

F 3. Verbs of **knowing and perceiving**

πῶς ; οὐ γὰρ οἶδα δεσπότην κεκτημένος
How so?   I did not know indeed that I had a master

τοὺς φιλτάτους γὰρ οἶδα νῦν ὄντας πικρούς
For I know that our dearest are now hostile (bitter)

ὁρῶμεν ἀνθοῦν πέλαγος Αἰγαῖον νεκροῖς
We behold the Aegean sea blossoming with the dead

G. **Final clauses**

1. εἴπω τι δῆτα κἄλλ᾽, ἵν᾽ ὀργίζῃ πλέον ;
Am I then to say other things that you may rage the more?

ἠκούσατ᾽ ἵνα μάθοιτε διὰ τέλους τὸ πᾶν
You listened so as to learn in the end all

2. ἡμεῖς πάρεσμεν ἔργα δράσοντες τάδε
We are here to do these deeds

οὐ μαρτυρήσων ἦλθον
I did not come to bear witness

ὡς μαρτυρήσων ἦλθεν
He came as though to bear witness

3. πέμψον τιν᾽ ὅστις σημανεῖ . . . ποίας τύχας ;
Send someone to report . . . what happenings?

H. Consecutive clauses

There are two constructions. The first expresses the *natural* result, the second the *actual* result.

1. ὥστε + *infinitive, so that, that.*
   The subject of the infinitive is in the accusative. If it is also the subject of the main verb it is omitted.
   Gives the *natural* result.
   Negative μή.

2. ὥστε + *indicative, and so.*
   ὥστε used in this way is a simple conjunction meaning *and so,* and has no grammatical effect on its clause.
   Gives the *actual* result.
   Negative οὐ.

K. Verbs of fearing

1. Fear for *present* or *past.*
   Verb of fearing + μή (Latin *ne*) and *indicative.*
   Negative οὐ.

2. Fear for *future.*
   Verb of fearing + μή and *subjunctive* in Primary sequence.
   + μή and *optative* or *subjunctive* in Secondary sequence.
   Negative οὐ.

3. *I am afraid to . . .*
   Verb of fearing + *infinitive* as in English.
   Negative μή.

4. Verb of precaution (*take care*) + ὅπως and *future indicative.*
   Negative μή.
   The verb of precaution, if 2nd person imperative, is often omitted.

H. Consecutive clauses

1. ἆρ' ἐστ' ἔτι ζῶν οὗτος, ὥστ' ἰδεῖν ἐμέ ;
Is he yet living, so that I can see him?

πῶς οὖν γένοιτ' ἂν ὥστε μήθ' ἡμᾶς θανεῖν
λαβεῖν θ' ἃ βουλόμεσθα ;
*How could it happen that we should not die
but should take what we want?*

2. βέβηκεν, ὥστε πᾶν ἐν ἡσύχῳ, ὦ πάτερ, ἔξεστι φωνεῖν
He has gone, and so, father, it is possible to tell everything in peace

K. Verbs of fearing

1. δεινῶς φοβοῦμαι μὴ βλέπων ὁ μάντις ἦν
I am terribly afraid that the seer had sight

2. δέδοικα δ' ὦ πρεσβῦτα μὴ πληγῶν δέῃ
I am afraid, old man, that you will need blows

3. πᾶς τις φοβεῖται φῶς λιπεῖν τόδ' ἡλίου
Every one is afraid to leave the light of the sun

4. [σκόπει] ὅπως δὲ τοῦτο μὴ διδάξεις μηδένα [1]
(See) that you teach no one this

[1] See negatives Par. 100 (p. 293).

L. Indirect questions

These are treated like ὅτι construction in indirect statements. (F 2).
Verb of asking + direct or indirect interrogative, (Par. 88-91),
        and *indicative* or *optative* according to sequence.
By Graphic Construction *indicative* can always be used.
The tense used is that of the actual question.
Negative οὐ.
εἰ, *if, whether*, can introduce a question. Negative with εἰ is sometimes μή.
ἤ, *or*, can introduce a second question.
ἢ οὔ or ἢ μή are both used for *or not*.
Indirect deliberative questions are in *subjunctive* or *optative* according to sequence. Negative μή.

M. Indirect command

1. κελεύω, *I order*
   πείθω, *I persuade* } + accusative with *infinitive*. Negative μή.

2. παραγγέλλω, *I give orders*
   (military)
   παραινέω, *I advise*
   προστάσσω, *I instruct* } + dative with *infinitive*. Negative μή.

L. Indirect questions

σὺ δ' οἶσθ' ὅς εἰμι κἀφ'[1] ὅτου πατρὸς γεγώς
κἀξ γῆς ὁποίας ἦλθον
*But you know who I am, and from what father born
and from what kind of land I came*

εἰδῶμεν εἰ νικῶμεν ἢ νικώμεθα
Let us learn if we are winning or losing

μένω δ' ἀκοῦσαι πῶς ἀγὼν κριθήσεται
I am waiting to learn how the contest will be settled

εὐθὺς παρ' ἡμῖν ἦν φόβος νεανικός
ὅθεν ποτ' εἴη φθόγγος
*Straightway among us there fell a youthful fear
of whence could come the sound.* (" πόθεν ἐστί," " whence comes " ...)

---

[1] κἀφ' for καὶ ἀπό.

M. Indirect command

1. τοῦτον κελεύω πάντα σημαίνειν ἐμοί
   I order this man to reveal everything to me

2. καὶ σοὶ παραινῶ πατέρα μὴ στυγεῖν, τέκνον
   And you I warn not to hate your father, child

N. Indefinite construction

This is used for sentences of general application, often marked by *ever* in English, e.g. *whoever, whatever, if at any time.* English alters the pronoun or conjunction, Greek the *mood*, to express indefinite application.

1. For Primary time use *subjunctive* + ἄν. Negative μή.

   Note. εἰ + ἄν = ἐάν, or ἤν, *if ever.* Cf. Conditionals, P 6.
   ὅτε + ἄν = ὅταν, *whenever.*
   ὁπότε + ἄν = ὁπόταν, *whenever.*
   ἐπειδή + ἄν = ἐπειδάν, *whenever, as soon as.*

2. For Secondary time use *optative* without ἄν. Negative μή. Cf. Conditionals, P 7.

O. Temporal clauses

1. *When* and *since.* ὅτε, ἐπειδή, ἀφ' οὗ, ἐξ οὗ
   Indicative unless indefinite. See E and N.

2. *Before.*
   πρίν after affirmative sentence means *before* and takes *accusative and infinitive.* No negative found.
   Nominative and infinitive is used if the subjects of the main verb and of the infinitive are the same.

3. *Until.*
   πρίν after a *negative,* ἕως, μέχρι οὗ.
   For *past* time use *indicative.* Negative οὐ.
   For *future* time use *subjunctive with* ἄν. Negative μή.

N. Indefinite construction

1. μαντεύομαι γὰρ ὡς ἂν ἡγῆται θεός
   I prophesy in whatever way the god directs

   ἅπας δὲ τραχὺς ὅστις ἂν νέον κρατῇ
   Every man is harsh who is newly in power

2. ἀλλ' εἴ τι μὴ φέροιμεν ὤτρυνεν φέρειν
   But if ever we were not bringing anything, he urged us to bring it

O. Temporal clauses

1. ἐπεὶ τὸ κλεινὸν ἤλθομεν Φοίβου πέδον
   When we reached the famous plain of Phoebus

2. εἰ σωφρονεῖ τις, πρὶν λέγειν βουλεύεται
   If a man is prudent he reflects before he speaks

3. οὐκ ἦν ἀλέξημ' οὐδὲν πρίν γ' ἐγώ σφισιν ἔδειξα.
   There was no relief till I showed them.

   ἕως δ' ἂν οὖν
   πρὸς τοῦ παρόντος ἐκμάθῃς ἔχ' ἐλπίδα
   Until you learn from one who was present, have hope

   μηδένα νομίζετ' εὐτυχεῖν πρὶν ἂν θάνῃ
   Call no one happy till he is dead

P. Conditional clauses

Protasis (*if* clause), negative μή. **Apodosis** (main clause), negative οὐ.

(1) Future, near and vivid. (Latin indicative.)

Protasis (μή).	Apodosis (οὐ).
ἐάν ⎫ + present or aorist ἤν ⎭ subjunctive. (εἰ + future indicative is rare.)	Future indicative.

Note. English often uses present for future in *if* clauses. Latin and Greek are more precise.

(2) Future, more remote. (Latin present subjunctive.)

εἰ + present or aorist optative.	Present or aorist optative + ἄν.
	ἄν can not stand first in its clause.

(3) Present and past, openly stated. (Latin indicative.)

εἰ + suitable tense of the indicative.	Indicative, any suitable tense.

(4) Present, implying non-fulfilment. (Latin imperfect subjunctive.)

εἰ + imperfect indicative.	Imperfect indicative + ἄν.

(5) Past, implying non-fulfilment. (Latin pluperfect subjunctive.)

εἰ + aorist indicative.	Aorist or imperfect indicative + ἄν.

Note. The aorist indicative denotes past time. The imperfect denotes present or past continuous time.

In the subjunctive and optative the present denotes continuing action and the aorist simple action. The distinction is not one of present or past time.

(6) WISH OR COMMAND in apodosis. Use the appropriate mood.

P. Conditional clauses

(1) Future, vivid

ἐὰν φεύγῃ διώξω.
If he flees I shall follow.

ἥξουσιν αὖθις ἢν ἔχωμεν τὴν Πύλον.
They will come again if we hold Pylos.

ἀποκτενεῖς γὰρ εἴ με γῆς ἔξω βαλεῖς.
You will kill me if you cast me from the land.

(2) Future, remote

εἰ φύγοι διώξαιμι ἄν.
If he fled I should follow.

μάθοιμ' ἂν εἰ λέγοι τις ἐμφανῆ λόγον.
I should learn if someone would say a clear word.

(3) Present and past, open

εἰ φεύγει διώκω.
If he is fleeing I am following.

φιλοῦσι πάντες εἴ σὺ τὴν ψυχὴν φιλεῖς.
All love their life if you love yours.

εἰ ἔφυγεν ἐδίωξα.
If he fled I followed.

ἀλλ' εἰ τόδ' ἦν ἀληθὲς ἐψεύσθην ἐγώ.
But if this was true I was deceived.

(4) Present, unfulfilled

εἰ ἔφευγεν ἐδίωκον ἄν.
If he were fleeing I should be following.

εἰ μὴ γὰρ ἦν Χρύσιππος οὐκ ἂν ἦν Στοά.
If there were no Chrysippus there would be no Porch (Stoicism).

(5) Past, unfulfilled

εἰ ἔφυγεν ἐδίωξα ἄν.
If he had fled I should have followed.

οὐδ' ἱκόμην ἔγωγ' ἄν, εἴ σὺ μὴ 'κάλεις.
I should not have come if you had not been calling.

(6) Apodosis not a statement.

κάκιστ' ἀπολοίμην Ξανθίαν εἰ μὴ φιλῶ.
May I perish wretchedly if I don't love Xanthias!

(7) Conditions of general or indefinite application, *if ever, if any one.* These follow the rules for the indefinite construction N.

	Protasis	Apodosis
Present.	ἐάν + subjunctive.	Present Indicative.
Past	εἰ + optative.	Imperfect Indicative.

Q. Conditional clauses in indirect speech

Protasis μή. Apodosis οὐ.

1. ὅτι construction.
   No change need be made to conditional sentences as expressed in direct speech,
   but after a secondary tense, as ἔλεξεν,

   Present, future and perfect indicative [1] *may* change to *same tense of optative.* Secondary tenses remain unchanged.

   ἐάν + subjunctive may change to εἰ + *optative.*

   ἄν must be included if it is found in the direct speech.

2. Accusative and infinitive construction.

   (*a*) Protasis as above for ὅτι construction (Q 1).

   (*b*) Apodosis *accusative and infinitive* (or nominative if same subject as main verb).

   Use same tense of the infinitive as in the indicative or optative of direct speech.
   Present infinitive represents present and imperfect indicative.
   ἄν must be included if it is found in the direct speech.

   [1] The primary tenses.

(7) **Present,** indefinite or general

ἐὰν φύγῃ διώκουσιν
If ever he flees they follow

μισοῦσι τοὺς αἰνοῦντας ἢν αἰνῶσ' ἄγαν
Men hate those who praise if they praise too much

Past, indefinite

εἰ φεύγοι ἐδίωκον
If ever he fled they would follow

ἀλλ' εἴ τι μὴ φέροιμεν ὤτρυνεν φέρειν
If we failed to bring anything he would urge us to bring it

Q. Conditional clauses in indirect speech

Direct

ἐὰν φύγωσι διώξει
If they flee he will follow

Indirect

1. ἔλεξεν ὅτι $\begin{cases} ἐὰν φύγωσι διώξει \\ εἰ φύγοιεν διώξοι \end{cases}$ (unchanged, by graphic construction)

2. ἔφη   αὐτὸς $\begin{cases} ἐὰν φύγωσι \\ εἰ φύγοιεν \end{cases}$ διώξειν

Direct

εἰ φύγοι διώκοιεν ἄν
If he were to flee they would follow

Indirect

1. ἔλεξεν ὅτι εἰ φύγοι διώκοιεν ἄν

2. ἔφη αὐτοὺς εἰ φύγοι ἂν διώκειν

Direct

εἰ ἔφυγον ἐδίωξεν ἄν
If they had fled he would have followed

Indirect

1. ἔλεξεν ὅτι εἰ ἔφυγον ἐδίωξεν ἄν

2. ἔφη αὐτὸς εἰ ἔφυγον διῶξαι ἄν

R. Potential sentences

May, might and other English modals expressing *possibility* are translated in the same way as the corresponding conditionals (P 2 and 5).

1. *Future.* Optative with ἄν. Negative οὐ.

2. *Past.* Indicative, past tenses with ἄν. Negative οὐ.

S. Concessive clauses

Even if, although.

1. καί, or μηδέ if negative + εἰ or ἐάν. (καί + ἐάν = κἄν).
Treat as ordinary conditional.

2. καίπερ, *although, even though*, takes a participle.

Further examples of wishes, conditionals and allied constructions
(Syntax D and P-S)

1. εἰ μὲν κτενεῖς τόνδ', οἶκον οἰκήσεις μόνος
If you kill him you will live in the house alone (P 7)

2. ἢν δ' αὐτὰ μὴ πράσσωμεν ὡς ἐγὼ θέλω
πῦ σ' αὖθις ὀψόμεσθα¹ ;
If we do not do these things as I wish, where shall we see you again? (P 1)

3. γελᾷ δ' ὁ μῶρος κἄν τι μὴ γελοῖον ᾖ
The fool laughs even if it is not a laughing matter (S 1)

4. ἢν ἐγγὺς ἔλθῃ θάνατος, οὐδεὶς βούλεται
θνήσκειν
If ever death comes near, no one is willing to die (P 7)

5. θέλοις ἄν, εἰ σώσαιμί σ', ἀγγεῖλαί τί μοι ;
Would you be willing, if I saved you, to carry a message for me? (P 2)

6. θρόνων γὰρ εἰ λαβοίμεθ' εὐτυχοῖμεν ἄν
If we could but seize the throne we should be happy (P 2)

---

¹ -μεσθα for -μεθα, poetical.

R. Potential sentences

1. καὶ πῶς γένοιτ᾽ ἂν ἐν δίκῃ τύπτειν φίλον ;
   And how could it be just to beat a friend?

   οὐκ ἂν πιθοίμην τοῖσι σοῖς κόμποις ἐγώ
   I would never trust your boastful words

2. τούτου τις ἄν σοι τἀνδρὸς ¹ ἦν προνούστερος ;
   Who could have been kinder to you than this man?

S. Concessive clauses

1. ἀρετὴ δὲ κἂν θάνῃ τις οὐκ ἀπόλλυται
   Virtue, even if a man die, perishes not

2. πείθου γυναιξὶ καίπερ οὐ στέργων ὅμως
   Yield to women all the same, though you like it not

Further examples of wishes, conditionals and allied constructions
(Syntax D and P-S)

7. εἰ γὰρ θρόνων λαβοίμεθ᾽· εὐτυχοῖμεν ἄν
   Would we might seize the throne (D 1)! Then should we be happy (R 1)

8. οἶκος αὐτός, εἰ φθόγγην λάβοι
   σαφέστατ᾽ ἂν λέξειεν.
   The house itself, if it could find a voice, would speak most clearly (P 2)

9. ὦ φίλτατ᾽, εἰ γὰρ τοῦτο κατθάνοιμ᾽ ἰδών
   Dear one, would that I might die on seeing this! (D 1)

10. δὶς εἰς τὸν αὐτὸν ποταμὸν οὐκ ἂν ἐμβαίης
    You could never step twice into the same river (R 1)

11. ἀλλ᾽ ὃν πόλις στήσειε, τοῦδε χρὴ κλύειν
    But whomsoever the city appointed, to him must we hearken (N 2)

12. εἰ μόνος ἐσώθη μᾶλλον ἂν ζηλωτὸς ἦν
    εἰ δ᾽ ἄλοχον ἄγεται, κακὸν ἔχων ἥκει μέγα
    If he alone had been saved he would have been more enviable (P 5)
    But if he is bringing his wife he has come with a great evil (P 3)

¹ τοῦ ἀνδρός. Compar. gen.

Table of irregular verbs

		ACTIVE OR MIDDLE			PASSIVE MEANING		
Verb	Meaning	Future	Aorist	Perfect	Future	Aorist	Perfect
αἰνέω¹	Praise	αἰνέσω	ᾔνεσα	ᾔνεκα	αἰνεθήσομαι	ᾐνέθην	ᾔνημαι
αἱρέω	Take	αἱρήσω	εἷλον	ᾕρηκα	αἱρεθήσομαι	ᾑρέθην	ᾕρημαι
αἴρω	Raise	ἀρῶ	ἦρα	ἦρκα	ἀρθήσομαι	ἤρθην	ἦρμαι
αἰσθάνομαι	Perceive	αἰσθήσομαι	ᾐσθόμην	ᾔσθημαι			
ἀκούω	Hear	ἀκούσομαι	ἤκουσα	ἀκήκοα	ἀκουσθήσομαι	ἠκούσθην	ἤκουσμαι
ἁμαρτάνω	Err	ἁμαρτήσομαι	ἥμαρτον	ἡμάρτηκα	ἁμαρτηθήσομαι	ἡμαρτήθην	ἡμάρτημαι
ἀνοίγνυμι Imperf. ἀνέῳγον	Open	ἀνοίξω	ἀνέῳξα	ἀνέῳχα	ἀνοιχθήσομαι	ἀνεῴχθην	ἀνέῳγμαι
ἅπτω	Kindle	ἅψω	ἧψα		ἁφθήσομαι	ἥφθην	ἧμμαι
ἅπτομαι	Touch	ἅψομαι	ἡψάμην				
αὐξάνω	Increase (trans.); Pass. and Mid.: Grow (intrans.)	αὐξήσω	ηὔξησα	ηὔξηκα	αὐξήσομαι	ηὐξόμην / ηὐξήθην	ηὔξημαι
ἀφικνοῦμαι	Arrive	ἀφίξομαι	ἀφικόμην	ἀφῖγμαι			
-βαίνω	Go	βήσομαι	ἔβην	βέβηκα			
βάλλω	Throw	βαλῶ	ἔβαλον	βέβληκα	βληθήσομαι	ἐβλήθην	βέβλημαι
βούλομαι	Wish	βουλήσομαι	ἐβουλήθην	βεβούλημαι			
γαμέω	Marry (of a man)	γαμέω	ἔγημα	γεγάμηκα			
γαμοῦμαι	Marry (of a woman)	γαμοῦμαι	ἐγημάμην	γεγάμημαι			
γίγνομαι	Become	γενήσομαι	ἐγενόμην	γεγένημαι γέγονα			

The middle is not usually given as it almost invariably follows the active in future and aorist, and the perfect is identical with the passive

314

¹ Present indicative is given uncontracted, to show the stem vowels. It should, of course, only be used contracted.

Table of irregular verbs—*continued*

		ACTIVE OR MIDDLE			PASSIVE MEANING		
Verb	Meaning	Future	Aorist	Perfect	Future	Aorist	Perfect
γιγνώσκω	Get to know	γνώσομαι	ἔγνων	ἔγνωκα	γνωσθήσομαι	ἐγνώσθην	ἔγνωσμαι
δάκνω	Bite	δήξομαι	ἔδακον	δέδηχα	δηχθήσομαι	ἐδήχθην	δέδηγμαι
δείκνυμι	Show	δείξω	ἔδειξα	δέδειχα	δειχθήσομαι	ἐδείχθην	δέδειγμαι
δέχομαι	Receive	δέξομαι	ἐδεξάμην	δέδεγμαι			
δέω	Bind	δήσω	ἔδησα	δέδεκα	δεθήσομαι	ἐδέθην	δέδεμαι
δέω	Lack	δεήσω	ἐδέησα	δεδέηκα	δεήσομαι	ἐδεήθην	δεδέημαι
διδάσκω	Teach	διδάξω	ἐδίδαξα	δεδίδαχα	διδάξομαι / διδαχθήσομαι	ἐδιδάχθην	δεδίδαγμαι
δύναμαι	Be able	δυνήσομαι	ἐδυνήθην	δεδύνημαι			
ἐάω	Allow	ἐάσω	εἴασα	εἴακα	ἐάσομαι	εἰάθην	εἴαμαι
ἐθέλω	Wish	ἐθελήσω	ἠθέλησα	ἠθέληκα			
ἐλαύνω	Drive	ἐλῶ -ᾷς, ἐλᾷ κ.τ.λ.	ἤλασα	ἐλήλακα	ἐλαθήσομαι	ἠλάθην	ἐλήλαμαι
ἕλκω	Drag	ἕλξω	εἵλκυσα	εἵλκυκα		εἱλκύσθην	εἵλκυσμαι
ἕπομαι Imperf. εἱπόμην	Follow	ἕψομαι	ἑσπόμην				
ἐρωτάω	Ask	ἐρωτήσω / ἐρήσομαι	ἠρώτησα / ἠρόμην	ἠρώτηκα	ἐρωτηθήσομαι	ἠρωτήθην	ἠρώτημαι
εὑρίσκω	Find	εὑρήσω	ηὗρον	ηὕρηκα	εὑρεθήσομαι	ηὑρέθην	ηὕρημαι
ἔχω Imperf. εἶχον	Have	ἕξω / σχήσω	ἔσχον	ἔσχηκα	ἕξομαι / σχήσομαι		ἔσχημαι
θάπτω	Bury	θάψω	ἔθαψα		ταφήσομαι / τεθάψομαι	ἐτάφην	τέθαμμαι
-θνῄσκω	Die	-θανοῦμαι	-ἔθανον	τέθνηκα			
καθαίρω	Purify	καθαρῶ -εῖς	ἐκάθηρα		καθαροῦμαι / καθανθήσομαι	ἐκαθάρθην	κεκάθαρμαι
καίω	Burn	καύσω / καύσομαι	ἔκαυσα	κέκαυκα	καυθήσομαι	ἐκαύθην	κέκαυμαι

315

Table of irregular verbs—continued

		ACTIVE OR MIDDLE			PASSIVE MEANING		
Verb	**Meaning**	**Future**	**Aorist**	**Perfect**	**Future**	**Aorist**	**Perfect**
καλέω	Call	καλῶ -εῖς -εῖ	ἐκάλεσα	κέκληκα	κληθήσομαι	ἐκλήθην	κέκλημαι
κλέπτω	Steal	κλέψω κλέψομαι	ἔκλεψα	κέκλοφα	κλεφθήσομαι	ἐκλέφθην ἐκλάπην	κέκλεμμαι
-κτείνω	Kill	-κτενῶ	ἔκτεινα	ἔκτονα	see θνῄσκω		
κτάομαι	Acquire	κτήσομαι	ἐκτησάμην	κέκτημαι		ἐκτήθην	κέκτημαι
λαγχάνω	Get by lot	λήξομαι	ἔλαχον	εἴληχα		ἐλήχθην	εἴληγμαι
λαμβάνω	Get	λήψομαι	ἔλαβον	εἴληφα	ληφθήσομαι	ἐλήφθην	εἴλημμαι
λανθάνω	Lie hid	λήσω	ἔλαθον	λέληθα			
ἐπι-λανθάνομαι	Forget	ἐπιλήσομαι	ἐπελαθόμην	ἐπιλέλησμαι			ἐπιλέλησμαι
λείπω	Leave	λείψω	ἔλιπον	λέλοιπα	λειφθήσομαι	ἐλείφθην	λέλειμμαι
μανθάνω	Learn	μαθήσομαι	ἔμαθον	μεμάθηκα			
μάχομαι	Fight	μαχοῦμαι	ἐμαχεσάμην	μεμάχημαι			
μίγνυμι	Mix	μίξω[1]	ἔμιξα		μιχθήσομαι	ἐμίχθην	μέμιγμαι
μιμνῄσκω	Remind	μνήσω	ἔμνησα		μνησθήσομαι	ἐμνήσθην	μέμνημαι
νομίζω	Think	νομιῶ -εῖς -εῖ κτλ.	ἐνόμισα	νενόμικα	νομισθήσομαι νομιοῦμαι νομιοῦμαι	ἐνομίσθην	νενόμισμαι
οἴομαι (οἶμαι)	Think	οἰήσομαι	ᾠήθην				
ἀπ-όλλυμι Imperf. ἀπωλλυν	Destroy	ἀπολῶ -εῖς -εῖ κτλ.	ἀπώλεσα	ἀπολώλεκα	ἀπολοῦμαι	ἀπωλόμην	ἀπόλωλα
					All passive in meaning, *perish*		
ὄμνυμι	Swear	ὀμοῦμαι	ὤμοσα	ὀμώμοκα	ὀμοθήσομαι	ὠμόθην	ὀμώμο(σ)μαι
πάσχω	Suffer	πείσομαι	ἔπαθον	πέπονθα			
πείθω	Persuade	πείσω	ἔπεισα	πέπεικα	πεισθήσομαι	ἐπείσθην	πέπεισμαι
πείθομαι	Obey (w. dative)	πείσομαι	ἐπιθόμην (poetical)	πέποιθα			
πίμπλημι	Fill	πλήσω	ἔπλησα	πέπληκα	πλησθήσομαι	ἐπλήσθην	πέπλησμαι
πίνω	Drink	πίομαι	ἔπιον	πέπωκα			
πίπτω	Fall	πεσοῦμαι	ἔπεσον	πέπτωκα			
πλέω	Sail	πλεύσομαι	ἔπλευσα	πέπλευκα			

[1] Sometimes μείξω and ει for ι throughout.

		ACTIVE OR MIDDLE			PASSIVE MEANING		
Verb	Meaning	Future	Aorist	Perfect	Future	Aorist	Perfect
πυνθάνομαι	Enquire, hear	πεύσομαι	ἐπυθόμην	πέπυσμαι			
ῥήγνυμι	Break	ῥήξω	ἔρρηξα		ῥαγήσομαι	ἐρράγην	ἔρρωγα
στέλλω	Despatch	στελῶ (-έω)	ἔστειλα	ἔσταλκα	σταλήσομαι	ἐστάλην	ἔσταλμαι::
στρέφω	Turn	στρέψω	ἔστρεψα		στραφήσομαι στρέψομαι	ἐστράφην ἐστρέφθην	ἔστραμμαι
τείνω	Stretch	τενῶ (-εω)	ἔτεινα	τέτακα			
τέμνω	Cut	τεμῶ (-εω)	ἔτεμον	τέτμηκα	τμηθήσομαι	ἐτμήθην	τέτμημαι
τίκτω	Bring forth	τέξομαι	ἔτεκον				
τιτρώσκω	Wound	τρώσω	ἔτρωσα		τρωθήσομαι	ἐτρώθην	τέτρωμαι
τρέπω	Turn	τρέψω	ἔτρεψα	τέτροφα	τρέψομαι	ἐτράπην ἐτρέφθην	τέτραμμαι
τρέφω	Nourish	θρέψω	ἔθρεψα	τέτροφα	θρέψομαι	ἐτράφην	τέθραμμαι
τυγχάνω	Happen, hit	τεύξομαι	ἔτυχον	τετύχηκα			
ὑποσχέομαι	Promise	ὑποσχή-σομαι	ὑπεσχόμην	ὑπέσχημαι			
φαίνω	Show	φανῶ (-έω)	ἔφηνα	πέφαγκα	φανοῦμαι	ἐφάνην	πέφασμαι
φεύγω	Flee	φεύξομαι	ἔφυγον	πέφευγα			
φοβέομαι	Fear, be afraid	φοβήσομαι			φοβηθήσομαι	ἐφοβήθην ἐφθάρην	πεφόβημαι ἔφθαρμαι
δια-φθείρω	Destroy	-φθερῶ (έω)	-έφθειρα	ἔφθαρκα	φθαρήσομαι		
χαίρω	Rejoice	χαιρήσω	ἐχάρην	κεχάρηκα			
χάσκω	Gape	χανοῦμαι (εο)	ἔχανον	κέχηνα			
χράομαι	Use	χρήσομαι	ἐχρησάμην	κέχρημαι			
ὠθέω	Push	ὤσω	ἔωσα		ὠσθήσομαι	ἐώσθην	ἔωσμαι

Delphi

ENGLISH INTO GREEK

Words or phrases not contained in the English into Greek vocabulary can be found by referring to the Greek version on which the English passage is based. When in difficulty a paraphrase must be used, and a word for word translation is often best avoided.

Grammatical forms are shown more fully in the Greek-English vocabulary. Familiarity with the grammar section, pages 139 to 313, is assumed. Frequent reference must be made to the table of irregular verbs, pages 314 to 317, until they are perfectly known.

Sunium

I. GREECE AND ATHENS

1. *Greece*

Greece (ἡ Ἑλλάς) is in Europe. Its inhabitants were long ago called Hellēnes. We admire them for their love of freedom, of truth, and of beauty.

This book will tell you some of the things which they said, or wrote, or did.

No part of Greece is far from the sea. It has many harbours, and near it are many islands.

Greece is not a large country. It contains many mountains, but not many plains, and no long rivers. The mountains cut off the Greeks from one another, so that they distrust their neighbours. Among the most famous of their city-states are Sparta, Athens, Thebes, Argos, Corinth. These were often at war with each other, seldom at peace.

2. *Sparta and Athens*

Sparta is sometimes called Lacedaemon. It is some distance from the sea. It bred strong women fitted to be mothers of brave men. Its soldiers were strong, for they practised the art of war from their youth.

Athens, on the other hand, is near the sea. Its citizens learned as sailors or merchants to use ships. They also used their ships in fighting: and thus they became powerful at sea.

3. *Athens : the Acropolis*

It is easier to get to Athens by sea than by land. The traveller by sea arrives at Piraeus, the harbour of Athens, which is five miles distant from the city. In the heart of Athens rises the Acropolis. On the top of the Acropolis are temples, one of which is the Parthenon, or temple of the Virgin Goddess, Athena. The Parthenon has many pillars : and beautiful statues, the work of Pheidias. Some of these statues show a procession in honour of Athena. Her priest gives a *peplus* * to a boy, who brings it to

* ornamental robe.

the goddess, and many go with the boy, on foot or on horseback. The other gods watch the procession : Zeus, Hera, Hephaestus, and even Ares, the god of war.

4. Athens (continued) : market-place and theatre

The market-place of Athens is full of purchasers, for it is now mid-day. They are examining the olive-oil, vinegar, charcoal for the fire, and fish, and conversing with one another, eager, as always, to hear or to say some new thing. A sophist is teaching [1] wisdom to others, as he claims.

The theatre is open to the sky, and looks towards the sea and Salamis. It is called the theatre of Dionysus, the god in whose honour the plays were performed. Some plays are tragedies, which cause tears : others are comedies, which cause laughter.

II. GODS AND GODDESSES

5. Zeus, Hera, Athena, Poseidon

Zeus was called " the father of gods and men " by the Greeks. He lives on the top of Mount Olympus, and with him are the other gods : they advise, but he decides. With his thunderbolt he punishes the guilty.

Hera is his sister, and also his wife. She is honoured at Argos.

Athena is honoured at Athens. She was born from the head of her father Zeus. An owl sits on her helmet : the owl is the emblem of wisdom, and Athena is the goddess of wisdom.

Poseidon is the god of the sea. He rides in a chariot drawn by sea-monsters. He carries a trident as an emblem of his power. He—so they say—causes earthquakes.

6. Apollo, Artemis, Hermes, Demeter, Aphrodite

Apollo, or Phoebus, is the god of light. He is the patron of youth, and presides over their sports and games. He is also the god of prophecy ; his priestess lives at Delphi and is able to prophesy the future. When the gods feast, Apollo plays his harp and leads the dancers.

Artemis is the sister of Apollo, and is a great huntress.

---

[1] Teaching takes two accs.

Hermes was born in Arcadia, a land of flocks and herds. As messenger of the gods, he brings their commands to men. He also leads the dead to the world below.

Demeter taught men how to cultivate corn. Her daughter was Persephone.

Aphrodite is the goddess of love. Her son is Eros. The other goddesses were resentful when Paris, in the beauty contest, awarded the apple to Aphrodite.

III. HEROES

7. *Heracles and Theseus*

Hera sent snakes to destroy Heracles, but he was able to kill them though still an infant. Heracles was a friend of men, and did many things to make their lives happier. He performed twelve labours : in one of which he slew the lion of Nemea. He carried a club, and had round his shoulders a lion's skin.

Theseus was almost a second Heracles. He went to Crete, and killed the Minotaur, a savage monster. He also made the road from Corinth to Athens safe for travellers. He loved Ariadne.

8. *Agamemnon, Achilles, Odysseus*

Agamemnon, the son of Atreus, led the Greeks to Troy, as Helen, the wife of his brother Menelaus, had been carried off by Paris, son of the king of Troy. Agamemnon, on his return home, was killed by Clytemnestra his wife.

Achilles, the son of Peleus, was the bravest warrior among the Greeks at Troy. When his friend Patroclus was killed by the Trojan Hector, Achilles slew Hector, and avenged his friend.

Odysseus was son of Laertes, king of Ithaca, a little island. Odysseus was resourceful amid dangers on his way home from Troy. He then slew the suitors who wished to marry his wife Penelope, while he was absent.

IV. LEGENDS

9. *The Argonauts*

Aeetes, King of Colchis, had a golden fleece, which was guarded by a fire-breathing dragon. Jason offered to bring this to his father Pelias, and built a ship, called the *Argo*. On board the *Argo* went some of the bravest Greeks, among whom was Heracles. On its way to Colchis, the *Argo* had to pass the Symplegades at the entrance of the Black Sea. These were rocks which clashed against one another from time to time. Jason sent a dove, to see if it could get through the rocks. It came through, but its tail-feathers were cut off by the rocks as they came together.

10. *The Argonauts (continued)*

When the Argonauts reached Colchis, Jason asked Aeetes for the golden fleece. Aeetes promised to give it if Jason would first yoke the fierce bulls which the king had. Jason learnt how to do this from Medea, daughter of the King of Colchis. She was in love with him ; and he promised he would marry her, and take her to Greece. So he yoked the bulls, and by means of Medea's ointment he suffered no harm either [1] from bulls or [1] dragon. He then went back to Greece with Medea, on board the *Argo*.

11. *Perseus and Andromeda, Deucalion and Pyrrha*

Cepheus, king of Aethiopia, gave his daughter Andromeda to be devoured by a sea-monster. This was sent by the gods to punish him for the pride of his wife, who had boasted that she was lovelier than the sea-nymphs, the Nereides. But Perseus came to the rock, fought and killed the monster, and set Andromeda free.

Deucalion was the husband of Pyrrha. When Zeus wished to destroy the human race because of its wickedness, he spared only Deucalion and Pyrrha. They constructed a vessel, and when the rains came which covered the earth, they were carried safely over the sea in their ark.

12. *Orpheus, Prometheus, the Sphinx*

Orpheus played the harp so beautifully that even rocks and trees followed him as he played. His wife, Eurydice, died : but Orpheus induced the god of the lower world to let her go back to earth. On the way up, he turned to look at her. Thus, by his longing for her, she was again lost.

Prometheus gave to mankind the gift of fire : and was punished by Zeus, who nailed him to a rock in Caucasus, and sent an eagle to gnaw his liver.

The Sphinx was a monster, half-woman, half-lioness. She asked all

---

[1] either... οὔτε ... οὔτε.

who came to her to guess a riddle.   Oedipus was not at a loss, for he realised that man can be two-footed, three-footed and four-footed.

V. FABLES AND FICTION

13. *The frogs and their king*

The frogs asked Zeus to send them a king, who could keep them in order.   Zeus at first sent them a log of wood.   They were alarmed when this fell into their pond, but afterwards, as it did nothing, they despised it.   They asked for a more worthy king.   This time Zeus decided to send them a water-snake, so fierce that it caught and devoured them.   The moral is : better to have no ruler than a wicked one.

14. *The lion, the ass, and the fox went into partnership*

A lion, an ass, and a fox, went into partnership.   They killed some game, and proceeded to divide the spoil.   The ass made the division.   He made three equal parts, and gave one part to each.   But the lion was so angry that he killed the ass.   The fox began to divide what they had taken, and made two portions.   One, very large, he gave to the lion.   The other portion, very small, he kept for himself.   The fox explained that the fate of the ass taught him to make so wise a division.

15. *Voyage to the moon*

For some days and nights we travelled in our air-ship until as night fell we came to a land from which shone a bright light.   Making fast our ship, we went ashore.   Nothing could be seen by day, but when night came on other islands appeared in the sky : among these was one which had cities, seas, and woods : it was our earth.   We decided to explore the land to which we had come, as it was inhabited and cultivated, and presently encountered men mounted on large birds ; the birds had broad wings like the sails of a ship.   These Bird-Men used to patrol the country, and bring any strangers to the king.   Seeing us he guessed us to be Greeks, and we admitted it.

16. *Metamorphoses*

Palaestra's mistress intended to change herself into a bird, and fly away to her lover.   And so it was : the woman anointed herself with an unguent, and immediately wings began to sprout from her shoulders.   And as I

watched I saw her nose become like a beak.   She was now the bird which
we call a crow.   I could hardly trust my eyes, but was amazed at the sight.

I then proceeded to smear myself with some of the same ointment.
But I was not changed into a bird.   No : I acquired a tail : my fingers
and toes were changed into hooves.   My face grew broad.   My man's
voice had disappeared.   I realised that I had been turned into an ass.

VI. HOME LIFE

17. *The Homeric age*

Odysseus, Ajax (*Aías*), and Phoenix were sent by the Greek army to
the tent of Achilles before Troy, to bring about friendship between him
and Agamemnon.   When they came to his tent, they found him playing
the harp.   They sat down, and Patroclus gave them wine to drink.
Achilles offered them meat, which was then roasted at the fire.   They
would not partake of food until they had sacrificed to Zeus and the other
gods.

Telemachus, son of Odysseus, went to King Menelaus at Sparta, to
learn news of his father.   The servants of the king met him, and brought
him to the palace.   After bathing, he was anointed with olive oil, and the
king entertained him at dinner.   Then Helen came, and worked at her
wool.

18. *At Athens*

Socrates paid a visit to the house of Callias, to see Protagoras, the
Sophist.   The porter admitted us, and we found Protagoras surrounded
by a number of pupils, who walked about with him, and listened as he
walked and talked.   When he turned in his walk, they moved to one side
or the other, and took care not to get in his way.

19. *Training of a wife*

I asked Ischomachus how he trained his young wife to be a good house-
keeper.   He said that some training was necessary, for when she became
his wife she had been taught to see little, hear little, and ask no questions.
She may have known how to apportion the wool to her handmaidens to
spin.   She also had some knowledge of cookery, a valuable acquisition
for both men and women.   He asked her to say why he had married *her*,

and why her parents had entrusted her to *him*. She replied that it was because they were fitted to join together in partnership, and make a happy home.

20. *The joy of seeing a well-ordered household*

Marriage will bring to a wife some pleasures that are all her own. For example, she will convert a maidservant who knows nothing about spinning into a useful servant : she will also be able to correct those who need correction, and she will have the pleasure of making them more efficient. But the chief joy which she will experience will be that of making her husband her devoted servant. And the more effective she becomes in managing the home and looking after the children, the higher she will stand in his esteem.

21. *Diversions at a banquet*

When the tables had been removed, and the guests had poured a libation and sung a hymn to Apollo, a man came in to entertain us. With him were a flute girl, a dancing girl, and a handsome boy, good at playing the zither and at dancing. The flute girl accompanied the dancing girl on the flute. The boy handed to her hoops, which, as she danced, she threw into the air, and caught.

VII. SPORT AND GAMES

22. *In the heroic age*

In the funeral games over the body of Patroclus, one of the competitions was a boxing match. Epeus entered the ring, confident of victory. Euryalus followed. The fight was short. Epeus struck Euryalus a blow, which caused him first to leap in the air, and then to fall, as a fish leaps, and then disappears in the sea.

At the court of Alcinous in Phaeacia Odysseus, somewhat unwillingly, took part in the sports. He threw the quoit further than any Phaeacian. He then challenged them to box, wrestle, or race him. It was plain that if they had thought him a more inexperienced athlete they would have accepted his challenge.

23. *Hunting a wild boar.*

Adrastus came to the court of King Croesus. He had killed his own brother, and his father had driven him from home. Croesus received him

Olympia

kindly, and soon after, when a boar hunt was organised at the request of the people of Mysia, whose lands the boar was ravaging, Croesus allowed Adrastus to go, and to take care of Atys, son of Croesus. So Adrastus and Atys took part in the hunt, though Croesus had had a dream warning him of the coming death of Atys. A chance thrust of Adrastus' spear, intended for the boar, struck Atys, and killed him.

24. *The Olympic games*

The Olympic games were held every fourth year, at Olympia in Elis, on the banks of the river Alpheus, likewise the Pythian games at Delphi. The month during which they were held was sacred, and a truce was observed while the games lasted. Pindar has written many odes in praise of the victors. Sophocles tells us how Orestes hit the turning post in the chariot race. He fell tangled in the reins and was killed.

VIII. SEA : SEA FIGHTS : ISLANDS

25. *Battle of Salamis*

Aristides came from Aegina to Salamis, and told the Greeks that they were completely surrounded by the Persians. So the Greeks made ready for battle. At daybreak, Themistocles ordered the ships to put to sea : as they put out, the Persians began to attack them.

Artemisia, queen of Caria, fighting for the Persians, had a double success. She was pursued by an Athenian ship. In front of her lay a Persian ship, which she rammed and sank. The Athenian commander thought she was a deserter from the Persian cause, and desisted from the pursuit. Xerxes, on the other hand, loudly praised Artemisia for her courage. He did not believe that she was deserting, nor that she would sink a friendly ship.

26. *Battle between Peloponnesian ships and a force of Athenian ships under Phormio*

The Peloponnesian ships were drawn up in a circle, with bows outwards and sterns inwards. The Athenian ships were in a single line, and sailed round the enemy, driving him into a narrower space. When the wind arose, the enemy's ships fell into confusion, and the crews kept pushing off the other ships with poles. The sailors were clumsy and could not prevent collisions, but merely shouted and swore. At this moment Phormio gave the signal for attack. The Athenians won the victory.

27. The battle of Aegospotami

The Dardanelles ('Ελλήσποντος) at Aegospotami, which lies opposite Lampsacus, is about a mile and a half across. The Athenians offered battle to Lysander, but he declined. A few days later, he sent out his scouts to watch the Athenians. When they had gone ashore, and were widely scattered in search of food, his scouts raised up a shield as a signal. Lysander attacked. Conon, the Athenian admiral, promptly recalled his men, but they were too far away. Nearly every Athenian ship was captured.

28. Crete and its ruler Minos

Minos, the ruler of Cnossus in Crete, was the first to maintain a navy in Greece. He ruled over the Cyclades, and he kept down the pirates. Piracy was frequent in early Greece. The pirates could fall on a city unprotected by walls, and plunder it. When the pirates had been suppressed the revenues came instead to Minos.

IX. LAND BATTLES AND SIEGES

29. Marathon

The battle of Marathon lasted several hours. The Greek centre was forced in by the Persians, and driven in flight. But the Greek wings were victorious, and turned to attack the Persians in the centre. Here, too, the Greeks prevailed, and carried their pursuit to the water's edge, where the Persian ships were drawn up. Some fierce fighting ensued in the attack on the ships, and a number of Greeks lost their lives in struggling for the ships.

30. Battle of Tegea : Lacedaemonians v. Argives and allies

Before the battle began, the leaders of the allies of Argos exhorted their men to fight bravely, and to defeat the Spartans in the Peloponnese itself. But to the Spartans a brief reminder of their discipline was thought to be better than many words. The Argives advanced rapidly, the

Spartans slowly. The Spartan advance was kept steady by the music of many flutes, which helped them to keep time, and Agis, King of Sparta, was victorious. The enemy withdrew in haste. As usual with Spartans, the pursuit was not long continued.

31. *Battle of Leuctra*

The Thebans were easily superior to the Spartans in a cavalry engagement, for the Spartans were not well-trained in such a form of fighting. Epaminondas, who led the Thebans, argued that, if he could defeat those Spartans who stood round their king Cleombrotus, the rest could not give him much trouble. By this time the cavalry engagement was over, and the Spartan horse, in their retreat, obstructed the advance of their own infantry. First the Spartan right gave way, then the left, for the Thebans were in mass formation. There were many casualties, and the Spartans asked for an armistice to enable them to take up their dead.

32. *Battle of Issus*

The Persian left were soon defeated, but the Greek mercenaries serving Darius were not so easily overcome. However, help came from the Macedonian right wing. Also, Darius, when he saw his left give way, turned his chariot, and fled. Alexander pursued while daylight lasted. When night fell he returned, bringing with him the chariot of Darius and his shield. He also took by assault the Persian camp, in which he found Darius' mother and wife. On the next day he congratulated those who had distinguished themselves in the fight.

33. *Siege of Troy*

When Agememnon had collected an army to go to Troy and recover Helen, the wife of Menelaus, he assembled his army at Aulis, and thence he sailed to Troy. Drawing up his ships, he built a wall to protect them. A battle was fought in the plain, and the Trojans began to set fire to the Greek ships within the wall. Patroclus now appeared, being sent by Achilles to help the Greeks. On the death of Patroclus, Achilles himself entered the fray and chased Hector round the walls of Troy. Finally, Troy was taken by the stratagem of the Wooden Horse. The siege of Troy lasted ten years.

34. *Siege of Plataea*

The Spartans, under their king Archidamus, built a wall round Plataea, which was an ally of Athens. The Plataeans had deposited their wives and children, and the old and infirm, for safety at Athens. About 600 were left in the town itself : and of these about 200 succeeded, one dark and stormy night, in getting over the wall, crossing the ditch, which was frozen over, and in making their way to Athens.

35. *Night attack during the siege of Syracuse*

Demosthenes, Nicias, and others in command of the Athenians, set out by night to capture Epipolae, a fortress of Syracuse. They were at first successful, but when reinforcements came up under Gylippus they had to retreat. The light of the moon was not distinct enough to enable them to see who was friend, who was foe : and this confusion made it easier for the Syracusans to overcome them, especially as the Syracusans knew the ground.

X. TRAVEL

36. *The adventures of Democedes*

Darius, King of Persia, sustained an injury during a hunt. As the Egyptian doctors failed to cure him, he sent for Democedes, who was a native of Croton in Italy. His father's violent temper had caused him to leave home. He went first to Aegina, where he speedily outstripped the local practitioners : Athens offered him a larger fee than Aegina, but Polycrates of Samos offered him still more. When Polycrates was put to death by the Persians, Democedes lost his freedom, and was a slave in Sardis when Darius heard of his skill.

37. *The founding of Cyrene*

Battus was the son of a native of the island of Thera. He received his name from his habit of stammering. When he went to Delphi to consult the oracle about this defect, the priestess told him that she could do nothing for his voice : but she bade him go to Libya to found a colony there. Battus was disappointed that the god assigned him such an impossible task. The assistance of Thera was obtained for him. The settlers went first to an island off the coast of Libya, and then to a fertile region in Libya, not far from Cyrene.

38. *The Scythians are attacked by Darius*

Before invading the land of the Scythians with his army, Darius ordered the Ionians who had built the bridge over the Danube to break it down. But the leader of the Mytileneans warned him that the Scythians lived in

caravans, with no cultivation or settled cities. It might be impossible to
find them and defeat them. It would be better to keep the bridge as a
safe line of retreat, and not lose their way and come to grief.

39. *The Royal Road from Sardis to Susa*

The conveying of news in the Persian Empire was done speedily. At
every stage in the journey there is a horse and rider. Each is stationed a
day's ride from the next. Nothing stops them, not snow nor rain, nor
heat, nor darkness. They cover the allotted distance at full speed. The
first passes on the message to the second, the second to the third, and so
on, like torch-bearers in Greece. The first tidings received at Susa
about Xerxes was that he had captured Athens. The next, however,
conveyed the news of his defeat at Salamis.

40. *Alexander and Porus*

Porus, after being defeated by Alexander, dismounted from his elephant
and asked his old friend Meroes to bring him to Alexander. But Alexander
did not treat him harshly. He checked his horse in front of the army in
amazement at Porus's splendid stature and proud bearing. Then he said
to him : " We two have fought each other as two kings for the throne.
I shall treat you as a king, for that is what you would wish."

41. *Alexander's army refuses to advance*

The country beyond the Hyphasis was said to be fruitful, and Alexander was eager to advance. But the Macedonians felt that before them
lay the prospect of more and more toils and dangers. They announced
their intention of refusing to advance, even if Alexander himself led the
way. He asked them if they were dissatisfied with the results they had
gained. " To Macedonia," he said, " we have added Ionia, Egypt and
Babylon." But all rejoiced when he announced his intention to turn
back.

42. *Great Britain as described by Strabo*

Britain is a three-cornered island producing corn, silver and iron.
They do not use hounds in warfare, but fight mostly from chariots. They
are less civilised than the Gauls, and some do not even know how to make
cheese. In other respects they resemble the Gauls. The weather is rainy,
and there is persistent fog. They are well supplied with herds, and export
many things to Gaul. On many days the sun is visible for only a few
hours. The island lies opposite Gaul.

XI. FRIENDSHIP

43. *Theseus and Pirithous*

Pirithous, king of the Lapithae, had heard a great deal about Theseus's reputation for strength and bravery. Wishing to test whether it was true, he drove Theseus's cattle away, and then waited to meet his pursuer. But on beholding the beauty of Theseus, Pirithous held out his hand and promised to submit to any penalty he might inflict. Then they each gladly accepted the other as friend and ally.

44. *Achilles and Patroclus*

Patroclus, son of Menoetius, went to live with Peleus, and became a comrade of Achilles, son of Peleus. With Achilles he went to Troy. When the Greek ships were set on fire, Achilles gave him his own suit of armour, and sent him to fight for the Greeks. Patroclus pursued the Trojans to the city wall, but was killed by Hector. Achilles mourned for his friend, and celebrated games in his honour.

45. *Socrates and Alcibiades*

Socrates and Alcibiades were brought together as soldiers in the campaign round Potidaea. Alcibiades tells us that in bearing the fatigues of the campaign Socrates, though the older man, was ahead of him, and indeed of everyone in the army. In regard to food and drink Socrates was the most moderate of men. Also, in the retreat from Delium in Boeotia, Socrates, who was on foot and in full armour, showed no fear, but looked round with perfect calmness on friend and foe alike.

46. *The Sacred Band of warriors at Thebes*

The Sacred Band consisted of 300 young Thebans, for whom their native town provided food and lodging in the citadel. They were personal friends. This made them feel shame at the thought of giving way·in battle, for they would be in the presence of intimate friends. There were once two men thus joined in friendship, and one of them was about to be pierced by the spear of an enemy through the back. He asked, however, to be stabbed through the chest, as he did not wish his friend to have the shame of seeing him lying dead with a wound in his back.

47. *Glaucus of Sparta and his friend from Miletus*

Glaucus of Sparta had a great reputation for honesty. A man from Miletus came to him one day : he was about to sell his estate, and wished to arrange for the safe deposit of a large sum of money. " Take these tallies," he said, " and keep them carefully : and when men come bearing the corresponding tallies, pay them the money which I now deposit with you." Glaucus agreed : but when the men came asking for the money he pretended to have forgotten. However, the Oracle of Delphi advised him to repay the money. It said, " The god of justice has a son who pursues wrongdoers, and punishes them."

48. *Damon and Phintias, of Syracuse*

In the days of Dionysius, tyrant of Syracuse, Phintias was accused of conspiring against the life of Dionysius, and was sentenced to death. He asked to be allowed the remainder of that day, in which to put his affairs in order. If his request were granted, he said, he would get his friend Damon to stand surety for him, in case he himself failed to return before the end of the day. Damon agreed to this. Just at sunset, when Damon was about to be executed, Phintias reappeared. Dionysius was so touched that he asked to join in their friendship.

49. *Alexander and Clitus*

Clitus disliked Alexander because he had adopted Persian habits, and listened to flatterers. So their friendship, which had been very close, became less so. At a banquet, Clitus said to Alexander : " Your triumphs are not so magnificent as your toadies make out, most of your successes are due to the ordinary Macedonian private." The end came when Clitus claimed to have saved Alexander's life at the battle of the Granicus. The king leaped up, snatched a spear from the hand of a guardsman, and Clitus fell dead to the ground.

50. *Orestes and Pylades*

After the death of his father Agamemnon, Orestes was sent secretly to Phocis, where he was guarded by the father of his friend Pylades. In company with Pylades, Orestes set out to avenge himself on his mother. When the Furies pursued Orestes, Pylades stood by him. The two friends went together to the land of the Tauri, to fetch back from that land the image of the goddess Artemis.

XII. GREAT MEN

51. *Aristides*

After Marathon, the Athenians were jealous of anyone whose fame outshone that of his fellows. For this reason they banished Aristides. The custom was to write a name on potsherds or *ostraka* : hence the word " ostracised ". Any citizen could write a name on an ostrakon. A common Athenian brought his potsherd to Aristides, taking him to be an ordinary bystander, and asked him to write " Aristides " on it. When Aristides asked, " Has Aristides done you any injury? " he said, " None at all, but I am tired of hearing him called ' The Just '." Aristides did as he was desired.

52. *Themistocles*

The Spartans were not usually cowards in the face of danger, but when the Persian fleet approached they wanted to withdraw to the Isthmus. This plan would have meant the overthrow of Greece, and Themistocles opposed it. He even threatened that the Athenians would sail away to Italy. He said that the Athenians had abandoned their city, not wanting to face slavery for the sake of lifeless possessions. It was not fair to taunt men who owned two hundred triremes with being without a city.

53. *Pericles*

The greatest glory of Athens, which chiefly moved the admiration of the world, was the splendour of her public monuments, many of which were erected by Pericles. His enemies attacked him for erecting these out of money paid by the allies of Athens, but he explained that Athens was not called upon to render an account of the money which she spent upon the monuments, so long as she carried out the war on behalf of the allies who contributed the money. The works erected by Pericles were of imposing beauty, and it is astounding to hear of the speed with which the work was done.

54. *Plato*

Plato was greeted with extraordinary marks of honour when he came to Sicily. He did so at the request of Dion, a relative of Dionysius, tyrant of Syracuse. Dion hoped that Plato would help to remove from the tyranny its absolute character, and make Dionysius into a constitutional ruler. Dionysius received Plato with great honour, going so far as to offer sacrifice to the gods as for some great good fortune. There was also a crowd anxious to learn about philosophy.

55. *Plato (continued)*

But the people soon began to speak ill of both Dion and his friend

Plato. For it seemed to them that Plato's philosophy was casting a spell on the tyrant. For what other reason should he have sent away his body-guard, hoping to gain happiness through geometry alone? They were vexed that one Sophist should be undermining the power of Dionysius. In this way they aroused the suspicion of the tyrant.

56. *Demosthenes*

Demosthenes, at the end of his life, had fled from the Macedonians, and was in the temple of Poseidon in the island of Calauria. Archias, an Athenian working for the Macedonians, sought to persuade him to leave the sanctuary. But Demosthenes refused. Looking at Archias, who had been an actor, he said, " Archias, you have never convinced me by your acting, and you will not now convince me by your promises." He took a pen as if to write, and put it to his lips. There was poison in the pen, and soon he ceased to breathe. After his death, the Athenians repented that they had not taken his advice.

XIII. LOVE OF COUNTRY

57. *Codrus*

Codrus, King of Athens, knew that the oracle had said that if the Athenian king were killed by the Spartans, then the Athenians would win. The Spartans also knew this, and tried not to lay hands on Codrus. Codrus therefore went out to collect wood disguised as a woodcutter. He wounded a soldier with his axe and was instantly despatched. If the oracle had not been fulfilled the Athenians would not have been victorious.

58. *Thermopylae*

On the approach of Xerxes, many of the Greeks retreated to the Isthmus of Corinth. But Leonidas, king of Sparta, resolved to stand his ground. Xerxes sent scouts to report on the number and conduct of the Greeks. The scouts reported that some of the Greeks were drilling, while others were combing their hair. Demaratus, a Spartan exile, told Xerxes that Spartans when about to risk their lives, always comb their hair. The Spartans, to the number of 300, were attacked from the rear as well as in front, and they perished to a man.

59. *Speech of Pericles over the first Athenians to die in the Peloponnesian War*

" These men died in the manner in which it befits Athenians to die. You, the survivors, must show a resolution as unyielding as theirs. You must realise the greatness of Athens : brave men who knew their duty have made her great. . . . These men who have fallen have received, in return for the offering of their lives, a renown that grows not old. Heroes have the whole earth for their tomb : in lands far from their own there is a record of them not inscribed on any tablet, but written in the hearts of men."

60. *The scene at Athens on the arrival of news of Philip's advance*

Evening came, and with it the news that Philip held Elatea. Athens became a scene of confusion. . . . Next day the Senate met : the public assembly, too, was convened. Views on the crisis were invited : but no one rose in his place. Repeated requests produced no response, till at last I rose in my place. I said, " Philip is displaying his strength at our doors, in order to encourage his friends and terrify his enemies. Set aside your fears, and send to Eleusis cavalry and infantry, to encourage our forces in Thebes to speak their minds openly."

A

ἀγαθός, -ή, -όν, adj., *good, brave.*
  Comp. ἀμείνων, ἄριστος (Par. 37).
'Αγάθων, ὁ, *Agathon.*
'Αγαμέμνων, ὁ, *Agamemnon.*
ἀγανακτῶ(εω), v.n., *be indignant.*
ἀγαπητός, -ή, -όν, adj., *beloved,*
  giving grounds for thanks (ἀγαπητόν
  ἐστι).
ἀγγελία, ἡ, 1, *message.*
ἀγγέλλω, v.a., *announce.*
ἄγγελος, ὁ, 2, *messenger.*
ἀγέλη, ἡ, 1, *herd.*
ἀγήραντος, -ον, adj., *ageless.*
ἀγήρως, -ων, adj., *immortal, undying.*
ἅγιος, -α, -ον, adj., *holy, sacred.*
ἄγκυρα, ἡ, 1, *anchor.*
ἀγορά, ἡ, 1, *market-place, agora.*
ἀγορεύω, v.a. and n., *speak.* Par. 71.
ἄγρα, ἡ, 1, *booty, prey, hunting.*
ἀγράμματος, -ον, adj., *illiterate.*
ἄγραφος, -ον, adj., *unwritten.*
ἄγριος, -α, -ον,, adj., *wild.*
ἀγριότης, -τητος, ἡ, 3, *fierceness.*
ἀγρός, ὁ, 2, *field, country.*
ἀγρυπνία, ἡ, 1, *sleeplessness.*
ἄγχω, v.a., *strangle.*
ἄγω, v.a., *bring, lead, conduct, drive.*
ἀγών, -ῶνος, ὁ, 3, *contest, struggle,*
  athletic contest.
ἀγωνίζομαι, v.dep., *contend, fight.*
ἀδελφή, ἡ, 1, *sister.*
ἀδελφός, ὁ, 2, *brother.*
ἀδικία, ἡ, 1, *injustice.*
ἀδικῶ(εω), v.a., *injure.*
ἀδόλως, adv., *honestly, without guile.*
ἀδύνατος, -ον, adj., *impossible.*
Ἄδραστος, ὁ, 2, *Adrastus.*
ᾄδω, v.n., *sing.*

"Αδωνις, -ιδος, ὁ, 3, *Adonis.*
ἀεί, adv., *always.* ἀεὶ ... ποτε,
  constantly.
ἀείμνηστος, -ον, adj., *ever to be*
  remembered.
ἀεροδρομῶ (εω), v.n., *sail in the air.*
ἀετός, ὁ, 2, *eagle.*
ἀηδών, -όνος, ἡ, 3, *nightingale.*
ἀήρ, -έρος, ὁ, 3, *air.* Plur. *climate.*
ἀθάνατος, -ον, adj., *immortal.*
'Αθηνᾶ, ἡ, 1, *Athena.*
'Αθῆναι, αἱ, 1, *Athens.* 'Αθήναζε, *to*
  Athens. 'Αθήνηθεν, *from Athens.*
  'Αθήνησι, *at Athens.*
'Αθηναῖος, -α, -ον, adj., *Athenian.*
ἆθλον τό, 2, *prize in a contest.*
ἆθλος, ὁ, 2, *contest, labour.*
ἀθλῶ(εω), v.n., *compete.*
ἀθροίζω, v.a. *muster.*
αἰαῖ, *alas!*
Αἴας, -αντος, ὁ, 3, *Ajax, Aias.*
Αἰγαῖος, -α, -ον, adj., *Aegean.*
Αἰγεύς, -έως, ὁ, 3, *Aegeus, father of*
  Theseus.
Αἴγινα, ἡ, 1, *Aegina.*
Αἰγινήτης, ὁ, 1, *Aeginetan, native of*
  Aegina.
Αἴγισθος, ὁ, 2, *Aegisthus.*
Αἰγὸς ποταμοί, οἱ, *Aegospotami.*
Αἰγύπτιος, -α, -ον, adj., *Egyptian.*
Αἴγυπτος, ἡ, 2, *Egypt.*
Ἄιδης, ὁ, 1, *Hades, lord of the lower*
  world. Also "Αδης.
εἰς Ἄιδου, ἐν Ἄιδου, supply οἶκον
  or οἴκῳ, *to hell, in hell.*
αἰδοῦμαι(εο), v.n., *feel shame before,*
  respect.
'Αιήτης, ὁ, 1, *Aeetes, king of Colchis.*
Αἰθιοπία, ἡ, 1, *Aethiopia.*

αἴνιγμα, -ατος, τό, 3, *riddle.*
αἴξ, αἰγός, ὁ, ἡ, 3, *goat.*
αἵρεσις, -εως, ἡ, 3, *choice.*
αἱροῦμαι(εο) v., mid. *choose.*
αἱρῶ(εω), v.a., *take.* ᾿Ὰ
αἰσθάνομαι, v. mid., *perceive.*
ἀΐσσω, v.n., *rush forward.*
αἰσχρός, -α, -ον, adj., *base.*
Ἀισχύλος, ὁ, 2, *Aeschylus.*
αἰτία, ἡ, 1, *cause.*
αἴτιος, -α, -ον, adj., *guilty of, responsible.*
αἰτῶ(εω), v.a., *ask, beg.*
αἰχμή, ἡ, 1, *point of a weapon.*
ἀκάτιον, τό, 2, *boat.*
ἀκίνδυνος, -ον, adj., *free from danger.*
ἀκίνητος, -ον, adj., *immovable.*
ἀκμάζω, v.n. *be at one's prime.*
ἀκόλουθος, ὁ, 2, *servant, attendant.*
ἀκολουθῶ(εω), v.a., *follow,* w. dat.
ἀκοντίζω, v.a., *hurl a javelin.*
ἀκόντιον, τό, 2, *javelin.*
ἀκούω, v.a., *hear, hear of, be spoken of, reputed.*
ἄκρα, ἡ, 1, *summit.*
ἀκρόαμα, -ατος, τό, 3, *anything heard,* plur. *players or singers.*
Ἀκρόπολις, -εως, ἡ, 3, *Acropolis,* esp. of Athens.
ἄκρος, -α, -ον, adj., *high, topmost.*
ἀκροῶμαι(αο),v. mid., *listen to, obey.*
ἄκων, -οντος, ὁ, 3, *javelin.*
Ἀλέξανδρος, ὁ, 2, *Alexander the Great; Paris, son of Priam.*
ἀλέξημα, -ατος, τό, 3, *respite, help.*
ἀλήθεια, ἡ, 1, *truth.*
ἀληθεύω, v.n., *tell the truth.*
ἀληθής, -ές, adj., *true.*
ἁλίσκω, v.a., *capture;* par. 72.
Ἀλκιβιάδης, ὁ, 1, *Alcibiades.*
Ἀλκμήνη, ἡ, 1, *Alcmena, mother of Heracles.*
ἀλλά, conj., *but.*
ἀλλάσσω, v.a., *I change, get rid of.*

ἀλλήλους, -ας, -α, recip. pron., *one another.*
ἅλλομαι, ἡλάμην, v. mid., *leap.*
ἄλλη . . . ἄλλη, adv., *in different directions.*
ἄλλος, -η, -ον, pron., *other, another.*
οἱ ἄλλοι, *the rest.*
ἄλλοτε, adv., *sometimes.*
ἅλμα, -ατος, τό, 3, *leap.*
ἄλοχος, ἡ, 2, *wife.*
ἄλσος, -ους, τό, 3, *grove.*
Ἀλφεῖος, ὁ, 2, *Alpheus, river flowing by Olympia.*
ἄλφιτα, -ων, τά, 2, *barley cakes.*
ἀλώπηξ, -εκος, ἡ, 3, *fox.*
ἅλωσις, -εως, ἡ, 3, *capture.*
ἅμα, adv., *at once, at the same time, as soon as.*
Ἀμάζων,-ονος, ἡ, 3, *amazon, female warrior.*
ἀμαθής, -ές, adj., *ignorant.*
ἅμαξα, ἡ, 1, *waggon.*
ἁμαρτάνω, v.a. or n., *miss the mark, fail, err, sin,* w. gen.
ἀμείβομαι, v. mid., *make reply, answer, exchange.*
Ἀμεινίας, -ου, ὁ, 1, *Ameinias.*
ἀμείνων, comp. adj., from ἀγαθός.
ἄμεμπτος, -ον, adj., *blameless.*
ἄμπελος, ἡ, 2, *vine.*
ἀμπελών, -ῶνος, ὁ, 3, *vineyard.*
ἀμύνω, v.a., *ward off;* ἀμύνομαι, *defend oneself.*
ἀμφί, prep. w. acc., *about, with, following.*
ἀμφότερος, -α, -ον, pron., *both.*
ἄμφω, ἀμφοῖν, pron., *both.*
ἄν, conditional particle. Syntax N, O, P, Q, R (pp. 306-12).
ἀνά, prep., *up to, along.* Table, p. 278.
ἀναβλέπω, v.n., *look up.*
ἀναγκάζω, v.a., *compel.*
ἀνάγω, v.a., *lead up, lead out to sea.* Middle, *put out to sea.*
ἀναδίδωμι, v.a., *give up, hand over.*

ἀνάθημα,-ατος, τό, 3, *offering, monument.*

ἀναιρῶ(εω), v.a., *remove, kill, destroy.*

ἀνακαλῶ(εω), v.a., *call up.*

ἀνακρούω, v.a. and n., *back water.*

ἀναλίσκω, v.a., *spend*, aor. ἀνήλωσα.

ἀναμιμνήσκω, v.a., *remind*, pass. *remember.*

ἄναξ, -ακτος, ὁ, 3, *king.*

ἀνάξιος, -ον, adj., *unworthy.*

ἀναπαύω, v.a. *bring to rest,* mid. *rest.*

ἀναπέμπω, v.a., *send up.*

ἀναρπάζω, v.a., *catch up.*

ἀναρρίπτω, v.a., *throw up.*

ἀναρχία, ἡ, 1, *lawlessness.*

ἀναστρέφω, v.a., *turn, turn up, turn round, overthrow.*

ἀνατείνω, v.a., *stretch out.*

ἀνατέλλω, v.n., *rise.*

ἀνατίθημι, v.a., *set up, dedicate.*

ἀναφέρω, v.a., *bring up, raise.*

ἀναχάσκω, v.n., *gape open, yawn.*

ἀναχωρῶ(εω), v.n., *withdraw, go back.*

ἀνδραποδίζω, v.a., *enslave.*

ἀνδράποδον, τό, 2, *slave.*

ἀνδρεία, ἡ, 1, *courage.*

ἀνδρεῖος, -α, -ον, adj., *brave.*

ἀνδρείως, adv., *bravely.*

ἀνδρηλατῶ(εω), v.a., *banish* (poetical).

ἀνδριάς, -άντος, ὁ, 3, *statue.*

ἀνδροῦμαι(οο), v.pass., *grow to manhood.*

ἀνέλκω, v.a., *draw up.*

ἄνεμος, ὁ, 2, *wind.*

ἀνεπιστήμων, -ον, adj., *ignorant.*

ἀνέρχομαι, v. dep., *come up.*

ἄνευ, prep. with gen., *without.*

ἀνήρ, ἀνδρός, ὁ, 3, *man.*

ἀνθίσταμαι, intrans. tenses p. 250, *resist, stand up to.*

ἄνθραξ, -ακος, ὁ, *coal, charcoal.*

ἄνθρωπος, ὁ or ἡ, 2, *man, human being* (Latin *homo*).

ἄνθος, -ους, τό, 3, *flower.*

ἀνθῶ(εω), v.n., *flower.*

ἀνίημι, v.a., *let go, release.*

ἀνίσταμαι, intrans. tenses, *stand up.*

ἀνίσχειν, v.n., *rise.*

ἀνοίγνυμι, v.a., *open.*

ἀνταγωνίζομαι, v. mid., *struggle against, compete with.*

ἀντανάγω, v.a. and n., *put to sea.*

ἀντέχω, v.n. *hold out, resist,* mid. w. gen, *hold on to, clutch.*

ἀντί, prep. w. gen., *instead of.*

ἄντιον, adv., *opposite, against.*

ἀντιλέγω, v.n., *oppose.*

ἄνω, adv., *above, up.*

ἄνωθεν, adv., *from above.*

ἄξιος, -α, -ον, adj., *worthy,* w. gen.

ἀξίωμα, -ατος, τό, 3, *reputation*

ἀξιῶ(οω), v.a. and n., *think fit, consent to.* Mid., *ask.*

ἀοίδιμος, -ον, adj., *famed in song.*

ἀπαγγέλλω, v.a., *announce, report.*

ἀπαλλάσσομαι, v. mid., *depart from, get clear.*

ἀπαντῶ(αω), v.n., *meet,* with dative.

ἄπας, ἄπασα, ἄπαν, adj., *all, whole, every.*

ἀπειθής, -ές, adj., *disobedient.*

ἀπειλῶ(εω), v.a., *threaten.*

ἀπειρία, ἡ, 1, *inexperience.*

ἄπειρος, -ον, adj., *inexperienced.*

ἀπέχω, v.n. *be distant, keep away from.*

ἀπήνη, ἡ, 1, *chariot.*

ἄπιστος, -ον, adj., *unfaithful, untrustworthy, incredible.*

ἀπλήρωτος, -ον, adj., *unsatisfied.*

ἁπλοῦς, -ῆ, -οῦν (contracted o throughout), *innocent, simple.*

ἀποβάλλω, v.a. *throw away, lose.*

ἀποδίδωμι, v.a., *give back.*

ἀπό, prep., w. gen. *from, away from.*

ἀποδείκνυμι, v.a., *show, render.*

ἀποδύω, v.a. *strip off,* mid., *undress.*

ἀποθνήσκω, v.n., *die, am killed* (Par. 71).

ἀποθρώσκω, v.n., *leap from.*

ἀποικία, ἡ, 1, *colony.*

ἀποκάμνω, v.n., *grow weary.*

ἀποκλείω, v.a., *shut off.*

ἀποκόπτω, v.a., *cut off.*

ἀποκρίνομαι, v. dep., *answer.*

ἀποκτείνω, v.a., *kill.*

ἀπολαύω, v.a., *enjoy, reap the fruits.*

ἀπολείπω, v.a., *leave behind.*

ἄπολις, -ι, adj., *stateless.*

ἀπόλλυμι, v.a. *destroy*, mid. *perish*, (Par. 69).

ἀπολύω, v.a., *acquit.*

ἀπονέμω, v.a., *award, distribute.*

ἀποπλέω, v.n., *sail away.*

ἀπορία, ἡ, 1, *want, lack*, often with gen., *difficulty.*

ἀπορῶ(εω), v. with gen., *lack, be without ; be at a loss.*

ἀποστρέφω, v.a., *turn away.*

ἀποσφάλλω, v.a., *cause to fail.*

ἀποσφάττω, v.a., *kill, put to death.*

ἀποτέμνω, v.a., *divide.*

ἀποτίθημι, v.a., *put away, bury.*

ἀποτρέχω, v.n., *run away.*

ἀποφέρω, v.a., *carry away.*

ἅπτομαι, v. mid., *touch*, with gen.

ἀπωθῶ(εω), v.a. *push away*, mid. *reject.*

ἆρα, interrogative particle.

ἄρα, particle, *then, so then.*

ἀργάλεος, -α, -ον, adj., *painful, grievous* (poetical).

Ἀργεῖος, ὁ, 2, *native of Argos, Argive.*

Ἀργοναῦται, οἱ, 1, *the Argonauts.*

Ἄργος, τό, 3, *Argos.*

ἀργός, -ή, -όν, adj., *lazy.*

ἀργύριον, τό, 2, *silver, money.*

Ἀργώ, ἡ, 3, *the ship Argo* (Par. 23).

ἀρετή, ἡ, 1, *virtue, valour, excellence.*

Ἄρης, voc. Ἄρες, acc. Ἄρη, gen. Ἄρεως, dat. Ἄρει, ὁ, 3, *Ares, god of war.*

ἄρθρον, τό, 2, *joint.*

ἀριθμός, ὁ, 2, *number.*

ἀρίσημος, -ον, adj., *very notable.*

Ἀριστείδης, ὁ, 1, *Aristeides.*

ἀριστερά, ἡ, 1, *the left hand.*

ἀριστερός, -ά, -όν, adj., *left.*

ἀριστεύω, v.n., *be brave.*

ἄριστος, superl. adj., *best*; see ἀγαθός.

Ἀριστοτέλης, ὁ, 3, *Aristotle.*

Ἀριστοφάνης, ὁ, 1, *Aristophanes.*

Ἀρίων, -ονος, ὁ, 3, *the minstrel Arion.*

Ἀρκαδία, ἡ, 1, *Arcadia, a district in the Peloponnese.*

ἅρμα, -ατος, τό, 3, *chariot.*

ἁρματηλάτης, ὁ, 1, *charioteer.*

ἀρνοῦμαι(εο), v. mid., *deny.*

ἄροτος, ὁ, 2, *tillage, corn land.*

ἀρουραῖος, -α, -ον, adj., *of the country.*

ἁρπάζω, v.a., *seize, carry off, plunder.*

ἁρπακτήρ, -ῆρος, 3, *robber.*

ἄρρην, -εν, adj., gen. -ενος, *male.*

ἄρσην, -εν, as above.

Ἄρτεμις, ἡ, -ιδος, 3, *Artemis.*

Ἀρτεμισία, ἡ, 1, *Artemisia, Queen of Caria.*

ἄρτι, adv., *lately, just now.*

ἀρχή, ἡ, 1, *rule, empire, beginning.*

ἄρχομαι, v. mid., *begin*, with gen.

ἄρχω, v.a., *rule*, with gen.

ἄρχων, -οντος, ὁ, 3, *ruler, magistrate.*

ἀρῶ(οω), v.a., *plough.*

ἀσέληνος, -ον, adj., *moonless.*

ἀσθενής, -ές, adj., *weak.*

ἀσιτῶ(εω), v.n., *go hungry.*

ἀσκῶ(εω), v.n., *practise, train.*

ἀσπάζομαι, v. mid., *greet, salute.*

ἀσπίς, -ίδος, ἡ, 3, *shield.*

ἀστήρ, -τέρος, ὁ, 3, *star.*

ἄστικος, -η, -ον, adj., *of the city.*

ἀστράγαλος, ὁ, 2, *ankle bone* ; pl. *dice.*

ἄστυ, -εως, τό, 3, *city* (Par. 16).

ἀσφαλής, -ές, adj., *safe.*

ἄταφος, -ον, adj., *unburied.*

ἀτείχιστος, -ον, adj., *unwalled.*

ἀτελής, -ές, adj., *incomplete, uncompleted, ineffective.*

ἀτιμάζω, v.a., *dishonour.*

ἄτιμος, -ον, adj., *without honour.*

"Ατοσσα, ἡ, 1, *Atossa.*

'Ατρεύς, -έως, ὁ, 3, *Atreus, father of Agamemnon.*

ἅττω, see ἀΐσσω.

"Ατυς, ὁ, 3, *Atys, son of Croesus.*

αὐθάδης, -ες, adj., *self-willed, obstinate.*

αὖθις, adv., *again.*

αὐξάνω, v.a. *increase,* passive *grow.*

αὔλειος, -α, -ον, adj., *of the court.*

αὐλή, ἡ, 1, *hall, court.*

αὐλητής, ὁ, 1, *fluteplayer.*

αὐλητρίς, -ίδος, ἡ, 3, *fluteplayer.*

'Αυλίς, -ίδος, ἡ, 3, *Aulis,* whence the Greeks set sail for Troy.

αὐλῶ(εω), v.n., *play the flute.*

ἄϋπνος, -ον, adj., *sleepless, wakeful.*

ἀϋτή, ἡ, 1, *trumpet blast.*

αὐτίκα, adv., *forthwith, for the moment.*

αὐτομολῶ(εω), v.n., *desert.*

αὐτός, *self,* oblique cases 3rd pers. pron. (Pars. 47 and 94 (3)).

αὐτοῦ, adv., *there.*

αὐχῶ(εω), v.n., *boast.*

ἀφαιρῶ(εω), v.a., *take away.*

ἀφανίζω, v.a., *cause to disappear.*

ἀφίημι, v.a., *let go, remit, release, set aside, leave.*

ἀφικνοῦμαι(εο), v.n., *arrive.*

ἀφίστημι, v.a., *cause to revolt.* Intrans. *revolt.*

ἀφοβῶς, adv., *without fear.*

ἀφορῶ(αω), v.a. and n., *look, see.*

'Αφροδίτη, ἡ, 1, *Aphrodite, goddess of love.*

ἀφρός, ὁ, 2, *sea-foam, foam.*

ἄφνω, adv., *suddenly.*

'Αχαιοί, οἱ, 2, *the Achaeans.* Used in Homer for the Greeks.[1]

ἀχθάνομαι, v. pass., *be vexed.*

ἄχθομαι, v. mid., *grieve.*

ἄχρηστος, -ον, adj., *useless.*

ἄψυχος, -ον, adj., *lifeless.*

ἄωρος, -ον, adj., *untimely.*

B

Βαβυλών, -ῶνος, ἡ, 3, *Babylon.*

βαδίζω, v.n., *walk.*

βάθος, -ους, τό, 3, *depth.*

βαθύς, -εῖα, -ύ, adj., *deep.*

βαίνω, v.n., *go, walk* (Par. 72).

βαιός, -ά, -όν, adj., *short, brief.*

βακτηρία, ἡ, 1, *staff, stick, rod.*

βακχιάδαι, οἱ, 1, *the Bacchiadae.*

βάλλω, v.a., *throw, hurl, pelt* (Par. 68).

βάρβαρος, -α, -ον, adj., *barbarian, non-Greek.*

βαρέως, adv., *grievously.*

βαρέως φέρω, v.a., *resent, feel sorrow, vexation, resentment.*

βαρύβρομος -ον, adj., *deep-sounding.*

βασιλεύς, -έως, ὁ, 3, *king.*

βασιλεύω, v.n., *be king* ; with gen.

βασιλικός, -ή, -όν, adj., *kingly.*

βασίλισσα, ἡ, 1, *queen.*

βάτος, ἡ, 2, *thorn.*

βατραχός, ὁ, 2, *frog.*

Βάττος, ὁ, 2, *Battus.*

βέβαιος, -α, -ον, adj., *firm, secure.*

βέλος, τό, 3, *dart.*

βέλτιστος, superl. of ἀγαθός *very good.*

βία, ἡ, 1, *violence, force.*

βιάζω, v.a., *constrain.*

βίαιος, -ον, adj., *violent.*

βίβλος, ἡ, 2. *book.*

[1] Particularly Achilles' and Agamemnon's men.

βίος, ὁ, 2, life, sustenance.
βιῶ(όω), v.n., live.
βλαστάνω, v.n., grow.
βλέπω, v.a. and n., look, see, look at.
βλέφαρον, τό, 2, eyelid.
βοή, ἡ, 1, shout.
βοηθῶ(έω), v.a., go to help, with dat.
βοηλασία, ἡ, 1, driving off of oxen.
βολή, ἡ, 1, throwing, cast.
βορά, ἡ, 1, food.
βορρᾶς or βορέας, -οῦ, 1, North wind.
βόσκημα, -ατος, τό, 3, fatted beast, pl. cattle.
βοτάνη, ἡ, 1, plant.
βούλευμα, -ατος, τό 3, plan.
βουλευτήριον, τό, 2, council hall.
βουλεύω, v.a. counsel, mid. take counsel, consider.
βουλή, ἡ, counsel, council.
βούλομαι, v. dep., I wish, want.
βοῦς, ἡ or ὁ, 3, cow or ox (Par. 18).
βοῶ(άω), v.n., shout.
βραδέως, adv., slowly.
βραχύς,-εῖα, -ύ, adj., short, shallow.
Βρεταννική, ἡ, 1, Britain.
βρέφος, -ους, τό, 3, babe, infant.
βωμός, ὁ, 2, altar.

Γ

γάλα, τό, 3, milk.
γάμος, ὁ, 2, marriage, generally pl.
γαμῶ(έω), v.a. marry, mid. marry (for a woman). Irreg.
γάρ, connecting particle, for.
γαστήρ, -τρός, ἡ, belly (Par. 20).
γεγονώς, -υῖα, -ός, partic. of γίγνομαι, born, become.
γείτων, -ονος, ὁ or ἡ, 3, neighbour.
γελοῖος, -α, -ον, adj., laughable.
γελῶ(άω), v.n., laugh.
γενεά, ἡ, 1, race, family.
γενναῖος, -α, -ον, adj., famous, noble.
γεννῶ(άω), v.a., beget.
γεννῶμαι(αο), pass., be born.

γένος, τό, 3, race, family.
γέρων, -οντος, ὁ, 3, old man.
γεύομαι, v. dep., taste, w. gen.
γέφυρα, ἡ, 1, bridge.
γεώλοφος, -ον, adj., hilly.
γεωμετρία, ἡ, 1, geometry.
γεωμετρῶ(έω), v.n., practise geometry.
γεωργία, ἡ, 1, tillage, farming.
γεωργός, ὁ, 2, farmer.
γεωργῶ(έω), v.a., till.
γῆ, ἡ, 1, earth, land.
γηράσκω, v.n., grow old.
γηροβοσκός, ὁ, 2, support for old age.
γίγας, -αντος, ὁ, 3, giant.
γίγνομαι, v.n., become, come into being.
γιγνώσκω, v.a., know.
Γλαῦκος, ὁ, 2, Glaucus.
γλαῦξ, -κός, ἡ, 3, owl.
γλυκύμηλον, τό, 2, sweet apple. (-μαλον in Aeolic).
γλυκύς, -εῖα, -ύ, adj., sweet.
γλύφω, v.a., carve (of a sculptor).
γνώμη, ἡ, 1, mind.
γονεύς, -έως, ὁ, 3, parent.
γόνυ, -ατος, τό, 3, knee.
Γρανικός, ὁ, the river Granicus, in N.W. of Asia Minor.
γραῦς, ἡ, 3, old woman. (Par. 18).
γράφω, v.a., write.
γρύπος, -η, -ον, adj., hooked.
γυμνάζεσθαι,, v. dep., take exercise.
γυμνάσιον, τό, 2, place for physical exercise, gymnasium.
γυμνικός, -ή, -όν, adj., athletic.
γυμνός, -ή, -όν, adj., bare, exposed.
γυῖον, τό, 2, limb.
γυνή,-αικός, ἡ, 3, woman.
γύψ, γυπός, ὁ, 3, vulture.

Δ

δαίμων, -ονος, ὁ, 3, god, divinity
δαιμόνιος, -α, -ον, adj., divine.
δάκνω, v.a., bite.

δάκρυ, }
δάκρυον, } τό, 3 or 2, *tear.*

δακρύω, v.n., *weep.*

δάκτυλος, ὁ, 2, *finger.*

Δάμων, -ωνος, ὁ, 3, *Damon of Syracuse.*

Δανάη, ἡ, 1, *Danaë, mother of Perseus.*

Δαρεῖος, ὁ, 2, *Darius, king of Persia.*

δάς, δᾳδός, ἡ, 3, *torch.*

δάφνη, ἡ, 1, *laurel, bay.*

δέ, conj. *but, and,* μὲν . . . δέ, *on the one hand . . . on the other hand.*

δέδοικα, perf. for pres. v.a., *fear.*

δεῖ, v. impersonal. From δέω, *I need,* hence (Par. 99), *it is necessary, should, ought.*

δείκνυμι, v.a. *show.*

δειλαῖος, -α, -ον, adj., *wretched, miserable* (poetical).

δειλιῶ(αω), v.n., *be cowardly.*

δεινός, -ή, -όν, adj., *terrible, monstrous, clever.*

δεῖπνον, τό, 2, *dinner, feast.*

δειπνῶ(εω), v.n., *dine.*

δείσας, aor. partic. from δέδοικα.

δέκα, num., *ten.*

δέκατος, ord. num., *tenth.*

δεκέτης, -ες, adj., *ten years old.*

δέλτοι, αἱ, 2, *tablets.*

δελφίς, -ῖνος, ὁ, 3, *dolphin.*

Δελφοί, αἱ, 2, *Delphi ;* the oracle of Apollo at the foot of Mt. Parnassus in Phocis.

Δελφοί, οἱ, 2, *the people of Delphi.*

δένδρον, τό, 2, *tree,* dat. pl. δένδρεσι.

δεξιός, -ά, -όν, adj., *on the right hand, skilful, clever.* ἡ δεξιά, *the right hand.*

δέομαι, v. mid., *need* (gen. of thing), *request, ask* (gen. of person).

δέπαστρον, τό, 2, *cup, goblet* (poetical).

δέρμα, -ατος, τό, 3, *skin, hide.*

δέρος, -ους, τό, 3, *fleece.*

δεσμωτήριον, τό, 2, *prison.*

δεσμώτης, ὁ, 1, *prisoner, captive.*

δέσποινα, ἡ, 1, *mistress, lady of the house.*

δεσπότης, ὁ, 1, *lord, master of the house.*

δεσποτικόν, τό, 2, *despotic character.*

Δευκαλίων, -ωνος, ὁ, 3, *Deucalion.*

δεύτερος, -α, -ον, ord. num., *second.*

δέχομαι, v. mid., *accept, welcome, receive.*

δέω, v.a., *bind.*

δή, particle, *in truth, indeed,* often ironical.

Δήλια, τά, 2, *the festival of Delian Apollo.*

Δῆλος, ἡ, 1, *the island of Delos.*

δῆλος, -η, -ον, adj., *plain.*

δηλῶ(οω), v.a., *make clear, show.*

δημαγωγός, ὁ, 2, *popular leader.*

Δημήτηρ, -τερ, -τρα, -τρος, -τρι, *Demeter.*

Δημοκήδης, ὁ, 1, *the physician Democedes.*

δημοκρατία, ἡ, 1, *democracy.*

δῆμος, ὁ, 2, *the people.*

Δημοσθένης, ὁ, 3, *Demosthenes* (1) *An Athenian general in the fifth century ;* (2) *the great Athenian orator of the fourth century* B.C.

δῆτα, particle, *pray.*

Δία, Διός, see Zeus.

διά, prep. with gen., *through ;* prep. with acc., *on account of.*

διαβαίνω, v.n., *go through, go across.*

διαβάλλω, v.a., *slander, traduce.*

διαβλέπω, v.n., *look across.*

διάγω, v.n., *spend time, live.*

διαδίδωμι, v.a., *hand out, publish.*

διάδοσις, -εως, ἡ, 3, *gift, distribution.*

διαιρῶ(εω), v.a., *divide.*

δίαιτα, ἡ, 1, *fare, diet.*

διάκενον, τό, 2, *gap, space.*

διακομίζω, v.a., *convey across.*

διακονία, ἡ, 1, *service.*

διάκονος, ὁ, 2, *servant.*
διακόσιοι, -αι, -α, num., *two hundred.*
διαλέγομαι, v. mid., *converse, talk.*
διαμένω, v.n., *remain, continue.*
διαπρεπής, -ές, adj., *notable.*
διαριθμῶ(εω), v.a., *reckon.*
διασπείρω, v.a., *scatter.*
διασπῶ(αω), v.a., *tear asunder.*
διασχίζω, v.a., *cleave.*
διατείνω, v.a. and n., *stretch, extend.*
διατελῶ(εω), v.a., *accomplish.*
διατηρῶ(εω), *preserve, watch over.*
δίαυλος, ὁ, 2, *double course ; race up the stadium and back.*
διαφαίνω, v.n., *show through.*
διαφέρω, v.a. and n., *spread abroad ; quarrel, differ.*
διαφθείρω, v.a., *destroy.*
διαφυλάσσω, v.a., *guard.*
διδάσκω, v.a., *teach.*
δίδωμι, v.a., *give.*
διεξέρχομαι, v. mid., *go through, explain.*
διεργάζομαι, v. mid., *destroy.*
διέρχομαι, v. mid., *go through.*
διέχω, v. n., *extend, be wide.*
διηγοῦμαι(εο), v. mid., *go through, explain.*
διίσταμαι, intrans., *be stationed apart.*
διισχυρίζομαι, v. mid., *assert.*
δίκαιος, -α, -ον, adj., *just.*
δικαιοσύνη, ἡ, 1, *justice.*
δικάστης, ὁ, 1, *arbiter, judge.*
δίκη, ἡ, 1, *justice, suit, penalty.*
δίκην λαμβάνειν, *avenge.*
δίμορφος, -ον, adj., *of two shapes.*
διό, conj., *wherefore.*
Διογένης, ὁ, 3, *Diogenes.*
διοικῶ(έω), v.a. and n., *keep house, manage.*
Διονύσιος, ὁ, 2, *Dionysius, tyrant of Syracuse.*
Διόνυσος, ὁ, 2, *Dionysus or Bacchus, god of wine.*
διπλάσιος, -α, -ον, adj., *double.*

διπλοῦς, -ῆ, -οῦν (contr. o), *double.*
δίπους, -ουν ; -οδος, adj., *two-footed.*
δίς, adv., *twice.*
δίσκος, ὁ, 2, *quoit.*
διωθῶ(εω), v.a., *thrust out.*
διώκω, v.a., *pursue.*
δίωξις, ἡ, 3, *pursuit.*
δόκησις, ἡ, 3, *appearance.*
δόκιμος, -ον, adj., *famous.*
δοκῶ(εω), v.n., *seem, think, resolve.*
δοκεῖ μοι, *it seems good to me.*
δόλιχος, ὁ (i.e. δρόμος), *long-distance race.*
δόξα, ἡ, 1, *reputation.*
δορά, ἡ, 1, *skin, hide.*
δόρυ, -ατος, τό, 3, also δορός and δορί, gen. and dat., *spear.*
δορυφόρος, -ον, adj., *bearing a spear.* οἱ δ., *tyrant's bodyguard.*
δουλεία, ἡ, 1, *slavery.*
δουλεύω, v.a., *am a slave, serve.*
δοῦλος, ὁ, 2, *slave.*
δουλοῦμαι(οο), v. mid., *enslave.*
δουλῶ(οω), v.a. *enslave.*
δράκων, -οντος, ὁ, 3, *snake, dragon.*
δρᾶμα, -ατος, τό, 3, *drama, play.*
δρέπανον, τό, 2, *axe.*
δρόμος, ὁ, 2, *running, race.*
δρῶ(αω), v.a., *do, act.*
δύναμαι, v. mid., *am able* (Par. 85).
ἴσον δύναται, *be equivalent.*
δύναμις, -εως, ἡ, 3, *power, strength.*
δυνατός, -η, -ον, adj., *powerful, mighty ; possible.*
δύνω, v.n., *set, sink.*
δύο, δυοῖν, num., *two.*
δυσκίνητος, -ον, adj., *hard to move.*
δυσμενής, -ές, adj., *hostile.*
δυσμή, ἡ, 1, *sunset.*
δυστυχής, -ές, adj., *unlucky.*
δυστυχῶ(εω), v.n., *be unlucky.*
δυσχεραίνω, v.n., *be angry.*
δυσχωρία, ἡ, 1, *difficult ground.*
δώδεκα, num., *twelve.*
δωδεκέτης, -ες, adj., *twelve years old.*

δωμάτιον, τό, 2, room, chamber.
δῶρον, τό, 2, gift.

E

ἔα, exclam., ah!
ἐάν, if.
ἑαυτόν, refl. pron., himself.
ἑβδομός, ordin. num., seventh.
ἐγγενής, -ές, adj., akin, related.
ἐγγράφω, v.a., write in or on.
ἐγγυητής, ὁ, 1, guarantor.
ἐγγύς, adv., and as prep. w. gen., near.
ἐγείρω, v.a., awaken.
ἐγκαταλείπω, v.a., leave behind.
ἐγκλίνω, v.a., lean on; v.n., give way.
ἐγκωμιάζω, v.a., praise.
ἐγχειρίζω, v.a., entrust.
ἐγχέω, v.a., pour in.
ἐγώ, pers. pron., I (Par. 46).
ἔδος, -ους, τό, 3, shrine, abode, temple.
ἕδρα, ἡ, 1, seat.
ἐδώλιον, τό, 2, seat of a ship.
ἔθνος, -ους, τό, 3, nation, tribe.
ἐθέλω, imperf., ἤθελον, v.a., wish, want.
ἔθος, -ους, τό, 3, custom.
εἰδέναι, infin. of οἶδα, know (Par. 73).
εἶδον, str. aor. of ὁρῶ, see (Pars. 71 and 72).
εἰκάζω, v.a., conjecture, guess to be.
εἰκός, τὸ (neut. partic. of ἔοικα, be likely), likelihood.
εἰκοσάμηνος, -η, -ον, adj., twenty months old.
εἴκοσι, num., twenty.
εἰκοστός, ord. num., twentieth.
εἰκών, -όνος, ἡ, 3, image.
εἶμι, v.n., I shall go; and as fut. of ἔρχομαι, (Par. 81).
εἰμί, v.n., be (Par. 79).
εἶναι, infin. of εἰμί, be (Par. 79).

εἵποντο, see ἕπομαι
εἶπον, aor. of verb of saying (Pars. 71 and 72).
εἰρήνη, ἡ, 1, peace.
εἰς, prep. with acc., in, into.
εἷς, μία, ἕν, numeral, one.
εἰσαγγέλλω, v.a., bring in news, announce.
εἰσάγω, v.a., lead in.
εἰσαεί, adv., for ever.
εἰσαθρῶ(εω), v.a., see into, look at.
εἰσβάλλω, v.n., invade, with εἰς.
εἴσοδος, ἡ, 2, way in.
εἰσφέρω, v.a., contribute.
εἴσω, adv., inside.
εἶτα, adv., next.
εἰώθα, perf. for proof, pluperf. for past, be accustomed.
ἐκ, ἐξ, prep. w. gen., out of, from.
ἕκαστος, -η, -ον, adj., every, each.
ἕκαστος καθ' ἕκαστον, each by itself.
ἑκάτερος, -α, -ον, adj., each of two, each side.
ἑκατόν, num., one hundred.
ἐκβαίνω, v.n., go out.
ἐκβάλλω, v.a., throw out, exile, throw overboard.
'Εκβάτανα, τά, 2, Ecbatana, in Persia.
ἐκδέχομαι, v. mid., receive from.
ἐκδύω, v.a., take from, strip.
ἐκεῖ, adv., there.
ἐκεῖνος, -η, -ο, dem. pron., that.
ἐκεχειρία, ἡ, 1, truce.
ἐκκάμνω, v.n., be utterly weary.
ἐκκλέπτω, v.a., steal away.
ἐκκλησία, ἡ, 1, assembly.
ἐκκομίζω, v.a., take out, export.
ἐκκύπτω, v.n., emerge, " pop up ".
ἐκλανθάνομαι, v. mid., utterly forget.
ἐκλέγω, v.a., select.
ἐκλείπω, v.a., leave.
ἐκμανθάνω, v.a., learn.
ἐκπηδῶ(αω), v.n., leap out.
ἐκπίμπλημι, v.a., fill from.

ἔκπληξις, -εως, ἡ, amazement.
ἔκτος, ord. num., sixth.
ἐκτρίβω, v.a., rub out, destroy.
ἐκφαίνω, v.n., show forth, disclose.
ἐκφύομαι, v. pass., grow out.
ἐκχωρῶ(εω), v.n., go out.
ἑκών, partic., willingly. Par. 30.
ἐλάα, ἡ, 1, olive tree.
ἐλαῖον, τό, 2, olive oil.
Ἐλάτεια, ἡ, 1, Elatea. Town on the frontier of Attica and Boeotia.
ἐλαύνω, v.a., drive.
ἐλάχιστος, superl. of ὀλίγος.
ὡς ἐλάχιστα, as little as possible.
ἐλαχύς, -εῖα, -ύ, adj., small.
ἐλέγχω, v.a., test, prove, examine.
Ἑλένη, ἡ, 1, Helen of Troy, wife of Menelaus.
ἐλευθερία, ἡ, 1, freedom.
ἐλεύθερος, -α, -ον, adj., free.
ἐλευθερῶ(οω), v.a., set free.
Ἐλευσινάδε, to Eleusis.
ἐλεφαντινός, -ή, -όν, adj., made of ivory.
Ἑλλάς, -άδος, ἡ, 3, Greece.
Ἕλλην, -ηνος, ὁ, 3, a Greek.
οἱ Ἕλληνες, the Greeks.
Ἑλληνικός, -ή, -ον, adj., Greek.
Ἑλληνίς, -ίδος, ἡ, 3, Greek.
Ἑλλήσποντος, ὁ, 2, Hellespont, Dardanelles.
ἐλπίζω, v.a., hope.
ἐλπίς, -ίδος, ἡ, 3, hope.
ἐμαυτόν, refl. pron., myself.
ἐμβαίνω, v.n., go into.
ἐμβάλλω, v.a., throw in, attack.
ἔμμισθος, -ον, adj., hired.
ἔμπαλιν, adv., back again.
ἐμπίπτω, v.n., fall in.
ἐκποδών, adv., out of the way.
ἐμποδών, adv., in the way, w. dat.
ἐμπόριον, τό, 2, trading station.
ἔμπορος, ὁ, 2, trader.
ἔμπροσθε(ν), adv., in front.
ἐμφανής, -ές, adj., visible, clear.

ἔμφρων, -ον, adj., sane, in one's senses.
ἐν, prep., see table, p. 280.
ἐναντίος, -α, -ον, adj., opposite, contrary.
ἐναντιοῦμαι(οο), v. mid., oppose, with dat.
ἐναποθνήσκω, v.n., die in (a place).
ἐνδίδωμι, v.n., give in.
ἐνδίκως, adv., justly.
ἔνδον, adv., within.
Ἐνδυμίων, -ωνος, ὁ, 3, Endymion.
ἐνδύομαι, v. dep., put on, don.
ἔνειμι, v.n., be in.
ἕνεκα, adv., because of (p. 284).
ἔνθα, adv., there, where, then.
ἔνθα καὶ ἔνθα, this way and that.
ἐνθάδε, adv., on this side, here.
ἔνθαπερ, adv., where.
ἐνθυμοῦμαι(εο), v. mid., consider.
ἐνιαύσιος, -ον, adj., yearly.
ἐνιαυτός, ὁ, 2, year.
ἔνιοι, -αι, -α, adj., some, a few.
ἐννέα, num., nine.
ἐνοικῶ(εω), v.a., dwell in.
ἐνοχλῶ(εω), v.a., trouble, entangle.
ἐνταῦθα, adv., here.
ἐντεῦθεν, adv., thereupon.
ἐντίθημι, v.a., place in, implant.
ἐντίκτω, v.a., give birth in.
ἐντόνως, adv., vehemently.
ἐντός, adv., inside.
ἐντυγχάνω, v.n., happen on.
ἐνύπνιον, τό, 2, dream.
ἐξ, prep. with gen. out of, from.
ἕξ, num., six.
ἐξαίφνης, adv., suddenly.
ἐξαργυρῶ(εω), v.a., convert into money.
ἐξελαύνω, v.a., drive out.
ἐξελέγχω, v.a., test.
ἐξέρχομαι, v.n., come out.
ἔξεστι, v. impers., it is possible.
ἐξευρίσκω, v.a., find out.
ἐξοπίσω, adv., hereafter.

GREEK-ENGLISH VOCABULARY 349

ἐξοπλίζω, v.a., equip.
ἐξοστρακίζω, v.a., ostracise, banish.
ἐξοστρακισμός, ὁ, 2, ostracism.
ἐξωθῶ(εω), v.a., thrust aside.
ἔξω, adv., outside.
ἐπαγγέλλομαι, v. mid., promise.
ἔπαθλον, τό, 2, reward, prize.
ἔπαινος, ὁ, 2, praise.
ἐπαινῶ(εω), v.a., praise.
ἐπακούω, v.n., hearken, obey.
Ἐπαμεινώνδας, -ου, ὁ, 1, Epaminondas of Thebes.
ἐπανέρχομαι, v. mid., come back.
ἐπανθῶ (εω), v.n., bloom.
ἐπαράσσω, v.a., close, slam.
ἐπεί, conj., since, when, w. indic.
ἐπειδή, conj., when, w. indic.
ἔπειμι (εἶμι), v.n., come against.
Ἔπειος, ὁ, 2, Epeus, a boxer.
ἔπειτα, adv., then, afterwards.
ἐπέκεινα, adv., beyond.
ἐπεκχωρῶ (εω), v.n., advance
against.
ἐπερείδω, v.a., push against, support
oneself on.
ἐπέχω, v.a. and n., check, stop.
ἐπί, prep., acc., towards.
gen., on, in the time of.
dat., on, at, p. 280.
ἐπιβαίνω, v.n., walk upon, mount, set
foot on, with gen.
ἐπιβουλεύω, v.n., plot against.
ἐπιγίγνομαι, v. mid., come next,
follow.
ἐπιγραφή, ἡ. 1, inscription.
ἐπιδείκνυμι, v.a., show.
ἐπιθυμία, ἡ 1, desire.
ἐπιθυμῶ(εω), v.a., desire.
ἐκικεῖμαι, w. dat., attack. (Par. 83).
ἐπικίνδυνος, -ον, adj., dangerous.
ἐπικοσμῶ(εω), v.a., adorn, praise.
ἐπιλαμβάνομαι, v. mid., w. gen.,
seize hold of.
ἐπίλεκτος, -ον, adj., chosen.
ἐπιμελοῦμαι(εο), v. mid., supervise.

ἐπιπλέω, v.a., sail against.
Ἐπίπολαι, αἱ, 1, Epipolae, a fortified
plateau at Syracuse.
ἐπίσημος, -ον, adj., conspicuous.
ἐπισκοπῶ(εω), v.a., watch over,
supervise, examine.
ἐπίσταμαι, v. mid., know (Par. 84).
ἐπιστέλλω, v.a., send a message to.
ἐπιστήμων, -ον,adj., acquainted with,
with knowledge of ; with gen.
ἐπιστραφῆναι, str. aor. pass. of
ἐπιστρέφω, v. a., turn back.
ἐπιτελῶ(εω), v.a. carry out.
ἐπιτήδειος, -α, -ον, adj., necessary,
friend.
τὰ ἐπιτήδεια, provisions.
ἐπιτηρῶ(εω), v.a., watch over.
ἐπιτρέπω, v.a., entrust.
ἐπίτροπος, ὁ, 2, guardian, trustee.
ἐπιφανής, -ές, adj., conspicuous.
ἐπιφλέγω, v.n., flame upon.
ἐπιχείρησις, -εως, ἡ, 3, attempt.
ἐπιχειρῶ(εω), v.a., attempt.
ἐπιχώριος, -α, -ον, adj., native of
the country.
ἐπιψαύω, v.a., touch ; with gen.
ἕπομαι, v. mid., follow ; with dat.
ἔπομβρος, -ον adj., rainy.
ἔπος, -ους, τό, 3, word.
ἐποτρύνω, v.a., urge on.
ἑπτά, num., seven.
ἐργάζομαι, v. mid., work.
ἐργασία, ἡ, 1, labour.
ἐργάτης, ὁ, 1, labourer.
ἔργον, τό, 2, deed, work.
ἔρεισμα, -ατος, τό, 3, bulwark.
Ἐρετριεῖς, οἱ, 3, people of Eretria in
Euboea.
ἐρεύθομαι, v. mid., blush.
ἐρίζω, v.n., strive, compete.
Ἐρινύς ἡ, 3, Erinys, Fury.
ἔριον, τό, 2, wool.
ἔρομαι,v.mid.,ask. (ἐρωτάω,p.315).
ἐρρωμένως, adv., vigorously.
ἔρχομαι, v. dep., come (Par. 71).

ἐρῶ(άω), v.a., *love*; with gen.
ἔρως, -ωτος, ὁ, 3, *love*.
ἐρώτημα, -ατος, τό, 3, *question*.
ἐρωτῶ(άω), v.a., *ask a question*.
ἐς, prep., for εἰς.
ἐσακοντίζω for εἰσ-, v.a., *hurl a javelin at*.
ἐσθής, -ῆτος, ἡ, 3, *clothes, raiment*.
ἐσθίω, v.a., *eat* (Par. 71).
ἐσθλός, -ή, όν, adj., *noble* (poetical).
ἑσπέρα, ἡ, 1, *evening*.
ἕσπερος, -α, -ον, adj., *western, of the evening*.
ἑστιῶ(άω), v.a., *feast, entertain*.
ἐσχατία, ἡ, 1, *remote part, end*.
ἔσχατος, -η, -ον, adj., *furthest, last*.
ἑταῖρος, ὁ, 2, *comrade*.
ἔτι, adv., *yet, still, even*.
ἑτοῖμος, -η, -ον, adj., *ready*.
ἔτος, -ους, τό, 3, *year*.
εὖ, adv., *well*.
Εὔβοια, ἡ, 1, *Euboea*.
εὐγενής, -ές, adj., *well-born*.
εὐδαιμονῶ(έω), v.n., *be happy*.
εὐδαίμων, -ον, adj., *happy, fortunate*.
εὐδόκιμος, -ον, adj., *famous*.
εὐδοκιμῶ(έω), v.n., *be in good repute*.
εὐεργετῶ (έω), v.a., *benefit*, w. dat.
εὐήθεια, ἡ, 1, *innocence, simplicity*.
εὐθύς, adv., *immediately*.
εὐκληΐζω, v.a., *glorify* (poetical).
εὐλαβοῦμαι(έο), v. mid., *be cautious*.
εὐλογία, ἡ, 1, *fame*.
εὐμαθής, -ές, adj., *quick at learning*.
εὐμαρής, -ές, adj., *easy, convenient*.
Εὔξεινος, ὁ, 2, *the Euxine or Black Sea*; euphemistically for "*kind to strangers*".
εὐπείθεια, ἡ, 1, *obedience*.
εὔπορος, -ον, adj., *well-provided*.
εὐπορῶ(έω), v.n., *be well provided*.
Εὐριπίδης, -ου, ὁ, 1, *Euripides*.
εὑρίσκω, v.a., *discover, find*.
Εὐρύαλος, ὁ, 2, *Euryalus*.

Εὐρυδίκη, ἡ, 1, *Eurydice, wife of Orpheus*.
Εὐρώπη, ἡ, 1, *Europe*.
εὐτάκτως, adv., *in good order*.
εὐτρεπίζω, v.a., *arrange*.
εὐτύχημα, -ατος, τό, 3, *stroke of good luck*.
εὐτυχής, -ές, adj., *lucky, fortunate*.
εὐτυχῶ(έω), v.n., *be lucky*.
εὐφεγγής, -ές, adj., *bright* (poetical).
εὐφημῶ(έω), v.n., *shout in triumph*.
εὐφραίνω, v.a., *comfort, please*.
εὐφυής, -ές, adj., *of good breed, well-formed*.
εὐχείρωτος, -ον, adj., *easy to overcome*.
εὐχή, ἡ, 1, *prayer*.
εὔψυχος, -ον, adj., *courageous*.
εὐώνυμος, -ον, adj., *of good name or omen*; euphemistically for *left*, side of bad omen.
ἐφίστημι, v.a., *set over, halt*; intrans., *stand over, appear*.
ἔφοδος, ἡ, 2, *attack, assault*.
ἐφ' ᾧ, *on condition that*, with future.
ἐφ' for ἐπί before an aspirate.
Ἐφέσιος, α, ον, adj., *native of Ephesus, Ephesian*.
ἐφορμῶ(έω), v.a., *be anchored against*; used of a blockading fleet.
ἔχω, v.a., *have*; v.n. with adv. *to be*, οὕτως ἔχειν, *to be thus*.
ἔχθρα, ἡ, 1, *enmity*.
ἐχθρός, -ά, -όν, adj., *hostile*.
ἐχθρῶς, adv., *in hostile manner, cruelly*.
ἐῶ(άω), v.a., *allow, leave alone*.
ἔωθα for εἴωθα, *be wont*.
ἑῷος, -α, -ον, adj., *eastern, of the morning*.
ἕως, ἡ, 3, *dawn*; acc. ἕω, gen. ἕω, dat. ἕῳ.
ἕως, conj., *while, still, until*. Syntax E, p. 296, and O 3, p. 306.

Z

ζεύγνυμι, v.a., *join, yoke.*
Ζεύς, Διός, ὁ, 3, *Zeus, king of the gods* (Par. 23).
ζηλωτός, -όν, adj., *enviable.*
ζητῶ(εω), v.a., *seek.*
ζῶ(-αω), v.n., *live* (Par. 71).
ζωή, ἡ, 1, *life.*
ζῷον, τό, 2, *living creature, animal;* in art, *figure.*

H

ἤ, *or, than* : ἤ . . . ἤ, *either . . . or.*
ἦ δ'ὅς, *said he* (Par. 80, note).
ᾗ, adv., *whithersoever, where.*
ἡβῶ(αω) v.n., *be in one's prime.*
ἡγεμονία, ἡ, 1, *leadership, supremacy.*
ἡγεμών, -όνος, ὁ, 3, *leader.*
ἡγοῦμαι(εο), v.n., *think, consider ; lead,* with dat.
ἡδέως, adv., *pleasantly.*
ἤδη, adv., *already.*
ἡδονή, ἡ, 1, *pleasure.*
ἡδύς, -εῖα, -ύ, adj., *sweet, pleasant.*
'Ηετίων, -ωνος, ὁ, 3, *Eetion.*
ἥκω, v.n., *have come.*
ἠλακάτη, ἡ, 1, *distaff.*
'Ηλέκτρα, ἡ, 1, *Electra, daughter of Agamemnon, and sister of Orestes.*
ἡλικία, ἡ, 1, *age, military age, contemporaries.*
ἥλιος, ὁ, 2, *the sun, Helios.*
'Ηλις, -ιδος, ἡ, 3, *Elis,* in N.W. Peloponnese.
ἡμεῖς, pers. pron., *we* (Par. 46).
ἡμέρα, ἡ, 1, *day ;* ἡμέρας, gen., *by day.*
ἡμερήσιος, -α, -ον, adj., *of one day, for a day.*
ἡμέτερος, -α, -ον, pron. adj., *our.*
ἡμίονος, ὁ, 2, *mule,* i.e. *half-donkey.*
ἥμισυς, -εῖα, -υ, adj., *half ;* τὰ ἡμίση, *half.*
ἡνία, ἡ, 1, *rein.*
ἧπαρ, ἥπατος, τό, 3, *liver.*

ἤπειρος, ἡ, 2, *continent, mainland.*
ἤπιος, -α, -ον, adj., *gentle.*
"Ηρα, ἡ, 1, *Hera, queen of the gods.*
'Ηράκλειτος, ὁ, 2, *Heracleitus.*
'Ηρακλῆς, ὁ, *Heracles* (Latin *Hercules*) (Par. 23).
ἠρέμα, adv., *gently.*
'Ησίοδος, ὁ, 2, *the poet Hesiod.*
ἧσσον, adv., *less.*
ἡσσῶ(αω), v.a., *defeat.*
ἡσυχάζω, v.n., *keep quiet, remain inactive.*
ἡσυχῇ, adv., *quietly.*
ἥσυχος, ὁ, 2, *quiet.*

Θ

θ' for τε before an aspirated vowel.
θάλαμος, ὁ, 2, *bridal chamber.*
θάλασσα (or θάλαττα), ἡ, 1, *the sea.*
θαλάσσιος, -α, -ον, adj., *of the sea.*
θαλασσοκράτωρ, -τορος, ὁ, *ruler of the sea, sea-power.*
θαλασσοκρατῶ(εω), v.n., *hold control of the sea.*
θάνατος, ὁ, 2, *death.*
θάπτω, v.a., *I bury.*
θαρρῶ(εω), v.n., *be of good courage.*
θάρρει, imper., *be of good cheer.*
θαῦμα, -ατος, τό, 3, *marvel ;* plur., *juggler's tricks,* or *mountebank's gambols.*
θαυμάζω, v.a., *wonder at.*
θαυμαστός, -ή, -όν, adj., *marvellous.*
θέα, ἡ, 1, *spectacle, sight.*
θέατρον, τό, 2, *theatre.*
θεῖος, -α, -ον, adj., *divine ;* τὰ θεῖα, *the gods.*
θέλω, v.a., *wish, want.*
θεός, ὁ or ἡ, 2, *god or goddess.*
θεράπαινα, ἡ, 1, *handmaid.*
θεραπεία, ἡ, 1, *service.*
θεραπεύω, v.a., *tend, cultivate.*
θεράπων, -οντος, ὁ, 3, *servant.*
θερίζω, v.a., *reap.*
θερμότης, -τητος, ἡ, 3, *warmth.*

θέρος, τό, 3, summer.
θεσπίζω, v.a., declare by oracle, prophesy.
Θεσσαλία, ή, 1, Thessaly.
Θεσσαλός, ὁ, 2, Thessalian.
θεῶμαι(αο), v.a., gaze at.
θεωρῶ(εω), v.a., see.
Θῆβαι, αἱ, 1, Thebes, capital of Boeotia.
Θηβαῖος, -α, -ον, adj., native of Thebes.
θήκη, ή, 1, tomb.
θήρ, ὁ, 3, beast, brute.
Θήρα, ή, 1, the island of Thera.
θήρα, ή, 1, prey.
Θηραῖος, -α, -ον, adj., native of Thera.
θηρεύω, v.a., hunt, chase.
θήριον, τό, 2, beast, brute.
θησαυρός, ὁ, 2, treasure.
θιγγάνω, v.a., touch, w. gen.
θνήσκω, v.n., die (Par. 71).
θνητός, -ή, -όν, adj., mortal.
θοῦρος, adj., impetuous. Poetical.
θράσος, -ους, τό, 3, courage, boldness.
θρασύς, εῖα, -ύ, adj., bold.
θρόνος, ὁ, 2, throne, rule: often plur.
θρίξ, ή, gen. τριχός, hair (Par. 22).
θυγάτηρ, ή, 3, daughter (Par. 20).
θυμοειδής, -ές, adj., spirited.
θυμός, ὁ, 2, spirit.
θύρα, ή, 1, door.
θυρωρός, ὁ, door-keeper.
θυσία, ή, 1, festival.
θύω, v.a., sacrifice.
θῶραξ, -ακος, ὁ, 3, breastplate.

I

Ἰαπετός, ὁ, 2, Iapetus, father of Prometheus.
ἴασμα, -ατος, τό, 3, cure, remedy.
Ἰάσων, -ονος, ὁ, 3, Jason, leader of the Argonauts.
ἰατρός, ὁ, 2, surgeon, physician.

ἰδίᾳ, adv., individually.
ἴδιος, -α, -ον, adj., one's own, private.
ἰδού, behold! (imper. aor. mid. of εἶδον).
ἱδρώς, -ῶτος, ὁ, 3, sweat.
ἱέρεια, ή, 1, priestess.
ἱερεύς, -έως, ὁ, 3, priest.
ἱερομηνία, ή, 1, the holy time of the month, when hostilities were suspended.
ἱερόν, τό, 2, temple.
ἱερός, -ά, -όν, adj., holy, sacred.
ἵζομαι, v. mid., sit.
Ἰθάκη, ή, 1, Ithaca, island home of Odysseus.
ἱκανός, -ή, -όν, adj., sufficient.
ἱκετεύω, v.a., supplicate, implore.
ἱκέτης, ὁ, 1, suppliant.
Ἴλιον, τό, 2, Ilion, Troy.
ἱμάτιον, τό, 2, outer garment, cloak.
Ἰνδός, ὁ, 2, an Indian.
ἴον, τό, 2, violet.
ἰοστέφανος, -ον, adj., violet-crowned.
ἱππεύς, -έως, ὁ, 3, horseman.
ἱππικός, -ή, -όν, adj., to do with horses.
Ἱππογῦπαι, οἱ, 1, vulture cavalry.
ἱππόδαμος, -ον, adj., horse-taming.
ἱππομαχία, ή, 1, cavalry engagement.
ἵππος, ὁ, 2, horse
ἱπποτοξόται, οἱ, 1, mounted bowmen.
Ἴσθμια, τά, 2, Isthmian games.
ἰσθμός, ὁ, 2, isthmus.
ἴσος, -η, -ον, adj., equal, even.
Ἱστιαῖος, ὁ, 2, Histiaeus, leader of Ionian revolt.
ἵστημι, v.a., I make to stand. For trans. and intrans. tenses, p. 250.
ἱστίον, τό, 2, sail.
ἱστορία, ή, 1, history.
ἰσχάς, -άδα, ή, 3, dried fig.
Ἰσχόμαχος, ὁ, 2, Ischomachus.

ἰσχόφωνος, -ον, adj., *stammering* (from ἴσχω, *hold, check*, and φωνή, *voice*).

ἰσχυρός -ά, -όν adj., *strong, violent.*

ἴσως, adv., *perhaps.*

'Ιταλία, ἡ, 1, *Italy.*

'Ιφιγένεια, ἡ, 1, *Iphigenia, daughter of Agamemnon and Clytemnestra.*

ἰχθύς, -ύος, ὁ, 3, *fish.*

ἴχνος, -ους, τό, 3, *tread, foot- or hoof-print.*

'Ιωλκός, ἡ, 2, *Iolcus in Thessaly,* whence the Argonauts set sail.

ἰῶμαι(αο), v. mid., *heal, cure.*

"Ιωνες, οἱ, 3, *the Ionians.*

'Ιωνία, ἡ, 1, *Ionia.* The west coast of Asia Minor

Κ

κ.τ.λ. =καὶ τὸ λοιπόν, *et cetera.*

καί, conj., *and.* Joins words and sentences. Adv., *also, even.*

καὶ μήν, *furthermore, and now.*

τε . . . καί, *both . . . and.*

καὶ . . . δέ, *and also.*

καὶ δὴ καί, *and even.*

Καδμεία, ἡ, 1, *the Cadmea, citadel of Thebes.*

καθ' for κατά, before aspirate.

καθαίρω, v.a., *purify.*

καθαιρῶ(εω), v.a., *drag down, destroy.*

κάθαπερ, adv., *just as, like.*

καθαρός, -ά, -όν, adj., *pure.*

καθάρσια, τά, 2, *rites of purification.*

καθεύδω, v.n., *sleep.*

κάθημαι, v. mid., *sit* (Par. 82).

καθίζομαι, v. mid., *sit down.*

καθίημι, v.a., *put down, drop* (Par. 78).

καθίστημι, v.a., *appoint, establish, make.* Intrans., *become.*

καθορῶ(αω),, v.a., *observe, descry.*

καθώς, adv., *as.*

καινός, -ή, -όν, adj., *new, fresh.*

καινότης, -τητος, ἡ, 3, *freshness.*

καιρός, ὁ, 2, *time, opportunity.*

καίω, v.a. *burn*, p. 315.

κακοπαθῶ(εω), v.n., *suffer harm.*

κακός, ἡ, -όν, *bad.*

κάλαμος, ὁ, 2, *a reed-pen.*

Καλαυρία, ἡ, 1, *island of Calauria,* off Troezen, in the Saronic Gulf.

Καλλίας, ὁ, 1, *Callias.*

κάλλος, -ους, τό, 3, *beauty.*

καλός, -ή, -όν, adj., *beautiful, good, noble* (Par. 35).

Καλυδώνιος, -ά, -ον, adj., *of Calydon,* in W. Greece.

καλύπτω, v.a., *hide.*

καλῶ(εω), v.a., *call.*

κάμνω, v.n., *be weary, be ill.*

κάμπτω, v.a., *turn round.*

κάνιστρον, τό, 2, *wicker basket.*

Κανωβικός, -ή, -όν, adj., *of Canopus,* in Egypt.

κάπρος, ο, 2, *wild boar.*

καρδία, ἡ, 1, *heart.*

Κᾶρες, οἱ, 3, *the Carians.*

καρπός, ὁ, 2, *fruit.*

καρτερός, -ά, -όν, adj., *strong, violent.*

καρτερῶ(εω), v.n., *hold out, endure.*

Καρχηδόνιοι, οἱ, 2, *native of* Καρχηδών, *Carthage ; Carthaginians.*

Κασσιόπεια, ἡ, 1, *Cassiopea.*

Κάστωρ, -ορος, ὁ 3, *Castor, brother of Polydeuces* (Latin *Pollux*).

κατά, prep. with acc., *according to, by.* w. gen., *down from, against* p. 281.

καταβαίνω, v.n., *go down.*

κατάγνυμι, v.a., *break in pieces.*

κατάδρυμος, -ον, adj., *wooded.*

καταδύω, v.a., *sink.*

καταζεύγνυμι, v.a., *yoke.*

καταισχύνω, v.a., *put to shame.*

κατακαίω, v.a., *burn up.*

κατακεῖμαι, v. mid., *lie down.*

κατακλείω, v.a., *shut up.*

κατακλύζω, v.a., *deluge.*

κατακοιμίζω, v.a., *lull to sleep.*

κατ-ακούω, v.a., *hear.*
καταλείπω, v.a., *leave behind.*
καταλοχίζω, v.a., *set in ambush.*
καταλύω, v.a., *destroy utterly.*
κατανύω, v.a., *accomplish.*
καταπίνω, v.a., *swallow, drink down.*
καταπίπτω, v.n., *fall down.*
καταπλέω, v.n., *sail to shore.*
καταπλήσσω, v.a., *amaze, dismay.*
κατασκάπτω, v.a., *dig, demolish.*
κατασκευάζω, v.a., *prepare.*
κατασκευή, ἡ, 1, *display.*
κατάσκοπος, ὁ, 2, *scout.*
κατασπῶ(αω), v.a., *drag down.*
καταστρέφω, v.a., *upturn, overthrow.*
κατάστρωμα, -ατος, τό, 3, *deck of a ship.*
κατατίθημι, v.a., *put down, deposit.*
καταφανής, -ές, adj., *visible, obvious.*
καταφέρω, v.a., *bear back.*
καταφεύγω, v.n., *flee for refuge.*
καταφρονῶ(εω), v.a., *despise,* w.gen.
καταφρόνησις, -εως, ἡ, 3, *contempt.*
κατείργω, v.a., *rein in, check, prevent.*
κατεπάδω, v.a., *enchant.*
κατεργάζομαι, v. mid., *complete.*
κατέρχομαι, v.n., *go back, go home.*
κατεσθίω, v.a., *eat.*
κατέχω, v.a., *check, prevail.*
κατηγορῶ(εω), v.a. *accuse,* acc. of thing, gen. of person.
κατθανεῖν, poetical for καταθανεῖν, *die* ; see ἀποθνῄσκω, (Par. 71).
κατοικτείρω, v.a., *pity.*
κατοικῶ(εω), v.n., *dwell.*
κάτοπτρον, τό, 2, *mirror.*
κατορύσσω, v.a., *bury.*
κάτω, adv., *below.*
Καύκασος, ὁ, 2, *Caucasus.*
καῦμα, -ατος, τό, 3, *heat.*
κεῖμαι, v. mid., *lie* (Par. 83).
κέλευμα, -ατος, τό, 3, *boatswain's call.*
κελευστής, ὁ, 1, *boatswain.*
κελεύω, v.a., *order.*
κέλης, -ητος, ὁ, 3, *riding horse.*

Κελτική, ἡ, 1, *Gaul.*
κέντρον, τό, 2, *goad.*
κέρας, -ατος, τό, 3, *horn, wing of an army* ; also gen. κέρως, dat. κέρᾳ, in meaning, *wing of army.*
κεράτινος, -η, -ον, adj., *horny.*
κεραυνός, ὁ, 2, *thunderbolt.*
κέρδος, -ους, τό, 3, *gain, profit.*
κεφαλή, ἡ, 1, *head.*
κήδω, v.a., *trouble* ; κέκηδε, intrans., *is troubled.*
κηλῶ(εω), v.a., *soothe, charm.*
κῆρυξ, -υκος, ὁ, 3, *herald.*
κηρύσσω, v.a., *announce.*
κῆτος, -ους, τό, 3, *sea-monster.*
Κηφεύς, -έως, ὁ, *Cepheus, father of Andromeda.*
κιβώτιον, τό, 2, *chest, box.*
κιθάρα, ἡ, 1, *harp.*
κιθαρίζω, v.n., *play the harp.*
κιθαριστρία, ἡ, 1, *girl harpist.*
κιθαρῳδός, ὁ, 2, *one who sings to the harp.*
Κίλιξ, -ικος, ὁ, 3, *native of Cilicia.*
κινδυνεύω, v.a. and n., *risk, be in danger.*
κίνδυνος, ὁ, 2, *danger.*
Κινύρας, ὁ, 1, *Cinyras.*
κισσός, ὁ, (κιττός), 2, *ivy.*
κλαίω, v.n. and a., *weep.*
κλεινός, -ή, -όν, adj., *famous.*
κλείω, v.a., *shut.*
Κλεόμβροτος, ὁ, 2, *Cleombrotus, a king of Sparta.*
κλέος, -ους, τό, 3, *fame, glory.*
κλέπτω, v.a., *steel.*
κλῆρος, ὁ, 2, *lot.*
κλῇς, κληδός, ἡ, 3, *key, bolt.*
κλῖμαξ, -ακος, ἡ, 3, *ladder.*
κλισία, ἡ, 1, *tent.*
Κλυταιμνήστρα, ἡ, 1, *Clytaemnestra, wife of Agamemnon.*
κλυδώνιον, τό, 2, *wave* (poetical).
κλυτός, -ή, -όν, adj., *famous*
κλύω, v.a., *hear, obey* (poetical).

Κόδρος, ὁ, 2, *Codrus, king of Athens.*
κοιμῶ(αω), v.a., *lull to rest* ; mid.,
  sleep.
κοινῇ, adv., *in common.*
κοινός, -ή, -όν, adj., *common.*
κοινωνῶ(εω), v.a., *share,* w. gen.
κοινωνία, ἡ, 1, *partnership.*
κοινωνός, ὁ, 2, *partner.*
κολάζω, v.a., *punish.*
κόλαξ, -ακος, ὁ, 3, *flatterer.*
Κολχίς, -ιδος, ἡ, 3, *Colchis,* S. of
  Black Sea.
Κόλχοι, οἱ, 2, *Colchians.*
κολωνός, ὁ, 2, *hill.*
κόμη, ἡ, 1, *hair.*
κομίζω, v.a., *carry, convey, bring.*
κόμπος, ὁ, 2, *boast.*
κόνις, -εως, ἡ, 3, *dust.*
κοντός, ὁ, 2, *ship's pole.*
κόπτω, v.a., *cut, strike.*
κόραξ, -ακος, ὁ, 3, *crow.*
Κορίνθιος, ὁ, 2, *Corinthian.*
Κόρινθος, ἡ, 2, *Corinth.*
κόρος ὁ, 2, *satiety.*
κορυφή, ἡ, 1, *height, summit.*
κόσμος, ὁ, 2, *order* ; *the world* ;
  κόσμῳ, *in order.*
κοσμῶ(εω), v.a., *set in order, adorn.*
κότινος, ὁ, or ἡ 2, *wild olive.*
κούφως, adv., *lightly,* from κοῦφος,
  -η, -ον, *light.*
κράνος, -ους, τό, 3, *helmet.*
κράτος, -ους, τό, 3, *mastery, power.*
κρατῶ(εω), v.a., *hold sway, prevail* ;
  w. gen.
κρέας, κρέως, τό, 3, *meat.*
Κρέων, -οντος, ὁ, *Creon, brother-in-
  law of Oedipus.*
Κρής, ὁ, 3, *a Cretan.*
Κρήτη, ἡ, 1, *Crete.*
κρίνω, v.a., *decide, adjudge.*
Κρισαῖος, -α, -ον, adj., *of Crisa,* in
  Phocis, near Delphi.
κριτής, ὁ, 1, *judge.*

Κροτωνιάτης, ὁ, 1, *native of Croton*
  in S. Italy.
κρούω, v.a., *knock at the door.*
κρύπτω, v.a., *hide, conceal.*
κρύσταλλος, ὁ, 2, *ice.*
κτείνω, v.a., *kill,* poetic. For ἀποκτ.
κτενίζω, v.a., *comb.*
κτῆμα, -ατος, τό, 3, *possession.*
κτῆνος, -ους, τό, 3, *ox or sheep,* pl.
  cattle.
κτῶμαι(αο), v. mid., *acquire, possess.*
κυάνεος, -α, -ον, adj., *dark blue.*
κυβερνήτης, ὁ, 1, *helmsman.*
Κυκλάδες, αἱ, 3,   *The   Cyclades*
  islands.
κύκλος, ὁ, 2, *circle.*
κυκλῶ(οω), v.a., *encircle.*
κύλιξ, ἡ, 3, *drinking cup.*
κῦμα, -ατος, τό, 3, *wave.*
κυνηγεσία, ἡ, 1, *the chase.*
κυνηγέτις, -ιδος,[1] ἡ, 3, *huntress.*
Κύπρος, ἡ, 2, *Cyprus.*
Κυρήνη, ἡ, *Cyrene,* in N. Africa.
κύριος, -α, -ον, adj., *having control.*
κύτος, -ους, τό, 3, *hollow, hold,
  belly.*
κύων, ὁ or ἡ, 3, *dog* (Par. 19).
Κώης, ὁ, 1, *Coes,* of Mytilene in
  Lesbos.
κωλύω, v.a., *hinder.*
κωμαστής, ὁ, 1, *reveller.*
κώμη, ἡ, 1, *village.*
κωμῳδία, ἡ, 1, *comedy.*
κωμῳδοποιός, ὁ, 2, *comic poet.*
κώπη, ἡ, 1, *oar.*

Λ

λαβύρινθος, ὁ, 2, *labyrinth.*
λαγχάνω, v.a., *obtain.* Often by
  chance. W. gen.
Λαέρτης, ὁ, 1, *Laertes, father of
  Odysseus.*
λαισήϊον, τό, 2, *buckler* (poetical).

[1] Fem. tradenames in -ις decline -ιδος, cf αὐλητρίς (Par. 9).

Λακεδαιμόνιοι, οἱ, 2, *the Lace-daemonians, Spartans.*
Λακεδαίμων, -ονος, ἡ, 3, *Lacedae-mon*, the province of Sparta.
λαλῶ(εω), v.n., *speak.*
λαμβάνω, v.a., *take* (Par. 68, p. 236).
λαμπαδηφορία, ἡ, 1, *torch race.*
λαμπρός, -ά, -όν, adj., *brilliant, famous, obvious.*
λάμπω, v.n., *shine.*
Λάμψακος, ὁ, 2, *Lampsacus*, on the Hellespont.
λανθάνω, v.a., *escape notice of.*
λανθανομαι, mid., w. gen., *forget.*
λαός, ὁ, 2, *people* (poetical).
λάρναξ, -ακος, ἡ, 3, *an ark ; or chest in which children were exposed.*
λέαινα, ἡ, ι, *lioness.*
λέγω, v.a., *say* (Par. 71).
λείπω, v.a., *leave.*
λεκιθίτης, ὁ, 1, *a bread made of pulse.*
λεπτός, -ή, -όν, adj., *fine, subtle.*
Λέριος, ὁ, 2, *a man from the island of Leros in the Aegean.*
λέσχη, ἡ, 1, *place for discussion, lounge, club-room.*
λευκός, -ή, -όν, adj., *white.*
λέων, -οντος, ὁ, 3, *lion.*
Λεωνίδας, ὁ, *Leonidas, king of the Spartans, who led the 300 at Thermopylae.*
Λήδα, ἡ, 1, *Leda, mother of Helen, Castor and Pollux, also of Cly-taemnestra.*
λήθη, ἡ, 1, *forgetfulness, oblivion.*
ληστεία, ἡ, 1, *piracy*
ληστής, ὁ, 1, *robber, bandit, pirate.*
Λητώ, -ους, ἡ, 3, *Leto, mother of Apollo and Artemis* (Par. 23).
Λιβύη, ἡ, 1, *Libya*, N. Africa, west of Egypt.
λίθινος, -η, -ον, adj., *of stone, or marble.*
λίθος, ὁ, 2, *stone, marble.*

λιμήν, -ένος, ὁ, 3, *harbour.*
λίμνη, ἡ, 1, *lake, marsh.*
λιμός, ὁ, 2, *hunger.*
λίνον, τό, 2, *thread.*
λιπαρός, -α, -ον, adj., *bright, shining* (poetical).
λογάς, -άδος, ὁ, 3, *picked man.*
λογίζομαι, v. mid., *reason, reckon.*
λόγος, ὁ, 2, *word, fame, account.*
λόγχη, ἡ, 1, *spear shaft, spear.*
λοιδορία, ἡ, 1, *abuse.*
λοιδορῶ(εω), v.a., *abuse.*
λοιπός,-ή, -όν, adj., *remaining, rest.*
καὶ τὸ λοιπόν, *and the rest*, etc., abbreviated κ.τ.λ.
λουτρόν,τό, 2, *b th.*
λούω, v.a., *wash* ; mid. *take a bath.*
λόφος, ὁ, 2, *hill.*
λόχος, ὁ, 2, *body of men, company* ; also *an ambush.*
λυγρός, -ά, -όν, adj., *pitiable, wretched* (poetical).
Λυδοί, οἱ, 2, *the Lydians.*
λυπῶ(εω), v.a., *vex, annoy* ; pass. *grieve.*
λύρα, ἡ, 1, *lyre.*
Λύσανδρος, ὁ, 2, *Lysander.* Spartan admiral at end of Peloponnesian War.
λύω, v.a., *loose, set free, solve* ; mid. *ransom.*

M

Μαῖα, ἡ, 1, *Maia, mother of Hermes.*
Μακεδών, -όνος, ὁ, 3, *a Macedonian.*
μακρός, -ά, -όν, adj., *long.*
μάλα, adv., *very.*
μαλακός, -ή, -όν, adj., *soft, weak.*
μαλθακός, -ή, -όν, adj., *soft.*
μᾶλλον, adv., *more.*
μαλλός, ὁ, 2, *wool, fleece.*
μαλο-, see μηλο-.
μανθάνω, v.a., *learn.*
μαντεύομαι, v. mid., *prophesy.*

GREEK-ENGLISH VOCABULARY 357

μαντικός, -ή, -όν, adj., of a seer ;
ἡ μαντική, the prophetic art.
Μαντινεῖς, οἱ, 3, the Mantineans.
μάντις, -εως, ὁ or ἡ, a seer.
Μαραθών, -ῶνος, ὁ, 3, Marathon.
μάρναμαι, v. dep., fight. Poetical.
μαρτυρῶ(εω), v.a., bear witness.
μάστιξ, -ιγος, ἡ, 3, whip.
μάτην, adv., in vain.
μάχη, ἡ, 1, battle.
μάχομαι, v. mid., fight, with dat.
μεγαλοπρεπῶς, adv., magnificently.
μέγας, μεγάλη, μέγα, adj., great
(Par. 26).
μέγεθος, -ους, τό, 3, greatness, size.
μέγιστος, superl. of μέγας, (Par.
35).
μεθίστημι, v.a., change, remove.
μεθύω v.n., be drunk.
μείζων, comp. of μέγας (Par. 36).
μέλας, μέλαινα, μέλαν adj., black.
μέλει, impers. v., concern. Often
turn by care for (Par. 99).
μελέτη, ἡ, 1, practice, training.
μελετῶ(αω), v.a., practise.
μέλι, -ιτος, τό, 3, honey.
μέλλω, v.n., intend, or futurity, be
about to.
μέμνημαι, see μιμνήσκω.
μεμπτός, -ή, -όν, adj., worthy of
blame.
μέμφομαι, v. mid., blame, acc. of
thing, dat. of pers., occasionally
dat. of thing.
μέν, particle, for contrast, on the one
hand ; with δέ, on the other hand.
Μενέλαος, ὁ, 2, Menelaus, king of
Sparta.
Μενοίτιος, ὁ, Menoetius, father of
Patroclus.
μένω, v.n., remain.
Μερόης, ὁ, 1, Meroes, an Indian.
μερίς, -ίδος, ἡ, 3, part, slice.
μέρος, -ους, τό, 3, part, turn.
μεσημβρία, ἡ, 1, mid-day.

μεσόγαια, ἡ, 1, inland.
μέσος, -η, -ον, adj., in the middle,
middle (Par. 93).
μεστός, -ή, -όν; adj., full of, with
gen.
μετά, prep. (see p. 281), with acc.,
after ; with gen., with.
μεταβάλλω, v.a., change.
μετανάστασις, -εως, ἡ, 3, removal,
exile.
μεταξύ, adv., in the midst ; prep.
with gen., between.
μεταπέμπομαι, v. mid., summon.
μετέπειτα, adv., afterwards.
μετέρχομαι, v. mid., go after, pursue.
μέτριος, -α, -ον, adj., moderate.
μετρίως, adv., moderately.
μέτρον, τό, 2, measure, metre.
μεχρί οὗ, until (Syntax O 3, p. 306).
μή, negative (Syntax, Par. 100, p.
293).
μηδαμῶς, adv., in no way.
Μήδεια, ἡ, 1, Medea, daughter of
Aeëtes.
μηδέποτε, never.
μηλοδροπεύς, -έως, ὁ, 3, apple picker.
μῆλον, τό, 2, apple.
μηλοτρόφος, -ον, adj., sheep-rearing.
μήν, particle, verily, indeed. καί
μήν, often introduces a new fact
or person.
μήν, μηνός, ὁ, 3, month.
μηρός, ὁ, 2, thigh.
μήτηρ, μητρός, ἡ, 3, mother (Par. 20).
μικρός, -ά, -όν, adj., small.
Μιλήσιος, ὁ, 2, native of Miletus.
μιμνήσκω, v.a., remind, pass. remember. Perf. pars., μέμνημαι. W. gen.
Μινώταυρος, ὁ, 2, Minotaur.
μίσθιος, -α, -ον, adj., hired.
μίσθος, ὁ, 2, fee, reward.
μισθοφόρος, ὁ, 2, mercenary.
μισθοῦμαι(οο), v. mid., hire.
μισῶ(εω), v.a., hate.

μνᾶ, acc. μνᾶν, gen. μνᾶς dat. μνᾷ.
a mina = 100 drachmae, and $\frac{1}{60}$
of a talent.
μνήμη, ἡ, 1, memorial.
μνηστήρ, -τῆρος, ὁ, 3, wooer, suitor.
μόγις, adv., with difficulty.
μόλις, adv., with difficulty.
μονή, ἡ, 1, stay, lodging.
μόνιμος, -η, -ον, adj., steadfast.
μονομαχία, ἡ, 1, single combat.
μόνον, adv., only ; οὐ μόνον . . . not
only . . . ἀλλὰ καί but also . . .
μόνος, -η, -ον, adj., alone, single.
μόρος, ὁ, fate.
Μοῦσα, ἡ, 1, Muse.
μουσικός, -ή, -όν, adj., of the muses,
musical ; ἡ μουσική (τεχνή, art),
music.
μῦθος, ὁ, 2, tale, story.
Μυκῆναι, αἱ, 1, Mycenae.
μυρίανδρος, -ον, adj., of 10,000 men.
μυριάς, -άδος, ἡ, 3, a myriad, 10,000.
μύριοι, num., 10,000.
Μυρμιδόνες, οἱ, 3, the Mymidons,
followers of Achilles.
μῦς, μυός, ὁ, 3, a mouse.
Μυσοί, οἱ, 2, the Mysians, natives of
Mysia, in N.W. Asia Minor.
Μυτιληναῖος, ὁ, 2, a man of Mytilene, (in the island of Lesbos).
μῶρος, -α, -ον, adj., foolish.

N

ναί, particle, yes.
ναυηγός, ὁ, 2, a shipwrecked man.
Ναύκρατις, -εως, ἡ, 3, Naucratis,
a city in the Egyptian Delta.
ναυμαχία, ἡ, 1, sea-fight.
ναυμαχῶ(εω), v.n., fight at sea.
ναυπηγός, ὁ, 2, ship-builder, ship-
wright.
ναῦς, νεώς, ἡ, 3, ship (Par. 18).
ναύτης, ὁ, 1, sailor.
ναυτικόν, τό, 2, fleet.
ναυτίλος, ὁ, 2, a sailor.

νεανίας, ὁ, 1, youth, young man.
νεανικός, -ή, -όν, adj., youthful.
Νεῖλος, ὁ, 2, the Nile.
νεκρός, ὁ, 2, a corpse.
Νέμεια, τά, 2, the Nemean games.
νέμω, v.a., allot, apportion, inhabit.
νέος, -α, -ον, adj., young.
νεουργός, -ον, adj., newly wrought.
νέρτερος, -α, -ον, adj., of the lower
world.
νέρτεροι, οἱ, the dead.
νῆις, -ιδος, adj., ignorant, with gen.
νήπιος, -α, -ον, adj., infantile, infant.
Νήρηδες, αἱ, 3, the Nereids.
νησιώτης, ὁ, 1, islander.
νῆσος, ἡ, 2, island.
νήφω, v.n., be sober.
νίκη, ἡ, 1, victory.
Νικίας, ὁ, 1, Nicias.
Νικοτέλης, -ους, 3, Nicoteles.
νικῶ(αω), v.a., conquer, prevail over,
win.
νιφετός, ὁ, 2, snowstorm.
νιφετώδης, -ες, adj., snowy.
νομίζω, v.a., think, consider.
νόμιμος, -η, -ον, adj., lawful, law-
abiding.
νομοθέτης, ὁ, 1, lawgiver.
νόμος, ὁ, 2, law, custom.
νόσος, ἡ, 2, disease.
νοσῶ(εω), v.n., be ill.
νοῶ(εω), v.a., bear in mind.
νυκτομαχία, ἡ, 1, battle at night.
νυμφή, ἡ, 1, nymph, bride.
νῦν, adv., now.
νύξ, νυκτός, ἡ, 3, night ; νυκτός, at
night.
νῶτον, τό, 2, back, rear.

Ξ

ξενία, ἡ, 1, entertainment (by a ξένος).
ξένιον, τό, 2, present.
ξένος, ὁ, 2, friend, guest, guest-friend,
stranger.

Ξενοφῶν, -ῶντος, ὁ, 3, *Xenophon, soldier and author.*
Ξέρξης, ὁ, 1, *Xerxes, king of Persia.*
ξίφος, -ους, τό, 3, *sword.*
ξόανον, τό, 2, *statue,* originally a wooden statue.
ξύλον, τό, 2, *wood, timber, log.*

Ο

ὁ, ἡ, τό, definite article, *the* (Par. 3).
ὀβελός, ὁ, 2, *spit for roasting.*
ὀγδοήκοντα, num., *eighty.*
ὄγδοος, ord. num., *eighth.*
ὁδοιπόρος, ὁ, 2, *wayfarer.*
ὁδός, ἡ, 2, *way, road.*
ὀδούς, -οντος, ὁ, 3, *tooth* (Par. 22).
ὀδύνη, ἡ, 1, *pain, anguish.*
ὀδύρομαι, v. mid., *bewail.*
'Οδύσσεια, ἡ, 1, *the Odyssey of Homer.*
'Οδυσσεύς, ὁ, 3, *Odysseus* (Latin *Ulysses* or *Ulixes*).
ὄζος, ὁ, 2, *bough, shoot.*
Οἴαγρος, ὁ, *Oeagrus, father of Orpheus.*
οἶδα, v.a., *know* (Par. 73).
οἶδμα, -ατος, τό, 3, *wave.*
οἴκειος, -α, -ον adj., *own.*
οἴκησις, -εως, ἡ, 3, *dwelling.*
οἰκητήρ, ὁ, 3, *settler.* Poetical.
οἰκία, ἡ, 1, *house.*
οἰκίζω, v.a., *found.*
οἰκοδομῶ(εω), v.a., *build.*
οἶκος, ὁ, 2, *house* ; οἴκοι, *at home* ; οἴκαδε, *homewards* ; οἴκοθεν, *from home.*
οἰκῶ(εω), v.a., *inhabit.*
οἶμαι, v. mid., *think.*
οἶνος, ὁ, 2, *wine.*
οἰνοχόος, ὁ, 2, *cupbearer.*
οἴομαι, v. dep., *think.*
οἶος, rel. pron., *such as.*
οἶός τ' εἶναι, *to be able.*
ὀϊστός, ὁ, 2, *arrow.*
οἴχομαι, v. mid., *depart, die, be gone.*

ὀκέλλω, v.a., *bring a ship to shore.*
ὀκνῶ(εω), v.a., *shrink.*
ὀκτώ, num., *eight.*
ὄλβιος, -α, -ον, adj., *blessed.*
ὀλιγαρχία, ἡ, 1, *oligarchy.*
ὀλίγος, -η, -ον, *few, small* (Par. 37).
οἱ ὀλίγοι, *oligarchs.*
ὄλλυμι, v.a., *destroy* ; mid., *perish*
ὄλωλα, *I have perished,* (p. 316).
ὅλος, -η, -ον, adj., *whole, complete.*
ὀλοφύρομαι, v. mid., *lament, bewail.*
'Ολυμπία, ἡ, 1, *Olympia,* in N.W. Peloponnese, where were held the Olympic games. 'Ολυμπίασι, *at Olympia.*
'Ολυμπιάς, -άδος, ἡ, 3, *an Olympiad,* i.e. four year period.
'Ολυμπιονίκης, ὁ, *a victor in the Olympic games.*
"Ολυμπος, ὁ, 2, Mt. Olympus. (1) in N. Greece. (2) in N.W. Asia Minor.
ὁμαλός, -ή, -όν, adj., *level, uniform.*
ὄμβρος, ὁ, 2, *rain.*
"Ομηρος, ὁ, 2, *Homer.*
ὅμηρος, ὁ, 2, *hostage.*
ὁμιλῶ(εω), v.a., *associate with,* w. dat.
ὁμίχλη, ἡ, 1, *mist.*
ὄμμα, -ατος, τό, 3, *eye.*
ὄμνυμι, v.a., *swear.*
ὁμοῖος, -α, -ον, adj., *like.*
ὁμοῖα φρονεῖν, *be in sympathy.*
ὄμορος, -ον, adj., *neighbouring.*
ὀμφαλόεις, -εσσα, -εν ; -εντα, etc., adj., *with a boss.*
ὅμως, adv., *nevertheless.*
ὄναρ, adv., *in a dream.*
ὀνειδίζω, v.a., *rebuke, blame.*
ὄνειρον, τό, 2, *dream.*
ὄνομα, -ατος, 3, *name.*
ὀνομάζω, v.a., *name.*
ὀνομαστί, *by name.*
ὀνομαστός, -ή, -όν, adj., *renowned.*
ὄνος, ὁ, 2, *ass.*
ὄνυξ, ὄνυχος, ὁ, 3, *nail.*

ὄξος, -ους, τό, 3, *vinegar.*
ὀξύς, -εῖα, -ύ, adj., *sharp.*
ὄπη, ἡ, 1, *chink.*
ὄπη, adv., *where ; how.*
ὄπισθεν, adv., *from behind.*
ὀπίσω, adv., *back.*
ὁπλή, ἡ, 1, *hoof.*
ὁπλίτης, ὁ, 1, *heavy armed foot-soldier, hoplite.*
ὅπλον, τό, 2, *weapon.*
ὁπόσος, -η, -ον, pron., *how great* ; pl., *how many* ; or rel., *as many as*
ὀπτῶ(αω), v.a., *roast, cook.*
ὅπου, adv., *where.*
ὀργή, ἡ, 1, *anger.*
ὀργίζω, v.a., *vex, incense* ; pass., *be angry.*
ὀργυία, ἡ, 1, *fathom.*
'Ορέστης, ὁ, 1, *Orestes, son of Agamemnon.*
ὄρθιος, -α, -ον, adj., *upright.*
ὀρθῶς, adv., *rightly.*
ὀρίζω, v.a., *define.*
ὅρκος, ὁ, 2, *oath, promise.*
ὁρμίζω, v.a., *bring to anchor.*
ὁρμῶ(αω), v.n., *rush.*
ὄρνις, -νιθος, ὁ or ἡ, 3, *bird.*
ὄρος, -ους, τό, 3, *mountain.*
ὀρχηστρίς, -ίδος, ἡ, 3, *female dancer.*
'Ορχομένιοι, οἱ, 2, *people of Orchomenos.*
ὀρχοῦμαι(εο), v. mid., *dance.*
ὁρῶ(αω), v.a., *see* (Pars. 71 and 72).
ὅς, ἥ, ὅ, rel. pron., *who, which.*
ὁσάκις, adv., *how many times.*
ὅσος, pron., *so much* ; ὅσῳ, with comp., *the more.*
ὅστις, ἥτις, ὅ τι, indef. rel. pron., *whoever.*
ὄστρακον, τό, 2, *potsherd.*
ὅτι, conj., *that, because* (Syntax F 2, p. 298).
οὐ, negative particle, *not.*
οὐδέ, negative, *and not, nor.*

οὐδείς, οὐδεμία, οὐδέν, pron., *no-one* (Par. 44).
οὐκέτι, adv., *no longer.*
οὖν, particle, *accordingly, therefore.*
οὐρά, ἡ, 1, *tail.*
οὐρανός, ὁ, 2, *sky, heaven.*
οὖς, ὠτός, τό, 3, *ear* (Par. 22).
οὐσία, ἡ, 1, *existence, property.*
οὔτε . . . οὔτε, *neither . . . nor.*
οὗτος, αὕτη, τοῦτο, dem. pron., *this.*
οὕτως, adv., *thus, so.*
ὀφείλω, v.a., *owe.*
ὀφθαλμός, ὁ, 2, *eye.*
ὄφις, -εως, ὁ, 3, *snake.*
ὄχημα, -ατος, τό, 3, *vehicle, carriage.*
ὄχθος, ὁ, 2, *river bank.*
ὀχοῦμαι(εο), v. mid., *ride.*
ὀχυρός, -ά, -όν, adj., *firm, lasting.*
ὀψέ, adv., *late.*
ὄψις, -εως, ἡ, 3, *view, vision.*
ὄψομαι, fut. ὁρῶ, *see.*

Π

πάγος, ὁ, 2, *hill.*
παιανίζω, v.n., *raise a song of victory.*
παιδαγωγός, ὁ, 2, *tutor, one who escorts a boy to school.*
παίδευμα, -ατος, τό, 3, *lesson, teaching.*
παιδευτής, ὁ, 1, *teacher.*
παιδεύω, v.a., *teach, train.*
παιδία, ἡ, 1, *play.*
παιδίον, τό, 2, *young child.*
παίζω, v.n., *play.*
παῖς, παιδός, ὁ or ἡ, 3, *child ; slave.*
παίω, v.a., *strike.*
παλάθη, ἡ, 1, *cake of preserved fruit.*
πάλαι, adv., *of old.*
παλαιός, -ά, -όν, adj., *of olden time, ancient, old.*
Παλαίστρα, ἡ, 1, *Palaestra.*
πάλη, ἡ, 1, *wrestling.*
πάλιν, adv., *back, again.*
πανταχόθεν, adv., *from every side.*
πανταχοῦ, adv., *everywhere.*

πάντη, adv., *in every way.*
παντοδαπός, -ή, -όν, adj., *of every kind.*
πάνυ, adv., *altogether, very.*
παρά, prep. with acc., *to the side of, along, contrary to* ; with gen., *from* ; with dat., *at.* (P. 281.)
παραβάλλω, v.a., *extend along.*
παραγγέλλω, v.a. *give orders.*
παραγίγνομαι, v. mid., *come to, be in, stand by.*
παράγω, v.a., *lead along.*
παραδίδωμι, v.a., *hand over.*
παραίνεσις -εως, ή, 3, *exhortation.*
παραινῶ(εω), v.a., *advise* with dat.
παραιτοῦμαι(εο), v. mid., *ask leave to decline.*
παρακαλῶ(εω), v.a., *exhort.*
Παράκλητος, ὁ, 2, *advocate, comforter.* From παρακαλῶ.
παραλαμβάνω, v.a., *take along.*
παράπαν, adv., *altogether.*
παραπλέω, v.a., *sail past.*
παραπλήσιος, -α, -ον, adj., *just like.*
παρασκευάζω, v.a., *get ready, provide.*
παρατάσσω, v.a., *arrange beside.*
παρατίθημι, v.a., *deposit, set by.*
παρειά, ή, 1, *cheek.*
πάρειμι, v.n., *be present.*
πάρεστι, v. impers., *it is possible.*
παρέρχομαι, v. mid., *pass by, come forward* (to speak).
παρέχω, v.a., *supply, afford, provide, cause* ; with adj., *show.*
παρθένος, ή, 2, *maiden.*
Παρθενών, -ῶνος, ὁ, 3, *Parthenon, temple of Athens.*
Πάρις, -ιδος, ὁ, 3, *Paris, son of Priam.*
παρίσταμαι, intrans. tenses, *be around, occur.*
Παρνασσός, ὁ, 2, *Mt. Parnassus,* in Phocis.
παροξύνω, v.a., *encourage.*

παρουσία, ή, 1, *presence.*
παρρησιάζομαι, v. mid., *speak freely.*
πᾶς, πᾶσα, πᾶν, adj., *all, the whole, every.*
πάσχω, v.n. and a., *suffer.*
πατάσσω, v.a., *strike.*
πατήρ, -τρός, ὁ, 3, *father* (Par. 20).
πατρίς, -ίδος, ή, 3, *native country.*
Πάτροκλος, ὁ, 2, *Patroclus, friend of Achilles.*
πατρῷος, -α, -ον, adj., *ancestral.*
πατῶ(εω), v.n., *tread.*
παυστήριος, adj., *one who checks, stays.*
παύω, v.a., *I stop,* trans. ; mid., *I stop (myself),* intrans.
παχύς, -εῖα, -ύ, adj., *fat, rich, thick.*
πεδιάς, -άδος, adj., *flat, level.*
πεδίον, τό, 2, *plain.*
πέδον, τό, 2, *ground,* poetical for πεδίον.
πεζομαχία, ή, 1, *infantry engagement.*
πεζός, -ή, -όν, adj., *on foot* ; ὁ πεζός, *an infantryman.*
πείθω, v.a., *persuade* ; mid. and pass., *be persuaded, obey,* with dat.
πειθώ, ή, 3, *persuasion* (Par. 23).
πεῖρα, ή, 1, *attempt, trial.*
Πειραιεύς, ὁ, 3, *the Piraeus, chief harbour of Athens* (Πειραιᾶ, Πειραιῶς, Πειραιεῖ) ; cf. βασιλεύς, (Par. 17, and 23).
πείρω, v.a., *pierce.*
πειρῶμαι(αο), v. mid., *try.*
Πεισίστρατος, ὁ, 2, *Pisistratus, tyrant of Athens in sixth century* B.C.
πείσομαι from πείθω or πάσχω
πέλαγος, -ους, τό, 3, *sea, ocean.*
πέλας, adv., *near.*
πελειάς, -άδος, ή, 3, *dove.*
πέλεκυς, ὁ, 3, *axe.* Par. 16.
Πελοπίδας, ὁ, 1, *Pelopidas, a famous Theban.*

Πελοποννήσιος, -α, -ον, adj., *of the Peloponnese.*
Πελοπόννησος, ἡ, 2, *Peloponnese.*
Πέλοψ, -οπος, ὁ, 3, *Pelops.*
πέμπτος, -η, -ον, ord. num., *fifth.*
πέμπω, v.a., *send, escort.*
πενθῶ(εω), v.n., *mourn.*
πένταθλον, τό, 2, *competition at the games.* The five exercises were ἅλμα, *jumping* ; δίσκος, *discus* ; δρόμος, *running* ; πάλη, *wrestling* ; πυγμή, *boxing.*
πέντε, num., *five.*
πεντεκαίδεκα, num., *fifteen.*
πέπλος, ὁ, 2, *robe, ceremonial robe in honour of Athene.*
περ, particle, *though.*
περαίνω, v.a., *accomplish.*
πέραν, adv., *on the other side of.*
περί, prep., *see* p. 282.
  with acc., *about* ;
  with gen., *concerning* ;
  with dat., *around.*
περιβάλλω, v.a., *throw around, wrap, cling to.*
περιγίγνομαι, v. mid., *to be left, survive.*
περίειμι (εἰμί), v.n., *survive, be superior.*
περίειμι (εἶμι), v.a., *go around.*
περιέχω, v.a., *surround.*
περιίστημι, v.a., *set around, surround* ; mid. and intrans., *stand around.*
περικάθημαι, v. mid., *sit around.*
Περικλῆς, ἡ, 3, *Pericles* (Par. 23).
περικλύζω, v.a., *wash around.*
περιπατῶ(εω), v.n., *walk about.*
περιπέτομαι, v. mid., *fly around.*
περιπλέω, v.a., *sail round.*
περισκοπῶ(εω), v.a., *look about.*
περισσός, -ή, -όν, adj., *superfluous, excessive.*
περισχίζω, v.a., *cut around, part.*
περιτειχίζω, v.a., *fortify.*

περιτίθημι, v.a., *bestow.*
Πέρσαι, οἱ, 1, *the Persians.*
Περσεύς, -έως, ὁ, 3, *Perseus.*
Περσεφόνη, ἡ, 1, *Persephone.*
πεσών, see πίπτω.
πέτομαι, v. mid., *fly.*
πέτρα, ἡ, 1, *stone, rock.*
πῆ, adv., *anywhere.*
πήγνυμι, v.a. and n., *fix, freeze.*
πηλός, ὁ, 2, *mud, clay.*
πηλώδης, -ες, adj., *muddy.*
Πηνελοπή, ἡ, 1, *Penelope, wife of Odysseus.*
πῆχυς, -εως, ὁ, 3, *cubit, fore-arm* (Par. 16).
πικρός, -ά, -όν, adj., *bitter.*
Πίνδαρος, ὁ, 2, *Pindar, Theban poet.*
πίνω, v.a., *drink,* (p. 316).
πίπτω, v.n., *fall.*
πιστεύω, v.n., *trust, be confident.*
πιστός, -ή, -όν, adj., *faithful.*
πίτυς, -υος, ἡ, 3, *pine tree.*
πίων, πῖον, adj., *fat, rich.*
Πλαταιεῖς, οἱ, 3, *the people of Plataea.*
πλάσσω, v.a., *form, mould.*
πλατύς, -εῖα, -ύ, adj., *broad, level.*
Πλάτων, -ωνος, ὁ, 3, *Plato.*
πλεῖστος, superl. of πολύς, (Par. 37).
πλευρόν τό, 2, *side, flank.*
πλέω, v.n., *sail* (p. 223 and 316).
πληγή, ἡ, 1, *blow.*
πλῆθος, -ους, τό, 3, *crowd, main body.*
πλήν, adv., *but, except* ; also prep. w. gen., *save.*
πλησιάζω, v.n., *draw near.*
πλησίον, adv., *near* ; ὁ πλησίον, *neighbour.*
πλοῖον, τό, 2, *ship, cargo-vessel.*
πλοῦς, (οο contracted), ὁ, 2, *voyage.*
πλοῦτος, ὁ, 2, *wealth.*
πλουτῶ(εω), *be wealthy.*
Πλούτων, -ωνος, ὁ, 3, *Pluto, Hades.*
πνέω, v.n., *breathe, blow* (see p. 223).
πνεῦμα, -ατος, τό, 3, *breath, breeze.*

ποδωκεία, ἡ, 1, racing, swiftness of foot.
πόθος, ὁ, 2, longing, desire.
ποίημα, -ατος, τό, 3, poem.
ποιητής, ὁ, 1, maker, poet.
ποιμήν, ὁ, 3, shepherd.
ποίμνη, ἡ, 1, flock.
ποῖος, interrog. and indef. pron., what kind?
ποιῶ(εω), v.a., do, make.
πολέμαρχος, ὁ, 2, general.
πολεμικῶς, adv., with ἔχω, I am warlike.
πολέμιος, ὁ, 2, enemy.
πόλεμος, ὁ, 2, war.
πολεμῶ(εω), v.n., make war.
πολιορκία, ἡ, 1, siege.
πολιορκῶ(εω), v.a., besiege.
πόλις, -εως, ἡ, 3, city.
πολίτης, ὁ, 1, citizen.
πολλάκις, adv., often.
Πολυδεύκης, ὁ, 1, Polydeuces, Pollux.
Πολυκράτης, -ους, ὁ, 3, Polycrates, tyrant of Samos.
πολύτροπος, ον, adj., of many wiles.
Πολύμνηστος, ὁ, 2, Polymnestus.
πολύς, πολλή, πολύ, adj., many, great, large (Par. 26). πολύ, adv., very, much.
πομπή, ἡ, 1, procession.
πονηρός, -ά, -όν, adj., base, evil, poor.
πόνος, ὁ, 2, labour, toil.
πόντιος, -α, -ον, adj., of the sea.
πόντος, ὁ, 2, sea. In particular Πόντος, the Black Sea, euphemistically called εὔξεινος, friendly.
ποντοπορῶ(εω,) v.n., cross the sea.
πονῶ(εω) and πονοῦμαι, v.n. and mid., toil, be in difficulties.
πορεία, ἡ, 1, road, journey.
πορεύομαι, v. mid., journey, walk.
πορθμεύω, v.a., ferry, convey across.
πορθμός, ὁ, 2, stretch of water.
πορθῶ(εω), v.a., ravage.

πορίζω, v.a., provide ; mid., procure for oneself.
πόρος, ὁ, 2, way.
πόρρω, adv., further on.
Ποσειδῶν, -ῶνος, ὁ, 3, Poseidon, god of the sea.
ποταμός, ὁ, 2, river.
ποτε, particle, ever, at any time.
πότερον, interrog., whether.
πότερος, interrog. pron., which of the two?
πούς, ποδός, ὁ, 3, foot (Par. 22).
πράσσω, v.a., do ; v.n., fare (Par. 64).
πρέπει, v. impers., it is fitting.
πρεπόντως, adv., properly.
πρέσβυς, -εως, ὁ, 3, old, old man (μ ε ι ι ε α l) ; pl., ambassadors (Par. 16)
πρεσβύτης, ὁ, 1, old man.
πρό, prep., see p. 282.
πρόβλημα, -ατος, τό, 3, protection.
πρόγονος, ὁ, 2, forebear.
προδίδωμι, v.a., betray.
προδοσία, ἡ, 1, treachery.
προέρχομαι, v.n., advance.
προθύμως, adv., eagerly.
πρόθυρον, τό, 2, porch, front hall.
προκαλοῦμαι(εο), v. mid., challenge.
πρόκειμαι, v. mid., lie in front, be allotted.
προκυκλῶ(εω), v.a., wheel in front.
προλέγω, v.a., say beforehand, prophesy. Par. 71 for προεῖπον, etc.
πρόμαχος, ὁ, 2, champion.
πρόνους, -νουν, adj., kindly-disposed.
πρόρριζος, -ον, adj., by the roots, utterly.
πρός, prep., see p. 282.
with acc., towards ;
with gen. from, πρὸς θεῶν, by the gods ; by.
with dat., at, in addition to.
προσαγορεύω, v.a., address, give the name of, call (Par. 71).
προσάγω, v.a., apply.
προσβάλλειν, v.a., attack, w. dat.

προσβολή, ἡ, 1, *attack.*
προσγελῶ(αω), v.a., *laugh at, smile at.*
προσδέχομαι, v. mid., *accept.*
πρόσειμι, v.n., *draw near.*
προσεῖπον, see προσαγορεύω.
προσήκω, v.n., *draw near, be related.*
  οἱ προσήκοντες, *relatives.*
  τὰ προσήκοντα, *affairs, duties.*
προσηλῶ(οω), v.a., *nail to, fasten to.*
προσημαίνω, v.a., *give a signal.*
πρόσθεν, adv., *in front.*
προσιππεύω, v.a., *ride up to.*
προσίσχω, v.n., *put in at.*
προσκαλῶ(εω), v.a., *invite, call.*
προσκεφάλαιον, τό, 2, *pillow.*
προσκυνῶ(εω), v.a., *greet.*
προσλαμβάνω, v.a., *take in addition.*
πρόσοδος, ἡ, 2, *revenue.*
προσόμοιος, -ον, adj., *like.*
προσπίπτω, v.n., *fall against,* w. dat.
προσπλέω, v.n., *sail towards, against.*
πρόσπολος, ὁ, 2, *attendant.*
προστατῶ(εω), v.a., *support, take charge of,* with gen.
πρόστάσσω, v.a., *command.*
προστίθημι, v.a., *add to, put in position, put up.*
προσφέρω, v.a., *bring up, offer.*
πρόσω, adv., *further on.*
πρόσωπον, τό, 2, *face.*
προτίθημι, v.a., *offer, put before, propose.*
πρύμνα, ἡ, 1, *ship's stern.*
πρώ, adv., *early.*
πρώρα, ἡ, 1, *ship's bow.*
Πρωταγόρας, ὁ, 1, *the sophist Protagoras.*
πρῶτον, adv., *first.*
πρῶτος, -η, -ον, ordin. num., *first.*
πρωτοστάτης, ὁ, 1, *in the first rank, first man on the right.*
πτερόν, τό, 2, *wing, feather.*
πτερῶ (οω), v.a., *fit with wings.*
πτήσσω, v.n., *crouch, cower before.*

πτολίεθρον, τό, 2, *city* (poetical).
πτύω, v.a., *spit.*
πυγμαχία, ἡ, 1, *boxing.*
πυγμάχος, ὁ, 2, *boxer.*
πυγμή, ἡ, 1, *boxing.*
πύλη, ἡ, 1, *gate.*
Πυθώ, ἡ, 3, *Pytho, Delphi.*
πυνθάνομαι, ἐπυθόμην, v. mid., *learn, enquire.*
πύξ, adv., *with fists, boxing.*
πυξίς, -ίδος, ἡ, 3, *box.*
πῦρ, πυρός, τό, 3, *fire.*
πύρνον, τό, 2, *wheaten bread.*
πῶς, interrog., *how?*
πως, *somehow.*

Ρ

ῥάδιος, -α, -ον, adj., *easy* (Par. 35).
ῥαθυμία, ἡ, 1, *inactivity.*
ῥαπίζω, v.a., *beat with rods.*
ῥᾶον, adv., *more easily* (Par. 35).
ῥέω, v.n., *flow.*
ῥήγνυμι, v.a., *break.*
ῥηθείς, -έντος, *spoken,* λέγω, (Par. 71).
ῥῆμα, -ατος, τό, 3, *word, order.*
Ῥήνεια, ἡ, 1, *the island Rheneia,* near Delos.
ῥήτωρ, -ορος, ὁ, 3, *speaker.*
ῥίζα, ἡ, 1, *root.*
ῥίπτω, v.a., *throw.*
ῥίς, ῥινός, ἡ, 3, *nostril, nose* (Par. 22).
ῥόδον, τό, 2, *rose.*
ῥοθιάς, gen. -άδος, adj. *dashing* (of oars).
ῥόπαλον, τό, 2, *club.*
ῥυθμός, ὁ, 2, *rhythm.*
Ῥωμαῖοι, οἱ, 2, *Romans.*
ῥώμη, ἡ, 1, *strength.*

Σ

Σαλαμίς, -ῖνος ἡ, 3, *Salamis.*
σάλπιγξ, -ιγγος, ἡ, 3, *trumpet.*
  ὑπὸ σάλπιγγος, *at the sound of the trumpet.*

Σάμιοι, οἱ, 2, the Samians.
Σάμος, ἡ, 2, the island of Samos.
Σάρδεις, αἱ, 3, the city of Sardis, in W. of Asia Minor.
σαφής, -ές, adj., clear.
σαφῶς, adv., clearly.
σεαυτόν, refl. pron., thyself.
σεισμός, ὁ, 2, earthquake.
σείω, v.a., shake.
σελήνη, ἡ, 1, the moon.
σέλινον, τό, 2, parsley.
σεμνός, -ή, -όν, adj., majestic, holy.
σῆμα, -ατος, τό, 3, sign, tomb.
σημαίνω, v.a., signal, signify.
σημεῖον, τό, 2, signal, emblem.
σίδηρον, τό, 2, iron.
σιδηροῦς, -ᾶ, -οῦν [1] (contr. ε), adj., of iron.
Σικελία, ἡ, 1, Sicily.
σιτίον, τό, 2, food.
σιτοποιός, -όν, adj., baker, bread-maker.
σῖτος, ὁ, 2, corn, grain.
σιωπῶ(αω), v.n., be silent.
σκάφη, ἡ, hull of a ship, ship.
σκεδάννυμι, v.a., scatter.
σκέπτομαι, v. mid., look, consider.
σκευή, ἡ, 1, dress, gear, robes.
σκηνῶ(οω), v.n., pitch a tent, settle.
σκῆπτρον, τό, 2, sceptre, staff.
σκόλοψ, -οπος, ὁ, 3, stake.
σκοπῶ(εω), v.a., look at, consider.
σκότος, -ους, τό, 3, darkness.
Σκυθικός, -ή, -όν, adj., Scythian.
σκώπτω, v.a., ridicule.
Σοῦσα, τά, 2, Susa, capital of the King of Persia.
σοφία, ἡ, 1, wisdom.
σοφιστής, ὁ, 1, a sophist, professional wise man.
Σοφοκλῆς, -κλέους, ὁ, 3, Sophocles (Par. 23).
σοφός, -ή, -όν, adj., wise.
σπάργανα, τά, 2, swaddling clothes.

Σπάρτη, ἡ, 1, Sparta.
Σπαρτιάτης, ὁ, 1, native of Sparta, Spartan.
σπείρω, v.a., scatter, sow.
σπένδω, ἔσπεισα, v.a., pour a libation.
σπεύδω, v.n., hasten.
σποδία, ἡ, 1, ashes.
σπονδαί, αἱ, 1, truce.
στάδιον, τό, 2, a stade (about 200 yards) race course (the course at Olympia was exactly a stade in length). Plur. often οἱ στάδιοι.
στέλλω, v.a., equip; mid., march, make an expedition.
στενός, -η, -ον, adj., narrow.
στέργω, v.n., acquiesce in, like.
στέρνον, τό, 2, chest.
στεροῦμαι(εο), v. pass., be deprived of, w. gen.
στέφανος, ὁ, 2, crown, garland.
στεφανῶ(οω), v.a., crown.
στήλη, ἡ, 1, monument (usually with inscription), post, turning post.
Στοά, ῆς, ἡ, 1, Porch. The Στωϊκοί, Stoic philosophers, taught in the Στοὰ ποικιλή (painted portico) at Athens.
στολή, ἡ, 1, raiment.
στόλος, ὁ, 2, fleet.
στόμα, -ατος, τό, 3, mouth.
στορέννυμι, v.a., lay low.
στρατεία, ἡ, 1, expedition.
στράτευμα, -ατος, τό, 3, army.
στρατηγίς, -ίδα, ἡ, adj., leading.
στρατηγός, ὁ, 2, general.
στρατιά, ἡ, 1, fleet, force ; military service.
στρεβλῶ(οω), v.a., wrench.
στρατιώτης, ὁ, 1, soldier.
στρατόπεδον, τό, 2, camp ; army.
στρέφω, v.a., turn, twist, p. 317.
Στρόφιος, ὁ, 2, Strophius the Phocian, father of Pylades.

[1] (Par. 26).

στυγῶ(εω), v.a., *hate.*
στῦλος, ὁ, 2, *pillar.*
σύ, personal pronoun, *thou.*
συγγνώμη, ἡ, 1, *pardon.*
συγκαλῶ(εω), v.a., *call together.*
συγκρούω, v.a., *clash together.*
συγχαίρω, v.n., *rejoice with.*
συζῶ (συν +ζάω), v.n., *live with.*
συλλαμβάνω, v.a., take *together,*
    catch.
συλλέγω, v.a., *collect, gather.*
συμβιῶ(οω), v.n. *live together.*
σύμβολον, τό, 2, *token, tally.*
συμβουλεύω, v.a., *advise,* acc. of
    thing, dat. of person.
συμμαχία, ἡ, 1, *alliance.*
σύμμαχος, ὁ, 2, *ally.*
συμπαίζω, v.a., *play with.*
σύμπαν, τό, 3, *the total.*
συμπαραστῶ(εω), v.a., *stand beside.*
συμπεριπατῶ(εω), v.n., *walk round*
    with.
συμπλέκω, v.a., twine *together,*
    grapple.
συμπλέω, v.n., *sail with.*
συμπίπτω, v.n., *fall with, fall in with.*
Συμπληγάδες, αἱ, 3, the *clashing*
    rocks, Symplegades.
σύμπτωσις, -εως, ἡ, 3, *coincidence*
    (*falling together*).
συμφεύγω, v.n., *flee.*
σύμφημι, v.n., *agree with.*
συμφορά, ἡ, 1, *misfortune.*
σύν, prep. with dat., *with, in company*
    with.
συναγείρω, v.a., *gather together.*
συνάγω, v.a., *bring together.*
σύνειμι, v.n., *be together.*
συνεμβολή, ἡ, 1, *the dip of the oars.*
συνεργάτης, ὁ, 1, *helper.*
συνεργῶ(εω), v.n., *work with.*
συνέρχομαι, v. mid., *go with, come*
    together.
συνίστημι, v.a., put *together,* in-
    trans., *be formed.*

σύνοδος, ἡ, 2, *encounter, gathering.*
συνοργίζομαι, v.n., *join in anger.*
συνορῶ(αω), v.a., *realise.*
συντάσσω, v.a., *arrange together.*
συντεκμαίρομαι, v. mid., *calculate.*
σύντροφος, ὁ, 2, *foster brother.*
Συρακόσιοι, οἱ, 2, *Syracusans.*
σῦριγξ, -ιγγος, ἡ, 3, *Pan pipe.*
σύς, ὁ, or ἡ, 3, *pig,* (Par. 15).
συσσιτῶ(εω), v.n., *mess with.*
συσσκοτίζω, v.n., *grow dark.*
συστρέφω, v.a., *form into a compact*
    body.
συσχολάζω, v.n., *spend leisure with.*
συφορβός, ὁ, 2, *swineherd.*
σφάζω, v.a., *sacrifice, slay.* (σφάττω).
σφαιροειδής, -ές, adj., *spherical.*
Σφίγξ, -ιγγός, ἡ, 3, *the Sphinx.*
σφόδρα, adv., *very, exceedingly.*
σφοδρός, -ά, -όν, adj., *vehement.*
σχῆμα, -ατος, τό, 3, *form, shape.*
σχολή, ἡ, 1, *leisure ; school.*
σώζω, v.a., *save, preserve.*
σῶμα, -ατος, τό, 3, *body.*
σωματοφύλαξ, -ακος, ὁ, 3, *body-*
    guard.
Σωκράτης, -ους, ὁ, 3, *Socrates* (Par.
    23).
σῶος, -α, -ον, adj., *safe.*
σωτήρ, -ῆρος, ὁ, 3, *saviour.*
σωτηρία, ἡ, 1, *safety.*
σώφρων, -ον, adj., of sound mind,
    prudent, sensible.
σωφρονῶ(εω). v.n., *be prudent.*

T

ταινία, ἡ, 1, *fillet, head-band.*
τάλαντον, τό, 2, talent (*weight, and*
    sum of money *corresponding,*
    =60 *minae*).
τάλαρος, ὁ, 2, *wool-basket.*
ταλασία, ἡ, 1, *wool spinning.*
ταμιεία, ἡ, 1, *housekeeping.*
τανύω, v.a., *stretch.*
τάξις, -εως, ἡ, 3, *rank.*

τάπης, -ητος, ὁ, 3, *rug, carpet*.
ταράσσω, v.a., *confuse, trouble, disturb*.
ταραχή, ἡ, 1, *confusion*.
τάσσω, v.a., *arrange*.
ταῦρος, ὁ, 2, *bull*.
ταύτῃ, adv., *there*.
τάφος, ὁ, 2, *tomb*.
ταφρός, ἡ, 2, *ditch*.
τάχος, -ους, τό, 3, *speed*.
ταχύς, -εῖα, -ύ, adj., *swift*.
ταχυτής, -τῆτος, ἡ, 3, *speed*.
τε, conj. enclitic, *and*, τε . . . καί,
   both . . . *and*. θ' before an aspirate.
τεθνεώς, -ῶτος, str. perf. partic. of
   θνήσκω, *die*.
τείχισμα, -ατος, τό, 3, *fortification*.
τεῖχος, -ους, τό, 3, *wall*.
τέκνον, τό, 2, *child*.
τέλειος, -α, -ον, adj., *complete, full-grown*.
τελευτή, ἡ, 1, *end*.
τελευτῶ(αω), v.a. and n., *end, finish*.
τελέως, adv., *completely*.
τέλος, τό, 3, *end* ; as adv., *finally*.
τελῶ(εω), v.a., *complete, pay, contribute, fulfil*.
τέμνω, v.a., *cut*.
τεναγώδης, -ες, adj., *marshy*.
τέρπω, v.a., *gladden*; mid., *enjoy*,
   w. dat.
τεσσαράκοντα, num., *forty*.
τέσσαρες, -α, num., *four*.
τέταρτος, -η, -ον, ord. num., *fourth*.
τετράγωνος, -ον, adj., *square*.
τετρακόσιοι, -αι, -α, num., *four hundred*.
τετράπους, -πουν, gen. -ποδος, adj.,
   four-footed.
τέτταρες, see τέσσαρες.
τέχνη, ἡ, 1, *art, skill, device*.
τέως, adv., *for a time*.
Τηλέμαχος, ὁ, 2, *Telemachus, son of Odysseus*.
τηνικαῦτα, adv., *then*.

τηρῶ (εω), v.a., *watch, guard, wait for*.
τῇδε, adv., *here*.
τίθημι, v.a., *place, put*.
τίκτω, ἔτεκον, v.a., *bear a child*.
τιμή, ἡ, 1, *honour*.
τίμιος, -α, -ον, adj., *honoured*.
τιμῶ(αω), v.a. *honour*.
τίς, τί, interrog. pron., *who? what?*
   (Pars. 50 and 95).
τις, τι, indef. pron., *any, a*.
τιτρώσκω, v.a., *wound*.
τοίνυν, adv., *accordingly*.
τοιοῦτος, τοιαύτη, τοιοῦτο, dem.
   pron., *such* (like οὗτος, Par. 45).
τόλμα, ἡ, 1, *daring*.
τολμῶ(αω), v. n., *dare.*
τόξον, τό, 2, *bow*.
τόπος, ὁ, 2, *place*.
τοσοῦτος, τοσαύτη, τοσοῦτο, (Par.
   45, οὗτος), *so great* ; pl., *so many*.
   ἐς τοσοῦτο. w. gen., *to such a pitch of*. τοσούτῳ, *so much*, w.
   comparatives.
τότε, adv., *then*.
τραγῳδία, ἡ, 1, *tragedy*.
τράπεζα, ἡ, 1, *table*.
Τραπεζούς, -οῦντος, ὁ, 3, *Trapezus, Trebizond*.
Τραπεζούντιοι, οἱ, 2, *people of Trapezus*.
τραυλός, -ή, -όν, adj., *lisping*.
τραῦμα, τό, 3, *wound*.
τραυματίας, -ου, ὁ, 1, *wounded man*.
τραυματίζω, v.a., *wound*.
τραχύς, -εῖα, -ύ, adj., *rough, difficult, harsh*.
τρεῖς, τρία, num., *three* (Par. 44).
τρέπω, v.a., *turn*.
τρέφω, v.a., *foster, bring up*.
τρέχω, v.n., *run*.
τρίαινα, ἡ, 1, *trident*.
τριάκοντα,, num., *thirty*.
τριακόσιοι, -αι, -α, num., *three hundred*.

368 GREEK-ENGLISH VOCABULARY

τρίβος, ή, 2, *path.*
τρίβω, v.a., *rub.*
τρίγων, -γωνος, ό, 3, *triangle.*
τριήρης, ή, *trireme, warship.* Like
σαφής, Par. 27.
τριήραρχος, ό, 2, *captain of a trireme.*
τρίπους, -ποδος, ό, 3, *tripod,* from
adj. τρίπους, -πουν, *three footed.*
τρίτος, -η, -ον, ord. num., *third.*
Τροία, ή, 1, *Troy.*
τρόπος, ό, 2, *manner, way.* τοῦτον
τὸν τρόπον, *in this way.*
τροφή, ή, 1, *nutriment, board.*
τροχός, ό, 2, *wheel, hoop.*
τρώγλη, ή, 1, *hole, crevice.*
τρώγω, v.a., *gnaw.*
τυγχάνω, v.n., *happen, meet with, hit;*
with gen. Opp. of ἁμαρτάνω.
τύμβος, ό, 2, *tomb.*
τύπτω, v.a., *hit.*
τυραννίς, -ίδος, ή, 3, *tyranny.*
τύραννος, ό, 2, *tyrant, absolute ruler.*
Τύρος, ή, 2, *Tyre.*
τυρός, ό, 2, *cheese.*
τυροποιῶ(εω), v.n., *make cheese.*
τύχη, ή, 1, *fortune.*

Υ

ὑβρίζω, v.a., *insult.*
ὑγιαίνω, v.n., *be well, in good health.*
ὑγιής, -ές, acc. m. -ᾶ, adj., *well,
healthy.*
ὕδρα, ή, 1, *water snake.*
ὕδωρ, -ατος, τό, 3, *water* (Par. 22).
ὑετός, ό, 2, *rain.*
υἱός, ό, 2 and 3, *son* (Par. 21).
ὕλη, ή, 1, *wood, forest.*
ὑμέναιος, ό, 2, *marriage song.*
ὑπέρ, prep., see p. 283.
with gen., *over, on behalf of.*
with acc., *beyond, above.*
ὑπερβαίνω, v.n., *go beyond, over.*
ὑπερβάλλω, v.a., *surpass.*
ὑπερέχω, v.n. *prevail, be powerful.*
ὑπέρθυρον, τό, 2, *lintel of a door.*

ὑπερμεγέθης, -ες, adj., *huge.*
ὑπέχω, v.n., *submit to,* with dat.
ὑπηρέτης, ό, 1, *attendant.*
ὑπισχνοῦμαι(εο), v. mid., *promise.*
ὕπνος, ό, 2, *sleep.*
ὑπό, prep. see p. 283; with gen., *by,
at the hands of, under.*
ὑποκρίνομαι, v. mid., *answer, act.*
ὑποκριτής, ό, 1, *actor.*
ὑπολαμβάνω, v.a., *take up, interrupt.*
ὑπομένω, v.a., *undergo, endure.*
ὑπομιμνήσκω, v.a., *remind.*
ὑπόσπονδος, -ον, adj., *under a truce.*
ὑποστρέφω, v.a. and n., *turn round*
ὑπουργῶ(εω), v.n., *collaborate.*
ὑποψία, ή, 1, *suspicion.*
ὕστατος, -η, -ον, adj., *last.*
ὑστεραῖος, -α, -ον, adj., *next.*
τῇ δὲ ὑστεραίᾳ, *on the next day.*
ὕστερον, adv., *later.*
ὕστερος, -α, -ον, comp. adj., *later,
inferior.*
Ὕφασις, ό, *the river Hyphasis,* in the
Punjab.
ὑψηλός, -ή, -όν, adj., *high.*
ὕψιστος, -η, -ον, adj., *highest.*
ὕψος, -ους, τό, 3, *height.*

Φ

Φαίακες, οἱ, 3, *the Phaeacians.*
φαίνω, v.a., *show.*
φαίνομαι v. mid., *appear, seem.*
φάλαγξ, -αγγος, ή, 3, *phalanx, close
formation.*
φανερός, -ά, ον, adj., *clear, plain,
evident.*
φάος, poetical for φῶς.
φαρέτρα, ή, 1, *quiver.*
φάρμακον, τό, 2, *drug, ointment,
poison.*
φάτνη, ή, 1, *manger.*
φαῦλος, -η, -ον, adj., *paltry, mean.*
φαύλως, adv., *poorly, inadequately.*
φέγγος, -ους, τό, 3, *light.*
Φειδίας, ό, 1, *Phidias, the sculptor.*

φέροικος, -ον, adj., *carrying their homes* (of the Scythians who lived in waggons).
φέρω, v.a., *carry, bear* p. 238 and 244.
φεύγω, v.a., *flee from, flee.*
φήμη, ἡ, 1, *reputation, report.*
φημί, v.a., *say* (Par. 80).
φθάνω, v.n. and a. *anticipate,* w. partic.
φθίμενος, -η, -ον, adj., *dead* (poetical).
φθόγγη, ἡ, 1, *voice.*
φθόγγος, ὁ, 2, *sound, voice.*
φθόνος, ὁ, 2, *envy.*
φιλάνθρωπος, -ον, adj., *kind-hearted.*
φιλάργυρος, -ον, adj., *avaricious.*
φιλελλήν, -εν, gen. ἡνος, adj., *friendly to the Greeks.*
φίλεργος, adj., *energetic.*
φίλημα, -ατος, τό, 3, *kiss.*
φιλία, ἡ, 1, *friendship.*
φιλικῶς, adv., *in friendly fashion.*
φίλοινος, -ον, adj., *fond of wine.*
φιλονεικία, ἡ 1, *rivalry.*
φίλος, -η, -ον, adj., *friendly, loving.*
φιλοσοφία, ἡ, 1, *philosophy.*
φιλοφροσύνη, ἡ, 1, *loving kindness.*
φίλτατος, superl. of φίλος.
φιλῶ(εω) v.a., *love.*
Φιντίας, ὁ, 1, *Phintias, friend of Damon.*
φόβος, ὁ, 2, *fear.*
φοβοῦμαι(εο), v. mid. and pass., *fear, be frightened.*
φοῖνιξ, -ικος, ὁ, 3, *date palm.*
Φοίνικες, οἱ, 3, *the Phoenicians.*
φοιτῶ(αω), v.n., *go regularly, frequent, keep coming.*
φονεύω, v.a., *kill.*
φόρμιγξ, -ιγγος, ἡ, 3, *lyre.*
φορμίζω, v.n., *play the lyre.*
Φορμίων, ωνος, ὁ, 3, *Phormio, an Athenian admiral.*

φόρος, ὁ, 2, *tribute.*
φορτίον, τό, 2, *cargo.*
φρήν, φρενός, ἡ, 3, *mind,* pl. *wits.*
φροντίζω, v.a., *think.*
φρονῶ(εω), v.n., *think, form an opinion* ; μέγα φρονῶ, *be proud.* φρονῶ τά τινος *to sympathise with.*
φρουρῶ(εω), v.a., *guard.*
φρυγανισμός, ὁ, 2, *gathering firewood.*
φρύγανον, το 2, *firewood.*
φυγή, ἡ, 1, *flight.*
φύλαξ, -ακος, ὁ, 3, *guard.*
φυλάσσω, v.a., *guard.*
φύλλον, τό, 2, *leaf.*
φυσῶ(αω), v.n., *blow.*
Φωκυλίδης, ὁ, 1, *Phocylides* (wrote maxims in verse).
Φωκεύς, -έως, ὁ, 3, *a Phocian.*
φωνή, ἡ, 1, *voice.*
φωνῶ(εω), v.a., *call.*
φῶς, φωτός, τό, 3, *light.*

X

χαίρω, v.n., *rejoice.* χαῖρε, imper., *hail, farewell.*
χαλεπός, -ή, -όν, adj., *difficult, hard.*
χαλκόπους, -πουν, gen. -ποδος, adj., *with feet of bronze.*
χαλκός, ὁ, 2, *bronze.*
χαλκοῦς, -ῆ, -οῦν,¹ adj. (contr. ε), *of bronze.*
χαλῶ(αω), v.a., *loosen.*
χαμαί, adv., *on the ground.*
χαρά, ἡ, 1, *joy.*
χάρις, -ιτος, ἡ, 3, *grace, beauty, charm, kindness, favour, thanks.*
χάριν, following a gen., *for the sake of.*
χάσκω, v.n., *gape.*
χεῖλος, -ους, τό, 3, *lip.*
χειμέριος, -α,-ον, adj., *wintry, stormy.*
χειμών, -ῶνος, ὁ, 3, *winter, storm.*
χείρ, χειρός, ἡ, 3, *hand* (Par. 22).

¹ See Par. 19, note.

χειροήθης, -ες, adj., *tame, domesticated.*

χελιδών, -όνος, ἡ, 3, *swallow.*

χελώνη, ἡ, 1, *tortoise.*

Χερρόνησος, ἡ, *the Chersonese* (the peninsula of Thrace which runs along the Hellespont) ; also **Χερσόνησος.**

χιλιάς, -άδος, ἡ, 3, *a thousand.*

χίλιοι, -αι, -α, num., *a thousand.*

χλωρός, -ά, -όν, adj., *pale, green.*

χορδή, ἡ, 1, *string of a musical instrument.*

χορός, ὁ, 2, *dance.*

χόω, v.a., *pile up a mole.*

χρή, impers. v., *it is necessary, ought, should* (Par. 99).

χρήζω, v.a., *need* (with gen.).

χρῆμα, -ατος, τό, 3, *thing,* pl. *money.*

χρησμός, ὁ, 2, *oracle.*

χρηστός, -ή, -όν, adj., *good, worthy.*

Χριστός, ὁ, 2, *Christ (the anointed).*

χρίω, v.a., *anoint.*

χρόνος, ὁ, 2, *time* ; χρόνῳ ποτε, *long ago.*

χρυσόμαλλος, -ον, adj., *with golden wool.*

χρυσός, ὁ, 2, *gold.*

χρυσοῦς,-ῆ,-οῦν, adj.,*golden*(Par. 26).

χρυσοφόρος, -ον, adj., *wearing gold, gold-clad.*

χρῶμα, -ατος, τό, 3, *colour.*

χρῶμαι(αο), v. mid., *use, enjoy,* w. dat. *treat.*

χρώς, χρωτός, ἡ, 3, *flesh.*

χῶ(χόω), v.a., *pile up a dyke.*

χῶμα, -ατος, τό, 3, *dyke, mole.*

χώρα, ἡ, 1, *country.*

χώριον, τό, 2, *place, fort.*

χωρῶ(εω), v.n., *go.*

Ψ

ψηφίζομαι, v. mid., *vote.*

ψόφος, ὁ, 2, *noise.*

ψυχή, ἡ, 1, *soul, spirit.*

ψῦχος, -ους, τό, 3, *cold.*

Ω

ᾠδή, ἡ, 1, *ode, song.*

ὠθῶ(εω), v.a., *push, thrust.*

ὠνητός, -ή, -όν, adj., *bought.*

ὠνοῦμαι(εο), v. mid., *buy.*

ὥρα, ἡ, 1, *hour, season.*

ὡραῖος, -α, -ον, adj., *beautiful.*

ὡς, conj., *as, as though* ; *that* ; *in order that* ; *since.* (Syntax F 2, G 1, G 2, pp. 298–300).

ὡς τάχιστα, *as soon as possible.*

ὡς, prep. with acc., *to (of people).*

ὡσαύτως, adv., *in the same way.*

ὥσπερ, adv., *as, just as, as though.*

ὥστε, conj., *so as, so that.* Syntax H, p. 302.

ὦτα, see οὖς.

ὠφέλιμος, -η, -ον, adj., *useful.*

ὤφελον, -ες, -ε, *ought (for wishes).* Syntax, D 2 and 3, pp. 296–7.

ENGLISH—GREEK VOCABULARY

a, a certain, τις, τι encl.
abandon, καταλείπω.
about (concerning), περί, with gen.
about (round), περί, with acc.
about, I am, (intend) to, μέλλω.
absolute (ruler), τύραννος, ὁ. αὐτο-
κράτωρ, adj.
accept, I, δέχομαι, v. dep.
accompany, I, ὁμιλῶ(εω), σύνειμι,
with dat.
accuse, I, κατηγορῶ(εω), with gen.
Achilles, Ἀχιλλεύς.
acquire, I, κτῶμαι(αο), v. dep.
acquisition, κτῆσις, ἡ.
Acropolis, Ἀκρόπολις, ἡ.
admiral, ναύαρχος, ὁ.
admiration, θαῦμα, τό.
admire, I, θαυμάζω.
Aeginetan, Αἰγινήτης, ὁ.
Adrastus, Ἄδραστος, ὁ.
advance, I, προβαίνω, προχωρῶ
(εω).
adventure, τόλμημα, τό.
advice, παραίνεσις, ἡ.
advise, I, συμβουλεύω, with dat.
Aeëtes, Αἰήτης, ὁ.
Aegina, Αἴγίνη.
Aegospotami, Αἰγὸς ποταμοί, οἱ.
Aethiopia, Αἰθιοπία, ἡ.
afterwards, ἔπειτα, ὕστερον.
against, κατά, with gen., πρός with
acc.
Agamemnon, Ἀγαμέμνων, ὁ.
Agis, Ἄγις, ὁ.
air, ἀήρ, ὁ.
airship, I fly in an, ἀεροδρομῶ(εω).
Ajax, Αἴας, gen. Αἴαντος.
alarm, φόβος, ὁ.
alarm, I, φοβῶ(εω).

Alcibiades, Ἀλκιβιάδης, ὁ.
Alcinous, Ἀλκίνους, ὁ.
Alexander, Ἀλέξανδρος, ὁ.
allot, I, νέμω.
allow, I, ἐῶ(αω).
ally, σύμμαχος, ὁ.
almost, σχεδόν τι, μόνον οὐ.
Alpheus, Ἀλφειός, ὁ.
also, καί.
always, ἀεί.
among, μετά, with gen.
Andromeda, Ἀνδρομέδα, ἡ.
anger, ὀργή, ἡ.
angry, ὀργισθείς.
announce, I, ἀγγέλλω.
anoint, I, ἀλείφω.
any, τις, encl.
Aphrodite, Ἀφροδίτη, ἡ.
Apollo, Ἀπόλλων, ὁ.
appear, I, φαίνομαι, v. dep.
apportion, I, νέμω.
approach, I, πρόσειμι, προσέρχομαι.
approach, εἴσοδος, ἡ. πρόσοδος, ἡ.
Arcadia, Ἀρκαδία, ἡ.
Archias, Ἀρχίας, ὁ.
Archidamus, Ἀρχίδαμος, ὁ.
Ares, Ἄρης, ὁ.
Argo, Ἀργώ, ἡ.
Argonauts, Ἀργοναῦται, οἱ.
Argos, Ἄργος, τό.
argue, I, διαλέγομαι, v. dep.
Ariadne, Ἀριάδνη, ἡ.
Aristides, Ἀριστείδης, ὁ.
Aristophanes, Ἀριστοφάνης, ὁ.
Aristotle, Ἀριστοτέλης, ὁ.
armistice, ἐκεχειρία, ἡ.
armour, ὅπλα, τά.
army, στρατός, ὁ. στρατόπεδον, τό.
art, τέχνη, ἡ.

Artemisia, 'Αρτεμισία, ἡ.
ashore, I run, ὀκέλλω, with acc.
ask a question, I, ἐρωτῶ(αω).
ask a favour, I, αἰτῶ(εω).
ass, ὄνος, ὁ.
assault, προσβολή, ἡ.
assembly, ἐκκλησία, ἡ.
assistance, ὠφέλεια, ἡ. βοήθεια, ἡ.
Athena, 'Αθηνᾶ.
Athenian, 'Αθηναῖος, ὁ.
Athens, 'Αθῆναι; *at Athens*, 'Αθήνησι.
Atreus, 'Ατρεύς, ὁ.
attack, προσβολή, ἡ.
attack, I, ἔπειμι, ἐπέρχομαι.
attempt, πεῖρα, ἡ.
attempt, I, πειρῶμαι(αο), ἐπιχειρῶ (εω).
Atys, "Ατυς, ὁ.
Aulis, Αὖλις, ἡ.
avenge, I, δίκην λαμβάνω, with gen. of person avenged.

back, νῶτον, τό.
back, adv., ὀπίσω.
bank, ὄχθος, ὁ.
banquet, ἑορτή, ἡ.
battle, μάχη, ἡ.
Battus, Βάττος, ὁ.
beak, ῥύγχος, τό.
beautiful, καλός, -ή, -όν.
beauty, κάλλος, τό. τὸ καλόν.
because of, διά, with acc.
become, I, γίγνομαι. v. dep.
befits, it, πρέπει, with dat. of person.
before, adv., πρότερον.
before, conj., πρίν.
before, prep., πρὸ, with gen.
begin, I, ἄρχομαι.
between, μεταξὺ, with gen.
beyond, πέραν, with gen.
bid (order), I, κελεύω.
birdman, ὀρνιθάνθρωπος, ὁ.
Black Sea, Εὔξεινος, ὁ.

boar, κάπρος, ὁ.
board (on), ἐπὶ, with gen.
boast, I, κομπάζω.
boat hook, κόντος, ὁ.
body, σῶμα, τό.
Boeotia, Βοιωτία, ἡ.
book, βίβλος, ἡ, or βιβλίον, τό.
born, I am, γίγνομαι, v. dep.
bow, τόξον, τό.
box, I, πυκτεύω.
boxing-match, πυγμαχία, ἡ.
boy, παῖς, ὁ.
brave, ἀνδρεῖος, -α, -ον.
break down, I, κατάγνυμι.
bridge, γέφυρα, ἡ.
bright, λαμπρός, -ά, -όν.
bring, I, φέρω ; *bring in*, εἰσφέρω ; *bring with*, συμφέρω.
Britain, Βρεταννική, ἡ.
broad, πλατύς, -εῖα, -ύ.
brook, I (stand), ὑπομένω.
brother, ἀδελφός.
build, οἰκοδομῶ(εω)
bull, ταῦρος, ὁ.
but, δέ, ἀλλά ; *meaning except*, πλήν, with gen.
bystander, ὁ παρών.

call, I, καλῶ(εω).
Callias, Καλλίας, ὁ.
camp, στρατόπεδον, τό.
campaign, στρατεία, ἡ.
carefully, ἐπιμελῶς.
carry off, I, ἀποφέρω.
casualties, τραυματίαι, οἱ.
Caucasus, Καύκασος, ὁ.
cavalry engagement, ἱππομαχία, ἡ.
celebrate, a festival, I, ἄγω.
Celt, Κέλτος, ὁ.
centre, of an army, τὸ μέσον.
chance, τύχη, ἡ.
chance, I, τυγχάνω.
change, I, ἀλλάσσω.
charcoal, ἄνθραξ, ὁ, usually in pl.
chariot, ἅρμα, τό, ἀπήνη, ἡ.

child, παῖς, ὁ or ἡ.
citadel, ἄκρα, ἡ.
city, πόλις, ἡ.
civilised, ἥμερος, -α, -ον.
Cleombrotus, Κλεόμβροτος, ὁ.
Clitus, Κλεῖτος, ὁ.
club, ῥόπαλον, τό. κορύνη, ἡ.
Clytemnestra, Κλυταιμνήστρα, ἡ.
Cnossus, Κνωσσός, ἡ.
Codrus, Κόδρος, ὁ.
collect, I, συλλέγω.
colony, ἀποικία, ἡ.
comb, κτείς, ὁ. I comb, κτενίζω.
comedy, κωμῳδία, ἡ.
comely, ὡραῖος, -α, -ον. καλός, -ή,
   -όν.
commander, ἡγεμών, ὁ.
competitor, ἀγωνιζόμενος, ὁ.
completely, παντελῶς.
compulsion, ἀνάγκη, ἡ.
confusion, ταραχή, ἡ.
Conon, Κόνων, ὁ.
construct, I, ποιῶ(εω), οἰκοδομῶ
   (εω).
consult, I, βουλεύομαι.
contain, I, ἔχω.
contest, ἀγών, ὁ. ἆθλος, ὁ.
continue, I, διατελῶ(εω).
control, I, κρατῶ(εω), κατέχω.
convert, I, πείθω.
convince, I, ἐξελέγχω.
cookery, ὀψοποιϊκή, ἡ.
Corinth, Κόρινθος, ἡ.
corn, σῖτος, ὁ.
country, ἀγρός, ὁ ; native country,
   πατρίς, ἡ.
court, αὐλή, ἡ.
cover, I, καλύπτω, κρύπτω.
cradle, in the, ἐν σπαργάνοις.
creation, γένεσις, ἡ.
Crete, Κρήτη, ἡ.
crew of a ship, ἄνδρες, οἱ. ναῦται, οἱ.
Croesus, Κροῖσος, ὁ.
cross, I, διαβαίνω.
Croton, Κροτών, ὁ.

crow, κόραξ, ὁ.
crown, στέφανος, ὁ. I crown,
   στερανῶ(οω).
cruel, ὠμός, -ή, -όν. ἄγριος, -α, -ον.
cultivate, I, γεωργῶ(εω).
cure, I, ἰῶμαι(αο).
custom, ἔθος, τό.
cut off, I, ἀποτέμνω.
Cyclades, Κυκλάδες, αἱ.

Damon, Δάμων, ὁ.
dance, dancing, χορός, ὁ.
dance, I, ὀρχοῦμαι(εο).
Danube, Ἴστρος, ὁ.
Dardanelles, Ἑλλήσποντος, ὁ.
Darius, Δαρεῖος, ὁ.
dark, σκοτεινός, -όν. ἀσέληνος, -ον.
daughter, θυγάτηρ, ἡ.
dawn, ἕως, ἡ.
day, ἡμέρα, ἡ.
dead, νεκροί, οἱ. οἱ τεθνηκότες.
death, θάνατος, ὁ.
decide, I, κρίνω.
deep, βαθύς, -εῖα, -ύ.
defeat, I, νικῶ(αω), ἡττῶ(αω).
Delium, Δήλιον, τό.
Delphi, Δελφοί, αἱ.
Delphians, Δελφοί, οἱ.
Demeter, Δημήτηρ, ἡ.
Democedes, Δημοκήδης, ὁ.
Demosthenes, Δημοσθένης, ὁ.
desert, I, αὐτομολῶ(εω).
deserter, αὐτόμολος, ὁ.
deposit, I, κατατίθημι.
despise, I, καταφρονῶ(εω), with
   gen.
destroy, I, διαφθείρω.
devoted, πιστός, -ή, -όν.
devour, I, κατεσθίω.
dinner, δεῖπνον, τό.
Dionysius, Διονύσιος, ὁ.
Dionysus, Διόνυσος, ὁ.
disappear, I, ἀφανίζομαι, οἴχομαι.
disaster, συμφορά, ἡ.
discipline, μελέτη, ἡ.

discover, I, εὑρίσκω.
disgrace, αἰσχύνη, ἡ.
distance, use ἀπέχω, am distant.
distrust, I, ἀπειθῶ(εω).
ditch, τάφρος, ἡ.
do, I, ποιῶ(εω), πράσσω, δρῶ(αω).
dog, κύων, ὁ or ἡ.
doubt, I, ἀπορῶ(εω).
dove, πελειάς, ἡ.
dragon, δράκων, ὁ.
dream, ἐνύπνιον, τό.
drill, I, γυμνάζω, v.a.
drink, I, πίνω.
drive, I, ἐλαύνω.
during, ἐν, with dat.
duties, τὰ δέοντα.

each, ἕκαστος, -η, -ον.
eager, πρόθυμος, -ον.
early, πρῴ, adv.
earth, γῆ, ἡ ; on the earth, χαμαί.
earthquake, σεισμός, ὁ.
easily, ῥᾳδίως.
easy, ῥᾴδιος, -α, -ον.
education, παιδεία, ἡ.
Egypt, Αἴγυπτος, ἡ.
Egyptian, Αἰγύπτιος, -α, -ον.
embellish, I, κοσμῶ(εω).
emblem, σημεῖον, τό.
empire, ἀρχή, ἡ.
encounter, I, ἀπαντῶ(αω).
encourage, I, παροξύνω.
end, τέλος, τό.   τελευτή, ἡ.
end, I, v.a. ; παύω, καταλύω.
  v.a. and n., τελευτῶ(αω).
enter, I, εἰσέρχομαι, εἴσειμι.
entertain, I, ξενίζω.
entrust, I, ἐπιτρέπω.
Epaminondas, Ἐπαμεινώνδας, ὁ.
Epeus, Ἐπειός, ὁ.
equal, ἴσος, -η, -ον.
Eros, Ἔρως, ὁ.
especially, μάλιστα, ἄλλως τε καί.
estate, οὐσία, ἡ.
Europe, Εὐρώπη, ἡ.

Euryalus, Εὐρύαλος, ὁ.
Eurybiades, Εὐρυβιάδης, ὁ.
Euxine Sea (Black Sea), Εὔξεινος
  πόντος, ὁ.
evening, ἑσπέρα, ἡ.
every, πᾶς, πᾶς τις, ἕκαστος.
evildoers, πονηροί, οἱ.
examine, I, ἐξετάζω.
example, παράδειγμα, τό.
except, πλήν, with gen.
expel, I, ἐκβάλλω.
experience, ἐμπειρία.
experience, I, πάσχω, χρῶμαι(αο).
export, I, ἐξάγω.
expose, I, ἐκτίθημι.
extraordinary, περισσός, -ή, -όν.

face, πρόσωπον, τό.
fail, I, ἁμαρτάνω.
fall, I, πίπτω.
fame, δόξα, ἡ. ἀξίωμα, τό.
famous, λαμπρός, -ά, -όν. ἐπίσημος,
  -ον.
fasten, I, πήγνυμι. I fasten to,
  προσάπτω.
fat, πίων.
fate, μοῖρα, ἡ. δαίμων, ὁ. τύχη, ἡ.
father, πατήρ, ὁ.
fear, φόβος, ὁ.
feast, ἑορτή, ἡ.
feel, I, αἰσθάνομαι.
fellows, one's, οἱ συνόντες, οἱ ἑταῖροι.
fertile, ἄφθονος, -ον.
fetch, I, φέρω, κομίζω.
field, ἀγρός, ὁ, ἄρουρα, ἡ.
fight, μάχη, ἡ. I fight, μάχομαι.
find, I, εὑρίσκω.
finger, δάκτυλος, ὁ.
fire, πῦρ, τό.
fire-breathing, πυρπνόος, -ον.
first, πρῶτος, -η, -ον.
fish, ἰχθύς, ὁ.
flatterer, κόλαξ, ὁ.
flee, I, φεύγω.
flight, φυγή, ἡ.

flock, ποίμνη, ἡ. ποίμνιον, τό.
fly, I, πέτομαι, v. dep.
foe, πολέμιος, ὁ. ἐναντίος, ὁ.
foot, πούς, ὁ ; on foot, πεζός, -ή, -όν.
foremost, πρῶτος, ἐν τοῖς
  ἔμπροσθεν.
forget, I, λανθάνομαι.
forgive, I, συγγιγνώσκω, with dat.
fortress, τείχισμα, τό.
four, τέσσαρες, τέσσαρα.
four hundred, τετρακόσιοι.
four-footed, τετράπους, -πουν.
fox, ἀλώπηξ, ἡ.
free, ἐλεύθερος, -α, -ον.
freedom, ἐλευθερία, ἡ.
frequent, I, ὁμιλῶ(εω), with dat.
friend, φίλος, -η, -ον.
friendship, φιλία, ἡ.
frighten, I, φοβῶ(εω).
front, in, ἔμπροσθε.
frozen over, use πέπηγα, from πήγνυμι.
full, μεστός, -ή, -όν, with gen.
Furies, Εὐμενίδες, αἱ.
further, adv., πορρωτέρω.

game (beasts and birds), θήρα, ἡ.
game (play), παιδία, ἡ.
games, ἀγών, ὁ. ἄθλοι, οἱ.
garden, κῆπος, ὁ.
general, στρατηγός, ὁ.
get, I, λαμβάνω, κτῶμαι(αο).
gift, δῶρον, τό. δωρεά, ἡ.
give birth to, I, τίκτω.
give way, I, ἐγκλίνω.
Glaucus, Γλαῦκος, ὁ.
glory, δόξα, ἡ. κλέος, τό.
go, I, ἔρχομαι, βαίνω. I shall go,
  εἶμι.
god, θεός, ὁ. δαίμων, ὁ.
goddess, θεός, ἡ.
gold, χρυσός, ὁ.
golden, χρυσοῦς, -ῆ, -οῦν.
grant, I, δίδωμι.
grave, τάφος, ὁ.

great, μέγας, μεγάλη, μέγα.
greeks, Ἕλληνες, οἱ.
ground, γῆ, πέδον.
grow, I, αὐξάνομαι.
guard, φύλαξ, ὁ.
guard, I, φυλάσσω.
guardsman, σωματοφύλαξ, ὁ.
guess, I, εἰκάζω ; of a riddle, λύω.
guest, ξένος, ὁ.
Gylippus, Γύλιππος, ὁ.

habit, ἔθος, τό.
hairs, θρίξ, ἡ, ; usually in pl., αἱ
  τρίχες.
half, ἥμισυς, -εῖα, -υ.
hand, χείρ, ἡ.
handmaiden, θεράπαινα, ἡ
happy, εὐδαίμων, -ον.
harbour, λιμήν, ὁ.
harp, κιθάρα, ἡ. I play the harp,
  κιθαρίζω.
haste, in, ταχέως.
have, I, ἔχω, ἐστί μοι.
hear, I, ἀκούω, ἀκροῶμαι(αο), with
  gen. of person.
heart, καρδία, ἡ.
heat, θερμότης, ἡ.
Hector, Ἕκτωρ, ὁ.
Helen, Ἑλένη, ἡ.
helmet, κράνος, τό.
Hephaestus, Ἥφαιστος, ὁ.
Hera, Ἥρα, ἡ.
Heracles, Ἡρακλῆς, ὁ.
herd, ἀγέλη, ἡ.
here, ἐνθάδε, ἐνταῦθα.
Hermes, Ἑρμῆς, ὁ.
hero, ἀνήρ ἄριστος ; ἥρως =demi
  god.
Herodotus, Ἡρόδοτος, ὁ.
high, ὑψηλός, -ή, -όν.
hire, μισθός, ὁ.
historian, συγγραφεύς, ὁ.
home, οἶκος, ὁ. οἰκία, ἡ.
Homer, Ὅμηρος, ὁ.
honesty, πίστις, ἡ.

honour, τιμή, ἡ. I honour, τιμῶ(αω).
hoof, ὁπλή, ἡ.
hope, ἐλπίς, ἡ.
horn (wing of an army), κέρας, τό.
horse, ἵππος, ὁ.
horseman, cavalryman, ἱππεύς, ὁ.
housekeeping, ταμιεία, ἡ.
human, ἀνθρώπινος, -η, -ον.
hunt, I, θηρεύω, κυνηγετῶ(εω).
huntress, κυνηγέτις.
hymn, ὕμνος, ὁ.
Hyphasis, Ὕφασις, ὁ.

I, ἐγώ.
idle, ἀργός, -ή, -όν.
Iliad, Ἰλιάς, ἡ.
in, ἐν, with dat.
induce, I, προτρέπω.
infirm, ἀσθενής, -ες.
inhabitants, οἱ οἰκοῦντες.
injury, βλάβη, ἡ.
intention, βουλή, ἡ.
interior, the, τὸ ἔνδον, τὸ ἔσω.
invite, καλῶ(εω).
Ionia, Ἰωνία, ἡ.
island, νῆσος, ἡ.
Ischomachus, Ἰσχόμαχος, ὁ.
Ithaca, Ἰθάκη, ἡ.

Jason, Ἰάσων, ὁ.
javelin, ἄκων, ὁ. ἀκόντιον, τό.
jealousy, φθόνος, ὁ.
join, I, συνίσταμαι.
journey, ὁδός, ἡ. πορεία, ἡ.
joy, χαρά, ἡ. ἡδονή, ἡ.
judge, δικαστής, ὁ. κριτής, ὁ.
jump, I, πηδῶ(αω), ἄλλομαι.
just, δίκαιος, -α, -ον.
justice, δίκη, ἡ. δικαιοσύνη, ἡ.

keep, I, φυλάσσω, τηρῶ(εω).
kill, I, ἀποκτείνω, φονεύω, δια-
    φθείρω.
kindly, φιλικός, -ή, -όν.
king, βασιλεύς, ὁ.

know, I, γιγνώσκω, ἐπίσταμαι.
knowledge, γνῶσις, ἡ. μάθημα, τό.

labours (of Heracles), πόνοι, οἱ.
Lacedaemon(Sparta),Λακεδαίμων,ἡ.
Laertes, Λαέρτης, ὁ.
Lampsacus, Λάμψακος, ὁ.
land, γῆ, ἡ. χώρα, ἡ.
Lapithae, Λάπιθαι, οἱ.
large, μέγας, μεγάλη, μέγα.
last, I, μένω, διατελῶ(εω).
last, adj., ὕστατος, -η, -ον.
later, ὕστερον.
laughter, γέλως, ὁ.
law, νόμος, ὁ.
lawgiver, νομοθέτης, ὁ.
lay down, I, κατατίθημι.
lead, I, ἄγω.
leap, I, πηδῶ(αω).
leap, ἅλμα, τό. πήδημα, τό.
learn, I, μανθάνω, ἐπίσταμαι, v.
    dep. Par. 84.
left (hand), ἀριστερός, -ά, -όν. εὐώ-
    νυμος, -ον.
lend, I, δανείζω.
let, I, ἐῶ(αω).
libation, σπονδή, ἡ.
Libya, Λιβύη, ἡ.
life, βίος, ὁ. ζωή, ἡ.
light, φέγγος, τό. φῶς, τό.
like, παρόμοιος, ον.
lion, λέων, ὁ.
lioness, λέαινα, ἡ.
little, μικρός, -ά, -όν. A little, μικρόν
    τι.
log, ξύλον, τό.
look, I, βλέπω, ἀθρῶ(εω).
lose, I, ἀπόλλυμι, ἀποβάλλω.
love, I, ἐρῶ(αω), with gen.
low-lying, χθαμαλός, -ή, -όν.
Lycurgus, Λυκοῦργος, ὁ.
Lysander, Λύσανδρος, ὁ.

maiden, παρθένος, ἡ. κόρη, ἡ.
maintain, I, τρέφω.

man, ἀνήρ, ὁ (Latin *vir*)
ἄνθρωπος, ὁ or ἡ (Latin *homo*).
manage, I, διαχειρίζω.
many, πολύς, συχνός. *The many,*
οἱ πολλοί.
Marathon, Μαραθών, ὁ.
market-place, ἀγορά, ἡ.
marry, I, γαμῶ(εω).
meat, κρέας, τό.
meet, I, ἀπαντῶ(αω), with dat. ;
ἐντυγχάνω, with dat.
memorial, μνημεῖον, τό.
Menelaus, Μενέλεως, (gen. Μενέ-
λεω), ὁ.
messenger, ἄγγελος, ὁ.
mile, about 8 stades.
Miletus, Μίλητος, ἡ.
milk, γάλα, τό.
Minos, Μίνως, ὁ, (gen. Μίνωος).
Minotaur, Μινώταυρος, ὁ.
mistress, δέσποινα, ἡ.
moderate, μέτριος, -α, -ον.
moment (fit), καιρός, ὁ.
monster (sea), κῆτος, τό.
more, adj. πλείων, πλέον.
more, adv., πλεῖον or πλέον, μᾶλλον.
mother, μήτηρ, ἡ.
mourn, I, πενθῶ(εω).
mouse, μῦς, ὁ or ἡ.
Mysians, Μῦσοι, οἱ.

nail to, I, προσηλῶ(οω).
narrow, στενός, -ή, -όν.
nature, φύσις, ἡ.
navy, τὸ ναυτικόν or αἱ νῆες.
near, ἐγγὺς or πλησίον, with gen.
nearly, ὅσον οὐ, μάλιστα.
necessary, ἀναγκαῖος, -ον.
neighbours, οἱ πλησίον, οἱ ὅμοροι (of
adjoining countries).
Nemea, Νεμέα, ἡ.
Nemean games, Νέμεια, τά.
new, νέος, -α, -ον.
news, καινόν τι, τὰ ἀγγελλόμενα.
next, ὁ ἐπιγιγνόμενος.

Nicias, Νικίας, ὁ.
night, νύξ, ἡ.
none, no-one, οὐδείς, οὐδεμία, οὐδέν.
not, οὐ, οὐκ, οὐχ, μή. (Par. 100).
note = take notice of, I, προσέχω τὸν
νοῦν, with dat.
nothing, οὐδέν.
now, νῦν.
number, ἀριθμός, ὁ.
number, I, ἀριθμῶ(εω).

observe, I, ὁρῶ(αω).
obstruct, I, βλάπτω, ἐμποδίζω.
occupation, ἀσχολία, ἡ.
Odysseus, Ὀδυσσεύς, ὁ.
offer, I, προκαλοῦμαι(εο), ἐπαγγέλλομαι.
often, πολλάκις.
ointment, χρῖσμα, τό.
older, πρεσβύτερος, -α, -ον.
olive oil, ἔλαιον, τό.
Olympia, Ὀλυμπία, ἡ.
Olympus, Ὄλυμπος, ὁ.
once = once for all, ἅπαξ.
once = formerly, πάλαι.
only, μόνος, -η, -ον. ; *not only,* οὐ
μόνον.
open, I, ἀνοίγνυμι, (of a letter) λύω.
oppose, I, ἐναντιοῦμαι(οο), v. dep.
opposite, ἐναντίος, -ον.
oracle, μαντεῖον, τό. χρηστήριον,
τό.
order, I, κελεύω.
order = system, κόσμος, ὁ.
ordinary, ὁ τυχών.
organise, I, κοσμῶ(εω), τάσσω.
Orpheus, Ὀρφεύς, ὁ.
ostracise, I, ἐξοστρακίζω.
ostracism, ἐξοστρακισμός.
other, ἄλλος, -η, -ον.
our, ἡμέτερος, -α, -ον.
outstrip, I, ὑπερβάλλω.
outwards, ἔξω, ἐκτός.
over, ὑπέρ, with gen., ἐπί, with dat.
owl, γλαῦξ, ἡ.

own, one's, οἰκεῖος, -ον. ἴδιος, -α, -ον.

palace, βασίλειον, τό, usually in pl.
parent, γονεύς, ὁ.
Paris (son of Priam), Πάρις, ὁ.
part, μέρος, τό. μερίς, ἡ.
partake, I, μετέχω, with gen.
Parthenon, Παρθενών, ἡ.
partnership, κοινωνία, ἡ.
pass, I, πάρειμι.
pass, εἰσβολή, ἡ.
Patroclus, Πάτροκλος, ὁ.
patrol, I, περιπολῶ(εω).
patron, προστάτης, ὁ.
pay, μισθός, ὁ.
peace, εἰρήνη, ἡ.
Peleus, Πηλεύς, ὁ.
Pelias, Πελίας, ὁ.
Peloponnese, Πελοπόννησος, ἡ.
penalty, δίκη, ἡ. ζημία, ἡ.
Penelope, Πηνελόπη, ἡ.
pentathlon, πένταθλον, τό.
peplus, πέπλος, ὁ.
perform, I, πρασσω, ἐπιτελῶ(εω).
Pericles, Περικλῆς, ὁ (Περικλεᾶ, Περικλέους, Περικλεῖ).
Persephone, Περσεφόνη, ἡ.
Perseus, Περσεύς, ὁ.
Persia, Περσίς, ἡ.
Persians, Πέρσαι, οἱ.
Phaeacia, Φαιακία, ἡ.
Phidias, Φειδίας, ὁ.
Phintias, Φιντίας, ὁ.
Phocis, Φωκίς, ἡ.
Phoebus, Φοῖβος, ὁ.
Phoenix, Φοῖνιξ, ὁ.
Phormio, Φορμίων, ὁ.
pierce, I, πείρω.
pillar, στῦλος, ὁ.
pillow, προσκεφάλαιον, τό.
piracy, τὸ ληστικόν. ἡ λῃστεία.
Piraeus, Πειραιεύς, ὁ.
pirate, λῃστής, ὁ.
Pirithous, Πειρίθοος, ὁ.

plain, πεδίον, τό.
Plataea, Πλάταια, ἡ.
Plataeans, Πλαταιεῖς, οἱ.
pleasure, ἡδονή, ἡ.
plunder, λεία, ἡ. ἁρπαγή, ἡ.
plunder, I, διαρπάζω, πορθῶ(εω).
poison, φάρμακον, τό.
Poseidon, Ποσειδών, ὁ.
porter, θυρωρός, ὁ.
pour, I, χέω.
powerful, δυνατός, -ή, -όν, -or use κράτος, τό.
practice, μελέτη, ἡ. ἐμπειρία, ἡ.
presently = soon, δι' ὀλίγου, αὐτίκα.
preside, I, ἐπιστατῶ(εω), with dat.
Priam, Πρίαμος, ὁ.
priest, ἱερεύς, ὁ.
priestess, ἱέρεια, ἡ.
private, ἴδιος, -α, -ον. οἰκεῖος, ον.
prize, ἆθλον, τό. ἔπαθλον, τό.
proceed, I, προβαίνω.
procession, πομπή, ἡ.
Prometheus, Προμηθεύς, ὁ.
prompt, πρόθυμος, -ον.
Protagoras, Πρωταγόρας, ὁ.
protect, I, φυλάσσω.
provide, I, παρέχω.
publicly, δημοσίᾳ, κοινῇ.
punish, I, κολάζω.
pupil, μαθητής, ὁ.
purchase, I, ὠνοῦμαι(εο).
pursue, I, διώκω.
Pyrrha, Πύρρα, ἡ.

quarrel, I, ἐρίζω.
queen, βασίλισσα, ἡ.
quoit, δίσκος, ὁ.

race, δρόμος, ὁ.
rain, ὄμβρος, ὁ. ὑετός, ὁ.
raise up, I, ἀνεγείρω.
ram, I, ἐμβάλλω (εἰς with acc. ; or dat.).
rapidly, ταχέως.
ravage, I, ἄγω καὶ φέρω.

ENGLISH-GREEK VOCABULARY 379

read aloud, I, ἀναγιγνώσκω.
ready, ἑτοῖμος, -η, -ον.
reappear, I, ἀναφαίνομαι.
recall, I, ἀνακαλῶ(εω).
recover, I, ἀναλαμβάνω, κομίζομαι.
refuse, I, οὐκ ἐθέλω.
reign, I, βασιλεύω, ἄρχω.
reinforcements, βοήθεια, ἡ.
remainder, λοιπός, -ή, -όν.
remind, I, ἀναμιμνήσκω.
remit, I, ἀφίημι.
remove, I, ἀφίστημι, ἐκβάλλω.
repent, I, μεταμέλει μοι.
reply, I, ἀποκρίνομαι.
request, I, αἰτῶ(εω).
retreat, I, ἀναχωρῶ(εω).
return, I, κατέρχομαι.
ride, I, ἱππεύω, ἐλαύνω.
riddle, αἴνιγμα, τό.
right (hand), δεξιός, -ά, -όν.
ring, δακτύλιος, ὁ.
rise, I, ἀνίσταμαι.
risk, κίνδυνος, ὁ.
river, ποταμός, ὁ.
road, ὁδός, ἡ.
roast, I, ὀπτῶ(αω).
rock, πέτρα, ἡ.
round, ἀμφί or περί, with acc.
rough, τραχύς, -εῖα, -ύ.

sacred, ἱερός, -ά, -όν.
sacrifice, θυσία, ἡ.
safe, ἀσφαλής, -ές.
sail, ἱστίον, τό.
sail, I, πλέω.
Salamis, Σαλαμίς, ἡ.
same, ὁ αὐτός.
sanctuary, τὸ ἱερόν.
Sardis, Σάρδεις, αἱ.
savage, ἄγριος, -α, -ον.
scatter, I, σκεδάννυμι.
scout, σκοπός, ὁ.
sea, θάλασσα, ἡ.
second, δεύτερος, -α, -ον.
see, I, ὁρῶ(αω), ἀθρῶ(εω).

servant, θεράπων, ὁ. θεράπαινα, ἡ.
  δοῦλος, ὁ or ἡ. ὑπηρέτης, ὁ.
set free, I, ἐλευθερῶ(οω).
settler, μέτοικος, ὁ.
several, πολλοί, οὐκ ὀλίγοι.
show, I, δείκνυμι.
shield, ἀσπίς, ἡ.
ship, ναῦς, ἡ. πλοῖον, τό.
ship of war, τριήρης, ἡ.
short, βραχύς, -εῖα, -ύ.
shoulder, ὦμος, ὁ.
side, πλεῦρον, τό. πλευρά, ἡ.
siege, πολιορκία, ἡ.
signal, σημεῖον, τό.
silver, ἄργυρος, ὁ.
sing, I, ᾄδω.
single, ἁπλοῦς, ῆ, -οῦν
sister, ἀδελφή, ἡ.
sit, I, καθίζομαι. κάθημαι.
six hundred, ἑξακόσιοι, -αι, -α.
sky, οὐρανός, ὁ.
slave-girl, θεράπαινα, ἡ. δούλη, ἡ.
slave, I am a, δουλεύω.
slay, I, ἀποκτείνω, φονεύω.
sleep, ὕπνος, ὁ.
slowly, βραδέως.
smear, I, ἀλείφω.
snow, χιών, ἡ.
so that, ὥστε, with indic. or infin.
Socrates, Σωκράτης, ὁ.
soldier, στρατιώτης, ὁ.
sometimes, ἔσθ' ὅτε.
soon, τάχα, δι' ὀλίγου.
sophist, σοφιστής, ὁ.
spare, I, φείδομαι, with gen.
speed, τάχος, τό. ταχύτης, ἡ.
splendour, λαμπρότης, ἡ.
spoil, λεία, ἡ. ἁρπαγή, ἡ.
sprout, I, βλαστάνω.
spy, κατάσκοπος, ὁ.
stab, I, κεντῶ(εω), τιτρώσκω.
stade, στάδιον, τό.
staff, σκῆπτρον, τό. βακτηρία, ἡ.
stand, I, ἵσταμαι. I stand up,
  ἀνίσταμαι.

statue, εἰκών, ἡ. ἀνδριάς, ὁ.
   ἄγαλμα, τό.
stay, I, μένω.
steady, μόνιμος, -η, -ον.
stranger, ξένος, ὁ.
strangle, I, ἄγχω.
strength, ἰσχύς, ἡ.
stretch out, I, προτείνω.
strong, ἰσχυρός, -ά, -όν.
submit, I, εἴκω.
succeed, I, εὐτυχῶ(εω), κατορθῶ
   (οω).
suffer, I, πάσχω.
suitor, μνηστήρ, ὁ.
Susa, Σοῦσα, τά.
sustain, I, φέρω, τρέφω, ὑπομένω.
Symplegades, Συμπληγάδες, αἱ.
Syracusan, Συρακόσιος, -α, -ον.
Syracuse, Συρακοῦσαι, αἱ.

tablet (memorial), στηλή, ἡ.
tail, οὐρά, ἡ.
take, I, λαμβάνω.
taken, I am, ἁλίσκομαι. (Par. 72).
talk, I, λέγω, διαλέγομαι.
tally, σύμβολον, τό.
teacher, διδάσκαλος, ὁ.
tear, δάκρυον, τό.
tear, I, σχίζω.
Telemachus, Τηλέμαχος, ὁ.
tent, κλισία, ἡ.
terrify, I, φοβῶ(εω).
theatre, θέατρον, τό.
Thebes, Θῆβαι, αἱ.
Themistocles, Θεμιστοκλῆς, ὁ.
Theseus, Θησεύς, ὁ.
Thessaly, Θεσσαλία, ἡ.
third, τρίτος, -η, -ον.
though, καίπερ, with partic. ; εἰ καί.
three, τρεῖς, τρία.
throw, I, βάλλω.
thrust, I, ὠθῶ(εω).
thus, οὕτως.
tired, I am, κάμνω.
toady, κόλαξ, ὁ.

toe, δάκτυλος, ὁ.
toil, ἔργον, τό. πόνος, ὁ.
tomb, τάφος, ὁ.
too, καί.
top, ἄκρα, ἡ. κορυφή, ἡ.
torch, δάς, ἡ.
touch, I, ἅπτομαι, with gen.
trace, ἴχνος, τό.
tragedy, τραγῳδία, ἡ.
train, I, ἀσκῶ(εω).
traveller, use πορεύομαι.
tree, δένδρον, τό.
triangle, τρίγωνον, τό.
tribe, ἔθνος, τό.
trident, τρίαινα, ἡ.
Trojan, Τρωικός, -ή, -όν.
Troy, Τροία, ἡ. Ἴλιον, τό.
truce, σπονδαί, αἱ.
truth, ἀλήθεια, ἡ.
turn, I, στρέφω, v.a. Intrans., use
   middle.
tutor, διδάσκαλος, ὁ.
tutor, παιδαγωγός, ὁ, (slave who
   accompanies his pupil to and from
   school).
two, δύο.
two-footed, δίπους, δίπουν.
two hundred, διακόσιοι.

uncivilised, ἀνήμερος, -ον.
under, ὑπό with dat.
unprotected by walls, ἀτείχιστος, -ον.
unwilling, ἀκούσιος, οὐχ ἑκών.
useful, ὠφέλιμος, -η, -ον.
usual, εἰωθώς, -υῖα, -ός.

valuable, ἔντιμος, -ον.
vessel, ναῦς, ἡ. πλοῖον, τό.
victory, νίκη, ἡ.
vinegar, ὄξος, τό.
violent, βίαιος, -ον.
virgin, παρθένος, ἡ.
voice, φωνή, ἡ.

walk, I, περιπατῶ(εω).

wall, τεῖχος, τό.
warm, θερμός, -ή, -όν.
warn, I, νουθετῶ(εω).
warrior, see soldier.
watch, I, φυλάσσω.
water, ὕδωρ, τό.
way, ὁδός, ἡ.
when, ὅτε. When? πότε.
where, ὅπου. Where? ποῦ.
while, ἐν ᾧ.
who, ὅς, ἥ, ὅ. Who? τίς; What? τί.
wicked, πονηρός, -ά, -όν.
wife, γυνή, ἡ.
wine, οἶνος, ὁ.
wise, σοφός, -ή, -όν.
wish, I, βούλομαι, v. dep.
within, ἔνδον.
woman, γυνή, ἡ.
wood, ξύλον, τό.

wool, ἔριον, τό.
word, λόγος, ὁ.
work, ἔργον, τό. I work, ἐργάζομαι,
    v. dep.
wreath, στέφανος, ὁ.
wreathe, I, στεφανῶ(οω).
wrestle, I, παλαίω.
write, I, γράφω.

Xenophon, Ξενοφῶν, ὁ.
Xerxes, Ξέρξης, ὁ.

yet, ἔτι.
yoke, ζυγόν, τό.
young, νέος, -α, -ον.
youth, νεανίας, ὁ.

Zeus, Ζεύς (Δία, Διός, Διί).
zither, κιθάρα, ἡ.

GRAMMATICAL INDEX

The reference is by pages

Accusative
  absolute, 292
  uses, 290
Adjectives
  comparison, 193–5
  declension, 188–91
Adverbs
  comparison, 196
  formation, 195
  interrogative, etc., 284-6
Aorist
  meaning, 203
  paradigms, 240–4
  strong or 2nd, 234–37
Article
  declension, 177
  uses, 288–90
Augment
  uses, 203–5

Cases
  usages, 290–1
Commands
  direct, 294
  indirect, 304
Concessive clauses, 312
Conditional clauses, 308–12
Conjunctions
  indicative, 296
  temporal, 306
Consecutive clauses, 302
Consonants
  changes, 142–3, 230–4
  types, 142

Dative
  uses, 291

Dental stems
  nouns, 179–80
  verbs, 232–3

Fear, clauses, 302
Final clauses, 300

Genitive
  absolute, 292
  uses, 291
Guttural stems
  nouns, 179
  verbs, 230–1

Impersonal verbs, 292–3
Indefinite
  construction, 306, 310, 312
  pronouns, 202, 290
Infinitive, 292
  (*see statements, indirect*)
Interrogatives, 285–6
  (*see questions*)
Irregular nouns, 184–6
  verbs, 238–45
  verb table, 314–17

Knowing and perceiving, verbs, 300

Labial stems
  nouns, 179
  verbs, 232
Liquid stems
  nouns, 180–1
  verbs, 233–4

Middle voice, 203

Negatives, 293

383

Neuter nouns in -ος, 181
Nominative uses, 290
Nouns
  declensions   I, 175–6
             II, 177–8
  consonant III, 178–81
  vowel   III, 182–4
Numerals
  list, 197–8
  declension, 199

Optative, 203
ὅτι construction, 298, 310

Perfect
  reduplication, 204–5
  strong or 2nd, 237
Potential sentences, 312
Prepositions
  cases, meanings, 278–284
  compounded, 205
Pronouns
  correspondence, 285
  demonstrative, 199–200, 285, 289–90
  indefinite, 202, 290
  interrogative, 202, 290
  personal, 200
  position of 289–90
  possessive, 201, 289
  reflexive, 201
  relative, 202

Questions, 285–6
  direct, 294
  indirect, 304

Reduplication, 204–5

Statements
  direct, 294
  indirect, 298–300, 310

Temporal clauses, 306

Verbs in -μι
  δείκνυμι, 260–3
  δίδωμι, 256–9
  ἵημι, 264–67
  ἵστημι, 246–50
  τίθημι, 250–5
  irregular in -μι, 268–277
Verbs in -ω
  uncontracted, 206–17
  -αω contracted, 218–21
  -εω contracted, 222–5
  -οω contracted, 226–9
  dental stems, 232–3
  guttural stems, 230–1
  labial stems, 232
  liquid stems, 233–4

Wishes, 296, 312–3